# Handbook of Crime Correlates

# Handbook of Crime Correlates


**Lee Ellis**
Minot State University, Minot, North Dakota

**Kevin Beaver**
Florida State University, Tallahassee, Florida

**John Wright**
University of Cinncinati, Cinncinati, Ohio

AMSTERDAM • BOSTON • HEIDELBERG • LONDON • NEW YORK • OXFORD • PARIS
• SAN DIEGO • SAN FRANCISCO • SINGAPORE • SYDNEY • TOKYO

Academic Press is an imprint of Elsevier

Academic Press is an imprint of Elsevier
The Boulevard, Langford Lane, Kidlington, Oxford OX5 1GB, UK
525 B Street, Suite 1900, San Diego, California 92101-4495, USA
32 Jamestown Road, London NW1 7BY, UK

First edition 2009



**British Library Cataloguing in Publication Data**
A catalogue record for this book is available from the British Library

**Library of Congress Cataloguing in Publication Data**
A catalogue record for this book is available from the Library of Congress

ISBN–13: 978-0-12-373612-3

For information on all Academic Press publications
visit our website at books.elsevier.com

Printed and bound in the USA

09 10 11 12 10 9 8 7 6 5 4 3 2 1

# Contents

## 3. Ecological and Macro-Economic Factors



## 4. Family and Peer Factors

# Preface

In what size cities are crime rates the highest and lowest, or does the answer depend on what part of the world is being studied? Are there societies in which females are more involved in crime than males? Is child abuse victimization more common among offenders than among relatively law-abiding persons? What is the relationship between the state of the economy in a country and its crime rate? Are religious people involved in crime to a lesser or greater degree than nonreligious people, or does the answer depend on which religion is being considered? Do persistent offenders have brains that function differently than those of persons in general?

The above questions are among thousands that have been scientifically investigated by criminologists and other social/behavioral scientists over the past two centuries. This book has been organized and written to provide a documented summary of what is currently known (always with varing degrees of certainty) regarding variables associated with criminal (and delinquent) behavior. Additionally, evidence concerning closely related factors such as clinically-diagnosed antisocial personality disorder is also provided. In assembling the studies cited in this book, no restrictions were made regarding the types of variables examined nor the countries or time periods involved.

## CHAPTER STRUCTURE

The book consists of more than 400 tables pertaining to different variables that have been investigated regarding their possible relationship to criminality. These tables are organized into the following nine chapters:

Chapter 1 – Pervasiveness and Intra-Offending Relationships
Chapter 2 – Demographic Correlates
Chapter 3 – Ecological and Macro-Economic Factors
Chapter 4 – Family and Peer Factors
Chapter 5 – Institutional Factors
Chapter 6 – Personality and Behavioral Factors
Chapter 7 – Cognitive Factors
Chapter 8 – Biological Factors
Chapter 9 – Crime Victimization and Fear of Crime
Chapter 10 – Grand Summary

Accompanying each table is a narrative that provides a description of how each variable appears to be related to offending probabilities.

## LOCATING RELEVANT PUBLICATIONS

A variety of methods were used to locate scientific publications on criminality, including previously published reviews, internet searches, interlibrary loan material, and simply by thumbing through journals. Nevertheless, the most heavily relied on source was *Current Contents*. This electronic publication was searched each week by setting the search parameters so as to flag all publications containing words such as *crime*, *delinquency*, and *antisocial*, as well as related words such as *aggression* and *violence*. After visually screening these flagged publications, copies of the articles that appeared to be genuinely relevant were sought either directly from their authors or from library sources. In this way, approximately 25 new articles were identified every week.

A key feature of the scientific method is that current research builds on past research of a related nature. This feature has made it possible for us to rely fairly heavily on literature reviews in contemporary research reports to obtain information about past studies. If everything appeared accurate and credible in these secondary citations, they too were included in the book's tables. When doubts arose concerning the accuracy of a secondary citation or more details were needed, copies of the relevant primary sources were obtained.

## STRUCTURE OF THE TABLES

Virtually all studies linking variables to criminal and related behavior are presented within tables, even if only one relevant study was located. This allows readers to obtain a quick visual picture of the weight of evidence for a particular relationship that may be of interest. Accompanying each table is a narrative that provides a written description of the general nature of each variable's relationship to offending behavior according to the available research findings.

Most of the tables throughout this book have a very similar format. Along the left margin appears three possible options regarding a variable's relationship to criminality: *positive*, *not significant*, or *negative*. A positive relationship would be one in which increases in as a variable increases, involvement in crime also increases. A negative (or inverse) relationship would be one in which increases in a variable would be associated with decreases in offending.

Across the top of most tables, the following types of officially detected offense categories are identified: *violent crime*, *property crime*, *drug offenses*, *sex offenses*, *delinquency*, *general and adult offenses*, and *recidivism*. Two additional offense categories are listed across the top of most tables; these pertain to self-reported (rather than officially detected) offending: *overall offenses* and *illegal drug offenses*.

The above paragraph pertains to the book's "main tables". However, many variables will also have a second table pertaining to it. In these second tables, evidence regarding traits that are often associated with criminality is considered. Put another way, these secondary tables link variables not to criminality per se, but to variables that have been repeatedly found *related* to criminality. The clearest example is a clinical conditions known as *antisocial behavior* (or *antisocial personality disorder*) or its childhood manifestation, known as *conduct disorder*. Other examples that are considered in these secondary tables include *physical aggression*, *cognitive and personality factors*, *alcoholism*, *drug abuse* (regardless of legality), *mental illness*, *mental disorders*, *familial factors*, *physiological factors*, and *biochemical factors*.

To enable readers to look for possible cultural variations in the research findings, the country within which each study was conducted is indicated. When special subpopulations were sampled, racial or ethnic identifiers appear in parentheses immediately following the relevant citation.

Countries are organized with regard to the region of the world in which they are located. The regional categories used were as follows: *Africa*, *Asia*, *Europe*, *Latin America*, *Middle East*, *North America*, and *Oceania* (the latter encompassing primarily islands in the Pacific and Indian Oceans). In some cases, islands were subsumed under nearby continents. For example, Britain and Iceland were listed under *Europe*, while both Japan and Taiwan were considered part of *Asia*. All of the American countries and islands of the Caribbean in which Spanish or Portuguese are the dominant languages were subsumed under *Latin America*. Hawaii was considered part of *Oceania* when information was available for it specifically; otherwise its data were treated simply as part of the *United States*.

Over 99% of the research was based on human subjects. Most of the exceptions were in Chapter 8 on biology, especially pertaining to studies of aggression. Citations to studies of nonhuman animals are included in the tables according to species (or species type) rather than according to the country in which they lived.

## WHAT CONSTITUTES PUBLISHED RESEARCH

The basic criterion used for including research findings in this book was that the findings must have been published. The criteria used to consider a study as having been *published* included having appeared in the form of a journal article or book. Dissertations were also considered "published", but master's theses and conference papers were not unless they appeared in a formally bound proceedings book available through library sources. Material that was available only on the internet without paper copies being available through public library sources was not considered "published".

## THE BOOK'S ANALYTIC CHARACTER

We believe that this book constitutes a meta-analysis since it is a "a study of studies". Perhaps the best description for the approach taken by the book is that it is a *type* of meta-analysis which uses a *ballot-box* or vote-counting methodology (Hedges & Olkin 1985:47; Jarvis 1992:1252). What qualifies a study to "cast a vote" is the fact that it was published as an empirical investigation. Each "vote" can be for one of three outcomes: *positive*, *negative*, or *no significant difference*. Rather than attempting to adjust each study's finding according to the sample size on which the sample was based, each finding carries the same weight as all others. Nevertheless, in some of the narratives surrounding a table, comments are sometimes made to suggest that some qualitative assessments are in order.

There were three reasons the ballot-box approach was adopted instead of the more conventional (effect size) type of meta-analysis. First, the ballot-box approach is easier in the sense that one only needs to determine if a particular relationship is statistically significant and its "direction" (i.e., positive or negative). No adjustments had to be made for variations in a study's sample size or other measures of statistical power. Second, a conventional meta-analysis does not lend itself well to accommodating variations over time or from one culture to another. This is because the conventional meta-analysis involves pooling results from all of the available studies into a single statistic. Detecting temporal and especially cultural variations was something we considered important to preserve because one of the hoped-for outcomes of this book is to begin revealing the extent to which correlates of crime are culturally universal. Third, when compared to the more conventional type of meta-analysis, the vote-counting version lends itself to being much more easily updated as additional studies are reported.

## STATISTICAL SIGNIFICANCE

Despite its limitations, the concept of *statistical significance* has been, and continues to be, a valuable tool for scientists who must base nearly all of their research findings on samples. Throughout this book, we have relied on whatever statistical significance test a researcher used in a particular study unless specifically indicated otherwise. In the vast majority of cases, this means that the maximum degree of sampling error allowed was .05. Nearly all of the studies cited assumed the more conservative two-tailed version of whatever statistical text that was used. Where this was not the case, and the less conservative one-tailed test would have made the difference between significance and non-significance, both results are indicated within the relevant table.

## CITATION STYLE

Slight variations on the widely used American Psychological Association (APA) style of citation are employed throughout this book. The key features that deviate from the APA style are as follows:

To help reduce confusing citations to specific references, seemingly common last names for a citation's lead author is preceded with the author's initials (without periods or spaces between them). Thus, an article by *Smith* would be preceded with his/her initials, such as *AW Smith.*

To keep citations as brief as possible, an article, chapter, or book with three or more authors was simply referred to by the first author's last name (plus initials, if the name was common) and the notation *et al.* followed by the year of publication. No commas are used to separate authors and the year their work was published, although, in many instances, a page number is cited following the year of publication in order to assist readers wishing to verify a particular finding, especially in the case of lengthy publications.

## SPECIAL NOTATIONS AND QUALIFIERS

Few arbitrary symbols and notations are used anywhere in this book. The most common special notation employed in the tables is an asterisk (*). This symbol signifies that a particular study is cited more than once within that particular table. The two main reasons for multiple citations to a study within a table are these: First, one study may have investigated how a variable relates to two or more specific categories of crime. Second, a study might report results for two or more different countries. For each country, the nature of the relationship with the variable in question will be indicated following the asterisk.

Also appearing frequently after table citations are what are called *qualifiers.* A qualifier is a word or phrase that serves to delimit the nature of the sample or the specific type of offense focused on in a particular study. For example, if the subjects of a study were all of one racial or ethnic group, this would be indicated in parenthesis as a qualifier. Many other qualifiers appear after particular citations to provide information about the type of methodology used to obtain the data, such as indicating that a particular study of sex offenses were limited to just one type (e.g., child molestation).

Some studies were found to be based on data extending far back in time. Therefore, to give some time-dimension to the studies reviewed besides those associated with the year of publication a special notation is made following any study that was based on data collected prior to the 20th Century. Thus, if *19th Century* appears as a qualifier following a particular study, data for that study were obtained sometime in the 1800s.

# Acknowledgements

Persons who provided valuable assistance in organizing the tables and in assembling the references for this book are as follows: Derek Boyko, Elizabeth Deserly, Ryan Eberhardt, and Ashley Everson. Dr. Harry Hoffman assisted in locating references cited in this book, and Myrna Nelson assisted greating in editing.

Special gratitude is extended to Dr. Eugene Garfield of the Institute for Scientific Information for providing access to *Current Contents*. This publication was invaluable for keeping abreast of the research reports that formed the foundation for the present book.

Chapter 1

# Pervasiveness and Intra-Offending Relationships

**Contents**



The initial chapter of the book is devoted to exploring the pervasiveness of criminality and the relationships between various types of criminality. In other words, how extensive is criminal (and delinquent) behavior throughout the world? And, to what extent is one type of offending associated with another type.

## 1.1 PERVASIVENESS

Research pertaining to the prevalence of various categories of crime for different geographical locations and periods of time is summarized in the tables in this section of Chapter 1. Prevalence estimates are obtained by dividing the number of crimes in a given geographical area by the number of human inhabitants in that area. For comparison purposes, the results of these calculations are nearly always expressed in terms of the number of crimes per 100,000 inhabitants.

### 1.1.1 Prevalence Estimates for Homicide

The earliest known estimates for the prevalence of homicide (murder) extend back into some medieval European cities. Nationwide estimates for Europe, however, did not begin to appear until several centuries later. The findings from these historic studies are summarized in Table 1.1.1 along with estimates from more contemporary times.

Examination of Table 1.1.1 reveals that overall there has been a dramatic downturn in homicide rates from earlier centuries. This table also contains estimates of "virtual murder" in several preliterate societies. *Virtual murders* are murders in all respects except that they occur where no written laws exist. Estimates are derived from anthropological interviews of members of foraging or tribal populations about the circumstances surrounding the deaths of their friends and relatives. It should be noted that often only a few hundred persons are interviewed which typically yields results surrounding the death of no more than a few thousand persons. Such a limited number of deaths reported do not provide stable estimates because official murder rates are usually expressed in terms of rates per 100,000. Nevertheless, this research has provided an interesting (but cloudy) window into the prevalence of deaths due to violence in preliterate societies.

Comparisons across vastly different cultures should be tempered with the realization that modern emergency medical services have dramatically lowered the likelihood of death from wounds suffered in many assaults. One estimate was that the current homicide rate would be as much as five times higher if today's emergency medical services were the same as those provided as recently as half a century ago (A Harris et al. 2002).

**TABLE 1.1.1 Annual Prevalence Estimates of Homicide (per 100,000 Population).**

| Prevalence estimates per 100,000 | Tribe | Geographic units of analyses | |
|---|---|---|---|
| | | City | Country |
| 250+ | **OCEANIA** *Philippines*: Headland 1986:542 (Agta, foragers – 326) | | |
| 150–250 | **SOUTH AMERICA** *Columbia*: Melancon 1982:33 (Yanomamo, horticulture – 166) | **EUROPE** *Italy:* MB Becker 1976:288 (in Florence in 1460 – 168) | |
| 100–149 | | **EUROPE** *England*: Gurr 1981:313 (in Oxford in 1340 – 110) | |
| 70–99 | | **SOUTH AMERICA** *Columbia*: Griswold 2005 (in Medellin in 2004 – 71) | **EUROPE** *Italy:* Bonger 1936:113 (in 1881 – 71) |
| 40–69 | | **EUROPE** *England*: Hanawalt 1979 (in London in the 1500s – ∼44); *Sweden*: Osterberg 1992:77 (in Stockholm in 1460 – 52) | **EUROPE** *Hungary:* Bonger 1936:113 (in 1875 – 52); *Spain*: Bonger 1936:113 (in 1885 – 68) |
| 20–39 | | **EUROPE** *England*: Gurr 1981:313 (in London in 1234 – 25, in 1340 – 35); *Germany:* Schussler 1992 (in Nuremberg in the 1300 – 20–38) **NORTH AMERICA** *United States*: Gurr 1981:325 (in Chicago in 1970 – 26) | **EUROPE** *Sweden*: Osterberg 1996:44 (in 1550 – 33) |
| 10–19 | **AFRICA** *South Africa*: Thomson 1980:101 (Xhosa, horticulture – 19.3); *Uganda*: Bolton 1984:2 (Sebei, simple hearders – 11.6); Southall 1960:228 (several tribes, subsistence farmers – ∼6) | **EUROPE** *Germany*: EA Johnson 1982:361 (in Berlin in 1915 – 19); *Netherlands*: Spierenburg 1994:707 (in Amsterdam in 1655 – 11) **NORTH AMERICA** *United States*: Bohannan 1967:218 (in Miami, FL in 1948 – 11); Gurr 1981:325 (in Chicago in 1960 – 10) | **EUROPE** *Sweden:* EA Johnson & Monkkone 1996:9 (in 1830 – 13); Osterberg 1996:44 (in 1824 – 10) |
| 5–9 | **AFRICA** *Uganda*: Southall 1960:228 (several tribes, subsistence farmers – ∼6) | **EUROPE** *Germany:* Schussler 1992 (in Nuremberg in 1984 – 5) **NORTH AMERICA** *United States*: Gurr 1981:325 (in Chicago in 1940 – 8; Gurr 1981:325; in Boston in 1880 – 7, in 1990 – 6) | **ASIA** *Soviet Union*: Gondolf & Shestakov 1997:68 **EUROPE** *Ireland*: Bonger 1936:113 (in 1885 – 9); *Sweden*: Osterberg 1996:44 (in 1760 – 32) |
| 2–4 | **AFRICA** *South Africa*: Bohannan 1960:158 (Bantu, subsistence farming – 4.6); Fallers & Fallers 1960:71 (Basoga, subsistence farming – 4.0); Lee 1979:398 (!Kung, foragers – 29.3) | **ASIA** *China*: Gaylor & Lang 1997:54 (in Hong Kong from 1955 1992 – 2–4) **EUROPE** *England:* Gurr 1981:313 (in London in 1900 – 3, in 1970 – 4); *Germany*: EA Johnson 1982:361 (in Berlin in 1860 – 2); *Netherlands*: Spierenburg 1994:707 (in Amsterdam in 1800 – 4) **NORTH AMERICA** *United States*: Gurr 1981:325 (in Boston in 1852 – 3) | **EUROPE** *Germany:* EA Johnson 1982:361 (from 1875 – 1886 – 2); *Netherlands*: Bonger 1936:113 (in 1880 – 4); EA Johnson & Monkkone 1996:9 (in 1899 – 4) |
| 0–1 | | | |

### 1.1.2 Percentage Estimates for Frequently Occurring Types of Offenses

In statistical terms, murder is an extremely rare crime. For this reason, as noted in the preceding table, its occurrence is usually expressed in annual terms of per 100,000 population. Table 1.1.2 pertains to much more common types of offenses. Specifically, the percentage estimates (i.e., "per 100") of the following are summarized in this table: (a) recidivism, (b) overall self-reported offending, and (c) the self-reported use of illegal drugs.

Recidivism pertains to the commission of an additional offense after having committed an earlier offense (which is usually inferred based on a prior conviction). As one can see, the estimates of recidivism rates range from 30 to 90%, depending on the length of time following release from custody to whether or not parole revocations are included as part of the recidivism measure.

The studies of overall self-reported offending are derived from surveys in which subjects voluntarily report (usually anonymously) the number of illegal acts they recall having committed. Unless specified otherwise, these acts include both victimful crimes (such as assaults, thefts, and vandalism) and victimless offenses (such as drug use and curfew or truancy violations). Table 1.1.2 suggests that approximately 90% of people recall having committed at least one delinquent or criminal act by the time they have reached their 20s.

At least in recent decades, the single most frequently reported type of self-reported offense is drug-related (mainly the possession and use of prohibited drugs, especially marijuana). Table 1.1.2 shows that the percentage estimates of illegal drug use varies considerably from one country to another, and also vary considerably within countries and within subpopulations over time.

### 1.1.3 Percentage Estimates for Antisocial Behavior and Chronic Physical Aggression

In Table 1.1.3 one finds a summary of studies that were located in which empirical estimates were provided regarding the prevalence of antisocial behavior. As one can see, all estimates are under 10%, and they are usually closer to 2–5%. This is true for both childhood and early adolescent forms (known as childhood conduct disorders) and for the forms that emerge in late adolescence or adulthood (called antisocial behavior or psychopathy). Chronic physical aggression, on the other hand, has been estimated to be more common than antisocial behavior, although still under 10%.

### 1.1.4 Criminal Versatility

According to one study of female prisoners, those who were diagnosed as psychopathic were more likely than those who were nonpsychopathic to have committed a wide range of offenses (Table 1.1.4). A review of the literature of offenders generally reached the same conclusion regarding a link between psychopathy and crime versatility (Hemphill et al. 1998).

### 1.1.5 Sequences in Criminal Offending

A few studies of self-reported offending have examined the following question: Do drug offenses usually precede or follow involvement in other types of crime? As shown in Table 1.1.5, the pertinent studies have concluded that drug offenses usually follow the commission of other (usually victimful) types of offenses.

### 1.1.6 Trends in Delinquent/Criminal Offending

One study was located regarding trends in victimful offending. As shown in Table 1.1.6, this study concluded that in the United States, the rates of violent and property crimes decreased substantially between 1994 and 2003.

## 1.2 INTRA-OFFENDING RELATIONSHIPS

Numerous studies have been undertaken to determine whether or not the commission of one type of crime is associated with the commission of one or more other types. Results of these studies, along with research correlating involvement in crime with the diagnosis of an antisocial personality condition, are presented below.

### 1.2.1 Officially Detected Violent Crime and Self-Reported Offending or Antisocial Behavior

A few studies have investigated the connection between officially detected involvement in violent crime and either self-reported illegal drug use or a diagnosis of antisocial personality or behavior. As shown in Table 1.2.1, these studies have concluded that these phenomena are all positively correlated with one another.

### 1.2.2 Officially Detected Drug Crimes and Delinquency in General

As shown in Table 1.2.2, one study conducted in two countries found that persons arrested for marijuana possession are more likely than persons in general to also be arrested for delinquency.

### 1.2.3 Officially Detected Delinquency and Criminal or Antisocial Behavior

According to numerous studies of official delinquency, such behavior is positively correlated with a statistically

**TABLE 1.1.2 Prevalence Estimates for Frequently Occurring Types of Offenses.**

| Prevalence estimates | Officially detected offenses | Self-reported offenses | |
|---|---|---|---|
| | Recidivism | Overall offenses | Drug offenses |
| 90–100% | | | |
| 80–89% | **NORTH AMERICA** *United States*: Langan & Levin 2002* (juveniles, rearrested within three years) | **EUROPE** *Sweden: Nilsson et al. 2005* (87% adol)* | |
| 70–79% | | | |
| 60–69% | | | **NORTH AMERICA** *United States*: EW Patterson 1988 (61% marijuana use, college students); Cuomo et al. 1994 (64% marijuana use, college students) |
| 50–59% | **NORTH AMERICA** *United States*: Langen & Levin 2002* (juveniles, rearrested & reconvicted within three years); Langen & Levin 2002* (adults, reimprisoned within three years, released in 1994) | **NORTH AMERICA** *United States*: Kraut 1976 (shoplifting, college students); Klemke 1982 (shoplifiting) | **EUROPE** *England*: Ashton & Kamali 1995 (50% marijuana use, medical/nursing students) **NORTH AMERICA** *United States*: penergast 1994 (59% marijuana use,college students); Mangweth et al. 1997:456 (59% marijuana use, college students) |
| 40–49% | | | **NORTH AMERICA** *United States*: Mathias 1999:58 (40–50% for all illegal drug use, high school seniors 1975–1987) |
| 30–39% | **NORTH AMERICA** *United States*: Langen & Levin 2002* (juveniles, rearrested & returned to prison, within three years) | **EUROPE** *Sweden: Nilsson et al. 2005* (37% adol, self-reported arrest)* | **EUROPE** *Austria*: Mangweth et al. 1997:466 (37% marijuana use, college students); *Spain*: Lopez et al. 1989 (31% marijuana use, college students); Del Rio et al. 1994 (30% marijuana use, college students); Casanovas et al. 1996 (30% marijuana use, college students) **NORTH AMERICA** *United States*: Mathias 1999:58 (30–40% for all illegal drug use, high school seniors 1988–1991 & 1994–1997) |
| 20–29% | | | **EUROPE** *Spain*: Hinojal et al. 1983 (25% marijuana use, college students); Queipo et al. 1988 (25% marijuana use, college students); Soler et al. 1992 (24% marijuana use, college students); Herreros et al. 1997 (24% marijuana use, college students) **NORTH AMERICA** *United States*: Mathias 1999:58 (27% for all illegal drug use, high school seniors 1992) |
| 10–19% | | | **EUROPE** *Spain*: Rubio et al. 1984 (17% marijuana use, medical students) |
| 0–9% | | | |

**TABLE 1.1.3 Prevalence Estimates for Antisocial Behavior and Chronic Physical Aggression.**

| Nature of the relationship | Antisocial behavior | | Chronic physical aggression |
|---|---|---|---|
| | Childhood & early adol. | Late adol. & adulthood | |
| 0–10% | **NORTH AMERICA** *United States*: Lahey et al. 1999 (3.2%) | **NORTH AMERICA** *United States*: LN Robins et al. 1991 (3–5%); Reiger et al. 1993 (2–3%); Moran 1999 (2–3%); Goodwin & Hamilton 2003 (3–5%); W Compton et al. 2005 (3–5%) | **NORTH AMERICA** *Canada*: Brame et al. 2001 (5–10%) |
| 11–20% | | | |
| 21–30% | | | |
| 31–40% | | | |
| 41–50% | | | |
| 51–60% | | | |
| 61–70% | | | |
| 71–80% | | | |
| 81–90% | | | |
| 91–100% | | | |

**TABLE 1.1.5 Sequences in Criminal Offending and Criminality/Delinquent Behavior.**

| Nature of the relationship | Self-reported offenses |
|---|---|
| | Overall offenses |
| Drug offending first | |
| Not signif. | |
| Non-drug offending first | **NORTH AMERICA** *United States*: Elliott et al. 1988 (victimful delinquency); Apospori et al. 1995 (victimful delinquency); Bui et al. 2000:297 (victimful delinquency) |

**TABLE 1.1.6 Trends in Delinquent/Criminal Offending and Criminality/Delinquent Behavior.**

| Nature of the relationship | Officially detected offenses |
|---|---|
| | General or adult crime |
| General increase | |
| Not signif. or irregular | |
| General decrease | **NORTH AMERICA** *United States*: HN Snyder 2005 (47%, violent & property crimes, between 1994 and 2003) |

significant degree with adulthood criminality and with self-reported offending. Also, persons who have been diagnosed with antisocial personality disorder are more likely to be officially identified as delinquent than are their unidentified peers (Table 1.2.3).

**TABLE 1.1.4 Criminal Versatility and antisocial behavior or factors frequently linked to Criminality.**

| Nature of the relationship | Antisocial behavior |
|---|---|
| | Late adol. & adult |
| Positive | **NORTH AMERICA** *United States*: Salekin et al. 1997 (female prisoners, psychopaths) |
| Not signif. | |
| Negative | |

**TABLE 1.2.1 Officially Detected Violent Crimes and Self-Reported Offending or Antisocial Behavior.**

| Nature of the relationship | Self-reported offenses | Antisocial behavior |
|---|---|---|
| | Illegal drugs | Late adol. & adult |
| Positive | **EUROPE** *Denmark*: Brennan et al. 2000 **NORTH AMERICA** *United States*: Steadman et al. 1998 **OCEANIA** *Australia*: C Wallace et al. 2004 | **EUROPE** *Finland*: Eronen et al. 1996 (homicide) **NORTH AMERICA** *Canada*: Cote & Hodgins 1992 (homicide, male prisoners) |
| Not signif. | | |
| Negative | | |

**TABLE 1.2.2 Officially detected Drug Crimes and Delinquency in General.**

| Nature of the relationship | Officially detected offenses |
|---|---|
| | Delinquency |
| Positive | **EUROPE** *Belgium*: Vermeiren et al. 2004:572* (marijuana use) **NORTH AMERICA** *United States*: Vermeiren et al. 2004:572* (marijuana use) |
| Not signif. | |
| Negative | |

## 1.2.4 Adult Crimes, Official and Delinquency or Antisocial Behavior

Table 1.2.4 summarizes findings concerning the relationship between an official identification as an adult offender and (a) involvement in delinquency and (b) a diagnosis of antisocial personality. The available evidence suggests that these phenomena are positively correlated with a significant degree.

**TABLE 1.2.4 Adult Crimes, Official and Delinquency or Antisocial Behavior.**

| Nature of the relationship | Officially detected offenses | Antisocial personality | |
|---|---|---|---|
| | Delinquency | Child & young adol. | Adol. & adult |
| Positive | **NORTH AMERICA** *United States*: Wolfgang et al. 1972 (Blacks); PE Tracy & Kampf-Leonard 1996 | **NORTH AMERICA** *United States*: Zoccolillo & Rogers 1991 (adolescent girls, convicted in adulthood); RJ Sampson & Laub 1993 | **NORTH AMERICA** *United States*: Lahey et al. 1998 (males) |
| Not signif. | | | |
| Negative | | | |

## 1.2.5 Recidivism and Delinquency or Antisocial Behavior

According to a couple of studies, general involvement in delinquency and a diagnosis of as psychopathic is positively correlated with the probability of recidivism when one has been involved in crime (Table 1.2.5).

## 1.2.6 Self-Reported Offenses in General

All of the research undertaken to determine if self-reported offending is statistically associated with other

**TABLE 1.2.3 Officially detected Delinquency and Criminal or Antisocial Behavior.**

| Nature of the relationship | Officially detected offenses | Self-reported offenses | | Antisocial personality | |
|---|---|---|---|---|---|
| | General & adult offenses | Overall offenses | Illegal drugs | Child & young adol. | Adol. & adult |
| Positive | **NORTH AMERICA** *United States*: Wolfgang et al. 1972 (Blacks); PE Tracy & Kampf-Leonard 1996 | **OCEANIA** *Australia*: Carroll et al. 2006:524* (males) | **EUROPE** *Belgium*: Vermeiren et al. 2004:572* (marijuana use) **NORTH AMERICA** *United States*: Vermeiren et al. 2004:572* (marijuana use) **OCEANIA** *Australia*: Carroll et al. 2006:524* (males) | **NORTH AMERICA** *Canada*: Broidy et al. 2003; *United States*: Laub & Sampson 1988; Pakiz et al. 1997 **OCEANIA** *New Zealand*: JL White et al. 1990 | **EUROPE** *Belgium*: Vermeiren et al. 2004:572* **NORTH AMERICA** *United States*: Vermeiren et al. 2004:572* |
| Not signif. | | | | | |
| Negative | | | | | |

**TABLE 1.2.5** Recidivism and Delinquency or Antisocial Behavior.

| Nature of the relationship | Officially detected offenses | Antisocial behavior |
|---|---|---|
| | Delinquency | Late adol. & adult |
| Positive | NORTH AMERICA *United States*: Luchansky et al. 2006:91 (teens in substance abuse treatment) | NORTH AMERICA *Canada*: SD Hart et al. 1990 (violent offense recidivism) |
| Not signif. | | |
| Negative | | |

**TABLE 1.2.6** Self-Reported Offenses in General and Criminal or Antisocial Behavior.

| Nature of the relationship | Officially detected offenses | Self-reported offenses | Antisocial behavior | |
|---|---|---|---|---|
| | Delinquency | Illegal drugs | Child & young adol. | Adol. & adult |
| Positive | OCEANIA *Australia*: Carroll et al. 2006:524* (males) | EUROPE *Belgium*: Vermeiren et al. 2004:572* (marijuana use) NORTH AMERICA *United States*: Vermeiren et al. 2004:572* (marijuana use) | NORTH AMERICA *United States*: Herrenkohl et al. 2000 (violent delinquency, teacher rated) | EUROPE *Belgium*: Vermeiren et al. 2004:572* (delinquency) NORTH AMERICA *United States*: Vermeiren et al. 2004:572* (delinquency) |
| Not signif. | | | | |
| Negative | | | | |

measures of criminality and/or antisocial behavior is in agreement that the relationships are positive and significant (Table 1.2.6).

## 1.2.7 Self-Reported Drug Offenses

Considerable research has shown that self-reported offending is positively correlated with both official crime measures and with those of antisocial behavior (Table 1.2.7).

## 1.2.8 Conduct Disorders in Childhood and Early Adolescence

Conduct disorder is a childhood and young adolescent clinical condition that is obviously not itself criminal or delinquent. Among its main symptoms are defiance of authority (e.g., parents and teachers), aggression toward peers, and general disciplinary difficulties (Fergusson et al. 2003:56). As shown in Table 1.2.8, all of the available research on statistical connections between conduct disorders and later involvement in criminality and/or delinquency has suggested that significant positive correlations exist. The table also shows that conduct disorder is very consistently correlated with a diagnosis of antisocial personality or psychopathy as an adolescent or an adult.

## 1.2.9 Antisocial Personality in Later Adolescence and Adulthood

As one can see by viewing Table 1.2.9, the research findings have been unanimous in indicating that antisocial behavior is positively correlated with criminal offending. There is also a very solid connection between adult antisocial personality and childhood conduct disorders.

**TABLE 1.2.7** Self-Reported Drug Offenses and Criminal or Antisocial Behavior.

| Nature of the relationship | Officially detected offenses | | Antisocial behavior | |
|---|---|---|---|---|
| | Violent offenses | Delinquency | Child & young adol. | Late adol. & adult |
| Positive | **EUROPE** *Denmark*: Brennan et al. 2000 **NORTH AMERICA** *United States*: Steadman et al. 1998 **OCEANIA** *Australia*: C Wallace et al. 2004 | **EUROPE** *Belgium*: Vermeiren et al. 2004:572* (marijuana use) **NORTH AMERICA** *United States*: Vermeiren et al. 2004:572* (marijuana use) **OCEANIA** *Australia*: Carroll et al. 2006:524* (males) | **NORTH AMERICA** *Canada*: Boyle & Offord 1991; Reebye et al. 1995; *United States*: Bukstein et al. 1989 (clinical data); Regier et al. 1990; B Neighbors et al. 1992 (among delinquents); Disney et al. 1999; Sung et al. 2004; Button et al. 2006 (twins, clinical data) **OCEANIA** *New Zealand*: Arseneault et al. 2000 (clinical data); Moffitt et al. 2002 (males) | **NORTH AMERICA** *United States*: LN Robins et al. 1991; Loeber et al. 2002; Goodwin & Hamilton 2003; W Compton et al. 2005 |
| Not signif. | | | | |
| Negative | | | | |

**TABLE 1.2.8** Conduct Disorder in Childhood and Early Adolescence and Criminal or Antisocial Behavior.

| Nature of the relationship | Officially detected offenses | | Self-reported offenses | | Antisocial behavior |
|---|---|---|---|---|---|
| | Delinquency | General & adult offenses | Overall offenses | Illegal drugs | Late adol. & adult |
| Positive | **NORTH AMERICA** *Canada*: Broidy et al. 2003; *United States*: Laub & Sampson 1988; Pakiz et al. 1997 **OCEANIA** *New Zealand*: JL White et al. 1990 | **NORTH AMERICA** *United States*: RJ Sampson & Laub 1993; Lahey et al. 1999 (males) | **NORTH AMERICA** *United States*: Zoccolillo & Rogers 1991 (adol. girls, convicted as adults); Loeber & Hay 1997; Herrenkohl et al. 2000 (violent delinquency) **OCEANIA** *New Zealand*: Wright et al. 1999 (rated by parents/ teachers, delinquency in general) | **NORTH AMERICA** *Canada*: Boyle & Offord 1991; Reebye et al. 1995; *United States*: Bukstein et al. 1989 (clinical data); Regier et al. 1990; B Neighbors et al. 1992 (among delinquents); Disney et al. 1999; Sung et al. 2004; Button et al. 2006 (twins, clinical data) **OCEANIA** *New Zealand*: Arseneault et al. 2000 (clinical data); Moffitt et al. 2002* (males) | **EUROPE** *Britain*: Harrington et al. 1991; Fombonne et al. 2001 **NORTH AMERICA** *Canada*: Tremblay et al. 2003 (males); *United States*: L Robins 1978:611; Fergusson & Horwood 1998; Lahey et al. 1998; Goodwin & Hamilton 2003; Loeber et al. 2003; Grant et al. 2004b; Sareen et al. 2004 **OCEANIA** *New Zealand*: Moffitt 1993; Moffitt et al. 2002* |
| Not signif. | | | | | |
| Negative | | | | | |

**TABLE 1.2.9** Antisocial Personality in Later Adolescence and Adulthood and Criminal/Antisocial Behavior.

| Nature of the relationship | Officially detected offenses | | | Self-reported offenses | Antisocial behavior |
|---|---|---|---|---|---|
| | Violent offenses | Delinquency | Recidivism | Illegal drugs | Child & young adol. |
| Positive | **EUROPE** *Finland*: Eronen et al. 1996 (homicide) **NORTH AMERICA** *Canada*: Cote & Hodgins 1992 (homicide, male prisoners) | **EUROPE** *Belgium*: Vermeiren et al. 2004:572* **NORTH AMERICA** *United States*: Vermeiren et al. 2004:572* | **NORTH AMERICA** *Canada*: SD Hart et al. 1990 (violent offense recidivism); Serin 1996 (Canada, violent crimes, especially Factor 1 of the PCL-R) | **NORTH AMERICA** *United States*: Loeber et al. 2002; Goodwin & Hamilton 2003; W Compton et al. 2005 | **EUROPE** *Belgium*: Vermeiren et al. 2004:572*; *Britain*: Harrington et al. 1991; Fombonne et al. 2001 **NORTH AMERICA** *Canada*: Tremblay et al. 2003 (males); *United States*: L Robins 1978a:611; Fergusson & Horwood 1998; Lahey et al. 1998; Goodwin & Hamilton 2003; Loeber et al. 2003; Grant et al. 2004b; Sareen et al. 2004; Vermeiren et al. 2004:572* **OCEANIA** *New Zealand*: Moffitt 1993; Moffitt et al. 2002 |
| Not signif. | | | | | |
| Negative | | | | | |

Chapter 2

# Demographic Correlates

**Contents**



Demographic variables are those having to do with the basic characteristics of individuals comprising a given society. These characteristics include gender (sex), age, race/ethnicity, and social status. An enormous amount of criminological research has sought to determine how demographic variables are related to involvement in criminal behavior.

## 2.1 GENDER/SEX

In all human societies, a person's gender (or sex) is the single most common characteristic with which persons are identified (Ellis et al. 2008:xi). As a result, an enormous number of studies have sought to determine if gender is related to involvement in crime and delinquency. So numerous are the studies that citations to them are presented in numerous tables, with each table pertaining to a specific type of crime.

### 2.1.1 Gender and Homicide

The research on gender differences in the commission of homicide is voluminous and far-reaching geographically. As shown in Table 2.1.1, these studies have shown without exception that males are more likely than females to be identified by law enforcement as having committed homicide.

TABLE 2.1.1 Gender and Homicide and Criminal/Delinquent Behavior.

| Nature of any difference | Officially detected offenses |
|---|---|
| | Homicides |
| Males more | **AFRICA** *Egypt* : Okasha et al. 1975:34; *Nigeria*: Asuni 1969; *South Africa*: Meel 2003:218<br>**ASIA** *India*: Elwin 1950; Saran 1974; Varma 1978; *Japan*: Tamura 1980<br>**EUROPE** *Britain*: d'Orban 1990; Gibson & Klein 1961; West 1965 (followed by suicide); Given 1977 (13th Century); Monkkonen 1989 (19th Century); Barraclough & Harris 2002 (followed by suicide); *Finland*: Verkko 1951; *France*: Lecomte & Fornes 1998 (followed by suicide); *Iceland*: Gudjonsson & Petursson 1982; *Scotland*: Gillies 1976; *Sweden*: Gottlieb et al. 1987; von Hofer 1990:31 (18th–20th century)<br>**LATIN AMERICA** *Brazil*: Yearwood 1974<br>**MIDDLE EAST** *Israel*: Landau et al. 1974<br>**NORTH AMERICA** *Canada*: Moyer 1992:398; Gartner 1995:200; *United States*: Wolfgang 1958:31; Pokorny 1965; Wolfgang 1967:18; Voss & Hepburn 1968; Curtis 1977:164; Swigert & Farrell 1977:21; Messner 1985; Weiner & Wolfgang 1985:27; Goetting 1988; Monkkonen 2001; Jurik & Winn 1990; Spergel 1995:108 (gang-related); McKanna 1997:42 (19th Century); Monkkonen 2001; R Shelden et al. 2001 (gang-related); Batton 2004<br>**OCEANIA** *Australia*: Wallace 1986; Milroy et al. 1997 (followed by suicide); *New Zealand*: Moskowitz et al. 2006:424 (followed by suicide)<br>**INTERNATIONAL** *Multiple Preliterate Societies*: Bohannan 1960a:36; Bohannan 1960c:240; JH Beattie 1960:134; Fallers & Fallers 1960:76; Southall 1960:217; La Fontaine 1960:106; *Various Preindustrial Countries*: Verkko 1967:42; Konner 1982:274; Daly & Wilson 1990 |
| No signif. diff. | |
| Females more | |

## 2.1.2 Gender and Official Violent Offenses in General

Numerous studies have been conducted to determine if the sexes differ with respect to involvement in violent crime. As shown in Table 2.1.2, throughout the world, all of the available research has converged on the conclusion that males engage in more violence-laden offenses than do females.

## 2.1.3 Gender and Official Property Offenses

Are there gender differences in the commission of property crimes? Table 2.1.3 summarizes the findings, and suggests that for all crimes except shoplifting (where females appear to be more involved than males), there is a worldwide tendency for males to be more involved as offenders than females.

TABLE 2.1.2 Gender and Official Violent Offenses in General and Criminal/Delinquent Behavior.

| Nature of any difference | Officially detected offenses |
|---|---|
| | Violent offenses |
| Males more | **AFRICA** *Egypt*: Okasha et al. 1975:34; *Nigeria*: Asuni 1963; Asuni 1969; *South Africa*: Meel 2003:218<br>**ASIA** *India*: Elwin 1950; Saran 1974; Varma 1978; *Japan*: Tamura 1980<br>**EUROPE** *Britain*: d'Orban 1990; Gibson & Klein 1961; Given 1977 (13th century); Home Office Statistical Bulletin 1996; Monkkonen 2001; Min Yang 2007 (adults); *Denmark*: Brennan et al. 2000; *Finland*: Verkko 1951; Viemero 1996:94; M Cannon et al. 2002:499 (among schizophrenics); *Germany*: Goppinger 1983:365; Groebel 1983:80; *Netherlands*: Blokland 2005:52<br>**NORTH AMERICA** *Canada*: Hartnagel 1987:77; Boritch & Hagan 1990:575 (19th century); *United States*: Boelkins & Heiser 1970:31; Detre et al. 1975; Block 1977; Hindelang 1981:466; Steffensmeier & Cobb 1981; Tinkenberg & Ochberg 1981; Bainbridge & Crutchfield 1983:261; Wilson & Herrnstein 1985:108; Rivera & Widom 1990: Sommers & Baskin 1992:193; Zingraff et al. 1993:192; RB Felson 1996; Steffensmeier & Allan 1996; JF Short 1997:8; Piquero & Tibbetts 1999; Capaldi & Owen 2001 (serious domestic violence); Monkkonen 2001; Piquero & Tibbetts 1991; RB Felson & Cares 2005 (serious domestic violence)<br>**OCEANIA** *New Zealand*: Ritchie & Ritchie 1983:330; McGee et al. 1990 (among conduct disordered adol.)<br>**INTERNATIONAL** *Multiple Countries*: Kruttschnitt 1993; *Various Preindustrial Societies*: Bacon et al. 1963:292; Curtis 1974:160; Curtis 1977:164 |
| No signif. diff. | |
| Females more | |

TABLE 2.1.3 Gender and Official Property Offenses and Criminal/Delinquent Behavior.

| Nature of any difference | Officially detected offenses |
|---|---|
| | Property offenses |
| Males more | **EUROPE** *Britain*: Box & Hale 1984; *Denmark*: LA Baker et al. 1989:358; *Germany*: Goppinger 1978:365; *Netherlands*: Blokland 2005:52<br>**NORTH AMERICA** *Canada*: Tepperman 1977; Hartnagel 1987:77; Boritch & Hagan 1990:578 (nineteenth century); *United States*: Healy & Bronner 1926:278; Parmelee 1926:240; Riddle 1927; Hindelang et al. 1979; Simon 1979; Steffensmeier 1978; Steffensmeier 1980; Steffensmeier & Cobb 1981; Wilson & Herrnstein 1985:108; D Cox et al. 1990 (shoplifting); Weisburd et al. 1991 (white-collar fraud convictions); Chadwick & Top 1993:62<br>**OCEANIA** *New Zealand*: Ritchie & Ritchie 1983:330<br>**INTERNATIONAL** *Multiple Preindustrial Countries*: Bacon et al. 1963:292 |
| No signif. diff. | |
| Females more | **EUROPE** *Britain*: Farrington & Painter 2002 (shoplifting)<br>**NORTH AMERICA** *United States*: J Ray & Briar 1988 (shoplifting); Abelson 1989 (shoplifting, kleptomania); Klemke 1992 (shoplifting) |

## 2.1.4 Gender and Sexual Assault

Perhaps because the answer is so obvious, only a few studies were located which specifically documented that most sex offenses are committed by males (Table 2.1.4).

## 2.1.5 Gender and Official Drug Offenses

Using official data sources, several studies in various countries have been undertaken to assess whether the sexes differ in their involvement in drug offenses. As shown in Table 2.1.5, these studies have all concluded that males commit these offenses at higher rates than do females.

## 2.1.6 Gender and Official Delinquency in General

A large number of studies of official delinquency rates according to the sex of the offender have been undertaken. Table 2.1.6 clearly shows that all of these studies have drawn the same conclusion: Males exhibit higher overall delinquency involvement than do females.

## 2.1.7 Gender and Official Adult Offenses (or Offenses in General)

Studies that have sought to determine if males or females are more involved in adult offending are summarized in Table 2.1.7. This table shows that in all societies, males are more likely to be identified as criminals by the criminal justice system. Several of the studies cited in Table 2.1.7 reflect findings from arrest, conviction, and imprisonment data extending *back* prior to the twentieth century. Overall, this table provides little support for the assertion of Robbers

TABLE 2.1.4 Gender and Sexual Assault.

| Nature of any difference | Sexual assault | |
|---|---|---|
| | Officially detected | Victim reports |
| Males more | **NORTH AMERICA** *United States*: National Council on Crime and Delinquency 1976 (parolees); Groth & Burgess 1980:806 (rape); DE Russell 1994:67 (arrests for rape) | **NORTH AMERICA** *United States* |
| No signif. diff. | | |
| Females more | | |

TABLE 2.1.5 Gender and official Drug Offenses.

| Nature of any difference | Officially detected offenses |
|---|---|
| | Drug offenses |
| Males more | **ASIA** *China*: Wu 1996:238; *Taiwan*: Denq et al. 1996:357<br>**NORTH AMERICA** *United States*: Strimbu et al. 1973; Wechsler & McFadden 1976; Bainbridge & Crutchfield 1983:259; Forthun et al. 1999:80 (alcohol and marijuana, in high school); Greenfield et al. 2003; Luchansky et al. 2006:91 (receive treatment, mainly marijuana & alcohol)<br>**OCEANIA** *New Zealand*: Ritchie & Ritchie 1983:331 |
| No signif. diff. | |
| Females more | |

**TABLE 2.1.6 Gender and Official Delinquency in General.**

| Nature of any difference | Officially detected offenses |
|---|---|
| | Delinquency |
| Males more | **AFRICA** *Nigeria*: Asuni 1963<br>**ASIA** *India*: Hartjen & Kethineni 1993:71; *Soviet Union*: Connor 1970:286<br>**EUROPE** *Britain*: Mulligan et al. 1963; Cockburn & Maclay 1965; Scholfield 1965:149; Douglas et al. 1966; Palmai et al. 1967:1075; A Edwards 1973; Miller et al. 1974; Wadsworth 1979:103; Ouston 1984; Figueira-McDonough 1986; R West et al. 1990; *Finland*: Almqvist 1986:296; Rantakallio et al. 1995:115; *Norway*: Pedersen & Wichstrom 1995:554; Pedersen et al. 2001:422; *Poland*: Hersch 1937:865; *Spain*: Diaz 1994:312; *Sweden*: Elmhorn 1965:38; Sigvardsson et al. 1982; Magnusson 1988<br>**NORTH AMERICA** *Canada*: Linden & Fillmore 1981; McCarthy & Hagan 1987; *United States*: Roach 1937; Ackerson 1931; Maller 1933; Maller 1937; Radzinowicz 1937:91; Porterfield 1946; Schwartz 1949:12; Wattenberg & Saunders 1954; Gibbons & Griswold 1957; Mensh et al. 1959; Barker & Adams 1962; JC Ball 1962; Havighurst et al. 1962:69; Hathaway & Monchesi 1963; JC Ball et al. 1965; Wise 1967; RA Gordon 1973; Robins 1975:129; GF Jensen & Eve 1976; Tagaki & Platt 1978:14; Warren 1979; Kashani et al. 1980; Steffensmeier & Steffensmeier 1980a; Wilkinson 1980:27; Feyerherm 1981; Giallombardo 1982:46; Shannon 1982; Bainbridge & Crutchfield 1983:261; Roff & Wirt 1984; Tracy et al. 1985:6; J Wilson & Herrnstein 1985:106; H White et al. 1985:191; LeFlore 1988:637; Shelden & Chesney-Lind 1993:84; Streissguth et al. 1996 (prenatal alcohol exposed); Pakiz et al. 1997; CD Coles et al. 2000 (prenatal alcohol exposed)<br>**OCEANIA** *Hawaii*: Voss 1963:323; E Werner 1987:22; E Werner & Smith 1992:103; *Samoa*: R Freeman 1983 |
| No signif. diff. | |
| Females more | |

**TABLE 2.1.7 Gender and Official Adult Offenses (or Offenses in General).**

| Nature of any difference | Officially detected offenses |
|---|---|
| | General & adult offenses |
| Males more | **AFRICA** *Ghana*: Seidman & Eyison 1969:63; *Multiple African Countries*: Houchon 1967; Clifford 1969:240; Leslie 1969:170<br>**ASIA** *India*: Bhanot & Mishra 1978; R Simon & Sharma 1979:104 & 394; Nagla 1982; *Soviet Union*: Koerber 1935:5; Serio 1992b:10; Ogawa 1976:601; *Taiwan*: Chow 1964:27<br>**EUROPE** *Britain*: Cockburn & Maclay 1965; Mannheim 1965:678; Gatrell & Hadden 1972:389 (19th century); Beattie 1975 (18th century); Weiner 1975 (17th century); Zehr 1975 (18th century); Wadsworth 1979; Farrington 1981; Farrington 1987:47; Ouston 1984; Kolvin et al. 1988: J Stevenson & Goodman 2001; Farrington & Painter 2002 (burglary and vehicle theft); *Denmark*: Raine et al. 1997a; *Finland*: Pulkkinen 1988 (47% versus 16% by age 27); Rantakallio et al. 1995; Statistics Finland 2002; *Germany*: Wurtenberger & Koch 1976:479; *Hungary*: Hacker 1949; *Italy*: Giannini 1976:548; *Sweden*: Stattin & Magnusson 1989; Wikstrom 1990:77; Wikstrom 1991:71; *Multiple European Countries*: Quetelet 1842 (18th century); Lombroso 1911:181 (19th century)<br>**LATIN AMERICA** *Argentina*: DeFleur 1970:131; Blarduni 1976:154; *Venezuela*: Mayorca 1976<br>**MIDDLE EAST** *Israel*: Sherer 1992<br>**NORTH AMERICA** *Canada*: Szabo & Rico 1976:309; *United States*: Healy & Bronner 1926:255; Parmelee 1926:240; Kavanagh 1928:147; Gillin 1929:57; Gillin 1935:48; Radzinowicz 1937; Pollack 1950; East 1951:281; Gibbons & Griswold 1957; Eaton & Polk 1961:19; Barker & Adams 1962; Lunden 1964:68; A Shaw 1966:148; Reckless 1967:98; E Green 1970:480; Noblit & Burcart 1976; Schaffer 1976:102; Vinter et al. 1976:23; Weiss 1976; Norland & Shover 1977:21; Hamparian et al. 1978; Hindelang 1980; Steffensmeier & Steffensmeier 1980; Hindlang 1981; Shannon 1981; Steffensmeier & Cobb 1981; Warr 1982:196; Steffensmeier 1983; JQ Wilson & Herrnstein 1985:106; Stein et al. 1987; Bureau of the Census 1989 (imprisonment); Steffensmeier & Streifel 1991; R O'Brien 1999; Steffensmeier & Haynie 2000b; D'Unger et al. 2002:367; Juon et al. 2006; McGloin et al. 2006<br>**OCEANIA** *Australia*: O'Brien 1970:286; Blarduni 1976:154; *New Zealand*: Moffitt et al. 2001<br>**INTERNATIONAL** *Multiple Industrial Countries*: Bonger 1916 (19th century); Goppinger 1983:361; R Simon & Sharma 1979:104 & 394; Hurwitz & Christiansen 1983:260 |
| No signif. diff. | |
| Females more | |

TABLE 2.1.8 Gender and Recidivism and Criminal/ Delinquent Behavior.

| Nature of any difference | Officially detected offenses |
|---|---|
| | Recidivism |
| Males more | **ASIA** *Japan*: Ogawa 1976:601<br>**EUROPE** *Italy*: Giannini 1976:548; *Netherlands*: Blokland 2005:113<br>**NORTH AMERICA** *United States*: Unkovic & Ducsay 1969; Meade 1973; L Brown 1978:98; Brundage 1984; M Jacobs 1990; DO Lewis et al. 1991; Robins et al. 1991 (multiple arrests, among persons diagnosed with antisocial personality disorder); K Minor et al. 1997:337<br>**OCEANIA** *Australia*: Broadhurst et al. 1988; Broadhurst & Maller 1990 |
| No signif. diff. | **NORTH AMERICA** *United States*: C Thomas 1977:61; P Schmidt & White 1979; SD Gottfredson & DM Gottfredson 1979; J Carroll et al. 1982; Roundtree et al. 1984 |
| Females more | |

(2004:548) that there has been a "steady closing of the criminal gender gap year by year" (also see Adler 1975; R Simons 1975 for similar propositions).

## 2.1.8 Gender and Recidivism

Recidivism refers to an individual becoming involved in crime after having been previously involved. Operationalizing recidivism can be done in a variety of ways (e.g., re-arrest, reconviction, reimprisonment) after various lengths of time following prison release (e.g., six months, two years, five years). Studies that have investigated sex differences in recidivism rates are summarized in Table 2.1.8. Most studies have found males exhibiting higher rates of recidivism than females, although some studies failed to find a significant sex difference.

## 2.1.9 Gender and Self-Reported Offenses in General

Gender differences in self-reported offending have been widely studied. As shown in Table 2.1.9, they have revealed

TABLE 2.1.9 Gender and Self-Reported Offenses in General.

| Nature of any difference | Self-reported offenses |
|---|---|
| | Overall offenses |
| Males more | **ASIA** *India*: Hartjen & Kethineni 1993:46<br>**EUROPE** *Belgium*: Born & Gavray 1994:140; *Britain*: SB Eysenck 1981:34; D Riley & Shaw 1985; Bowling et al. 1994:51; Home Office Research & Statistics Department 1995; Newcombe et al. 1995:333; Home Office Statistical Bulletin 1996 (violent crime); G Palmer & Hollin 1996; Farrington et al. 1998 (length of criminal careers); Farrington & Painter 2002 (adol.); *Denmark*: Arnett & Jensen 1994:10 (shoplifting, vandalism); *Finland*: Aromaa 1994:27; *Germany*: Boers et al. 1994:352; Sutterer & Karger 1994:165; *Greece*: Spinellis et al. 1994:301; *Ireland*: McQuoid 1994:72; *Italy*: Gatti et al. 1994:273; *Netherlands*: Terlouw & Bruinsma 1994:109; *Spain*: Barberet et al. 1994:273; *Sweden*: Elmhorn 1965<br>**MIDDLE EAST** *Israel*: Sherer & Karnieli-Miller 2004:103 (sex offenses, adolescents)<br>**NORTH AMERICA** *Canada*: LeBlanc 1983; Hagan et al. 1985; Paetsch & Bertrand 1997:30; La Grange & Silverman 1999; Nakhaie et al. 2000; Higgins & Makin 2004; *United States*: Wallerstein & Wyle 1947; Schofield 1965:150; M Gold 1966:46; Voss 1966; Hirschi 1969; Hindelang 1971:526; Datesman et al. 1975; M Gold & Reimer 1975; Kratcoski & Kratcoski 1975; G Jensen & Eve 1976; Kraut 1976 (shoplifting, college students); Biron & La Blanc 1977 (delinquency); Cernkovich & Giordano 1979a; Cernkovich & Giordano 1979b; Cullen et al. 1979:306; RE Johnson 1979; Steffensmeier & Steffensmeier 1980; Hindelang et al. 1981; Canter 1982b; Klemke 1982 (shoplifting, adolescents); Lott et al. 1982:312 (sexual assault); W Wilkinson et al. 1982:228; Bainbridge & Crutchfield 1983; D Elliott et al. 1983; Sigelman et al. 1984:538; McGarrell & Flanagan 1985:Table 3.48; D Elliott et al. 1986:486; R Johnson 1986:69; Morash 1986; Cernkovich & Giordano 1987:306; Bjerregaard & Smith 1993 (violent crime among gang members); J Wood et al. 1993; Arnett & Jensen 1994:10 (shoplifting, vandalism); DS Elliott 1994:6; Kruttschnitt 1994 (violent crime); Marshall & Webb 1994:332; Felson 1996; Saner & Ellickson 1996; Burton et al. 1998; Gibbs et al. 1998 (delinquency); Alarid et al. 2000:178* (among prisoners, property crime); Herrenkohl et al. 2000 (adolescents, violent delinquency); Wright et al. 2001 (delinquency); Hay 2003; Tittle et al. 2003; Wiebe 2003; Higgins 2004; Liu & Kaplan 2004 (delinquency); Burt et al. 2006; Felson & Staff 2006; Higgins & Tewksbury 2006<br>**OCEANIA** *Australia*: McAllister & Makkai 1991; Rigby et al. 1989; Heaven 1996:748; Rigby & Cox 1996; *Hawaii*: Voss 1963:326; *New Zealand*: Moffitt et al. 1994:361; DM Fergusson et al. 2002 (violent and property offending) |
| No signif. diff. | **NORTH AMERICA** *Canada*: Santesso et al. 2006:319 (maternal-reported, males more but not significantly, $n=40$); *United States*: Alarid et al. 2000:178* (among prisoners, violent & drug offenses); Wainright & Patterson 2006:529 (delinquency) |
| Females more | |

TABLE 2.1.10 Gender and Self-Reported Courtship and Domestic Violence and Criminal/Delinquent Behavior.

| Nature of any difference | Self-reported offenses | |
|---|---|---|
| | Courtship (dating) violence | Domestic violence |
| Males more | **NORTH AMERICA** *United States*: Lott et al. 1982 (sexually assaulted a date); Makepeace 1983 (serious injury); Sigelman et al. 1984:538 (sexually assaulted a date); L Ellis et al. 1990:1210 (sexually assaulted a date); White & Koss 1991; Fee & Margolin 1995* (serious injury); Merrill & Hervig 1997* (serious injury) | **EUROPE** *Britain*: Dobash et al. 1992 (resulting in serious injury)<br>**NORTH AMERICA** *United States*: WG Goldberg & Tomlanovich 1994 (resulting in emergency room treatment); Stets & Straus 1990 (resulting in significant injury); Vivian & Langhinrichten-Rohling 1994 |
| No signif. diff. | **EUROPE** *Britain*: R West et al. 1990:479<br>**NORTH AMERICA** *United States*: Aries 1987; Marshall & Rose 1988; White & Koss 1991; Tontodonato & Crew 1992 | **EUROPE** *Britain*: Nazron 1995<br>**NORTH AMERICA** *United States*: Straus 1980; Straus & Gelles 1986; McNeely & Robinson-Simpson 1987; O'Leary et al. 1989* (serious injury); Pan et al. 1994 |
| Females more | **NORTH AMERICA** *United States*: Riggs et al. 1990<br>**NORTH AMERICA** *United States*: Sigelman et al. 1984; Riggs et al. 1990; Fee & Margolin 1995* (minor or no injury); Mervill & Hervig 1997* (minor injury) | **EUROPE** *Britain*: Archer & Ray 1989<br>**NORTH AMERICA** *United States*: O'Leary & Arias 1988; O'Leary et al. 1989* (minor injury); McNeely & Mann 1990; Magdol et al. 1997 |

overwhelmingly that males self-report greater involvement in crime and delinquency than do females. One study provided strong evidence that self-reports actually underestimate the degree to which males surpass females in offending mainly because females are more conscientious and complete in self-reporting their offenses than are males (Kim et al. 2000).

## 2.1.10 Gender and Self-Reported Courtship Violence and Domestic Violence

Research that has been undertaken to determine which sex is more likely to engage in courtship or domestic violence has reached mixed conclusions. These inconsistent findings appear to be mainly explainable in terms of two factors: the sexual nature and the injurious nature of the violence. As shown in Table 2.1.10, when courtship violence of a sexually motivated nature are potentially quite injurious to the victim, males are more likely to be the aggressor. However, when violence of a non-sexual nature occurs, females appear to be the more frequent aggressor, particularly when the attacks have little likelihood of causing serious injury.

## 2.1.11 Gender and Self-Reported Drug Offenses

Many studies have been undertaken to determine if a sex difference exists in the use of illegal drugs using self-reports. As one can see by viewing Table 2.1.11, the overwhelming majority of these studies have concluded that males surpass females in this regard. Nevertheless, a substantial minority of studies have either failed to find significant sex differences or have actually concluded that females are more prone to use illegal drugs than males.

## 2.1.12 Gender and Crime Versatility

One study was located pertaining to sex differences in crime versatility, meaning the extent to which offenses tend to be of a similar (or homogeneous) character rather than of a varied (or heterogeneous) character. Table 2.1.12 shows that males were found to be more versatile than females in the offenses they committed.

## 2.1.13 Gender and Antisocial Behavior in Childhood and Early Adolescence

A very large number of studies have been conducted in numerous countries to determine which sex is more likely to be diagnosed with conduct disorder. Table 2.1.13 shows that all but one of the findings have pointed to males as exhibiting conduct disorder more. The exception was a New Zealand study that separated conduct disorder involving aggression and that involving no aggression. This study concluded that only conduct disorder accompanied by aggression was exhibited by a greater proportion of males.

## 2.1.14 Gender and Antisocial Disorder in Late Adolescence and Adulthood

Research findings are extremely consistent in indicating that males are more likely than females to be diagnosed with antisocial personality or antisocial disorder (also referred to

TABLE 2.1.11 Gender and Self-Reported Drug Offenses and Criminal/Delinquent Behavior.

| Nature of any difference | Self-reported offenses<br>Illegal drugs |
|---|---|
| Males more | **ASIA** *Russia*: Knyazev 2004:313 (adolescents)<br>**EUROPE** *Belgium*: Born & Gavray 1994:140; *Britain*: Evans et al. 1974; *Germany*: Sutterer & Karger 1994:165; *Greece*: Spinellis et al. 1994:301; *Italy*: Gatti et al. 1994:273; *Spain*: Barberet et al. 1994:247; *Switzerland*: Killias et al. 1994:195; *Multiple European Countries*: VanReek & Adrinase 1994<br>**LATIN AMERICA** *Puerto Rico*: Latimer et al. 2004 (marijuana)<br>**NORTH AMERICA** *Canada*: Laforest 1969; Smart et al. 1970; Annis et al. 1971; Fejer 1971; Fejer et al. 1972; Boggs & Hughes 1973; Bakal et al. 1975; Currie et al. 1977; Killeen 1977; Hollander & Macurdy 1978; *United States*: Frumkin et al. 1969; Gossett et al. 1971; Hager et al. 1971; Milman & Su 1973; Galli & Stone 1975; Harrell & Cisin 1980; Gleaton & Smith 1981; Winfree et al. 1981; Fors & Rojeck 1983:216; Barnes & Welte 1986; Newcomb et al. 1987:424; R Simons et al. 1991:658; V Peters et al. 1992; Opland et al. 1995; Gottfredson & Koper 1996; Johanson et al. 1996; Liu & Kaplan 1996; Nagel et al. 1996:292; Zebrowski & Gregory 1996; Ousey & Maume 1997 (marijuana use); Ploeger 1997 (marijuana use); Wadsworth et al. 1997:567; Whitmore et al. 1997:92; Novins & Mitchell 1998 (marijuana & cocaine, adolescents); Disney et al. 1999 (adolescents, clinical diagnosis); JS Gray & Winterowd 2002 (Native Americans); ONDCP 2003 (marijuana); JM Wallace et al. 2003 (marijuana, adol.); Ohannessian et al. 2004 (marijuana dependency)<br>**OCEANIA** *Australia*: Levy & Pierce 1990 |
| No signif. diff. | **EUROPE** *Germany*: Boers et al. 1994:352<br>**NORTH AMERICA** *Canada*: Moyer & Fejer 1972; *United States*: Wechsler & Thum 1973; Prendergast 1974; Wexler 1975; Forslund 1977; L Johnston et al. 1985; Agnew & White 1992:486; Arnett & Jensen 1994:9 (marijuana); Gfellner & Hundleby 1994; I Marshall & Webb 1994:332; Winfree et al. 1994:163; Mieczkowski 1996:382<br>**OCEANIA** *Australia*: Pirkis et al. 2003:282 (adolescents, marijuana) |
| Females more | **EUROPE** *Denmark*: Arnett & Jensen 1994:9 (marijuana); *Finland*: Aromaa 1994:27; *Norway*: W Pedersen et al. 2001 (marijuana)<br>**NORTH AMERICA** *United States*: Donnermeyer et al. 1987 |

as psychopathy). According to Table 2.1.14, the supportive evidence comes from a substantial number of different countries.

### 2.1.15 Gender and Physical Aggression

Physical aggression is a common behavioral component in criminality, especially violent criminality. For this reason, it is relevant to ask whether sex differences in physical aggression exist. As shown in Table 2.1.15, nearly all of the research located in the content of searching for correlates of crime found males to be more prone toward physical aggression than females. For more evidence, see Ellis et al. (2008:705–708).

TABLE 2.1.12 Gender and Crime Versatility and Criminal/Delinquent Behavior.

| Nature of any difference | Officially-detected offenses<br>Crime versatility |
|---|---|
| Males more | **EUROPE** *Britain*: Soothill et al. 2000 |
| No signif. diff. | |
| Females more | |

## 2.2 AGE AND MATURATION

The age of individuals who engage in crime (including delinquency) has been widely studied. Findings from those studies are reviewed below.

### 2.2.1 Age and Official Delinquency/Crime

The association between age and official delinquent and criminal behavior has been widely studied. As shown in Table 2.2.1, studies have unanimously concluded that such behavior is most heavily concentrated in the second and third decades of life.

### 2.2.2 Age and Self-Reported Delinquency/Crime

Compared to official data, relatively few studies of age and self-reported crime and delinquency have been published. This is because most self-reported offending studies are based on data derived from high school and college students. Nevertheless, Table 2.2.2 shows that these studies reinforced the conclusion based on official data that offending is most common among persons in their teens and 20s.

### 2.2.3 Age of Onset of Offending

A large number of studies have been undertaken to determine if early or late onset of offending is predictive of

**TABLE 2.1.13 Gender and Antisocial Behavior in Childhood and Early Adolescence and Criminal/Delinquent Behavior.**

| Nature of any difference | Antisocial behavior |
|---|---|
| | **Child & early adol.** |
| Males more | **ASIA** *China*: Rutter et al. 1974:250; Ekblad 1990:787<br>**EUROPE** *Britain*: Rutter et al. 1970:205; P Graham & Rutter 1973; Leslie 1974; Cochrone 1979:204; Rushton et al. 1986; Rutter 1988; Thapar & McGuffin 1996:1113; *Finland*: Pulkkinen 1983:138; Almqvist 1986:296; *Germany*: Furtado et al. 2006; *Sweden*: Magnusson et al. 1975; *Netherlands*: Verhulst et al. 1990:424; Verhulst et al. 1997; *Norway*: Schulz Jorgensen et al. 1993; Backe-Hansen & Ogden 1996:340<br>**NORTH AMERICA** *Canada*: Offord et al. 1986:275; Marriage et al. 1986:688; Offord et al. 1987:834; Tremblay et al. 1988; Rae-Grant et al. 1989; Szatmari et al. 1989; Offord et al. 1991; Santesso et al. 2006; *United States*: Frisk et al. 1966:132; Widom 1977; Cairns & Cairns 1984; Roff & Wirt 1984; Jary & Stewart 1985:11; Richman et al. 1985a; Richman et al. 1985b; Offord et al. 1986; Robins 1986:385; Cohen et al. 1987; Velez 1989:862; Gresham & Elliot 1990; Gabel & Shindledecker 1991; L Robins et al. 1991:268; Lewinsohn et al. 1993; Loeber & Keenan 1994; Comings 1995:148; EO Johnson et al. 1995; Lavigne et al. 1996 (externalizing behavior); Marcus & Betzer 1996; McDermott 1996; Ellickson et al. 1997:989; Lahey et al. 1998; Disney et al. 1999 (clinical data); Lahey et al. 1999; Sanford 1999; Silverthorn & Frick 1999; Lahey et al. 2000 (externalizing behavior); McCabe et al. 2001; Gadow et al. 2002 (externalizing behavior); Dekovic et al. 2004 (adolescents); McCabe et al. 2004; Ohannessian et al. 2004 (self-report by adolescents)<br>**OCEANIA** *New* Zealand: JC Anderson et al. 1990; R McGee et al. 1990; L McGee et al. 1992* (with significant aggression) |
| No signif. diff. | **OCEANIA** *New Zealand*: L McGee et al. 1992* (without significant aggression) |
| Females more | |

**TABLE 2.1.14 Gender and Antisocial Disorder in Late Adolescence and Adulthood and Criminal/Delinquent Behavior.**

| Nature of any difference | Antisocial behavior |
|---|---|
| | **Late adol. & adult** |
| Males more | **EUROPE** *Britain*: Edelmann & Vivian 1988:583; *Denmark*: Cloninger et al. 1978; *Sweden*: Halldin 1984:511<br>**MIDDLE EAST** *Israel*: Dohrenwend et al. 1992: 949<br>**NORTH AMERICA** *Canada*: R Hare 1980; M Swanson et al. 1994; Forth et al. 1996; *United States*: Cloninger et al. 1975a; Cloninger et al. 1975b; Guze 1976; Mednick et al. 1977; L Robins 1978:264; L Robins 1991; Cantwell 1981:22; Cadoret et al. 1984:3; J Fox 1984; L Robins et al. 1984; L Robins 1986; Coolidge et al. 1990; L Robins et al. 1991:265; Cottler et al. 1995<br>**OCEANIA** *Australia*: Slutske et al. 1997 (twins); *New Zealand*: Mulder et al. 1994 |
| No signif. diff. | |
| Females more | |

**TABLE 2.1.15 Gender and Physical Aggression.**

| Nature of the relationship | Self-reported and observed by others |
|---|---|
| | **Physical aggression/violence/fighting** |
| Males more | **EUROPE** *Britain*: WM Craig 1998 (school age); *Estonia*: Peets & Kikas 2006 (young adol.); *Germany*: Scheithauer et al. 2006 (5$^{th}$–10$^{th}$ graders)<br>**MIDDLE EAST** *Israel*: Harel et al. 1997 (adolescents); Sherer & Karnieli-Miller 2004 (adolescents)<br>**NORTH AMERICA** *United States*: Olweus 1991 (prepubertal children, reported by teachers, bullying); Whitney & Smith 1993 (adolescents); NR Crick & Grotpeter 1995 (childhood); Farrell & Bruce 1997 (adolescents); Kingery et al. 1998 (adolescents, in school); Seals & Young 2003:742 (adolescents, bullying)<br>**OCEANIA** *New Zealand*: LD Owens 1996 (childhood); Woodward & Fergusson 2000 (adolescents, physical assaults) |
| No signif. diff. | **NORTH AMERICA** *Canada*: Santesso et al. 2006:319 (males greater but not significantly, $N=40$) |
| Females more | |

**TABLE 2.2.1** Age and Official Delinquency/Crime.

| Nature of the relationship | Officially detected offenses | | | | | |
|---|---|---|---|---|---|---|
| | Violent | Property | Drugs | Minor | General & major | Recidivism |
| Prior to second decade | | | | | | |
| During second & third decades | **EUROPE** *Britain*: McClintock 1963:98*; A Campbell 1995*; *Czechoslovakia*: Zapletal 1979; *Denmark*: K Christiansen & Jensen 1972:87; *Scotland*: Cormack 1976:91*; *Germany*: Goppinger 1983:334* **NORTH AMERICA** *Canada*: Hartnagel 1987:77*; Moyer 1992:396; *United States*: Schroeder 1936; Wolfgang 1958:65; Bensing & Schroeder 1960:70; Pittman & Handy 1964; Wolfgang 1967:19; Langberg 1967; A Henry & Short 1967:263; Ohmart 1967; Mulvihill & Tumin 1969; Wolfgang et al. 1972:123; Haefner & Broeker 1973; Wolfgang 1975:468; Somers 1976:812; Neuman 1979; Hindelang 1981:464*; Magnuson 1981:21; Monahan 1981a:105; Weiner & Wolfgang 1984:27; Cairns 1986:80; Morash 1986:55*; O'Carroll & Mercy 1986:33; Holinger 1987; Wolfgang et al. 1987*; Sommers & Baskin 1992:196; Britt 1994:181; A Campbell 1995* **OCEANIA** *Australia*: Wallace 1986 **INTERNATIONAL** *Multiple Countries*: Curtis 1977:164*; Axenroth 1983:169* | **EUROPE** *Britain*: McClintock 1963:100; McKissack 1967; McKissack 1973; Farrington 1982; *Denmark*: Christiansen & Jensen 1972:87*; *Scotland*: Cormack 1976:91*; *Germany*: Goppinger 1983:356* **NORTH AMERICA** *Canada*: Hartnagel 1987:77*; *United States*: Cameron 1964 (arrests, teens); Wolfgang et al. 1972:123*; Hindelang 1981:465*; Murrell & Lester 1981:12; Haskell & Yablonsky 1982:15; Gottfredson & Hirschi 1986*; Morash 1986:55* **OCEANIA** *Australia*: JF Brady & Mitchell 1971 (arrests, teens) **INTERNATIONAL** *Multiple Countries*: Axenroth 1983:169* | **ASIA** *Taiwan*: Denq et al. 1996: 357 | **EUROPE** *Britain*: Mannheim & Wilkins 1955; Gibbens & Ahrenfeldt 1966:40; West 1967; Edwards 1973; *Denmark*: Christiansen & Jensen 1972:86*; *Finland*: Rantakallio et al. 1995:115* *France*: Frey 1951; *Germany*: EA Johnson 1995:198 (nineteenth century); *Sweden*: Elmhorn 1965 **MIDDLE EAST** *Israel*: Shavit & Rattner 1988 **NORTH AMERICA** *United States*: East 1942; Eriksson 1944; Fleisher 1966:79; Elliott & Huizinga 1983 **OCEANIA** *Australia*: Walmsley et al. 1983:154 | **ASIA** *Soviet Union*: Callcott 1935:62; Connor 1970:286 **EUROPE** *Britain*: Goring 1913:211; Grunhut 1951:149; Benson 1952; Mannheim 1965:678; Gatrell & Hadden 1972:384 (nineteenth century); Farrington 1981; Farrington 1983; Farrington 1986; Farrington 1987:42; *Finland*: Rantakallio et al. 1995:115*; *France*: Besson 1961; *Germany*: Grassberger 1946; Rangol 1962; Wehner & Muller 1966; Nann 1967; *Netherlands*: Blokland 2005:109* (conviction, age 18–24); *Norway*: W Pederson & Wichstrom 1995:550; *Sweden*: Sveri 1960; Sveri 1965; Wikstrom 1990:66; *Multiple European Countries*: Lombroso 1918:183 (nineteenth century); Farrington & Wikstrom 1994:85 **LATIN AMERICA** *Argentina*: DeFleur 1970:131; Blarduni 1976:154 **NORTH AMERICA** *Canada*: Boyer et al. 1966; Szabo & Rico 1976:310; *Greenland*: Hurwitz & Christiansen 1983:212; Gartner 1995:207; *United States*: Gillin 1926:54; Duncan 1931; Glueck & Glueck 1937:106; Glueck & Glueck 1939:95; Wood & Waite 1941:229 (nineteenth century); Sellin 1959; Fleisher 1963:546; Lunden 1964:24; Hirschi 1969:236; Gold 1970:66; Wellford 1973; Gordon 1976; Cline 1980; G Jensen & Rojek 1980:70; Petersilia 1980:357; Faretro 1981:453; Hindelang 1981; Joubert et al. 1981:354; Hirschi & Gottfredson 1983; La Grange & White 1985:36; Gottfredson & Hirschi 1986; Greenwood 1986:155; Holden 1986; M Wolfgang et al. 1987*; PE Tracy et al. 1990 (peaks in mid to late teens); Arboleda-Florez & Holley 1991; Steffensmeier & Streifel 1991; D'Unger et al. 2002:367 | **EUROPE** *Netherlands*: Blokland 2005:37* (decreases with age) **NORTH AMERICA** *Untied States*: Cloninger & Guze 1973; Delaware Executive Department 1984; Dembo et al. 1995a:1444; Fendrich & Archer 1998; Luchansky et al. 2006:91 (substance abuse treatment, ages 14–17) **OCEANIA** *Australia*: Broadhurst & Maller 1990:90 |
| Fourth decade or later | | | | | | |
| No signif. diff. | | | | | | |

**TABLE 2.2.2** Age and Self-Reported Delinquency/Crime.

| Nature of the relationship | Self-report data | |
|---|---|---|
| | Overall offending | Illegal drugs |
| Prior to second decade | | |
| During second & third decades | **EUROPE** *Britain*: Farrington 1973; Farrington 1986:210; *Netherlands*: Blokland 2005:109 (self-report, age 14–24) **NORTH AMERICA** *United States*: A Rowe & Tittle 1977; DS Elliott et al. 1983; DS Elliott & Huizinza 1984; WD Osgood et al. 1989 (teens); DS Elliott 1994:6; Longshore & Turner 1998 (high criminal opportunity, force crimes) **INTERNATIONAL** *Multiple Countries*: Junger-Tas 1994b:374 | **LATIN AMERICA** *Puerto Rico*: LA Warner et al. 2001 (marijuana); Latimer et al. 2004 (high school, males) **NORTH AMERICA** *United States*: Kleinman & Lukoff 1978:196; DB Kandel 1991:387; Flewelling et al. 1994 **OCEANIA** *Australia*: McAllister & Makkai 1991 |
| Fourth decade or later | | |
| No signif. diff. | | |

subsequent offending. As shown in Table 2.2.3a, these studies have nearly unanimously concluded that regardless of the type of crime or how the crime is measured, early-onset offenders commit more subsequent offenses than do late-onset offenders. The one study that failed to find this pattern was based on a fairly small sample of recidivists after a one-year follow-up.

A couple of studies investigated whether persons diagnosed with childhood conduct disorders were more likely than other children to become involved in offending at an earlier or later ages. Table 2.2.3b shows that they are more likely to exhibit early onset offending.

### 2.2.4 Age of Onset of Offending According to Gender

A few studies have investigated the question of which sex most often exhibits the earliest onset of offending. Despite the fact that girls usually mature more rapidly than boys, Table 2.2.4 suggests that if a sex difference exists in the age of onset of offending, boys begin exhibiting such tendencies earlier than girls.

### 2.2.5 Age of Onset of Puberty (Early Maturation)

Research undertaken to determine if the age at which puberty begins is related to the involvement in crime and delinquency is limited. That which has been published has unanimously concluded that those who mature early offend significantly more often than do late maturers (Table 2.2.5a).

Despite the tendency for early maturers to be more involved in crime than late maturers, two studies of conduct disorder did not find this to be significantly associated with age of puberty. In other words, children with conduct disorder did not mature significantly earlier than did children in general. The relevant citations appear in Table 2.2.5b.

## 2.3 RACE/ETHNICITY AND IMMIGRANT STATUS

Despite many difficulties in classifying people according to race, ethnicity, and immigrant status, many studies have been undertaken to determine if crime varies according to these traits. Most of the pertinent research on race and ethnicity has been conducted in the United States owing to its high degree of diversity (Blue & Griffith 1995:579). Research on immigration and crime comes primarily from Europe.

Beginning in the 1930s, official crime statistics in the United States were maintained separately for "whites" and "nonwhites", with over 90% of the latter being blacks. In the 1970s, more elaborate racial/ethnic categories came to be used in most U.S. government statistics primarily to help monitor compliance with laws against discrimination in employment.

Seven tables are used to summarize the research findings on racial/ethnic differences in criminality. Because of their rank as the majority populations in both the United States and Europe, whites are the reference group in each table presented.

### 2.3.1 Nonwhite–White Comparisons

Only a few studies were located in which whites were compared to nonwhites, all of which were conducted in the

**TABLE 2.2.3a** Age of Onset of Offending and Criminal/Delinquent Behavior.

| Nature of the relationship | Officially detected offenses | | | | Self-reported offenses | |
|---|---|---|---|---|---|---|
| | Violent offenses | Delinquency | General & adult offenses | Recidivism | Overall offenses | Illegal drugs |
| Early onset positively associated with offending | **NORTH AMERICA** *United States*: Hamparian et al. 1985 | **EUROPE** *Britain*: Mannheim & Wilkins 1955; Farrington et al. 1990; *Poland*: Zabczyaska 1977; Farrington 1983; *Sweden*: Bohman et al. 1982; Stattin & Magnusson 1991 **NORTH AMERICA** *Canada*: Frechette & LeBlanc 1987; *United States*: AH Roberts et al. 1974; Kandel 1978; CL Hanson et al. 1984*; Blumstein et al. 1986; Hamparian 1987; Tolan 1987*; Tolan & Lorion 1988*; Tolan & Thomas 1995; Crowley et al. 1998:234 | **EUROPE** *Denmark*: B Mednick et al. 1990; *Sweden*: Magnusson & Bergman 1990 **NORTH AMERICA** *United States*: JJ Collins 1981 **OCEANIA** *Hawaii*: Werner & Smith 1992:107 | **EUROPE** *Netherlands*: Blokland 2005:113* (number of convictions) **NORTH AMERICA** *Canada*: Gendreau et al. 1979; *United States*: Sellin 1940; Unkovic & Ducsay 1969; Wolfgang et al. 1972; Ganzer & Sarason 1973; McGurk et al. 1978; McCord 1981b:215; Monahan 1981a; CL Hanson et al. 1984*; Roundtree et al. 1984; DW Wilson 1985; Tolan 1987*; Tolan & Lorion 1988*; Dembo et al. 1991; Wierson & Forehand 1995; Patterson & Yoerger 1997; Benda et al. 2001:95; Piquero & Chung 2001 | **EUROPE** *Britain*: Farrington 1983; Farrington 1992; *Netherlands*: Blokland 2005:113* (self-reports) **NORTH AMERICA** *United States*: Herrenkohl et al. 2000 (violent delinquency, teens) **OCEANIA** *New Zealand*: Moffitt 1990a | **NORTH AMERICA** *United States*: Halikas & Rimmer 1974; Jessor et al. 1980; Fleming et al. 1982; Mills & Noyes 1984; Yamaguchi & Kandel 1984: Robins & Przybeck 1985; Flannery et al. 1996 |
| No significant difference | | | | **NORTH AMERICA** *United States*: Niarhos & Routh 1992 (one year follow-up) | | |
| Late onset positively associated with offending | | | | | | |

**TABLE 2.2.3b** Age of Onset of Offending and Antisocial Behavior or Factors Frequently Linked to Criminality.

| Nature of the relationship | Antisocial behavior |
|---|---|
| | Child & early adol. |
| Early onset positively associated with offending | **NORTH AMERICA** *United States*: Hinshaw et al. 1993; Silverthorn & Frick 1999 (school age) |
| No significant difference | |
| Late onset pos. assoc. with offending | |

United States. As shown in Table 2.3.1, two studies of official violent crime concluded that nonwhites were more criminally involved than whites. The other study of self-reported drug use found no significant racial difference.

## 2.3.2 Black–White Comparisons

A remarkably large number of studies have explored differences between blacks and whites in criminality. The results are summarized in four tables: Table 2.3.2a pertains to officially detected violent offenses, Table 2.3.2b covers all other official offense statistics, Table 2.3.2c focuses on self-reported offenses, and Table 2.3.2d has to do with antisocial personality.

**TABLE 2.2.5b** Age of Onset of Puberty (Early Maturation) and Antisocial Behavior.

| Nature of the relationship | Antisocial behavior |
|---|---|
| | Child & early adol. |
| Positive | |
| Not signif. | **EUROPE** *Norway*: Wichstom 1998 (females); *Sweden*: Silbereisen et al. 1989 |
| Negative | |

### 2.3.2a Black–White Comparisons of Official Violent Offenses

According to all of the available evidence, blacks commit more violent offenses than do whites (Table 2.3.2a). The extent of the differences has usually exceeded a ratio of 3:1.

Additional evidence that blacks are substantially more involved in violent crime than whites has come from victimization surveys. In these studies, victims of crime are asked whether or not they had an opportunity to see the

**TABLE 2.2.4** Age of Onset of Offending According to Gender.

| Nature of the relationship | Officially detected offenses | | Self-reported offenses |
|---|---|---|---|
| | Delinquency | General & adult offenses | Overall offenses |
| Earlier onset for males | **EUROPE** *Netherlands*: Blokland 2005:51; *Sweden*: Stattin & Magnusson 1989 | | **NORTH AMERICA** *United States*: RA Johnson et al. 1997 (delinquency) |
| Not signif. related | | **NORTH AMERICA** *United States*: Piquero 2001 | |
| Earlier onset for females | | | |

**TABLE 2.2.5a** Age of Onset of Puberty (Early Maturation) and Criminal/Delinquent Behavior.

| Nature of the relationship | Officially detected offenses | Self-reported offenses |
|---|---|---|
| | Delinquency | Overall offenses |
| Positive | **NORTH AMERICA** *United States*: Flannery et al. 1983 (females); Graber et al. 1997 (females) | **NORTH AMERICA** *United States*: Beaver & Wright 2005<br>**OCEANIA** *New Zealand*: Caspi et al. 1993 (females) |
| Not signif. | | |
| Negative | | |

**TABLE 2.3.1 Nonwhite–White Comparisons and Criminal/Delinquent Behavior.**

| Nature of the relationship | Officially detected offenses | | Self-reported offenses |
|---|---|---|---|
| | Violent offenses | Property offenses | Illegal drugs |
| Nonwhites higher | **NORTH AMERICA** *United States*: Petee et al. 1997 (mass murder) | **NORTH AMERICA** *United States*: Weisburd et al. 1991 (white-collar fraud convictions) | |
| Not signif. diff. | | | **NORTH AMERICA** *United States*: Ousey & Maume 1997 (marijuana use) |
| Whites higher | | | |

offender. In the case of most assaults and robberies, victims are able to report the apparent race of the assailant. Analyses of these victim responses indicate that assault and robbery rates are at least three times higher for blacks than for whites (Hindelang 1978a:98; Hindelang 1981:468; Pope 1979:351; Blumstein & Cohen 1987; Wilbanks 1987; Flowers 1988; Wolfner & Gelles 1993:202).

Regarding officially detected offenses other than those of a violent nature, Table 2.3.5b indicates that blacks are significantly more involved than whites. The only qualification is that a minority of studies of recidivism have failed to reveal significant black–white differences.

In the case of self-reported offending, the evidence concerning black–white differences is much less consistent

**TABLE 2.3.2a Black–White Comparisons of Official Violent Offenses.**

| Nature of any difference | Officially detected offenses |
|---|---|
| | Violent |
| Blacks more | **EUROPE** *Britain*: Hood 1992:205<br>**MIDDLE EAST** *Israel*: Landau & Drapkin 1968:11; Shoham 1970:336<br>**NORTH AMERICA** *Canada*: Gartner 1995:206; *United States*: Stearns 1925; Brearley 1930; Bowler 1931:119; Brearley 1932; DePorte & Parkhurst 1935; Lottier 1938; Sutherland 1939:120; Harlan 1949; Vold 1952; Wolfgang 1958: 31; Bensing & Schroeder 1960:70; Wolfgang 1961; Sellin & Wolfgang 1964; Porkony 1965:480; Forslund 1966; A Henry & Short 1967:262; Langberg 1967; Wolfgang 1967:18; Voss & Hepburn 1968; Lalli & Turner 1968; Voss & Hepburn 1968:501; Mulvihill & Tumin 1969; Boudouris 1970; Block 1975; Wolfgang 1975:33; Mumford et al. 1976; Block 1977; Count-van Maner 1977; Lundsgaarde 1977; Shin et al. 1977; Dennis 1979:20; R Lane 1979:112 (19th century); R Parker & Smith 1979; Skogan 1979; Farley 1980; M Smith & Parker 1980; Gurr 1981:326 (19th & 20th centuries); Hindelang 1981:466; Tinklenberg & Ochberg 1981:123; Wolfgang & Weiner 1981; Messner 1982; Messner 1983a; Messner 1983b; Poussaint 1983; Riedel 1984; Weiner & Wolfgang 1984:28; K Williams 1984; Bankston et al. 1985; Block 1985; Hawkins 1985; Sampson 1985; Centers for Disease Control 1986 (males, homicide); Farley 1986; Harvey 1986; Hawkins 1986; Kruttschnitt et al. 1986; O'Carroll & Mercy 1986; Shai & Rosenwaike 1988 (males, homicides); Christoffel 1990; Rose & McClain 1990; Hammett et al. 1992; M Harer & Steffensmeier 1992; Sommers & Baskin 1992:194; CR Block 1993:305; Wolfner & Gelles 1993; Zingraff et al. 1993:192; DiIulio 1994; Huizinga et al. 1994 (adolescents); Hutson et al. 1995:1035; La Free 1995; Massey 1995; Harer & Steffensmeier 1996 (prison violence, males); La Free 1996; R Martinez 1996 (males, homicides); Singh & Yu 1996:562; Sorenson & Shen 1996:98; Hickey 1997 (serial killers); McKanna 1997:42 (19th century); JF Short 1997:8; Stanton et al. 1997:27; Bradshaw et al. 1998 (homicide); Verdugo 1998:113; Fingerhut et al. 1998; Martinez & Matthew 1998 (homicide); R Peterson & Krivo 1999; Snyder 1999 (adolescents); Hawkins et al. 2000 (adolescents); Krivo & Peterson 2000 (homicide); J Fox & Levin 2001; McNulty 2001; McNulty & Bellair 2003 (adolescents); A Walsh 2005<br>**OCEANIA** *Hawaii*: Blanchard & Blanchard 1983:167 |
| No signif. difference | |
| Whites more | |

**TABLE 2.3.2b** Black–White Comparisons of Official Criminal/Delinquent Behavior (Except Violent Offenses).

| Nature of the relationship | Officially detected offenses | | | | |
|---|---|---|---|---|---|
| | Property offenses | Drug offenses | Delinquency | General & adult offenses | Recidivism |
| Blacks higher | **NORTH AMERICA** *United States*: Cameron 1964 (arrests for shoplifting); Reppetto 1974; Skogan 1979 | **EUROPE** *Britain*: Home Office 1994:Table 7 **NORTH AMERICA** *United States*: Vaillant 1966; Mieczkowski 1996:362; Brownsberger 2000 (imprisonment) | **EUROPE** *Britain*: Batta et al. 1975; Mawby et al. 1979 **NORTH AMERICA** *United States*: Durea & Pataky 1937; Growdon 1950; Nagasawa 1965; Conger & Miller 1966:190; Segal 1966; Chambliss & Nagasawa 1969; C Shaw & McKay 1972; Wolfgang et al. 1972:55*; Gordon 1973; Gordon 1976; Jensen 1976; Calhoun 1977; Lundman et al. 1978; Stevens & Willis 1979; Jensen & Rojeck 1980:69; Cortes 1982:206; Plutchik 1983; Tracy et al. 1985:5; Westendorp et al. 1986; R Gordon 1987; Dembo 1988; LeFlore 1988:637; Kempf 1990; Kaplan & Busner 1992; Shelden & Chesney-Lind 1993:84; Bishop & Frazier 1996:392 **NORTH AMERICA** *Canada*: J Roberts & Doob 1997:479; *United States*: Gillin 1926:61; Chamberlain 1936; Lottier 1938; JB Johnson 1940; Levinger 1940:210; CR Shaw & McKay 1942; Bonger 1943; Lemert & Rosberg 1948; von Hentig 1948a; Barnes & Teeters 1951:173; Kephart 1954; Frumkin 1955; V Fox & Volakakis 1956; Kephart 1957; Taft & England 1964:106; ME Wolfgang 1964; Mannheim 1965:567; Forslund 1966; Sutherland & Cressey 1966:150; Bonger 1969:43; GB Johnson 1970; E Green 1970:480; ME Wolfgang & Cohen 1970; P Wolfgang et al. 1972*; Bennett & Perry 1975; Max & Downs 1975:vii; Hamparian et al. 1978; Hindelang 1978b; Silberman 1978:123; Hindelang 1981; H Jones 1981; Shannon 1981; Blumstein 1982; Chilton & Galvin 1985; Thornberry et al. 1985:14; Visher & Roth 1986; Blumstein & Cohen 1987; Tillman 1987; Jaynes & Williams 1989; AR Harris 1991; M Levin 1992; Eisenman 1995; LaFree 1995:175; R Kennedy 1997:23; R O'Brien 1999 **OCEANIA** *Hawaii*: Blanchard & Blanchard 1983:167 | **ASIA** *Israel*: Landau & Drapkin 1968:11 **EUROPE** *Britain*: Stevens & Willis 1979; DJ Smith 1983; Home Office 1984; Home Office 1989a:Table 4; D Smith 1994; DJ Smith 1995:1056; Smith 1997; *France*: Hirsch 1953; Tournier & Robert 1991 **MIDDLE EAST** *Israel*: Shoham 1966:80; Shoskolsky et al. 1970; Amir & Hovav 1976:167 | **NORTH AMERICA** *United States*: Kirkpatrick 1937; Unkovic & Ducsay 1969; Forslund 1970; Kassenbaum et al. 1971; P Wolfgang et al. 1972*; Meade 1973:481; Palmer & Carlson 1976; Delaware Executive Department 1984; Beck & Shipley 1989; Dembo et al. 1993; Smith & Akers 1993:286; Elliott 1994:14; Dembo et al. 1995a:1444; Dembo et al. 1996:46; Benedict & Huff-Corzine 1997 (males); Minor et al. 1997:337; Benda et al. 2000 |
| Not signif. | | | | | **NORTH AMERICA** *United States*: Roberts et al. 1974:838; Thomas 1977:60; Schmidt & White 1979; Boudouris 1983; Roundtree et al. 1984:57; Wierson & Forehand 1995:65 |
| Whites higher | | | | | |

**TABLE 2.3.2c Black–White Comparisons of Self-Reported Criminal/Delinquent Behavior.**

| Nature of the relationship | Self-reported offenses | |
|---|---|---|
| | Overall offenses | Illegal drugs |
| Blacks higher | **EUROPE** *Britain*: Newcombe et al. 1995:334<br>**NORTH AMERICA** *United States*: Baughman & Dahlstrom 1968; Williams & Gold 1972; Berger & Simon 1974:151; Fors & Rojek 1983:216; Elliott et al. 1986:486; Sampson 1986:881; Elliott et al. 1989; Elliott 1994:6; Marshall & Webb 1994:332; Ross 1995; Farrington et al. 1996:509; Kelley et al. 1997:6 | **NORTH AMERICA** *United States*: Brunswick 1969; Murray et al. 1987; Flewelling et al. 1994; Marshall & Webb 1994:337 |
| Not signif. | **EUROPE** *Britain*: Bowling et al. 1994:55; Graham & Bowling 1996<br>**NORTH AMERICA** *United States*: Lively et al. 1962; Gold, 1966; Epps 1967; Gould 1969:330; Chambliss & Nagasawa 1969; Gould 1969; Williams & Gold 1972; Elliott & Voss 1974; Gold & Reimer 1974; Elliott & Ageton 1980:104; Gold & Petronio 1980; Petronio 1980; Harris 1992:92; Peeples & Loeber 1994; Dembo et al. 1995b:271; Weber et al. 1995; Heimer 1997:814; Manolakes 1997:245 | **NORTH AMERICA** *United States*: Brook et al. 1977; Fors & Rojek 1983:213; Oetting & Beauvais 1990; Wallace & Bachman 1991:341; Gottfredson & Koper 1996; Johanson et al. 1996:526; Friedman & Ali 1997; Gottfredson & Koper 1997; Neumark & Anthony 1997:195 |
| Whites higher | **NORTH AMERICA** *United States*: Walberg et al. 1974; Mazur 1995:280; Evans et al. 1996:55; Felson & Staff 2006 | **EUROPE** *Britain*: Leitner et al. 1993:28<br>**NORTH AMERICA** *United States*: Globetti & Windham 1967; Preston 1968; Bloom et al. 1974; Prendergast 1974; Kandel et al. 1976b; Nyberg & McIntosh 1979; Harrell & Cisin 1980; Fors & Rojek 1983; Zucker & Harford 1983; Harford 1985; Harford 1986; Maddahian et al. 1986:76; Newcomb et al. 1987:424; Welte & Barnes 1987; Austin 1988; Mensch & Kandel 1988a; Palmer & Ringwalt 1988; Austin & Gilbert 1989; Prendergast et al. 1989; Oetting & Beauvais 1990; Anthony & Helzer 1991; Bachman et al. 1991a; Blum et al. 1992; Wallace & Bachman 1991:350; Bass & Kane-Williams 1993; Johnston et al. 1995:137; Mazur 1995:280; O'Donnell et al. 1995; Parker et al. 1995; Mieczkowski 1996:365; Farley 1997:90; Whitmore et al. 1997:93 |

than it is regarding official data. As shown in Table 2.3.2c, findings have been nearly evenly divided between those that suggest blacks have higher overall offending rates and those that suggest no significant black–white differences exist. In the case of self-reported illegal drug offenses, most studies have concluded that whites actually surpass blacks in offending.

What could account for the inconsistencies between official data and self-reported data regarding black–white offending rates? In all likelihood, several factors are responsible. One factor may be biases by the criminal justice system in terms of arresting and convicting blacks on the basis of less evidence than is true for whites. The evidence for such an effect has been mixed, but is certainly asserted by a number of writers (Turk 1969; Quinney 1970:142; Williams & Gold 1972; Schur 1973:121). Another factor involves the type of offenses focused on by official versus self-reported data. Specifically, self-reported data primarily involves relatively trivial and victimless offenses, such as marijuana use (Eaton & Polk 1961; Pope 1979:355; Schuster 1981:110). These offenses may well be more prevalent among white youth than among their black peers. In this regard, one study of high school students indicated that whites were more likely than blacks to report involvement in minor delinquency (e.g., stealing something worth a few dollars or smoking marijuana), but the reverse pattern emerged with relatively serious forms of delinquency (e.g., dealing in illegal drugs, using force to get money) (Peeples & Loeber 1994). Third, some research indicates that whites tend to provide more complete self-reported information about their offending histories than do blacks (Cernkovich et al. 2000:143; also see Leitner 1993:30).

Regarding black–white differences in being diagnosed as antisocial, Table 2.3.2d shows that most studies have found blacks exhibiting higher rates than whites, although some studies have failed to find significant differences. To account for the seeming inconsistencies, small sample sizes in some of the studies may be involved. It is also important

**TABLE 2.3.2d** Black–White Comparisons and Antisocial Behavior or Factors Frequently Linked to Criminality.

| Nature of the relationship | Antisocial behavior | | Aggressive behavior |
|---|---|---|---|
| | Child & early adol. | Late adol. & adult | |
| Blacks higher | **EUROPE** *Britain*: Rutter et al. 1974:250 **NORTH AMERICA** *United States*: Tuckman & Regan 1966; Wells et al. 1992:122; Fabrega et al. 1993; Callahan 1994 (males); Dodge et al. 1994:663; O'Donnell et al. 1995:530; McDermott & Spencer 1997 | **EUROPE** *Britain*: R Lynn 2002 **MIDDLE EAST** *Israel*: Dohrenwend et al. 1992:949 **NORTH AMERICA** *Canada*: Forth et al. 2003; *United States*: Robins 1978:265 | **EUROPE** *Britain*: Rutter et al. 1974 (mothers' reports) **NORTH AMERICA** *United States*: Tuddenham et al. 1974 (mothers' accounts) |
| Not signif. | **NORTH AMERICA** *United States*: Gabel & Shindledecker 1991:986; Robins & Price 1991; McLeod & Shanahan 1996:214; Christian et al. 1997 | **NORTH AMERICA** *United States*: Robins et al. 1984; Robins et al. 1991:265 (among prisoners) | |
| Whites higher | | | |

to distinguish between studies conducted among incarcerated populations and those conducted in populations at large, as noted in the following paragraph.

Three meta-analyses of black–white differences in psychopathy among prisoners have been published and all have concluded that no significant differences exist (Cooke et al. 2001; Skeem et al. 2004; McCoy & Edens 2006). This suggests that the criminal justice system is not racially discriminating in its incarceration policies toward persons with psychopathic traits. In other words, while psychopaths

**TABLE 2.3.3a** Hispanic–Anglo Comparisons and Criminal/Delinquent Behavior.

| Nature of the relationship | Officially detected offenses | | | | |
|---|---|---|---|---|---|
| | Violent offenses | Drug offenses | Delinquency | General & adult offenses | Recidivism |
| Hispanic higher | **NORTH AMERICA** *United States*: Bowler 1931:119; Pokorny 1965; Lundsgaarde 1977; Silberman 1978; Block 1985; Smith et al. 1986; Flowers 1988; Zahn 1987; Polednak 1989:273; Sommers & Baskin 1992:194; Huizinga et al. 1994 (urban, adol.); Martinez 1996; Smith et al. 1986:269; CR Block 1993:305; Hutson et al. 1995:1035; Sorenson & Shen 1996:98; Bradshaw et al. 1998 (Mexicans, homicide); Hawkins et al. 2000 (adolescents); Sampson et al. 2005 | **NORTH AMERICA** *United States*: Flowers 1988:99; Brownsberger 2000 (imprisonment eight times higher) | **NORTH AMERICA** *United States*: Eaton & Polk 1961:25; Conger & Miller 1966:190; Calhoun 1977; Jensen et al. 1977:254; Carrasquillo 1991; Kaplan & Busner 1992:770; Office of Juvenile Justice & Delinquency Prevention 1994; Kingery et al. 1995 | **NORTH AMERICA** *United States*: Lemert & Rosberg 1948; Wolfgang & Cohen 1970:34; Silberman 1978:123; Takagi & Platt 1978:10 | **NORTH AMERICA** *United States*: Benedict & Huff-Corzine 1997 |
| Not signif. | | | | | |
| White higher | | | | | |

TABLE 2.3.3b Hispanic–Anglo Comparisons and Criminal/Delinquent Behavior.

| Nature of the relationship | Self-reported offenses | |
|---|---|---|
| | Overall offenses | Illegal drugs |
| Hispanics higher | **NORTH AMERICA** *United States*: Marshall & Webb 1994:332; Kingery et al. 1995; Kelley et al. 1997:6; Vazsonyi & Flannery 1997 | **NORTH AMERICA** *United States*: Brunswick 1969; Bloom et al. 1974; Mott & Haurin 1988; Bachman et al. 1991; Chavez & Swaim 1992; Flewelling et al. 1994; Marshall & Webb 1994:332; Grunbaum et al. 1996:1300; Swaim et al. 1997:54 |
| Not signif. | **NORTH AMERICA** *United States*: Elliott & Voss 1974; Winfree et al. 1994:163; Felson & Staff 2006 | **NORTH AMERICA** *United States*: Barnes & Welte 1986; Maddahian et al. 1986:76; Newcomb & Bentler 1986; Kandel 1991:396; Wallace & Bachman 1991:337; Flannery et al. 1994; Winfree et al. 1994:163; Parker et al. 1995; Flannery et al. 1996; Mieczkowski 1996:365 |
| Anglos (non-Hispanic whites) higher | **NORTH AMERICA** *United States*: Weber et al. 1995:369 | **NORTH AMERICA** *United States*: Newcomb et al. 1987:424; Robins et al. 1991:265; Stewart & Brown 1995; Whitmore et al. 1997:93; Johnston et al. 2002 (Puerto Rican youth compared to white youth) |

are much more common in prison than in the general population, black and white psychopaths are equally likely to end up being imprisoned. This conclusion is far from the question of whether blacks and whites exhibit higher rates of psychopathy or childhood conduct disorders in the general (non-incarcerated) population.

Regarding black–white differences in physical aggression, two studies were located, both based on reports by mothers. According to these two studies, black children behaved more aggressively than did white children.

## 2.3.3 Hispanic–Anglo Comparisons

As the term has come to be used, an *Hispanic American* (*Latino/Latina*) is a resident of the United States whose ancestors immigrated from Spain, Portugal or from a Spanish- or Portuguese-speaking South or Central American country. Racially, the vast majority of Hispanics are considered whites. Thus, the terms *white non-Hispanics* or *Anglos* are used interchangeably to distinguish these individuals from nearly all Hispanics.

Table 2.3.3a summarizes the research comparing Hispanics and Anglos with respect to officially detected delinquent/criminal behavior. This table is very consistent in indicating that Hispanics have significantly higher crime rates. Differences are especially well documented for homicide, with Hispanic rates being roughly intermediate to the rates for Anglo Americans and black Americans (Bowler 1931:119; Zahn 1987; Polednak 1989:273; Martinez 1996:142; Smith et al. 1986:269; Bradshaw et al. 1998).

In the case of self-reports, the findings regarding any Hispanic–Anglo differences are mixed. Table 2.3.3b shows nearly as many studies suggesting that Anglos self-report offending as do Hispanics. However, it should be noted that most of the drug offenses for which Anglos report higher rates pertain to marijuana use (Flannery et al. 1996) or to under-age alcohol consumption (Robins et al. 1991:265). In the case of drugs such as heroin and cocaine, Hispanics have been found to exceed Anglos in self-reported usage (Johnston et al. 1993:127; Mieczkowski 1996:373). This latter observation is supported by data collected in hospital emergency rooms, where Hispanic visitation rates for overdosing on heroin and

TABLE 2.3.3c Hispanic–Anglo Comparisons and Antisocial Behavior or Factors Frequently Linked to Criminality.

| Nature of the relationship | Antisocial behavior |
|---|---|
| | Child & early adol. |
| Hispanics higher | **NORTH AMERICA** *United States*: Tuddenham et al. 1974 |
| No signif. diff. | **NORTH AMERICA** *United States*: Touliatos & Lindholm 1980:30 |
| Whites higher | |

**TABLE 2.3.4a** Native American–White Comparisons of Criminal/Delinquent Behavior.

| Nature of the relationship | Officially detected offenses | | | | | |
|---|---|---|---|---|---|---|
| | Violent offenses | Property offenses | Drug offenses | Delinquency | General & adult offenses | Recidivism |
| Native Americans higher | **NORTH AMERICA** *Canada*: Statistics Canada 1976; Westcott 1987; Moyer 1992:400; Silverman & Kennedy 1993; Doob et al. 1994; *United States*: Barnes & Teeters 1959:176; McCone 1966:147; Levy et al. 1969; Mail & McDonald 1980; French & Hornbuckle 1982; Kunitz 1990:659; Bachman 1991; Mills 1991; Bachman 1992; Hisnanick 1994:104; U.S. Indian Health Service 1994; Holden 1996; Young & French 1996 | | **NORTH AMERICA** *United States*: Flowers 1988:108 | **NORTH AMERICA** *United States*: Minnis 1963; Forslund & Meyers 1974; Chadwick et al. 1976 | **NORTH AMERICA** *Canada*: Hagan 1974; Schmeiser 1974:81; Verfun-Jones & Muirhead 1979; Hylton 1982; Jolly 1982; LaPrairie 1983; Correctional Service of Canada 1985; Hagan 1985; Havemann et al. 1985; Hartnagel 1987:89; LaPrairie 1990; Bonta et al. 1992:517; Trevethan 1993:9; Correctional Service of Canada 1994:19; Roberts & Doob 1997:479; *United States*: Stewart 1964; Reasons 1972; Jensen et al. 1977; Echo-Hawk 1979; Young 1991:66; LaFree 1995:175 | **NORTH AMERICA** *Canada*: Schmeiser 1974:81; Wormith & Goldstone 1984:15; Bonta 1989 |
| Not signif. diff. | **NORTH AMERICA** *United States*: Levy & Kunitz. 1969:128 | | | | | |
| Whites higher | | **NORTH AMERICA** *United States*: McCone 1966:147 | | | | |

cocaine far exceed the rates for Anglos (Mieczkowski 1996:382).

Regarding Hispanic–Anglo differences in rates of antisocial behavior, only two pertinent studies were located, both limited to children. One study found higher rates for Hispanics and the other study found no significant ethnic difference (Table 2.3.3c).

### 2.3.4 Native American–White Comparisons

Native Americans inhabited North and South America long before Columbus "discovered" America. Most anthropological evidence indicates that their ancestors were northern Asian nomads who hunted in modern-day Alaska over 20,000 years ago and then migrated into the rest of the Americas about 10,000 years ago as the last great Ice Age came to an end (Scupin & DeCourse 1998:149).

As one can see from viewing Table 2.3.4a, nearly all comparisons of the crime rates of Native Americans (also called aboriginal Americans, Amerindians) and whites have found the former to be over-represented. The over-representation of Native Americans is especially high for offenses linked to alcohol consumption, such as public drunkenness and disorderly conduct as well as serious forms of interpersonal violence (Nettler 1984:136). This conclusion has been reached based on studies in both the United States (Graves 1967; Jensen et al. 1977:252; Flowers 1978:106; Pope & McNeely 1981:13; Moyer 1992a:392) and Canada (Roberts & Doob 1997:490). It is worth noting that alcohol abuse is considerably higher among Native Americans than for any other racial/ethnic group in North America (Jensen et al. 1977:253; U.S. Indian Health Service 1978; Schinke et al. 1985; Mills 1991:12). Links between criminality and both alcohol consumption and alcoholism (independent of race/ethnicity) are discussed in Chapters 5 and 6, respectively.

Regarding self-reported offending, studies have found minimal differences in overall offending between Native Americans and whites. However, Table 2.3.4b shows that in the case of illegal drug use, all of the published studies agree that rates are considerably higher among Native Americans.

### 2.3.5 East Asian–White Comparisons

Table 2.3.5a summarizes findings from studies that have compared descendants of Pacific Rim Asian (Oriental) populations and white (European) populations. This table reveals that nearly all of the studies have shown descendants of East Asia (primarily Japanese, Chinese, and Koreans) to exhibit significantly lower crime rates than do whites. Most of these studies were conducted in the United States, showing that the rates of crime among Pacific Rim Asian Americans were typically about half the rates exhibited by white Americans.

In addition to the numerous studies of crime per se, a few studies have been published in which East Asians and whites were compared regarding symptoms of childhood conduct disorders. Table 2.3.5b shows that all of these studies have concluded that whites exhibit higher conduct disorder symptomology than do East Asians.

### 2.3.6 South Asian–White Comparisons

Another Asia/Pacific Islander group that has been compared to whites regarding crime rates are persons from India and Pakistan (and sometimes Bangladesh). Because these countries were former British colonies, sizable numbers of their citizens immigrated to England shortly before these countries became independent from the British Empire. Since the 1980s, South Asians have comprised about 3% of the entire English population (DJ Smith 1997:108). This migration has made it possible for several British studies to compare the crime rates for Indians and Pakistanis with those of the white indigenous majority. (In addition, one study in Israel compared Jews of predominantly European ancestry with a minority who traced their ancestry to southern Asia.) The results of these studies are shown in Table 2.3.6a. This table indicates that the results have been quite mixed with respect to any significant South Asian–White differences in officially detected criminality. Self-report studies, however, support the view that South Asians are more involved in crime than are whites.

A couple of studies of childhood conduct disorders compared persons of Indian and Pakistani descents with whites. These studies fail to be consistent in their findings (Table 2.3.6b).

### 2.3.7 Oceanic Islander–White Comparisons

Included in the category of Oceanic Islanders here are persons who reside in one of the numerous islands in the Pacific and Indian Oceans. Nearly all of the comparisons of crime rates among Oceanic Islanders and whites have been conducted in Australia, New Zealand, and Hawaii. Studies from Hawaii have been particularly interesting, because Hawaii contains a sizable proportion of whites along with both an Asian (Japanese) and a Pacific Island (native Hawaiian) population. Table 2.3.7 indicates that native Oceanic Islanders exhibit substantially higher crime rates than do whites.

### 2.3.8 Immigrant versus Non-immigrant Comparisons

A variable that is closely related to race/ethnicity is that of immigrant status (or the descendants of immigrant parents). Over the years, quite a number of studies have compared immigrants with non-immigrants regarding criminality. These studies are sometimes difficult to separate from ones on race and ethnicity, so the studies reported in Table 2.3.8a are ones in which the research focus was on the recent

**TABLE 2.3.4b** Native American–White Comparisons and Criminal/Delinquent Behavior.

| Nature of the relationship | Self-reported offenses | |
|---|---|---|
| | Overall offenses | Illegal drugs |
| Native Americans higher | **NORTH AMERICA** *United States*: Jensen et al. 1977 | **LATIN AMERICA** *Mexico*: Medina-Mora & Ortiz 1988 **NORTH AMERICA** *Canada*: Lalinec-Michaud et al. 1991; Gfellner & Hundleby 1995; *United States*: Cockerham et al. 1976; Cockerham 1977; Jensen et al. 1977; Kandel et al. 1976; Nyberg & McIntosh 1979; Oetting et al. 1980; Olsen & Baffi 1982; Winfree & Griffiths 1983; Fortenberry 1985; Winfree & Griffith 1985; Newcomb et al. 1987:424; Welte & Barnes 1987; Beauvais & Oetting 1988; Beauvais et al. 1989; Bachman et al. 1991a; Lalinec-Michaud et al. 1991; Wallace & Bachman 1991; Beauvais 1992a; Beauvais 1992b; Blum et al. 1992; Amey et al. 1996:1313; Zebrowski & Gregory 1996; Federman et al. 1997:75; Swaim et al. 1997:54; JM Wallace et al. 2003 (adolescents) |
| No signif. diff. | **NORTH AMERCIA** *United States*: Felson & Staff 2006 | |
| Whites higher | | |

**TABLE 2.3.5a** East Asian–White Comparisons and Criminal/Delinquent Behavior.

| Nature of the relationship | Officially detected offenses | | | Self-reported offenses | |
|---|---|---|---|---|---|
| | Violent offenses | Delinquency | General & adult offenses | Overall offenses | Illegal drugs |
| East Asians higher | | | | | |
| No significant difference | | | | **NORTH AMERICA** *United States*: Gould 1969*; Elliott & Voss 1974 | **NORTH AMERICA** *United States*: Maddahian et al. 1986:76 |
| Whites higher | **NORTH AMERICA** *United States*: CR Block 1993:305; Sorenson & Shen 1996:98; Hawkins et al. 2000 (adolescents); McNulty & Bellair 2003; RJ Sampson et al. 2005 **OCEANIA** *Hawaii*: Blanchard & Blanchard 1983:167 | **EUROPE** *Britain*: Batta 1975; Mawby et al. 1979; Batta et al. 2001 **NORTH AMERICA** *United States*: MacGill 1928; Hayner 1933; Abbott & Abbott 1968 **NORTH AMERICA** *United States*: M Gold 1963:186; Voss 1963:326; Chambliss & Nagasawa 1969*; Gould 1969* **OCEANIA** *Hawaii*: Voss 1963:323 | **EUROPE** *Britain*: DJ Smith 1983 **NORTH AMERICA** *United States*: Beach 1932:49; Hayner 1933; Hayner 1938; Barnes & Teeters 1959:176; Korn & McCorkle 1959:249; Sutherland & Cressey 1960:147; Kitano 1973; LaFree 1995:175 **OCEANIA** *Hawaii*: Lind 1930; Blanchard & Blanchard 1983:167 | | **NORTH AMERICA** *United States*: Chambliss & Nagasawa 1969*; Barnes & Welte 1986; Bachman et al. 1991b; Wallace & Bachman 1991:337; Amey et al. 1996:1313; Graham & Bowling 1996 |

**TABLE 2.3.5b** East Asian–White Comparisons and Antisocial Behavior or Factors Frequently Linked to Criminality.

| Nature of the relationship | Antisocial behavior |
|---|---|
| | Child & early adol. |
| East Asians higher | |
| Not signif. | |
| Whites higher | **NORTH AMERICA** *United States*: Touliatos & Lindholm 1980:30; O'Donnell et al. 1976:30; EAWells et al. 1992:122; L Chang et al. 1995 (among Chinese–Americans) **OCEANIA** *Hawaii*: Loo & Rapport 1998 |

**TABLE 2.3.6b** South Asian–White Comparisons and Antisocial Behavior or Factors Frequently Linked to Criminality.

| Nature of the relationship | Antisocial behavior |
|---|---|
| | Childhood & early adolescents |
| Southern Asians higher | **NORTH AMERICA** *United States*: Touliatos & Lindholm 1980:30 |
| No signif. difference | **EUROPE** *Britain*: R Cochrane 1979 |
| Whites higher | |

arrival into a host country, and only secondarily on the race/ethnicity of the immigrant.

Most of the studies of the relationship between immigration and crime have been conducted in Europe, where substantial immigration has occurred since the 1950s. In particular, Germany, Belgium, the Netherlands, and Sweden have had many immigrant workers from various Middle Eastern countries in recent decades. Also, France experienced substantial immigration from Algeria, a former French colony. Despite considerable speculation about a positive link between immigration and crime in North America during the late 19th and early 20th centuries, surprisingly little scientific research was ever published.

The typical design of the studies located involved comparing arrest rates of immigrants or their first generation descendants to rates for the host country's indigenous people (Waters 1999). Recognizing that young adult males are more likely to immigrate than most other age/gender

**TABLE 2.3.6a** South Asian–White Comparisons and Criminal/Delinquent Behavior.

| Nature of the relationship | Officially detected offenses | | Self-reported offenses | |
|---|---|---|---|---|
| | Delinquency | General & adult offenses | Overall offenses | Illegal drugs |
| Southern Asians higher | **EUROPE** *Britain*: Batta et al. 1975:39; Mawby et al. 1979; Batta et al. 1981:149* | **EUROPE** *Britain*: Batta et al. 1981:147* | **EUROPE** *Britain*: Bowling et al. 1994:55; Newcombe et al. 1995:334 | **EUROPE** *Britain*: Leitner et al. 1993:28; Ramsay & Percy 1996 |
| No signif. difference | **MIDDLE EAST** *Israel*: Amir & Hovav 1976:167 | **EUROPE** *Britain*: Home Office 1989a; DJ Smith 1995:1056; DJ Smith 1997:101; Home Office 1992 | | |
| Whites higher | **EUROPE** *Britain*: Wallis & Maliphant 1972 **MIDDLE EAST** *Israel*: Agranat Committee on Juvenile Delinquency 1956 | **MIDDLE EAST** *Israel*: Shoham 1966:80 | | |

**TABLE 2.3.7 Oceanic Islanders–White Comparisons of Criminal/Delinquent Behavior.**

| Nature of the relationship | Officially detected offenses | | | | Self-reported offenses | |
|---|---|---|---|---|---|---|
| | Violent offenses | Delinquency | General & adult offenses | Recidivism | Overall offenses | Illegal DRUGS |
| Oceanic Islanders higher | **OCEANIA** *Australia*: Ferrante et al. 1996 (aborigines); *New Zealand*: Al Simpson et al. 2003 (Maori, homicide) | **OCEANIA** *Australia*: Gale et al. 1990; *New Zealand*: Fifield & Donnell 1980; New Zealand Department of Statistics 1986; Norris & Lovell 1988 | **OCEANIA** *Australia*: Hall et al. 1994; Luke & Cunneen 1995; *New Zealand*: Ritchie & Ritchie 1983; Fergusson et al. 1993b; Fergusson et al. 1993c | **OCEANIA** *Australia*: Broadhurst et al. 1988; Broadhurst & Maller 1990 | **OCEANIA** *Hawaii*: Voss 1963:324; *New Zealand*: Fergusson et al. 1993 | **OCEANIA** *Hawaii*: Blanchard & Blanchard 1983:183; *New Zealand*: Moffitt et al. 1994:361; DM Fergusson et al. 2003:58 (Maori, marijuana) |
| Not signif. | | | | | | |
| Whites higher | | | | | | |

groups, some of the studies controlled for age and gender differences between the immigrant and indigenous populations before making comparisons, while others did not.

As one can see, most studies cited in Table 2.3.8a found crime and delinquency rates to be higher among immigrants and their descendants than among native populations. However, some researchers emphasized that the country of origin seemed to be more relevant than immigrant status per se (Brearley 1932:41; Zimmerman 1966). For example, a French study found that immigrants who came from other European countries had crime rates that were actually lower than the overall French average, but that immigrants from Algeria had higher crime rates than the overall French average (Desdevises 1980). Similarly, two British studies found that immigrants from various African countries had higher rates of crime than was true for the indigenous British population, while immigrants from Asian countries (mainly India and Pakistan) actually had somewhat lower rates (Batta et al. 1975; Mawby et al. 1979). Also, a study in Israel found that Jewish immigrants from Africa had higher rates of delinquency, while those from India had essentially the same rates of delinquency as did Jews of European or American descent (Amir & Hovav 1976:167).

The few comparisons made in the United States provide a mixed picture. One study in Chicago found that as the percentage of foreign born increased in various neighborhoods, the delinquency rates actually decreased (Bursik 1986:52). Again, emphasizing the importance of where immigrants originated, rather than their immigrant status per se, one study compared four groups of immigrants to the overall U.S. crime rate. It found no significant difference between the rates for European and Latino immigrants and the U.S. average. For immigrants from India and Pacific Rim countries, the rates were significantly lower than the U.S. average (Touliatos & Lindholm 1980:30).

Over the years, many American criminologists have asserted that immigrants exhibit higher crime rates than do non-immigrants while presenting very little evidence to support this conclusion (Sellin 1938; Shaw & McKay 1942; Shaw & McKay 1969; WB Miller 1990; O'Kane 1992; Mears 2001). Ironically, Table 2.3.8a shows that the majority of studies conducted in the United States have actually found *lower* rates of crime among immigrants than among non-immigrants. In the majority of studies conducted outside the U.S., however, the evidence suggests a positive relationship between immigrant status and criminal involvement.

A few studies have compared immigrants and non-immigrants regarding factors that are frequently linked to criminality. As shown in Table 2.3.8b, one study of conduct disorders and three studies of drug abuse (regardless of the illegality of the drugs) all concluded that these factors were more common among immigrants than among people indigenous to the country.

## 2.4 INDIVIDUAL SOCIAL STATUS

Social status (or class) refers to people's unequal access to scarce resources and to the respect and deference they receive when interacting with others. In contemporary societies, social status is usually measured in terms of three indicators: income (or wealth), occupational level, and years of education (Mayer & Jencks 1989:1441; Townsend 1989:244). Collectively, these three measures are often described as *socioeconomic status* (or *SES*).

Given that education, income, and occupational level are all indicators of social status, one might expect them to be

**TABLE 2.3.8a Immigrant versus Non-immigrant Comparisons and Criminal/Delinquent Behavior.**

| Nature of the relationship | Officially detected offenses | | | | | Self-reported offenses |
|---|---|---|---|---|---|---|
| | Violent offenses | Property offenses | Delinquency | General & adult offenses | Recidivism | Overall offenses |
| Immigrants higher | **NORTH AMERICA** *United States*: Odum 1927:220; Zimmerman 1966; Monkkonen 1989 (homicide); Rosenwaike & Hempstead 1990 (Puerto Rican Hispanic immigrants); Sorenson & Shen 1996:98 | **EUROPE** *Britain*: MJ Brown et al. 1972:259 | **EUROPE** *Belgium*: Lahalle 1981; *France*: Lahalle 1982; *Germany*: Albrecht & Pfeiffer 1979; Chaidou 1984; Mansel 1986; Traulsen 1988; *Netherlands*: Buikhulsen & Timmerman 1971; van der Hoeven 1986; Essers & van der Laan 1988; Terlouw & Suzanne 1989; Junger 1990; Junger & Polder 1992; Junger & Polder 1993:429; van de Wijngaart 1997; *Sweden*: Sveri 1973; Sveri 1980; *Switzerland*: Killias 1977; *Yugosolovia*: Todorovich 1970 **MIDDLE EAST** *Israel*: Shuval 1956; Shoham et al. 1970:96; Shichor 1973; Amir & Hovav 1976:167 **NORTH AMERICA** *United States*: Shaw & McKay 1972:153 **OCEANIA** *Australia*: Kraus 1975 | **EUROPE** *Belgium*: Liben 1963; *Britain*: Bottoms 1967; MJ Brown et al. 1972:262; *France*: Lahalle 1982; Tournier & Robert 1991; *Germany*: Wensky 1965; Nann 1967; Gebauer 1981; Kaiser 1985; Mansel 1988; Traulsen 1988; Kube & Koch 1990; Johnson 1995:179; *Netherlands*: van der Hoeven 1986; Grapendaal 1989; *Sweden*: Klemming 1967 Martens 1997; *Europe in general*: Killias 1989 **MIDDLE EAST** *Israel*: Shoham 1962 **NORTH AMERICA** *United States*: Gurr 1989 | | **EUROPE** *Belgium*: Junger-Tas 1977:82 |
| Not signif. | | | **EUROPE** *Netherlands*: Junger-Tas 1983; *Switzerland*: Queloz 1986 **NORTH AMERICA** *United States*: Chilton & Dussich 1974:75 | **EUROPE** *Austria*: Hanak et al. 1984 | **EUROPE** *Netherlands*: Blokland 2005:49 | **EUROPE** *Netherlands*: Junger & Polder 1992 |
| Non-immigrants higher | | **EUROPE** *Germany*: Zimmerman 1966 | **NORTH AMERICA** *United States*: Hayner 1933 (Japanese immigrants in Seattle) | **NORTH AMERICA** *United States*: Abbott 1915 (European immigrants); Taft 1936 (Europeam immigrants); Sellin 1938 (European immigrants); van Vechten 1941 (European immigrants); Von Hentig 1945:793 (European immigrants); Ferracuti 1968; McCord 1995 (European immigrants); Tonry 1997 (European immigrants); Butcher & Piehl 1998a (controlled for age, gender & employment status); Hagon & Palloni 1998; Hagan & Palloni 1999 (among Hispanic immigrants) **OCEANIA** *Hawaii*: Lind 1930 (Chinese immigrants) | | **EUROPE** *Germany*: Schumann et al. 1987 |

**TABLE 2.3.8b Immigrant versus Non-immigrant Comparisons for Antisocial Behavior or Factors Frequently Linked to Criminality.**

| Nature of the relationship | Antisocial behavior | Drug abuse |
|---|---|---|
| | Child & early adol. | |
| Immigrants higher | **NORTH AMERICA** *United States*: Touliatos & Lindholm 1980 | **EUROPE** *Netherlands*: Van de Wijngaart 1997 (second generation immigrants); *Sweden*: Hjern 2004 (second generation immigrants) **OCEANIA** *Australia*: J Chen et al. 2000 (Asian immigrants) |
| Not signif. | | |
| Non-immigrants higher | | |

strongly correlated with one another. However, research has shown them to be only modestly related (usually yielding correlations in the low to mid 30s) (Ellis 1993:16). When attempting to measure social status, some social scientists use just one of these indicators while others report all three measures separately or combine two or more indicators into some sort of overall composite status measure.

Another important issue surrounding the measurement of social status involves the fact that persons who are still in school or are just beginning to enter the workforce usually

**TABLE 2.4.1a Individual's Social Status (Composite or Unspecified) and Criminal/Delinquent Behavior.**

| Nature of the Relationship | Officially detected offenses | | | | Self-reported offenses |
|---|---|---|---|---|---|
| | Violent offenses | Property offenses | Delinquency | General & adult offenses | Overall offenses |
| Positive | | | | | |
| Not signif. | | | | | **NORTH AMERICA** *United States*: Polk et al. 1974 |
| Negative | **AFRICA** *Nigeria*: Asuni 1969; *South Africa*: Lamont 1961 **ASIA** *Ceylon*: Jayewardene 1960; Wood 1961; *Soviet Union*: Connor 1970 **EUROPE**: *Britain*: Morris & Blom-Cooper 1963; *Italy*: Franchini & Itrona 1961 **LATIN AMERICA** *Mexico*: Bustamento & Bravo 1957 **NORTH AMERICA** *United States*: Palmer 1962; Kaplan & Reich 1976; Greene & Wakefield 1979 | **NORTH AMERICA** *Canada*: Chimbos 1973 | **EUROPE** *Britain*: Farrington 1987:32 | **AFRICA** *Uganda*: Clinard & Abbott 1973 **EUROPE** *Denmark*: Wolf 1962; *Britain*: Baldwin, Bottoms, & Walker 1976; Dunlop & McCabe 1965; *Scotland*: Cormack 1976 **NORTH AMERICA** *United States*: Hollingshead 1947; Green 1970:480; Pownall 1969; President's Commission 1967; Robins et al. 1962; U.S. Bureau of the Census 1923 **OCEANIA** *Australia*: New South Wales Bureau 1974; *New Zealand*: Nixon 1974 | |

TABLE 2.4.1b Individual's Social Status (Composite or Unspecified) and Antisocial Behavior or Factors Frequently Linked to Criminality.

| Nature of the relationship | Antisocial behavior | |
|---|---|---|
| | Child & early adolescents | Late adolescents & adult |
| Positive | | |
| Not signif. | | |
| Negative | **NORTH AMERICA** *United States*: Dodge et al. 1994 **OCEANIA** *New Zealand*: Jaffee et al. 2006 | **NORTH AMERICA** *United States*: Vanyukov et al. 1993 |

do not yet have a social status of their own. Instead, their status is usually defined by that of their parents. This type of status is called *parental* (or *dependent*) *social status*. In the tables to follow, individual social status and dependent social status are considered separately.

## 2.4.1 Individual Social Status (Composite or Unspecified)

The initial two tables summarize findings from studies using composite or general social status measures. Thereafter, separate tables present summaries of individual findings for each of the three social status measures. As one can see, Table 2.4.1a suggests that there is a consistent negative correlation between social status and criminality except in the case of one study of self-reported illegal drug use, where no significant relationship was found.

The few available studies of antisocial behavior have concurred with those surrounding criminality that such

TABLE 2.4.2a Individual's Social Status (Years of Education) and Criminal/Delinquent Behavior.

| Nature of the relationship | Officially detected offenses | | | | Self-reported offenses | |
|---|---|---|---|---|---|---|
| | Violent offenses | Delinquency | General & adult offenses | Recidivism | Overall offenses | Illegal drugs |
| Positive | | | | | **NORTH AMERICA** *United States*: Manolakes 1997:248* (blacks) | |
| Not signif. | | | | **EUROPE** *Britain*: Simon 1971 | **EUROPE** *Netherlands*: Terlouw & Bruinsma 1994:119 | |
| Negative | **EUROPE** *Scotland*: Bannister 1976 **NORTH AMERICA** *United States*: Lalli & Turner 1968; Gelles 1979 | **AFRICA** *Ghana*: Weinberg 1964 **ASIA** *China*: Zhang et al. 1983:223; Fen & Dinghy 1986; Chen 1987 **NORTH AMERICA** *United States*: Hill 1935; Coffey 1983; J Tanner et al. 1999 **OCEANIA** *Hawaii*: Werner & Smith 1992:109 | **EUROPE** *Denmark*: McGarvery et al. 1981:362; *Germany*: Krober et al. 1993; Scheurer 1993; *Scotland*: Bannister 1976 **MIDDLE EAST** *Israel*: Shavit & Rattner 1988:1465 **NORTH AMERICA** *United States*: Thornberry et al. 1985; Beck et al. 1993 | **NORTH AMERICA** *United States*: Vold 1931; Kirby 1954; Arbuckle & Litwack 1960; SD Gottfredson & Gottfredson 1979; Roundtree et al. 1984 | **EUROPE** *Belgium*: Tunger-Tas 1977:80 **NORTH AMERICA** *United States*: Elliott & Voss 1974; Bachman et al. 1978; Thornberry & Farnsworth 1982; Terlouw & Bruinsma 1994:119 (violent offenses); Manolakes 1997:248* (whites); Lochner & Moretti 2004; Siennick 2007 | **NORTH AMERICA** *United States*: Newcomb & Bentler 1986; Weng et al. 1988; Fagan & Pabon 1990; Kaestner 1997:168 |

**TABLE 2.4.2b** Individual's Social Status (Years of Education) and Antisocial Behavior.

| Nature of the relationship | Antisocial behavior | |
|---|---|---|
| | Child & early adolescents | Late adolescents & adult |
| Positive | | |
| Not signif. | | |
| Negative | **EUROPE** *Sweden*: Stattin & Magnusson 1996:621 | **NORTH AMERICA** *United States*: Robins & Regier 1991 |

behavior is more prevalent in the lower social strata than in the upper social strata (Table 2.4.1b).

## 2.4.2 Individual Social Status (Years of Education)

According to Table 2.4.2a, the vast majority of studies have concluded that as an individual's years of education increase, his or her probability of criminal behavior decreases. The only exceptions had to do with two studies of self-reported offending and one study of recidivism.

The extent to which criminality has been shown to be associated with low levels of education can be gleaned from noting that whereas about three-fourths of adults in the United States in recent decades have completed high school (Carpini & Keeter 1991:594), only about one-third of persons in U.S. prisons have done so (Beck et al. 1993:3; Winters 1997:453).

Two studies of the relationship between years of education and antisocial behavior both concluded that a significant negative correlation existed (Table 2.4.2b).

## 2.4.3 Individual Social Status (Income/Wealth)

Many of the most popular theories of criminal behavior have focused on poverty as a major causal factor (Messner & South 1986:977). Therefore, it is important to determine if a relationship between income or wealth and criminality can be empirically established.

**TABLE 2.4.3** Individual Social Status (Income/Wealth) and Criminal/Delinquent Behavior.

| Nature of the relationship | Officially detected offenses | | | | Self-reported offenses | |
|---|---|---|---|---|---|---|
| | Violent offenses | Property offenses | Delinquency | General & adult offenses | Overall offenses | Illegal drugs |
| Positive | | | | | | |
| Not signif. | | | | | | **EUROPE** *Britain*: Buchmueller & Zuvekos 1988 **NORTH AMERICA** *United States*: Gill & Michaels 1992; Register & Williams 1992; Kaestner 1994 |
| Negative | **NORTH AMERICA** *United States*: Kaplan & Reich 1976 | **NORTH AMERICA** *United States*: Cameron 1964 (shoplifters); E Yates 1986 (shoplifters) | **NORTH AMERICA** *United States*: Laub & Sampson 1994:245 | **NORTH AMERICA** *United States*: Paez 1981:44 | **NORTH AMERICA** *Canada*: SW Baron 2003 (self-control statistically controlled); *United States*: JB Ray et al. 1983 (shoplifters); RH Moore 1984 (shoplifters); Laub & Sampson 1994:245 | |

**TABLE 2.4.4a Individual Social Status (Occupation) and Criminal/Delinquent Behavior.**

| Nature of the relationship | Officially detected offenses | | | Self-reported offenses |
|---|---|---|---|---|
| | Violent offenses | Delinquency | General & adult offenses | Overall offenses |
| Positive | | | | |
| Not signif. | | **EUROPE** *Britain*: Farrington 1997b:100* | | **EUROPE** *Britain*: Raine et al. 1995:1596 |
| Negative | **EUROPE**: *Britain*: Givern 1977 (thirteenth century); *Finland*: Verkko 1951 | **EUROPE** *Britain*: Ferguson 1952:33 **OCEANIA** *Hawaii*: Werner & Smith 1992:109 | **EUROPE** Willett 1971; Farrington 1997b:97* | **EUROPE** *Britain*: Farrington 1997b:97* **NORTH AMERICA** *United States*: Swanson et al. 1990 |

Table 2.4.3 summarizes the available findings pertaining to an individual's income and his/her involvement in criminal behavior. As one can see, all of the studies have found negative relationships except in the case of illegal drug use/possession, where no significant relationships have been documented.

### 2.4.4 Individual Social Status (Occupation)

A few studies have investigated links between occupational status and criminality. Table 2.4.4a shows that there is either a negative relationship or no relationship between these two variables.

## 2.5 PARENTAL SOCIAL STATUS

Parental (dependent) social status is determined not by an individual, but by his or her parents. Findings of any relationship between parental social status and criminality of offspring are presented in the following tables.

### 2.5.1 Parental Social Status (Composite or Unspecified)

Findings based on broad or nonspecific measures of parental social status are summarized in Table 2.5.1a. This table suggests that there is a negative relationship between parental status and offspring criminality except possibly in

**TABLE 2.5.1a Parental Social Status (Composite or Unspecified) and Criminal/Delinquent Behavior.**

| Nature of the relationship | Officially detected offenses | | Self-Reported Offenses | |
|---|---|---|---|---|
| | Delinquency | General & adult offenses | Overall offenses | Illegal drug use |
| Positive | | | | |
| Not signif. | | | **EUROPE** *Britain*: Riley & Shaw 1985 (delinquency) **NORTH AMERICA** *United States*: Cernkovich & Giordano 1992 (delinquency); Lynam et al. 1993 (males, delinquency) | |
| Negative | **EUROPE** *Finland*: Rantakallio et al. 1995 | **EUROPE** *Denmark*: Van Dusen et al. 1983 | **EUROPE** *Britain*: Graham & Bowling 1995 (females, delinquency); Flood-Page et al. 2000 (delinquency); Farrington & Painter 2002 (adolescents) **NORTH AMERICA** *United States*: Martens 1997 (delinquency); Piquero & Tibbetts 1999 | **NORTH AMERICA** *United States*: Brennan et al. 1986; Martin & Pritchard 1991 |

**TABLE 2.5.1b Parental Social Status (Composite or Unspecified) and Antisocial Behavior or Factors Frequently Linked to Criminality.**

| Nature of the relationship | Antisocial behavior | Physical aggression |
|---|---|---|
| | Child & early adol. | |
| Positive | | |
| Not signif. | **EUROPE** *Netherlands*: Dekovic 2003 | |
| Negative | **OCEANIA** *New Zealand*: Moffitt et al. 2001 | **NORTH AMERICA** *United States*: Gorman-Smith et al. 1996 (inner city youth) |

the case of overall self-reported delinquency, where the findings have been mixed.

Table 2.5.1b contains a limited amount of evidence on the relationship between parental social status and childhood conduct disorders and aggression in children. Two studies suggest that as parental status rises, the prevalence of these behavior patterns decreases, although one study failed to find a statistically significant relationship.

## 2.5.2 Parental Social Status (Years of Education)

A couple of studies were located regarding a possible relationship between the years of education achieved by parents and criminality among offspring. As shown in Table 2.5.2, these findings failed to be statistically significant except in the case of the father's education, which seemed to be negatively correlated with criminal involvement.

**TABLE 2.5.2a Parental Social Status (Years of Education) and Criminal/Delinquent Behavior.**

| Nature of the relationship | Officially detected offenses | |
|---|---|---|
| | Drug offenses | Delinquency |
| Positive | | |
| Not signif. | **NORTH AMERICA** *United States*: Forthun et al. 1999:80 (marijuana possession) | **EUROPE** *Britain*: Farrington & Painter 2002:50* (mother's education) |
| Negative | | **EUROPE** *Britain*: Farrington & Painter 2002:50* (father's education) |

**TABLE 2.5.2b Parental Social Status (Years of Education) and Clinical or Personality Traits Associated with Criminality.**

| Nature of the relationship | Antisocial behavior | Physical aggression |
|---|---|---|
| | Late adolescents & adult | |
| Positive | | |
| Not signif. | **OCEANIA** *New Zealand*: Miech et al. 1999:1111 | |
| Negative | **OCEANIA** *New Zealand*: Bardone et al. 1996:820 (female) | **NORTH AMERICA** *Canada*: Nagin & Tremblay 2001 (childhood aggression); Kokko et al. 2006:417 (childhood aggression) |

Table 2.5.2b summarizes the available findings concerning any links between parental years of education and offspring antisocial behavior and physical aggression. These findings tend to suggest that a negative correlation exists, although one study failed to find a statistically significant relationship.

**TABLE 2.5.3a Parental Social Status (Income/Wealth) and Criminal/Delinquent Behavior.**

| Nature of the relationship | Officially detected offenses | Self-reported offenses | |
|---|---|---|---|
| | Delinquency | Overall offenses | Illegal drugs |
| Positive | | | |
| Not signif. | | **NORTH AMERICA** *United States*: Wiebe 2006 | **NORTH AMERICA** *United States*: Pleger 1997 (marijuana use) |
| Negative | **EUROPE** *Britain*: Farrington & Painter 2002:50 (for boys) | **NORTH AMERICA** *United States*: TD Evans et al. 1995:208 (college students) | |

**TABLE 2.5.3b Parental Social Status (Income/Wealth) and Antisocial Behavior.**

| Nature of the Relationship | Antisocial behavior |
|---|---|
| | Child & early adol. |
| Positive | |
| Not signif. | |
| Negative | **NORTH AMERICA** *United States*: Attar et al. 1994; Samaan 2000 |

**TABLE 2.5.4 Parental social Status (Occupation) and Criminal/Delinquent Behavior.**

| Nature of the relationship | Officially detected offenses | |
|---|---|---|
| | Delinquency | General & adult offenses |
| Positive | | |
| Not signif. | | |
| Negative | **EUROPE** *Finland*: Rantakallio et al. 1992:1109 | **EUROPE** *Finland*: Rantakallio et al. 1995 (father's occupation) |

## 2.5.3 Parental Social Status (Income/Wealth)

Studies of how parental income or wealth might be associated with offspring criminality are in disagreement. A couple of studies reported any significant negative relationship while two other studies failed to find a significant relationship (Table 2.5.3a).

Two studies sought to determine if childhood conduct disorders were related to parental income. As shown in Table 2.5.3b, both of these studies concluded that the relationship was negative and statistically significant.

## 2.5.4 Parental Social Status (Occupation)

Two studies assessed the relationship between parental occupational status and offspring criminality. Both were based on official crime measures. As shown in Table 2.5.4, these studies both concluded that a significant negative correlation was present.

Chapter 3

# Ecological and Macro-Economic Factors

**Contents**



The term *ecology* is often used to refer to the study of plants and animals living in their natural habitats; but in the present context, only humans and their culturally-created environments are at issue. Ecological studies in criminology can be traced back to the European cartographic school of the early 1800s. Mapping variations in crime rates were later elaborated in the 1930s and 1940s in the United States primarily by members of the Chicago School.

Most ecological research in criminology attempts to link crime rates for various geopolitical regions to the cultural feature of these regions or to the demographic characteristics of their inhabitants. The regional entities most often studied by ecological social scientists are neighborhoods, cities, states, and sometimes even entire countries. Sometimes these units of analyses are studied at a single specific point in time while at other times they are followed over several years or even decades.

In considering the ecological variables associated with crime, it is useful to keep in mind a concept known as the *ecological fallacy*. This term refers to erroneously assuming that whatever statistical relationship exists between two variables at one level of analysis will necessarily hold for another level (Demo & Acock 1988:641). For example, just because it is well established that crime is much more common among persons who are in their teens and 20s (Table 2.2.1), populations with large proportions of persons in this age range may not have the highest crime rates.

## 3.1 DEMOGRAPHIC ECOLOGICAL FACTORS

Ecological variables of a demographic nature have to do primarily with such variables as the racial or ethnic composition of neighborhoods. Other factors that will be considered in this section are sex ratios, age distributions, and percent of foreign born individuals in various geographic regions.

### 3.1.1 Ethnic/Racial Heterogeneity/Diversity

The degree to which a country is comprised of more than one recognized ethnic or racial group is referred to as its ethnic/racial heterogeneity, the opposite of homogeneity. Table 3.1.1 shows that numerous studies have been undertaken to determine if geographical areas (most often neighborhoods in large cities) that are relatively heterogeneous have higher crime rates than relatively homogeneous areas. As one can see, the evidence is largely consistent in indicating that the more ethnically heterogeneous a population is, the higher its crime and delinquency rates tend to be. Interestingly, all of the exceptions so far have to do with violent offenses.

### 3.1.2 Asian Percentage

One study sought to determine if the percentage of an Asian population was associated with three different categories of crime (homicide, robbery, and thefts). As shown in Table 3.1.2, homicide and theft rates were negatively correlated with the percent of the population that was Asian, but there was no significant association between the Asian percent and robbery rates.

### 3.1.3 Black Percentage

Numerous studies have been conducted in the United States in which the proportions of black populations are correlated with the region's crime rate. As shown in Table 3.1.3, most of these studies have concluded that violent crime rates are significantly higher in neighborhoods and/or cities with the highest proportions of black residents, especially regarding violent offenses. Regarding property offenses, the studies are nearly evenly spilt between those that reported a positive correlation and those that reported no significant relationship.

### 3.1.4 Foreign Born/Immigrant Percentage

One more ecological variable that has some similarity with ethnic/racial composition is that of the proportion of a population that was born in another country. Table 3.1.4 presents results from these studies, most of which were conducted in Europe. The results are mixed but, if any relationship exists, it appears that as the percent of foreign born (or percent immigrant) increases so too do the crime and delinquency rates.

### 3.1.5 Hispanic Percentage

According to the available evidence, there is either no relationship between the percent of Hispanics in a population and the crime rate in the area or the relationship is positive. The relevant findings that were located are summarized in Table 3.1.5.

### 3.1.6 Native American Percentage

Only one study was found that sought to determine if the percentage of persons who are Native American (American Indian) was correlated with the areas' crime rates. It found a positive relationship, at least regarding violent crime (Table 3.1.6).

### 3.1.7 Sex Ratio

Two studies were located that investigated possible links between the percent of the population that was male and the crime rates in those populations. Table 3.1.7 shows that one study found no significant relationship, while the other study reported that for violent crime. The percent of males was positively linked but that it was not significantly linked to property crime rates.

### 3.1.8 Teenagers and Young Adults, Percent of Residents

Because criminal behavior is most common among persons in their teens and 20s, numerous studies have attempted to determine if the proportion of the population who is roughly between the ages of 15 and 30 is associated with high crime rates. Most of these studies have involved comparing neighborhoods in large metropolitan areas or comparing sizable numbers of large cities based on information about

**TABLE 3.1.1** Ethnic/Racial Heterogeneity/Diversity and Crime/Delinquency Rates.

| Nature of the relationship | Officially detected offenses | | | | Self-reported offenses |
|---|---|---|---|---|---|
| | Violent offenses | Property offenses | Delinquency | General & adult offenses | Overall offenses |
| Positive | **EUROPE** *Britain*: K Matthews et al. 2006:667 (neighborhood, emergency room admissions) **NORTH AMERICA** *United States*: Messner 1983a (cities); RJ Sampson 1985 (neighborhoods); DA Smith & Jarjoura 1988 (neighborhoods); RJ Sampson & Groves 1989 (neighborhoods); Skogan 1990 (neighborhoods) Miethe et al. 1991 (urban census tracts); RJ Sampson & Wilson 1995 (neighborhoods); Krivo & Peterson 1996 (urban neighborhoods); Bellair 1997 (neighborhoods); BD Warner & Rountree 1997:528 (neighborhoods); Rountree & Warner 1999 (neighborhoods); Veysey & Messner 1999 (neighborhoods); Hipp et al. 2004:1359* (climatic factors controlled); Hipp 2007:681 (census tracks) **INTERNATIONAL** *Multiple Countries*: J Braithwaite & Braithwaite 1980; Hansmann & Quigley 1982; Avison & Loring 1986 | **EUROPE** *Britain*: MJ Brown et al. 1972 (cities); *Sweden:* Dahlback 1998 (cities) **NORTH AMERICA** *United States*: Warner & Rountree 1997:528 (neighborhoods); Hipp et al. 2004:1359* (climatic factors controlled) | **EUROPE** *Yugoslavia*: Todorovich 1970 (cities) **NORTH AMERICA** *Canada*: Jarvis 1972 (neighborhoods); *United States*: Hooker 1945:23 (neighborhoods); Willie & Gershenovitz 1964:743 (neighborhoods) | **EUROPE** *Britain*: Hirschfield & Bowers 1997:113 (neighborhoods) | **NORTH AMERICA** *United States*: Morash 1983:323 (neighborhoods) |
| Not signif. | **INTERNATIONAL** *Multiple Countries*: Krohn et al. 1976; McDonald 1976; Messner 1986, 1989; Neapolitan 1994 | | | | |
| Negative | **NORTH AMERICA** *United States*: Shihadeh & Flynn 1996 (cities) | | | | |

**TABLE 3.1.2** Asian Percentage and Crime/Delinquency Rates.

| Nature of the relationship | Officially detected offenses | |
|---|---|---|
| | Violent offenses | Property offenses |
| Positive | | |
| Not signif. | **NORTH AMERICA** *United States*: Reid et al. 2005:769* (robberies, metropolitan areas) | |
| Negative | **NORTH AMERICA** *United States*: Reid et al. 2005:769* (homicides, metropolitan areas) | **NORTH AMERICA** *United States*: Reid et al. 2005:769* (metropolitan areas) |

TABLE 3.1.3 Black Percentage and Crime/Delinquency Rates.

| Nature of the relationship | Officially detected offenses | | | | Self-reported offenses |
|---|---|---|---|---|---|
| | Violent offenses | Property offenses | Delinquency | General & adult offenses | Illegal drugs |
| Positive | **NORTH AMERICA** *United States*: Gastil 1971:421 (states); Harries 1974 (neighborhoods); Danziger & Wheeler 1975:126 (cities); Freedman 1975:138 (cities); Choldin & Roncek 1976:25 (cities); J Fox 1976 (cities); J Blau & Blau 1982 (cities); Crutchfield et al. 1982:471 (cities); DeFronzo 1983:129 (cities); Messner 1983a:1002 (neighborhoods); Stack 1983:342 (states); Bailey 1984 (cities, homicides); DeFronzo 1984:208 (cities); Jackson 1984:179 (cities); Williams 1984:287 (cities); Bankston et al. 1985 (cities); Sampson 1985a:59* (cities); Huff-Corzine et al. 1986 (states); Lester 1986:106 (states); McDowall 1986:29 (longitudinal); Rosenfeld 1986:125 (cities); Sampson 1986b:293 (cities); Taylor & Covington 1988:572 (cities); Williams & Flewelling 1988 (cities); Bainbridge 1989:292 (cities); Browne & Williams 1989:84 (states); Chamlin 1989 (states, police homicides);Balkwell 1990:66 (cities); Fingerhut & Kleinman 1990 (states); Harer & Steffensmeier 1992:1041 (cities); Kleck & Patterson 1993 (cities); Rojek & Williams 1993:261 (cities); Lester 1994:8 (states); Kposowa et al. 1995 (counties in the South); Volkwein et al. 1995:663 (college campuses); Kovandzic et al. 1998:585 (cities); Whitney 1995 (states); Speer et al. 1998:308 (states); MR Lee 2000 (neighborhoods, homicides) | **NORTH AMERICA** *United States*: Danziger & Wheeler 1975:126 (cities); Freedman 1975:138 (cities); Stack 1983:342 (states); DeFronzo 1984:208 (cities); Jackson 1984:179 (cities); Byrne 1986:91 (cities); Kposwa et al. 1995:92 (cities) | **NORTH AMERICA** *United States*: Shaw & McKay 1942 (neighborhoods); Freedman 1975:140 (neighborhoods); Bates 1962:352 (neighborhoods) Bursik 1986:49 (cities) | **NORTH AMERICA** *United States*: Schuessler 1962 (cities); Schuessler & Slatin 1964 (cities); Quinney 1966 (cities); Harries 1974 (neighborhoods); Reppetto 1974 (cities); Choldin & Roncek 1976:25 (cities); Harris 1976 (cities); Stafford & Gibbs 1980 (cities); A Watts & Watts 1981; Liska & Chamlin 1984 (cities); Shihadeh & Ousey 1996 (neighborhoods) | |
| Not signif. | **NORTH AMERICA** *United States*: Parker & Smith 1979 (states); Smith & Parker 1980 (states); Messner & Tardiff 1986a:312 (neighborhoods) | **NORTH AMERICA** *United States*: Crutchfield et al. 1982:471 (cities); DeFronzo 1983:129 (cities); Rosenfeld 1986:125 (cities); Bainbridge 1989:292 (cities); Volkwein et al. 1995:663 (college campuses) | **NORTH AMERICA** *United States*: Bordua 1958/59 (cities) | **NORTH AMERICA** *United States*: Sampson 1985a* (cities, controls imposed for population size, poverty rate, & unemployment) | |
| Negative | | | | | **NORTH AMERICA** *United States*: DC Gottfredson et al. 1991:213 (neighborhoods) |

**TABLE 3.1.4** Foreign Born/Immigrant Percentage and Crime/Delinquency Rates.

| Nature of the relationship | Officially detected offenses | | | |
|---|---|---|---|---|
| | Violent offenses | Property offenses | Delinquency | General & adult offenses |
| Positive | **EUROPE** *France*: D Cohen & Johnson 1982:486 (nineteenth century, neighborhoods) | **NORTH AMERICA** *United States*: Hagan & Palloni 1998 (neighborhoods, Hispanic immigrants) | **EUROPE** *Germany*: EA Johnson & McHale 1980:397 (nineteenth century, cities) | **EUROPE** *Germany*: EA Johnson 1982:366 (nineteenth century, cities) **NORTH AMERICA** *United States*: Schuessler 1962:315 (cities); Lauritsen 2001 (neighborhood, victimization) |
| Not signif. | **NORTH AMERICA** *United States*: Lester 1994:8 (states) | **EUROPE** *France*: D Cohen & Johnson 1982:487 (nineteenth century, neighborhoods) | | **NORTH AMERICA** *United States*: Butcher & Piehl 1998b (city comparisons); LW Reid et al. 2005 (metropolitan areas, multiple demographic & economic controls) |

**TABLE 3.1.5** Hispanic Percentage and Crime/Delinquency Rates.

| Nature of the relationship | Officially detected offenses | |
|---|---|---|
| | Violent offenses | Property offenses |
| Positive | **NORTH AMERICA** *United States*: Kposowa et al. 1995 (counties); LW Reid et al. 2005:769* (robbery, metropolitan areas, no controls) | **NORTH AMERICA** *United States*: Hagan & Palloni 1998 (neighborhoods) |
| Not signif. | **NORTH AMERICA** *United States*: MT Lee et al. 2001 (time study, homicide); LW Reid et al. 2005:769* (homicide, metropolitan areas, no controls) | **NORTH AMERICA** *United States*: LW Reid et al. 2005:769* (metropolitan areas, no controls) |
| Negative | | |

**TABLE 3.1.6** Native American Percentage and Crime/Delinquency Rates.

| Nature of the relationship | Officially detected offenses |
|---|---|
| | Violent offenses |
| Positive | **NORTH AMERICA** *United States*: Kposowa et al. 1995 (counties) |
| Not signif. | |
| Negative | |

age distributions derived from census data. Somewhat varying age ranges have been used to designate teens and young adults, with the most common being those between 15 and 24 or between 15 and 29, although a few studies have also used 20–29 (Land et al. 1990b:928).

The results of these studies have been mixed as shown in Table 3.1.8. Many studies have found the relationship to be positive, but numerous ones have failed to confirm this general pattern, especially for violent crimes.

## 3.2 DRUG-RELATED AND WEAPONS-RELATED ECOLOGICAL FACTORS

Ecological research having to do with the control and use of drugs and with the availability of firearms has been conducted frequently in the field of criminology. This section will summarize the findings from these lines of inquiry.

**TABLE 3.1.7** Sex Ratio and Crime/Delinquency Rates.

| Nature of the relationship | Officially detected offenses | |
|---|---|---|
| | Violent offenses | Property offenses |
| Higher percent males | **EUROPE** *Netherlands*: Van Wilsen et al. 2006:238* | |
| No signif. diff. | **NORTH AMERICA** *United States*: Lester 1999 (states) | **EUROPE** *Netherlands*: Van Wilsen et al. 2006:238* |
| Higher percent females | | |

**TABLE 3.1.8** Teenagers and Young Adults, Percent of Residents and Crime/Delinquency Rates.

| Nature of the relationship | Officially detected offenses | | |
|---|---|---|---|
| | Violent offenses | Property offenses | General & adult offenses |
| Positive | **NORTH AMERICA** *United States*: Sagi & Wellford 1968; Gastil 1971 (states); Wellford 1973; Loftin & Hill 1974 (states); McDowall 1986:29 **INTERNATIONAL** *Multiple Countries*: Hansmann & Quigley 1982; Conklin & Simpson 1985; Pampel & Gartner 1995 | **EUROPE** *France*: Zehr 1976:59 (neighborhoods) **NORTH AMERICA** *United States*: Byrne 1986:91 (cities); Reid et al. 2005:769* (metropolitan areas, no controls, age 15–29) | **EUROPE** *Netherlands*: van Wilsen et al. 2006:236 (neighborhoods) **NORTH AMERICA** *United States*: Pogue 1975 (cities); Choldin & Roncek 1976:25 (cities) |
| Not signif. | **NORTH AMERICA** *United States*: Choldin & Roncek 1976:25 (cities); Parker & Smith 1979 (states); Smith & Parker 1980 (states); DeFronzo 1983 (cities); Messner 1983b (cities); Huff-Corzine et al. 1986 (states); Kovandzic et al. 1998:585 (cities); Reid et al. 2005:769* (metropolitan areas, no controls, age 15–29) **INTERNATIONAL** *Multiple Countries*: Messner 1989; Gartner 1990; Neapolitan 1994 | | **NORTH AMERICA** *Canada*: Furlong & Mehay 1981:53; *United States*: DeFronzo 1984:208 (cities) |
| Negative | **NORTH AMERICA** *United States*: Bailey 1984 (cities); Hannon 1997 (cities) | | |

## 3.2.1 Alcohol Consumption Per Capita (and Alcohol Availability)

Several studies have looked for evidence of a link between the amount of alcohol consumed in a region and that region's crime rate. Because alcohol is nearly always taxed, researchers have been able to fairly accurately calculate the per capita alcohol consumption by dividing the revenue derived from alcohol sales by the number of people (usually of legal drinking age).

Table 3.2.1 summarizes the results of these studies. Readers can see that most studies have found a significant positive correlation between per capita alcohol consumption and rates of violent crime. However, this positive relationship may not hold for property crimes.

One particularly novel study involved determining the number of alcoholics anonymous groups active in various countries and adjusting for the total adult population. The prevalence of these groups was found to be positively correlated with the homicide rates in the countries sampled.

**TABLE 3.2.1** Alcohol Consumption Per Capita (and Alcohol Availability) and Crime/Delinquency Rates.

| Nature of the relationship | Officially detected offenses | |
|---|---|---|
| | Violent offenses | Property offenses |
| Positive | **ASIA** *Russia*: Pridemore 2002 (homicide, provinces); Pridemore 2004 (homicide, time series) **EUROPE** *Finland*: Verkko 1946; *France*: Zehr 1976:90*; *Sweden*: Lenke 1989; von Hofer 1990:35 (nineteenth & twentieth centuries); *Multiple European Countries*: Rossow 2001 (14 countries, homicide) **NORTH AMERICA** *Canada*: Rossow 2004 (time series); *United States*: Cook & Moore 1993 (states); RN Parker 1998:15 **INTERNATIONAL** *Multiple Countries*: Bridges 2005 (21 countries, Alcoholics Anonymous groups per capita) | |
| Not signif. | **NORTH AMERICA** *United States*: Lester 1994:8 (states) | |
| Negative | | **EUROPE** *France*: Zehr 1976:45*; *Germany*: Zehr 1976:51* |

### 3.2.2 Tavern and Liquor Store Prevalence Per Capita (Alcohol Outlet Density)

An ecological variable closely related to per capita alcohol consumption is called *alcohol outlet density*, which refers to the number of taverns and/or liquor stores in an area (usually adjusted for the physical size of the area or the number of people living in it). These studies are nearly always conducted at neighborhood levels within large cities. Table 3.2.2 shows that nearly all studies have revealed that neighborhoods with the highest density of alcohol outlets per capita tend to have the highest crime rates.

It is also worth mentioning that some studies have controlled for the possible confounding influences of factors, such as gender and age compositions of the populations under study. These studies have found that part of the relationship between the alcohol outlet density and crime is best explained in terms of extraneous factors such as the proportion of young males living in high alcohol outlet density areas (Donnelly 1978). Nevertheless, even after controlling for this sort of confounding demographics, some of the alcohol consumption/availability-crime connection seems to remain, especially in the case of violent crime (Speer et al. 1998).

### 3.2.3 Penalties for Drug Possession

One ecological study compared assault rates according to the penalties imposed for marijuana possession. It concluded that regions where the penalties were the highest had relatively lower assault rates than regions with the most lenient penalties (Table 3.2.3).

**TABLE 3.2.3** Penalties for Drug Possession and Crime/Delinquency Rates.

| Nature of the relationship | Officially detected offenses |
|---|---|
| | Violent offenses |
| Positive | |
| Not signif. | |
| Negative | NORTH AMERICA *United States*: Markowitz 2005 (marijuana possession, assault) |

### 3.2.4 Price of (Tax on) Alcohol and Drugs

A few studies have investigated the possibility that increasing the price of alcohol (usually through the increase of taxes on alcohol purchases) or the price of various illegal drugs (usually by suppressing the supply) will impact the rate of crime. As shown in Table 3.2.4, these studies have fairly consistently shown that these measures are associated with some reduction in violent crimes (with the possible exception of rape).

### 3.2.5 Gun Ownership/Firearm Availability, Per Capita

According to most of the available evidence, as the proportion of a population owning firearms increases, the rate of crime tends to decrease (Table 3.2.5).

## 3.3 FAMILY-BASED ECOLOGICAL FACTORS

Ecological variables that are of a familial nature have to do with things such as divorce rates and the number of persons comprising households. Research findings in these areas

**TABLE 3.2.2** Tavern and Liquor Store Prevalence Per Capita (Alcohol Outlet Density) and Crime/Delinquency Rates.

| Nature of the relationship | Officially detected offenses | |
|---|---|---|
| | Violent offenses | General & adult offenses |
| Positive | NORTH AMERICA *United States*: Watts & Rabow 1983 (neighborhoods); Scribner et al. 1995 (neighborhoods, taverns & liquor stores); Speer et al. 1998:308 (neighborhoods); Scribner et al. 1999 (neighborhoods, homicides); Gyimah-Brempong 2001 (census tracks); Gruenewald et al. 2006 (zip codes, assaults) | NORTH AMERICA *Canada*: Engstad 1975 (neighborhoods, taverns); *United States*: Frisbie 1978 (neighborhoods, taverns); Roncek & Bell 1981 (neighborhoods, taverns); Roncek & Pravatiner 1989 (neighborhoods, taverns); Sherman et al. 1989 (neighborhoods/taverns); Roncek & Maier 1991 (neighborhoods, taverns) |
| Not signif. | NORTH AMERICA *United States*: Gorman et al. 1998 (neighborhoods) | |
| Negative | | |

**TABLE 3.2.4 Price of (Tax on) Alcohol and Drugs and Crime/Delinquency Rates.**

| Nature of the relationship | Officially detected offenses |
|---|---|
| | Violent offenses |
| Positive | |
| Not signif. | **NORTH AMERICA** *United States*: Markowitz 2005* (increase tax on alcohol, rape, states) |
| Negative | **EUROPE** *Britain*: K Matthews et al. 2006 (time-series, emergency room admissions for assault)<br>**NORTH AMERICA** *United States*: Markowitz 2005:41* (increase tax on alcohol & increase price of cocaine, assaults, states)<br>**INTERNATIONAL** *Multiple Countries*: Markowitz 2001 (increase tax on alcohol) |

**TABLE 3.2.5 Gun Ownership/Firearm Availability, Per Capita and Crime/Delinquency Rates.**

| Nature of the relationship | Officially detected offenses | |
|---|---|---|
| | Violent offenses | General & adult offenses |
| Positive | | |
| Not signif. | **NORTH AMERICA** *United States*: Clotfelter 1981 (longitudinal) | **NORTH AMERICA** *United States*: Bordua & Lizotte 1979 (cities, ownership by men) |
| Negative | **NORTH AMERICA** *United States*: Murray 1975 (states); Phillips & Votey 1976 (longitudinal); Kleck 1979 (longitudinal); Bordua 1986:187 (cities)<br>**INTERNATIONAL** *Several Countries*: Killias 1993; Krug et al. 1998 (industrial countries, homicide); Hemenway & Miller 2000 (industrial countries, homicides) | **NORTH AMERICA** *United States*: Bordua & Lizotte 1979 (cities; ownership by women); Clotfelter 1981 (longitudinal) |

present a generally consistent pattern with respect to being associated with criminal behavior.

### 3.3.1 Divorced or Single-Parent Households, Percent of Residents

Table 3.3.1 shows that nearly all studies have found that regions with relatively high rates of divorced or separated individuals have higher rates of crime than do regions with low divorce or separation rates. Nevertheless, there are a minority of studies that have failed to confirm this basic pattern, especially regarding property crimes.

### 3.3.2 Household Density, Per Capita

Household density is usually measured in terms of the number of persons divided by the square footage or number of rooms in each residential household. Table 3.3.2 is consistent with the conclusion that crime and delinquency are more common in geographical regions with relatively crowded households.

## 3.4 PHYSICAL, SOCIAL AND HEALTH-RELATED ECOLOGICAL FACTORS

A variety of ecological variables having to do with physical, social and health-related conditions have been investigated with respect to their possible relationship with criminality. The findings are summarized below.

### 3.4.1 City or County Population Size

A substantial number of studies have investigated the relationship between crime rates and the size of a city's population (or the size of the county encompassing a city). The findings are summarized in Table 3.4.1. As one can see, nearly all of the research suggests that as a city's (or county's) population increases, so too does its crime rate according to official statistics. Victimization data (which by-passes official crime data) have also indicated that the larger and more urban a city is, the higher its overall crime rate (Ennis 1967).

### 3.4.2 Disorganized Neighborhoods, Residents of Relatively Well Organized Neighborhoods

The two available studies both indicate that persons who live in disorganized neighborhoods experience higher rates of crime than do residents of relatively well-organized neighborhoods (Table 3.4.2).

### 3.4.3 Mortality Rates/Life Expectancy

A number of studies have examined the possibility of a relationship between the average life expectancy in an ecological region and its crime rate. Some of these studies have focused on overall mortality rates, whereas others have

**TABLE 3.3.1 Divorced or Single-Parent Households, Percent of Residents and Crime/Delinquency Rates.**

| Nature of the relationship | Officially detected offenses | | | |
|---|---|---|---|---|
| | Violent offenses | Property offenses | Delinquency | General & adult offenses |
| Positive | **NORTH AMERICA** *United States*: Choldin & Roncek 1976:25 (cities); Block 1979 (neighborhoods) Loftin 1980 (states); Blau & Blau 1982 (cities); Williams 1984 (cities); Sampson 1985 (cities); Lieberman & Smith 1986 (cities); Messner & Tardiff 1986 (neighborhoods); Sampson 1986b:293 (cities); Williams & Flewelling 1988 (cities); Bainbridge 1989:292 (cities); RJ Sampson & Groves 1989 (neighborhoods); Balkwell 1990:66 (cities); Land et al. 1990 (cities); Messner & Sampson 1991 (counties); Kowalski & Stark 1992 (cities); Messner & Golden 1992 (counties); Shihadeh & Steffensmeier 1994 (cities); Lester 1995:52 (states); Hannon 1997 (cities & states); KF Parker & McCall 1997 (neighborhoods); JA Phillips 1997:548 (neighborhoods); Kovandzic et al. 1998:585 (cities); Ousey 1999 (neighborhoods); KF Parker & Johns 2002 (neighborhoods); Hipp et al. 2004:1359* (climatic factors controlled); J Schwartz 2006:264 (homicide, counties, female headed household) **INTERNATIONAL** *Multiple Countries*: Lester & Yang 1998 (cross-national comparison); He et al. 2003 (cross-national comparison) | **NORTH AMERICA** *United States*: Hipp et al. 2004:1359* (climatic factors controlled); Reid et al. 2005:769* (metropolitan areas, no controls) | **EUROPE** *Germany*: EA Johnson & McHale 1980:397 (19th century, cities) **NORTH AMERICA** *United States*: Willie 1967 **OCEANIA** *Australia*: Kraus 1975 (cities) | **EUROPE** *Wales*: Giggs 1970 **NORTH AMERICA** *United States*: Choldin & Roncek 1976:24 (cities); Sampson 1983 (neighborhoods); Sampson 1986 (neighborhoods); Chamlin & Cochran 1997 |
| Not signif. | **NORTH AMERICA** *United States*: Kposowa et al. 1995 (homicide, counties); Reid et al. 2005:769* (metropolitan areas, no controls) | **NORTH AMERICA** *United States*: Lieberman & Smith 1986 (states); Bainbridge 1989:292 (cities) | | |
| Negative | **EUROPE** *France*: Gillis 1996 | | | |

**TABLE 3.3.2 Household Density Per Capita and Crime/Delinquency Rates.**

| Nature of the relationship | Officially detected offenses | |
|---|---|---|
| | Delinquency | General & adult offenses |
| Positive | **NORTH AMERICA** *United States*: Shaw & McKay 1942; Schmitt 1957; Bordua 1958; Schmitt 1966; Chilton & Dussich 1974:75; Freedman 1975:140 | **NORTH AMERICA** *United States*: Chilton 1964; Galle et al. 1972 |
| Not signif. | | |
| Negative | | |

**TABLE 3.4.1** City or County Population Size and Crime/Delinquency Rates.

| Nature of the relationship | Officially detected offenses | | |
|---|---|---|---|
| | Violent offenses | Property offenses | General & adult offenses |
| Positive | **NORTH AMERICA** *United States*: Harries 1974:100; Danziger & Wheeler 1975:126*; Messner 1982b; Messner 1983b; DeFronzo 1984:208; Jackson 1984:179; Loftin & Parker 1985; Sampson 1985:59; J Schwartz 2006:268 (counties) | **EUROPE** *Slovakia*: Michalek 1996 **NORTH AMERICA** *United States*: Danziger & Wheeler 1975:126*; DeFronzo 1984:208; Jackson 1984:179; Byrne 1986:91 | **EUROPE** *Netherlands*: van Wilsem et al. 2006:238 (cities) **NORTH AMERICA** *United States*: Ogburn 1935; Clinard 1942; Wolfgang 1968; Hoch 1974; Skogan 1974; Freedman 1975:138; Pogue 1975:33; Harries 1976:477; Mayhew & Levinger 1976; Pyle 1976; Crutchfield 1982:471; O'Brien 1983; Nolan 2004 |
| Not signif. | **NORTH AMERICA** *United States*: Gastil 1971; Blau & Blau 1982; Simpson 1985 | | |
| Negative | | | |

**TABLE 3.4.2** Disorganized Neighborhoods, Residents of and Crime/Delinquency Rates.

| Nature of the relationship | Officially detected offenses | Self-reported offenses |
|---|---|---|
| | Delinquency | Overall offenses |
| Positive | **NORTH AMERICA** *United States*: Vander Ven & Cullen 2004:285 | **NORTH AMERICA** *United States*: Herrenkohl et al. 2000 (violent offenses) |
| Not signif. | | |
| Negative | | |

studied infant mortality. As shown in Table 3.4.3, most of these studies have found mortality rates to be higher in geographical regions with the highest crime rates.

### 3.4.4 Neighborhood Conditions

Over the years, many studies have been conducted to determine if neighborhoods that are poorly maintained have higher rates of crime than well-maintained neighborhoods. The results of these studies are summarized in Table 3.4.4a, which is divided into two subtables due to the large number of relevant studies. For official data, nearly all of the research has shown that crime rates are lower in well-maintained neighborhoods.

**TABLE 3.4.3** Mortality Rates/Life Expectancy and Crime/Delinquency Rates.

| Nature of the relationship | Officially detected offenses | | | |
|---|---|---|---|---|
| | Violent offenses | Property offenses | Delinquency | General & adult offenses |
| Positive | **NORTH AMERICA** *United States*: Lester 1994:8 (states, infant mortality) **INTERNATIONAL** *Multiple Countries*: Conklin & Simpson 1985 (infant mortality) | **INTERNATIONAL** *Multiple Countries*: Shichor 1985 (infant mortality); Shichor 1990:69 (infant mortality) | **NORTH AMERICA** *United States*: Shaw & McKay 1972:99 (states) | **EUROPE** *Germany*: EA Johnson 1982:366 (nineteenth century, cities) |
| Not signif. | **INTERNATIONAL** *Multiple Countries*: Rahav 1990 (infant mortality); Shichor 1990 (infant mortality) | | | |
| Negative | | | | |

**TABLE 3.4.4a** Neighborhood Conditions and Crime/Delinquency Rates.

| Nature of the relationship | Officially detected offenses | | | | |
|---|---|---|---|---|---|
| | Violent offenses | Property offenses | Drug offenses | Delinquency | General & adult offenses |
| More offending in poorly maintained neighborhoods | **NORTH AMERICA** *United States*: District of Columbia Crime Commission 1969; Roncek 1981 (neighborhoods); WJ Wilson 1987; Williams & Flewelling 1988; Roncek & Maier 1991 (neighborhoods); Krivo & Peterson 1996 (neighborhoods); Reid et al. 2005:769* (metropolitan areas, no controls); De Coster et al. 2006 | **NORTH AMERICA** *United States*: Reid et al. 2005:769* (metropolitan areas, no controls) | **NORTH AMERICA** *United States*: Nurco et al. 1996 | **AFRICA** *Egypt*: El-Saaty 1946 **ASIA** *India*: Sheth 1961; *Japan*: Matsumoto 1970 **EUROPE** *Britain*: Bagot 1941; Mannheim 1948; Morris 1957; Wallis & Maliphant 1967; Timms 1971; A Edwards 1973; Baldwin et al. 1976; Farrington 1987a:32; Nagin & Land 1993:353; *Italy*: Cherchi et al. 1972; *Yugoslavia*: Todorovich 1970 **NORTH AMERICA** *Canada*: Jarvis 1972; Jarvis & Messinger 1974; *United States*: Shaw & McKay 1931; Sullenger 1936; Shaw & McKay 1942; Reinemann 1945; Dirksen 1948; Carr 1950; Barker 1954; Lander 1954; Bordua 1958; Polk 1958; Martin 1961; Bates 1962; Shannon 1963; Chilton 1964; Bloom 1966; Chilton 1967; Polk 1967; Rosen & Turner 1967; Singell 1967; Hardt 1968; Shaw & McKay 1969; Slatin 1969; Conlen 1971; DeFleur 1971; Quinney 1971; Galle et al. 1972; Spady 1972; Wolfgang et al. 1972; Kapsis 1978; Chilton & Dussich 1974:75; Garrett & Short 1975; Johnston et al. 1978; Bursik & Webb 1982; Brown 1985; Byrne & Sampson 1986; Stern & Smith 1995; LM Burton & Jarrett 2000 **OCEANIA** *Australia*: Vinson and Hormel 1972; Dunstan & Roberts 1977; Braithwaite 1979 | **EUROPE** *Britain*: TP Morris 1957; Timms 1971; Brown et al. 1972; Baldwin et al. 1976; Farrington 1993b:16; *Wales*: Giggs 1970 **NORTH AMERICA** *United States*: Quinney 1971; Bechdolt 1975; J Blau & Blau 1982 (metropolitan areas); Covington & Taylor 1989; Skogan 1990; Jarjoura & Triplett 1997 |
| Not signif. | | | | | |
| Less offending in poorly maintained neighborhoods | | | | | **EUROPE** *Netherlands*: van Wilsem et al. 2006:236 (when general economy is improving) |

**TABLE 3.4.4b** Neighborhood Conditions and Crime/Delinquency Rates.

| Nature of the relationship | Self-reported offenses | | Antisocial behavior |
|---|---|---|---|
| | Overall offenses | Illegal drugs | Child & early adol. |
| More offending in poorly maintained neighborhoods | **EUROPE** *Britain*: McDonald 1968; Farrington 1997b:97 **NORTH AMERICA** *United States*: Clark & Wenninger 1962; Johnston 1978; Stern & Smith 1995; RL Simons et al. 2002 (parental report); Cleveland 2003 (violent delinquency); Vazsonyi et al. 2006 (delinquency) **OCEANIA** *Australia*: G Smith 1975 | **NORTH AMERICA** *United States*: Blout and Dembo 1984; Dembo et al. 1985; R Sampson 1986:881; Dielman et al. 1990; Gifford & Hine 1990; Agnew & White 1992:486*; R Smart et al. 1994 | **NORTH AMERICA** *United States*: Coulton 1996 |
| Not signif. diff. | **EUROPE** *Sweden*: Elmhorn 1965 **NORTH AMERICA** *United States*: Hardt 1968; EM Johnson 1969; Agnew & White 1992:486* **OCEANIA** *Australia*: Braithwaite 1979 | | |
| Less offending in poorly maintained neighborhoods | **NORTH AMERICA** *United States*: DC Gottfredson et al. 1991 | | |

Table 3.4.4b shows that in the case of self-reported offending, the evidence must be considered mixed, although most of the studies concur that offending is more prevalent among residents of poorly kept neighborhoods.

### 3.4.5 Owner Occupied Housing, Per Capita

As shown in Table 3.4.5, nearly all of the available studies have concluded that as the proportion of owner-occupied homes (as opposed to those being rented) increases, crime and delinquency rates decrease. One study conducted in England identified two types of rental homes: privately owned and publicly owned. This study concluded that property crime rates were particularly high among those rental homes that were publicly owned.

### 3.4.6 Geographic Population Density

Population density is usually assessed in terms of the number of persons living within a square mile (or kilometer). As indicated in Table 3.4.6, the evidence is moderately consistent with the view that population density and

**TABLE 3.4.5** Owner Occupied Housing, Per Capita and Crime/Delinquency Rate.

| Nature of the relationship | Officially detected offenses | | | |
|---|---|---|---|---|
| | Violent offenses | Property offenses | Delinquency | General & adult offenses |
| Positive | | | | **NORTH AMERICA** *United States*: Schuessler 1962:315 (cities) |
| Not signif. | | | | |
| Negative | **EUROPE** *Britain*: MJ Brown et al. 1972:259* (neighborhoods) | **EUROPE** *Britain*: MJ Brown et al. 1972:259* (neighborhoods) **NORTH AMERICA** *United States*: Byrne 1986:91 (cities) | **NORTH AMERICA** *United States*: Reinemann 1945 (neighborhoods); Bordua 1958 (neighborhoods); Grieson 1972 (cities); Shaw & McKay 1972:149 (neighborhoods); Chilton & Dussich 1974:75 (neighborhoods); Bursik 1986:49 (neighborhoods) **OCEANIA** *Australia*: Kraus 1975 (neighborhoods) | **EUROPE** *Britain*: Baldwin et al. 1976 (neighborhoods); C Wong 1997:237 (neighborhoods) **NORTH AMERICA** *United States*: Schuerman & Kobrin 1986 (neighborhoods) |

**TABLE 3.4.6 Geographic Population Density and Crime/Delinquency Rates.**

| Nature of the relationship | Officially detected offenses | | | | | Self-reported Offenses |
|---|---|---|---|---|---|---|
| | Violent offenses | Property offenses | Sex offenses | Delinquency | General & adult offenses | Illegal Drugs |
| Positive | **NORTH AMERICA** *United States*: Bechdolt 1975; Choldin & Roncek 1976:25; Stack 1983:342*; DR Smith & Jarjoura 198; Williams & Flewelling 1988; Sampson & Lauritsen 1994 (states); Kposowa et al. 1995* (counties) **INTERNATIONAL** *Multiple Countries*: Kick & LaFree 1985 | **EUROPE** *Germany*: EA Johnson 1996:236 (nineteenth century) **NORTH AMERICA** *United States*: Stack 1983:342*; Jackson 1984:179; Schuerman & Kobrin 1986:70 | **NORTH AMERICA** *United States*: Booth et al. 1974 (rape); Perry & Simpson 1987:84 (rape, neighborhoods) | **EUROPE** *Sweden*: Jonsson 1967:210 (states) **NORTH AMERICA** *United States*: Hathaway & Monachesi 1963:80 (states); Galle et al. 1972 (states); Freedman 1975:140; Bursik 1986:47 | **NORTH AMERICA** *United States*: Wirth 1938 (urban areas); Schmitt 1957; Wolfgang 1968 (urban areas); Yancey 1972; Beasley & Antunes 1974 (urban areas); Gillis 1974; Freedman 1975:138; Mladenka & Hill 1976 (urban areas); JQ Wilson & Boland 1976 | **NORTH AMERICA** *Canada*: Gillis & Hagan 1982:521 |
| Not signif. | **ASIA** *India*: Bagley 1989 **EUROPE** *France*: D Cohen & Johnson 1982 (nineteenth century); *Germany*: EA Johnson 1996:239 (nineteenth century) **NORTH AMERICA** *United States*: Pressman & Carol 1971* (controlling for various SES & demographic variables); Danziger & Wheeler 1975:126; Spector 1975:400; Messner 1983b; W Bailey 1984; K Williams 1984; M Simpson 1985; Schuerman & Kobnin 1986:70; Lester 1994a:8 **INTERNATIONAL** *Multiple Societies*: Hansmann & Quigley 1982; Messner 1982; Conklin & Simpson 1985; Avison & Loring 1986; Messner 1989; Neapolitan 1994; Lester 1996 | **NORTH AMERICA** *United States*: Kposowa et al. 1995* (counties) | **NORTH AMERICA** *United States*: Pressman & Carol 1971* (rape, controlled for various SES & demographic variables) | | **NORTH AMERICA** *United States*: Kvalseth 1977 (neighborhoods) | |
| Negative | **NORTH AMERICA** *United States*: Shichor et al. 1979* (among 26 large cities, assault victimization data); Perry & Simpson 1987:84 (assault rate, neighborhoods) | | **NORTH AMERICA** *United States*: Shichor et al. 1979* (among 26 large cities, rape victimization data) | | | |

criminality are positively correlated, particularly in the case of delinquency and property crimes. In the case of violent crimes, the evidence is mixed, with most studies failing to find a significant relationship.

### 3.4.7 Lead Levels in the Environment

Lead is considered a neurological toxin that in extreme cases can have devastating effects on brain functioning. Some studies have reported higher rates of violent crime in geographical regions containing relatively high levels of lead (Table 3.4.7).

### 3.4.8 Left-Handed Percentage

In all known societies left-handers are a small minority when compared to right-handers (Raymond & Ponier 2004). According to one study, preliterate societies with the greatest percentages of left-handers have significantly higher murder rates (Table 3.4.8).

### 3.4.9 Linoleic Acid Consumption, Per Capita

Linoleic acid is a type of polyunsaturated fatty acid akin to the omega-6 fatty acids. It is primarily present in vegetable seeds and polyunsaturated margarines and is widely regarded as a healthy compound to consume. Nevertheless, Table 3.4.9 shows that one study found per capita consumption of this acid was positively associated with the rates of murder in the countries compared.

**TABLE 3.4.7** Lead Levels in the Environment and Crime/ Delinquency Rates.

| Nature of the relationship | Officially detected offenses |
|---|---|
| | Violent offenses |
| Positive | **NORTH AMERICA** *United States*: Nevin 2000:20 (time-series data); Stretesky & Lynch 2001 (counties, homicides) **INTERNATIONAL:** *Multiple Countries*: Nevin 2007 (time series) |
| Not signif. | |
| Negative | |

**TABLE 3.4.8** Left-Handed Percentage and Crime/ Delinquency Rates.

| Nature of the relationship | Officially detected offenses |
|---|---|
| | Violent offenses |
| Positive | **INTERNATIONAL** *Multiple Tribal Societies*: Faurie & Raymond 2005 (murder rates) |
| Not signif. | |
| Negative | |

**TABLE 3.4.9** Linoleic Acid Consumption, Per Capita and Crime/Delinquency Rates.

| Nature of the relationship | Officially detected offenses |
|---|---|
| | Violent offenses |
| Positive | **INTERNATIONAL** *Multiple Countries*: Hibbeln et al. 2004 (homicide) |
| Not signif. | |
| Negative | |

### 3.4.10 Police Presence, Per Capita

One study investigated the possible connection between the per capita presence of police officers in each county and the rate of violent crime in those counties. As shown in Table 3.4.10, a positive correlation was found.

### 3.4.11 Residential Instability/Mobility

Residential mobility refers to the frequency with which people in an area change the houses or apartments in which they live. As shown in Table 3.4.11a, many studies have investigated residential mobility in relation with crime and nearly all have found that officially detected crime rates are higher in neighborhoods, cities, and states where people change addresses most often.

In the case of self-reported offending and residential mobility, the available evidence is split between suggesting that the relationship is either positive or not significant (Table 3.4.11b).

**TABLE 3.4.10** Police Presence Per Capita and Crime/ Delinquency Rates.

| Nature of the relationship | Officially detected offenses |
|---|---|
| | Violent offenses |
| Positive | **NORTH AMERICA** *United States*: J Schwartz 2006:264 (counties) |
| Not signif. | |
| Negative | |

**TABLE 3.4.11a** Residential Mobility and Crime/Delinquency Rates.

| Nature of the relationship | Officially detected offenses | | | | |
|---|---|---|---|---|---|
| | Violent offenses | Property offenses | Delinquency | General & adult offenses | Recidivism |
| Positive | **NORTH AMERICA** *United States*: Crutchfield et al. 1982:471 (neighborhoods); DR Smith & Jarjoura 1988 (neighborhoods); Sampson & Lauritsen 1994 (neighborhoods); Kposowa et al. 1995* (neighborhoods); Lester 1995:52 (states); Hipp et al. 2004:1359* (climatic factors controlled) | **NORTH AMERICA** *United States*: Crutchfield et al. 1982:471 (neighborhoods); Stark et al. 1983:13 (neighborhoods); Kposowa et al. 1995* (counties); Hipp et al. 2004:1359* (climatic factors controlled) | **NORTH AMERICA** *Canada*: Jarvis 1972 (neighborhoods); *United States*: Shaw & McKay 1942 (neighborhoods); Longmoor & Young 1936 (neighborhoods); Sullenger 1936; Reiss 1951 (nighborhoods); Eaton & Polk 1961 (states); Lunden 1964:143; Shaw & McKay 1969 (neighborhoods); Wolfgang et al. 1972 (neighborhoods); Rathus & Siegel 1981 (neighborhoods) **OCEANIA** *New Zealand*: Henry et al. 1996 (neighborhoods) | **EUROPE** *Britain*: Farrington & West 1981 **NORTH AMERICA** *United States*: Clinard 1964 (neighborhoods); Felner et al. 1981 (neighborhoods) | **EUROPE** *Netherlands*: Buikhuisen & Hoekstra 1974:65 |
| Not signif. | **NORTH AMERICA** *United States*: Stark et al. 1983:13 | | | | |
| Negative | | | | | |

## 3.4.12 Seafood Consumption, Per Capita

According to one study, the per capita consumption of seafood in various counties is inversely associated with the murder rates in those countries (Table 3.4.12).

**TABLE 3.4.11b** Residential Mobility and Crime/Delinquency Rates.

| Nature of the relationship | Self-Reported Offenses | |
|---|---|---|
| | Overall offenses | Illegal drugs |
| Positive | **NORTH AMERICA** *United States*: Nye 1958; Farnworth 1984; Herrenkohl et al. 2000 (violent offenses, teens) | |
| Not signif. | **NORTH AMERICA** *United States*: Simcha-Fagan & Schwartz 1986:685 (neighborhoods) | **NORTH AMERICA** *United States*: Steffenhagen et al. 1969:95 |
| Negative | | |

## 3.4.13 Social Interactions between Residents

In one study, researchers sought to determine if the amount of social interaction between neighborhood residents was associated with the level of crime in those neighborhoods. Table 3.4.13 suggests that as the amount of social interactions increased, the level of crime decreased.

## 3.4.14 Technological Development/ Modernization/Industrialization

A concept that numerous ecological studies have examined with respect to crime rates is technological

**TABLE 3.4.12** Seafood Consumption, Per Capita and Crime/Delinquency Rates.

| Nature of the relationship | Officially detected offenses |
|---|---|
| | Violent crime |
| Positive | |
| Not signif. | |
| Negative | **INTERNATIONAL** *Multiple Countries*: Hibbeln 2001 (homicide) |

**TABLE 3.4.13 Social Interactions between Residents and Crime/Delinquency Rates.**

| Nature of the relationship | Officially detected offenses |
|---|---|
| | General & adult offenses |
| Positive | |
| Not signif. | |
| Negative | **NORTH AMERICA** *United States*: Velez 2001 (neighborhoods) |

development (also known as *modernization* and *industrialization*). The results of these studies are shown in Table 3.4.14. Findings for crime in general are mixed, with nearly half of the studies failing to find significant relationships. For violent offenses, however, the evidence largely indicates that the most technologically developed societies have significantly lower crime rates than do less developed societies. In the case of property offenses, the opposite pattern emerges.

### 3.4.15 Tourism and Gambling Regions

Areas that are major tourist attractions have been compared with regions that are rarely visited by tourists to determine if the former have higher crime rates. As shown in Table 3.4.15, most studies have found a significant positive correlation. Of course, one should keep in mind that tourism is associated with other ecological correlates of crime, such as urbanism and per capita alcohol consumption.

**TABLE 3.4.14 Technological Development/Modernization/Industrialization and Crime/Delinquency Rates.**

| Nature of the relationship | Officially detected offenses | | |
|---|---|---|---|
| | Violent offenses | Property offenses | General & adult offenses |
| Positive | **INTERNATIONAL** *Multiple Countries*: Quinney 1965; Krohn 1974; Rahav & Jaamdar 1982:456; Shichor 1985; Kick & LaFree 1985:45; Groves et al. 1985:72; Messner 1986; Shichor 1990 | | **INTERNATIONAL** *Multiple Countries*: Shelley 1981; Buendia 1990 |
| Not signif. | **LATIN AMERICA** *Columbia*: Bouley & Vaughn 1995 (Technology)<br>**INTERNATIONAL** *Multiple Countries*: Messner 1982b:237 | | **EUROPE** *France*: Zehr 1975:128; *Germany*: Zehr 1975:128; EA Johnson 1982:363 (nineteenth century) |
| Negative | | **INTERNATIONAL** *Multiple Countries*: P Wolf 1971; Krohn 1974; Kick & LaFree 1985:45; Shichor 1985; Shichor 1990 | |

**TABLE 3.4.15 Tourism and Gambling Regions and Crime/Delinquency Rates.**

| Nature of the relationship | Officially detected offenses | | |
|---|---|---|---|
| | Violent offenses | Property offenses | General & adult offenses |
| Positive | | **NORTH AMERICA** *United States*: WP Thompson 1996b:12<br>**NORTH AMERICA** *United States*: McPheters & Strong 1974; Sternlieb & Hughes 1983; Ochrym 1988; Ochrym 1990; WP Thompson et al. 1996a | **LATIN AMERICA** *Mexico*: Judd 1975<br>**OCEANIA** *Australia*: Walmsley et al. 1983; *Hawaii*: Fukunaga 1975; Chesney-Lind & Lind 1986 |
| Not signif. | **NORTH AMERICA** *United States*: WP Thompson 1996b:10 | | **NORTH AMERICA** *United States*: Albanese 1985 |
| Negative | | | |

**TABLE 3.4.16a** Urban/Rural Residency (Percent Urban) and Crime/Delinquency Rates.

| Nature of the relationship | Officially detected offenses | | | | |
|---|---|---|---|---|---|
| | Violent offenses | Property offenses | Drug offenses | Delinquency | General & adult offenses |
| Rates higher in urban than in rural areas | **EUROPE** *Finland*: Aromaa 1974 **NORTH AMERICA** *United States*: Brearley 1932:99; Frankel 1939; Gibbs 1979; Weiner & Wolfgang 1984:26; Archer & Gartner 1984:114; Gladstein & Slater 1988; Gladstein 1992; Reiss & Roth 1993:81; Kposowa et al. 1995*(counties); Hannon 1997:131; Stanton et al. 1997:276 | **NORTH AMERICA** *United States*: Tittle & Stafford 1992; Kposowa et al. 1995*(counties) | **NORTH AMERICA** *United States*: Helzer 1985; Tittle & Stafford 1992 | **EUROPE** *Denmark*: Christiansen 1970 **MIDDLE EAST** *Israel*: Rahav 1981 **NORTH AMERICA** *Canada*: Social Planning Council 1965; *United States*: Hayner 1933; Middleton & Wright 1941:141; Clark & Wenninger 1962; Slocum & Stone 1963; Kornhauser 1978 **INTERNATIONAL** *Multiple Countries*: Axenroth 1983:169 | **AFRICA** *Uganda*: Clinard & Abbott 1973:91; *Zambia*: Cifford 1966; *Multiple African Countries*: Houchon 1967 **ASIA** *Korea*: Axenroth 1983:169; *Taiwan*: Tsai et al. 1989 **EUROPE** *Denmark*: Christiansen 1970; Christiansen & Jensen 1972; *Britain*: McClintock & Avison 1968; Rutter & Quinton 1977; Hough & Mayhew 1983; *Finland*: Aromaa 1974; Rantakallio et al. 1995:117; *France*: Szabo 1960; Lodhi & Tilly 1973 (nineteenth century); *Poland*: Hersch 1945:179 **NORTH AMERICA** *Canada*: Szabo & Rico 1976:310; Johnson & Sacco 1990; Sacco et al. 1993; *United States*: Sorokin et al. 1931:298; Ogburn 1935; Sutherland 1939:44; Reckless 1940:81; Clinard 1942; Angell 1951:15; Morris 1957:58; Ferdinand 1964; Clinard 1964; Lunden 1964:134; Rushton & Mangus 1964; Boggs 1965; Lunden 1965; Wolfgang 1968:246; McLennan 1970; Schafer & Knudten 1970:215; Hoch 1974; Fisher 1975; Gibbs 1977; Skogan 1977; Jones 1981; Joubert et al. 1981; Lyerly & Skipper 1981; Shelley 1981; Laub 1983; Larson 1984; Elliott et al. 1986:489; Tittle & Stafford 1992; Killias 1994:203 **INTERNATIONAL** *Multiple Countries*: Clinard & Abbott 1973; Szabo 1977; Hurwitz & Christiansen 1983:191 |
| Not signif. | | **NORTH AMERICA** *United States*: Dentler & Monroe 1961:736 | | **NORTH AMERICA** *United States*: Rivera 1973:20 | **ASIA** *Soviet Union*: Shelley 1980:120 |
| Rates higher in rural than in urban area | | | | | |
| Suburban area intermediate to urban/ rural areas | **NORTH AMERICA** *United States*: Gibbs 1979; Stanton et al. 1997:276 | | | **NORTH AMERICA** *United States*: Garbarino et al. 1992; Walter et al. 1995 | **NORTH AMERICA** *United States*: Brown et al. 1984:448; Gibbs 1977; Sparks 1982; Elliott et al. 1986:489; Gladstein et al. 1992 |
| Not signif. | | | | | |
| Suburban area not intermediate | | | | | |

**TABLE 3.4.16b** Urban/Rural Residency (Percent Urban) and Crime/Delinquency Rates.

| Nature of the relationship | Self-reported offenses | | Antisocial behavior | |
|---|---|---|---|---|
| | Overall offenses | Illegal drugs | Child & early adol. | Late adol. & adult |
| Rates higher in urban than in rural areas | **EUROPE** *Norway*: Christie et al. 1965; *Spain*: Barberet et al. 1994:252; *Switzerland*: Killias et al. 1994:202 **NORTH AMERICA** *United States*: Clark & Wenninger 1962; Elliott et al. 1989; Winfree et al. 1994:163; Heimer 1997:814; Manolakes 1997:246 | **NORTH AMERICA** *Canada*: Moyer & Fejer 1972; *United States*: Kandel et al. 1976; Nyberg & McIntosh 1979; Gleaton & Smith 1981; Hahn 1982; Johnston et al. 1989; Pentz et al. 1989:3263; Leukefeld et al. 1992:105; Peters et al. 1992; Winfree et al. 1994:163; DS Miller & Miller 1997 | **EUROPE** *Britain*: Rutter et al. 1975; Kastrup 1977; *Norway*: Lavik 1977; Wichstrom et al. 1996 **NORTH AMERICA** *Canada:* Offord et al. 1986:275; Offord et al 1987:832 | **MIDDLE EAST** *Israel*: Dohren-wend et al. 1992:949 |
| Not signif. | | | | |
| Rates higher in rural than in urban area | | **EUROPE** *Spain*: Barberet et al. 1994:252 **NORTH AMERICA** *United States*: Johnston et al. 1993 | | |
| Suburban area intermediate to urban/rural areas | | | | |
| Not signif. | | | | |
| Suburban area not intermediate | **EUROPE** *Switzerland*: Killias et al. 1994:203 (see narrative) | **NORTH AMERICA** *United States*: Luthar & D'Avanzo 1999 (higher than inner-city youth, composite measure of drug use) | | |

**TABLE 3.5.1** Religious Membership, Percent of Population and Crime/Delinquency Rates.

| Nature of the relationship | Officially detected offenses | | |
|---|---|---|---|
| | Violent offenses | Property offenses | General & adult offenses |
| Positive | | | |
| Not signif. | **NORTH AMERICA** *United States*: Stark et al. 1983:14* (states) | | |
| Negative | **NORTH AMERICA** *United States*: Porterfield 1952 (states); RD Stark et al. 1980* (SMSAs); RD Stark et al. 1983* (SMSAs); D Lester 1988 (states, church attendance); Kposowa et al. 1995:100* (counties) **INTERNATIONAL** *Multiple Countries*: Ellis & Peterson 1996 | **NORTH AMERICA** *United States*: RD Stark et al. 1980* (SMSAs); RD Stark et al. 1983* (SMSAs); Bainbridge 1989 (cities); Kposowa et al. 1995:92* (counties) | **NORTH AMERICA** *United States*: Chamlin & Cochran 1997; Kposowa et al. 1995* (counties) |

TABLE 3.5.2 Fundamentalist, Percent of Population and Crime/Delinquency Rates.

| Nature of the relationship | Officially detected offenses |
|---|---|
| | Violent offenses |
| Positive | **NORTH AMERICA** *United States*: Lester 1995 (murder) |
| Not signif. | |
| Negative | |

### 3.4.16 Urban/Rural Residency (Percent Urban)

Many studies have addressed the question of whether crime rates are higher in cities or in rural areas. While definitions of what constitutes cities and rural areas vary somewhat from one study to another (Lachmann 1991:294), Table 3.4.16a shows that the findings based on official data have been largely consistent in indicating that crime rates are higher in urban than in rural areas. Some studies have separately identified suburban areas as a third category for comparison; these nearly always report suburban rates falling between the rates for urban and rural areas.

Regarding self-reported offending and antisocial behavior, evidence of an association with urban/rural residency is less clear-cut than it is for official data. Table 3.4.16b shows that several studies using this methodology have failed to find significant differences. To note the nature of some of these exceptional studies, one conducted in Switzerland, a country with few large cities, found that persons who grew up in intermediate-sized cities (10–50,000) self-reported higher involvement in crime and delinquency than did persons from larger cities (50,000+), although both surpassed the self-reported offense rates of persons growing up in the smallest communities (<10,000) (Killias et al. 1994:203). In one U.S. and one Spanish self-report study, the rates of drug offending were higher for youth growing up in rural communities than for those reared in larger cities (Johnston et al. 1993; Barberet et al. 1994:252).

All of the available studies of antisocial behavior have thus far found these disorders to be higher in urban areas than in rural areas (Rutter & Giller 1984:203).

## 3.5 RELIGIOUS ECOLOGICAL FACTORS

Possible connections between religiosity and criminality have been frequently investigated, although usually in terms of comparing individuals rather than geographical regions. Nevertheless, some geographical regions are more concentrated with highly religious people than other regions. The tables below summarize what these ecological studies have revealed.

### 3.5.1 Religious Membership, Percent of Population

As shown in Table 3.5.1, nearly all of the available research has converged on the conclusion that as religious membership in a geographical region increases, its crime rates tend to decrease.

### 3.5.2 Fundamentalist, Percent of Population

The one available study of a statistical relationship between Christian fundamentalism and crime concluded that as the percentage of fundamentalists in a population increases, so too does the murder rate (Table 3.5.2).

### 3.5.3 Catholic, Percent of Population

A few studies have calculated the relationship between the percent of a Catholic population and the prevalence of official crime. Table 3.5.3 shows that the findings have not been consistent, especially with regard to the prevalence of violent crimes.

TABLE 3.5.3 Catholic, Percent Of Population and Crime/Delinquency Rates.

| Nature of the relationship | Officially detected offenses | | |
|---|---|---|---|
| | Violent offenses | Property offenses | General & adult offenses |
| Positive | **INTERNATIONAL** *Multiple Countries*: Lester 1996 (states) | | |
| Not signif. | | **NORTH AMERICA** *United States*: DeFronzo 1984:208* (cities) | **INTERNATIONAL** *Multiple Countries*: Rotten 1986:360 |
| Negative | **NORTH AMERICA** DeFronzo 1984:208* (cities) | | |

## 3.6 SOCIOECONOMIC ECOLOGICAL FACTORS

How relevant are socioeconomic factors to an area's crime rate? Many researchers have sought an answer to this question. As the following subsection will illustrate, the findings from these studies suggest that there is no simple answer to this question.

### 3.6.1 Education of Residents, Average Level

One common ecological measure of socioeconomic status is the average years of education in the geographic regions being compared. As shown in Table 3.6.1, except in the case of property offenses (where no significant relationship has been found), most studies suggest that as the average years of education for a region increase, the region's crime rate tends to be lower.

### 3.6.2 Income of Residents, Median Level

One measure of a region's economic well-being has involved comparing neighborhoods or cities in terms of the average incomes of their residents. An average income is usually expressed in terms of annual median family (household) earnings.

As shown in Table 3.6.2, most studies have found that as the average income of a neighborhood or city increased, the rate of violent crime tended to decrease. Nonetheless, it would be difficult to generalize with any confidence about the average income of a geographic region and its crime rate.

### 3.6.3 Income/Economic Inequality, General

Numerous studies have sought to determine if the degree of income inequality in various geographic regions might be associated with the crime rates in those regions. As shown in Table 3.6.3, the findings have been mixed, especially for violent offenses, with some studies finding a positive correlation and others finding no significant correlation. As one considers crimes more generally, most research has concluded that the regions with the greatest income inequality tend to have the highest crime rates.

### 3.6.4 Poverty among Residents, Percent

Another way to assess the socioeconomic status of a neighborhood or city is to use a poverty index. Such an index has been developed mainly in the United States based on the assumption that a family of a given size needs a certain minimum income in order "to make ends meet". The exact amount of money for this index is adjusted every year for inflation. The proportion of families in a region whose income is below this monetary value is said to be living below the poverty line.

Table 3.6.4 reveals a mixed pattern, with most of the studies indicating either a positive relationship or the lack of any significant relationship. This pattern roughly concurs with two other traditional reviews of the literature

**TABLE 3.6.1** Education of Residents, Average Level and Crime/Delinquency Rates.

| Nature of the relationship | Officially detected offenses | | | | Self-reported offenses |
|---|---|---|---|---|---|
| | Violent offenses | Property offenses | Delinquency | General & adult offenses | Overall offenses |
| Positive | | | | | |
| Not signif. | **NORTH AMERICA** *United States*: Crutchfield et al. 1982:471 (cities) | **NORTH AMERICA** *United States*: Crutchfield et al. 1982:471 (cities); Lieberman & Smith 1986 (cities) | **NORTH AMERICA** *United States*: Bordua 1958 (neighborhoods) | | |
| Negative | **NORTH AMERICA** *United States*: Gastil 1971:424 (cities/ education); Block 1979 (neighborhoods); Lieberman & Smith 1986 (cities) | | **EUROPE** *Britain*: *Germany*: EA Johnson & McHale 1980:396 (nineteenth century cities) **NORTH AMERICA** *United States*: Chilton & Dussich 1974:75 (neighborhoods) | **NORTH AMERICA** *United States*: Schuessler & Slatin 1964:140 (cities); Gastil 1971:422 (states); Bukenya 2005 (counties) | **NORTH AMERICA** *United States*: DC Gottfredson et al. 1991:213 (neighborhoods) |

**TABLE 3.6.2** Income of Residents, Median Level and Crime/Delinquency Rates.

| Nature of the relationship | Officially detected offenses | | | | Self-reported offenses |
|---|---|---|---|---|---|
| | Violent offenses | Property offenses | Delinquency | General & adult offenses | Overall offenses |
| Positive | | **ASIA** *Hong Kong*: Gaylord & Lang 1997:61 (neighborhoods) **NORTH AMERICA** *United States*: DeFronzo 1984:208 (cities) **INTERNATIONAL** *Multiple Countries*: Krohn 1976:308; Rahav & Jaamdar 1982:457 | | | **NORTH AMERICA** *United States*: Johnstone 1978 (neighborhoods); DC Grottfredson et al. 1991:213 (neighborhoods) |
| Not signif. | **EUROPE** *Netherlands*: van Wilsem et al. 2006:238* (neighborhoods) **NORTH AMERICA** *United States*: DeFronzo 1983 (cities); Lester 1994:8 (states) | **NORTH AMERICA** *United States*: Bechdolt 1975 (neighborhoods); Kposowa et al. 1995:92 (cities) | | **NORTH AMERICA** *United States*: Pressman & Carol 1971 (cities); Allison 1972 (cities) | **NORTH AMERICA** *United States*: Simcha-Fagan & Schwartz 1986:685 (neighborhoods) |
| Negative | **NORTH AMERICA** *United States*: Gastil 1971:421 (states); Harries 1974 (cities); Greenberg et al. 1983 (cities); DeFronzo 1984:208 (cities); Sampson 1986:293 (cities); RB Taylor & Covington 1988 (cities); Williams & Flewelling 1988 (cities); Crutchfield 1989 (neighborhoods); Arthur 1991 (cities); Rojek & Williams 1993:261 (cities) **INTERNATIONAL** *Multiple Countries*: Krohn 1976:308; Rahav & Jaamder 1982:457; Groves et al. 1985:69; Lester 1996c | **EUROPE** *Netherlands*: van Wilsem et al. 2006:238* (neighborhoods) **NORTH AMERICA** *United States*: Fleisher 1966 (cities); Greenberg et al. 1983:385 (cities) **INTERNATIONAL** *Multiple Countries*: Wellford 1974 | **NORTH AMERICA** *Canada:* Social Planning Council 1965; *United States*: Bates 1962:351 (neighborhoods); Willie 1967 (neighborhoods); Simcha-Fagan & Schwartz 1986:685 (neighborhoods) | **EUROPE** *Britain*: Hirschfield & Bowers 1997:110 (neighborhoods) **NORTH AMERICA** *United States*: Schuessler 1962:315 (cities); Loftin 1985 (states); Harries 1976:476 (cities); Humphries & Wallace 1980 (cities); Smith & Parker 1980 (states) | |

**TABLE 3.6.3** Income/Economic Inequality, General and Crime/Delinquency Rates.

| Nature of the relationship | Officially detected offenses | | | Self-reported offenses |
|---|---|---|---|---|
| | Violent offenses | Property offenses | General & adult offenses | Overall offenses |
| Positive | **NORTH AMERICA** *United States*: JR Blau & PM Blau 1982 (cities); Carroll & Jackson 1983 (cities outside the South, Gini Index); Crutchfield 1989* (100 Seattle census tracts, homicide); Kposowa et al. 1995* (counties, homicides); Fowles & Merva 19968 **INTERNATIONAL** *Multiple Countries*: Fajnzylber et al. 2002 (murder & robbery) | **NORTH AMERICA** *United States*: Danziger & Wheeler 1975; Jacobs 1981 (SMSAs); Chamlin & Cochran 1997 (cities) | **NORTH AMERICA** *United States*: Liska & Chamlin 1984 (cities); JE Farley 1987 (neighborhoods); Harer & Steffensmeier 1992 (neighborhoods); LaFree & Drass 1996:628; Shihadeh & Ousey 1996 (neighborhoods); Hipp 2007 (census tracks, 19 large cities) | **NORTH AMERICA** *United States*: Herrenkohl et al. 2000 (violent offenses, teens) |
| Not signif. | **NORTH AMERICA** *United States*: Messner 1982a (SMSAs, homicide); Messner 1983b (cities, homicides, Gini Index); Bailey 1984 (cities, homicides, Gini Index); Chamlin 1989 (states, police killings); Crutchfield 1989* (100 Seattle census tracts, violent crimes except homicide); Kposowa et al. 1995* (counties, Gini index) | **NORTH AMERICA** *United States*: Kposowa et al. 1995* (counties, Gini index); Fowles & Merva 1996* | **NORTH AMERICA** *United States*: Kposowa et al. 1995* (counties) | |
| Negative | | | | |

**TABLE 3.6.4** Poverty among Residents, Percent in and Crime/Delinquency Rates.

| Nature of the relationship | Officially detected offenses | | | | | Self-reported offenses |
|---|---|---|---|---|---|---|
| | Violent offenses | Property offenses | Sex offenses | Delinquency | General & adult offenses | Overall offenses |
| Positive | **NORTH AMERICA** *United States*: McCarthy et al. 1975 (cities); KD Harries 1976 (cities); R Block 1979 (neighborhoods); Mladenka & Hill 1976* (cities); Loftin 1980 (states); J Blau & P Blau 1982* (cities); Messner 1982a (cities); Sampson & Castellano 1982 (cities); Messner 1983a (cities); Messner 1983b (SMSAs, homicide) Bailey 1984 (cities, homicide); DeFronzo 1984:208* (cities); Jackson 1984:179 (cities); Williams 1984 (cities); Loftin & Parker 1985 (cities); Sampson 1985a:60 (cities, homicide); Lieberman & Smith 1986* (cities); Messner & Tardiff 1986a (cities); Sampson 1986* (cities); Taylor & Convington 1988 (neighborhoods); Bainbridge 1989:292* (cities); Chamlin 1989 (states, killing of police) RN Parker 1989 (nighborhoods, homicide); EB Patterson 1991:769 (cities); Lester 1994a:8 (states); Kposowa et al. 1995:99* (cities); Chamlin & Cochran 1997 (cities); Warner & Rountree 1997:528* (neighborhoods); Kovandzic et al. 1998:585 (cities); MR Lee 2000 (neighborhoods, homicide); Steffensmeier & Haynie 2000a (cities); Steffensmeier & Haynie 2000b (cities); Warner & Fowler 2003 (neighborhoods); J Schwartz 2006 (counties, homicide) | **NORTH AMERICA** *United States*: Swimmer 1974* (cities); Lieberman & Smith 1986* (cities); Sampson 1986* (cities); Bainbridge 1989:292* (cities); Warner & Rountree 1997:528* (neighborhoods); Joong-Hwan Oh 2005:579* (larceny, central-city poverty rate) | **NORTH AMERICA** *United States*: Joong-Hwan Oh 2005:579* (rape, central-city poverty rate) | **NORTH AMERICA** *United States*: PR Miller 1967:39 (neighborhoods); Grieson 1972 (neighborhoods); CR Shaw & McKay 1972:147 (neighborhoods); Freedman 1975:140 (neighborhoods); Curry & Spergel 1988 (neighborhoods); DW Osgood & Chambers 2000 (counties) | **EUROPE** *Netherlands*: van Wilsem et al. 2006:237 (neighborhoods) **NORTH AMERICA** *United States*: Boggs 1965 (cities); Pogue 1975 (cities); Bellair 1997 (neighborhoods); RJ Sampson et al. 1997 (neighborhoods); Krivo & Peterson 2000 (neighborhoods); Lauritsen 2001 (neighborhoods) | **NORTH AMERICA** *United States*: Peeples & Loeber 1994 (neighborhoods) |
| Not signif. | **NORTH AMERICA** *United States*: Swimmer 1974* (cities); Blau & Blau 1982* (SMSAs) Crutchfield et al. 1982:471 (cities); Simpson 1985 (cities); Harer & Steffensmeier 1992:1041 (cities); Hipp 2007 (census tracks in 19 large cities, income inequality controlled) | **NORTH AMERICA** *United States*: Mladenka & Hill 1976* (cities); Crutchfield et al. 1982:471 (cities); DeFronzo 1984:208* (cities); Jackson 1984:179 (cities); Kposowa et al. 1995* (counties) | | | **NORTH AMERICA** *United States*: Allison 1972 (cities); Pressman & Carol 1971 (cities); Braithwaite 1981 (cities); AD Watts & Watts 1981 (cities) | |
| Negative | **NORTH AMERICA** *United States*: Messner 1982a (SMSAs, homicide rates); DeFronzo 1983 (cities); Bailey 1984 (cities); Rosenfeld 1986 (cities) | **NORTH AMERICA** *United States*: Jacobs 1981 (SMSAs) | | | | |

**TABLE 3.6.5a Occupational Level of Residents and Crime/Delinquency Rates.**

| Nature of the relationship | Officially detected offenses | |
|---|---|---|
| | Violent offenses | Delinquency |
| Positive | | |
| Not signif. | | |
| Negative | **NORTH AMERICA** *United States*: RJ Sampson 1986:293 (cities) | **EUROPE** *Britain*: A Edwards 1973 (neighborhoods) |

**TABLE 3.6.6 Unemployment Rates between Regions and Crime/Delinquency Rates.**

| Nature of the relationship | Officially detected offenses | | | | |
|---|---|---|---|---|---|
| | Violent offenses | Property offenses | Drug offenses | Delinquency | General & adult offenses |
| Positive | **EUROPE** *Britain*: MJ Brown et al. 1972:259* (neighborhoods); Box 1987:85* (cities) **NORTH AMERICA** *Canada*: Brantingham & Brantingham 1993:8 (states); *United States*: Gylys 1970* (cities); R Block 1979 (neighborhoods); Bechdolt 1975* (neighborhoods); Jackson 1984:179* (cities); Kposowa et al. 1995:92 (cities); D Lester 1995:52 (states); JA Phillips 1997:549 (cities); Kovandzic et al. 1998:585 (cities) **INTERNATIONAL** *Multiple Countries*: Krohn 1976:308 | **EUROPE** *Britain*: MJ Brown et al. 1972:259* (neighborhoods); Pyle 1982 (cities); Box 1987:85* (cities) **NORTH AMERICA** *Canada*: Avio & Clark 1976 (states); *United States*: Gylys 1970* (states); Sjoquist 1973 (cities); Hoch 1974* (states); DeFronzo 1983:129* (cities); Bechdolt 1975* (neighborhoods); Jackson 1984:179* (cities); Lieberman & Smith 1986 (cities); Kposowa et al. 1995 (cities) | **NORTH AMERICA** *United States*: PR Miller 1967:39 (cities) | **NORTH AMERICA** *United States*: Fleisher 1963 (cities); RJ Sampson et al. 1981 (neighborhoods) | **EUROPE** *Britain*: MJ Brown et al. 1972:259* (neighborhoods); Willis 1983 (cities) **NORTH AMERICA** *Canada*: M Ross 1973 (neighborhoods); *United States*: Rushton & Mangus 1964 (cities); Allison 1972 (cities); Harries 1974 (neighborhoods); Hemley 1974 (cities); Hoch 1974* (cities); Chapman 1976 (cities); Danziger 1976 (cities); Booth et al. 1977 (cities); Kvalseth 1977 (cities); Nagel 1977 (states); Carroll & Jackson 1983 (cities); Bukenya 2005 (counties) **OCEANIA** *Australia*: Kraus 1975 (cities) |
| Not signif. | **NORTH AMERICA** *United States*: Schuessler & Slatin 1964* (cities); Fleisher 1966 (cities); Ehrlich 1973* (states); Spector 1975 (cities); Crutchffield et al. 1982:471* (cities); Maggadino & Medoff 1982 (states); DeFronzo 1983:129* (cities); Lieberman & Smith 1990b* (cities); Land et al. 1990:941* (cities & states); Hannon 1997:131 (cities) **INTERNATIONAL** *Multiple Countries*: MacDonald 1976; Avison & Loring 1986 | **NORTH AMERICA** *United States*: Schuessler & Slatin 1964* (cities); Ehrlich 1973* (states); Swimmer 1974* (cities); Crutchfield et al. 1982:471* (cities); DeFronzo 1984:208* (cities); Cantor & Land 1985 (states); Neustrom et al. 1988 (cities); Allan & Steffenmeier 1989 (states); Neustrom & Norton 1995 (cities); Elliot & Ellingsworth 1997 (postal codes); Kleck & Chiricos 2002 (cities) | | | **EUROPE** *Britain*: Stevens & Willis 1979 (cities); Wadycki & Balkin 1979 (cities) **NORTH AMERICA** *United States*: Schuessler & Slatin 1964* (cities); Singell 1967 (cities); Gylys 1970 (states); Swimmer 1974* (cities); Danziger & Wheeler 1975:126 (cities); Pogue 1975 (cities); Spector 1975 (cities); Forst 1976 (states) **INTERNATIONAL** *Multiple Countries*: McDonald 1976 |
| Negative | **NORTH AMERICA** *United States*: Harries 1974 (cities); DeFronzo 1984:208* (cities); Sampson 1985a:58 (cities); Perry &Simpson 1987:84 (assaults, neighborhoods, no controls) | **INTERNATIONAL** *Multiple Countries*: Krohn 1976:308 | | | |

**TABLE 3.6.7 Unemployment Rates over Time and Crime/Delinquency Rates.**

| Nature of the relationship | Officially detected offenses | | | |
|---|---|---|---|---|
| | Violent offenses | Property offenses | Delinquency | General & adult offenses |
| Positive | **EUROPE** *Italy*: Preti & Miotto 1999 (homicide); *Sweden*: Brenner 1987 (homicide) **MIDDLE EAST** *Israel*: Fishman 1980 **NORTH AMERICA** *Canada*: Schissel 1992:420*; *United States*: Danziger & Wheeler 1975:123*; Land & Felson 1976*; LW Reid et al. 2005:769* (no controls, metropolitan areas) **OCEANIA** *Australia*: DE Lester 1992 (homicide) | **ASIA** *Taiwan*: Danq et al. 1994:277 **EUROPE** *Sweden*: Stack 1982 **MIDDLE EAST** *Israel*: Rahav 1982 **NORTH AMERICA** *Canada*: Ross 1973; *United States*: Glaser & Rice 1959:683; Fleisher 1963; Gibbs 1966:55; Yeager 1978; JA Fox 1982:127*; Cantor & Land 1985:329*; PS Grant & Martinez 1997 | **NORTH AMERICA** *United States*: Fleisher 1963; Singell 1967; HL Phillips et al. 1972; EA Allan & Steffenmeier 1989 (juveniles); Bellair & Roscigno 2000 (juveniles) | **EUROPE** *Britain*: Leveson 1976; Wolpin 1978a; Box & Hale 1985 **NORTH AMERICA** *Canada*: Furlong & Mehay 1981:52; *United States*: V Jones 1932; RM Simpson 1934; Dobbins & Bass 1958; Brennet 1971; WH Robinson 1974; L Phillips & Votey 1975; Orsagh 1979; Phillips 1981; JQ Wilson 1983:97; Cantor & Land 1985:329*; PJ Cook & Zarkin 1985; Votey & Phillips 1974:1069; Barlow et al. 1993:160 **OCEANIA** *Australia*: Naffine & Gale 1989 **INTERNATIONAL** *Multiple Countries*: Brenner 1976:54 |
| Not signif. | **NORTH AMERICA** *United States*: Land & Felson 1976; Hoenack & Weiler 1980; Danser & Laub 1981*; KJ Jones & Jones 1982; Cantor & Land 1985:329*; McDowall 1986:29; RN Parker & Horwitz 1986 **INTERNATIONAL** *Multiple Countries*: Neapolitan 1998:364 | | **NORTH AMERICA** *United States*: V Jones 1932; Calvin 1981 **OCEANIA** *Australia*: Kraus 1978:27 | **AFRICA** *Uganda*: Clinard & Abbott 1973 **EUROPE** *Britain*: Tarling 1982; Field 1990; C Smith 1995:472; *Sweden*: S Smith 1995:471 |
| Negative | **NORTH AMERICA** *Canada*: LW Kennedy et al. 1991; Schissel 1992:417*; Britt 1994*; Britt 1997* **INTERNATIONAL** *Multiple Countries*: Brenner 1976:54 | **EUROPE** *Germany*: Zehr 1976:51 (nineteenth century) **NORTH AMERICA** *United States*: LE Cohen et al. 1980; Britt 1994*; Britt 1997* | | **NORTH AMERICA** *United States*: Danziger & Wheeler 1975:123*; Forst 1976; Land & Felson 1976*; JA Fox 1978; Wadycki & Balkin 1979; Danser & Laub 1981*; Orsagh 1981; MJ Lynch et al. 1994:37 |

concerning poverty and crime rates (BE Patterson 1991; Chiricos 1987).

### 3.6.5 Occupational Level of Residents

Only two studies were located pertaining to the relation of the occupational level of persons living in geopolitical regions and the crime rates in those regions. Table 3.6.5a shows that in both cases, the relationship was inverse.

### 3.6.6 Unemployment Rate between Regions

Yet another economic measure that has been frequently studied in connection with crime is the unemployment rate. A number of studies have been undertaken to determine if these two variables are statistically associated. As shown in Table 3.6.6, pertinent studies have reached conflicting conclusions with about half suggesting that a positive correlation exists while most of the remaining half have concluded that no significant relationship was apparent. A few studies (particularly those involving violent offenses) even suggest that offending rates are lower in areas where the unemployment rates were the highest.

### 3.6.7 Unemployment Rate over Time

Many studies have sought to determine if changes in unemployment rates over time have any relationship with crime rates. Table 3.6.7 shows that the findings have been mixed, with most studies finding either no significant relationship or that increases in unemployment are associated with increases in crime.

TABLE 3.6.8 State of the Economy over Time and Crime/Delinquency Rates.

| Nature of the relationship | Officially detected offenses | | | |
|---|---|---|---|---|
| | Violent offenses | Property offenses | Delinquency | General & adult offenses |
| Positive (favorable economy) | **EUROPE** *Britain*: Mannheim 1940* **NORTH AMERICA** *United States*: Henry & Short 1954; Danziger & Wheeler 1975:125; Ehrlich 1975 **INTERNATIONAL** *Multiple Countries*: Brenner 1976:54 | **EUROPE** *Sweden*: Stack 1982 **NORTH AMERICA** *United States*: Ehrlich 1973; Land & Felson 1976 | **ASIA** *Japan*: Toby 1967:132*; Fujiki 1972* **NORTH AMERICA** *United States*: Bogen 1944; Wiers 1945; Reinemann 1947; Carr 1950; Lunden 1964:160 **INTERNATIONAL** *Multiple Countries*: United Nations Secretariat 1960:45 | **NORTH AMERICA** *United States*: Wagner 1936 |
| Not signif. | **EUROPE** *Sweden*: von Hofer 1990:39 **NORTH AMERICA** *United States*: McDowall 1986:29 | **EUROPE** *Germany*: Zehr 1976:54* (nineteenth century) | | **ASIA** *Japan*: Toby 1967:132*; Fujiki 1972* **NORTH AMERICA** *United States*: Sellin 1937 |
| Negative (poor economy) | **NORTH AMERICA** *United States*: MH Brenner 1979 (during recessions, homicide rates) | **EUROPE** *Britain*: DS Thomas 1925 (nineteenth century); Walker 1965:90; *France*: Zehr 1976:45*; *Sweden*: Sundin 1976:287 **NORTH AMERICA** *United States*: AF Henry & Hort 1954 | | **EUROPE** *Britain*: Mannheim 1940*; Gatrell & Hadden 1972:377 (nineteenth century); S Field 1990 **INTERNATIONAL** *Multiple Countries*: Brenner 1976:54 |

## 3.6.8 State of the Economy over Time

Studies undertaken to determine if the state of the economy over time is related to variations in the crime rate. The results are shown in Table 3.6.8. As one can see, the findings have been inconsistent. The only category of crime that all available studies suggest becomes higher whenever the economy improves is delinquency. Most studies of violent crime indicate that these offenses rise when favorable economic conditions occur.

TABLE 3.7.1 Day of the Week and Criminal/Delinquency Rates.

| Nature of the relationship | Officially detected offenses |
|---|---|
| | Violent offenses |
| Sunday | |
| Monday | |
| Tuesday | **ASIA** *Russia*: Pridemore 2004:1036* (lowest, homicide) |
| Wednesday | **ASIA** *Russia*: Pridemore 2004:1036* (lowest, homicide) |
| Thursday | |
| Friday | **ASIA** *Russia*: Pridemore 2004:1036* (highest, homicide) |
| Saturday | **ASIA** *Russia*: Pridemore 2004:1036* (highest, homicide) |

## 3.7 OTHER ECOLOGICAL FACTORS

Findings for a few remaining ecological variables that have been investigated in connection with crime are summarized below.

### 3.7.1 Day of the Week

One study of variations in crime according to the days of the week concluded that there were significant differences. These specifics are summarized in Table 3.7.1.

### 3.7.2 Average Temperature

Studies that have examined associations between the average temperature and crime rates in various geographical locations are shown in Table 3.7.2. They have consistently shown that areas with the highest average temperatures tend to have more crime. This may be interpreted as being

**TABLE 3.7.2 Average Temperature and Crime/Delinquency Rates.**

| Nature of the relationship | Officially detected offenses | | |
|---|---|---|---|
| | Violent offenses | Property offenses | Sex offenses |
| Positive | **NORTH AMERICA** *United States*: CA Anderson & Anderson 1984 (seasonal average, over time); DeFronzo 1984 (seasonal average, in SMSAs); Cotton 1986 (seasonal average, over time); Rotton 1993 (homicide, seasonal average, over time); Rotton & Cohn 2003* (yearly average, robbery) | **NORTH AMERICA** *United States*: Rotton & Cohn 2003* (yearly average, burglary & larceny) | **NORTH AMERICA** *United States*: Rotton 1993 (yearly average, sexual assault); Rotton & Cohn 2003* (yearly average, rape) |
| Not signif. | | | |

**TABLE 3.7.3 Distance from the Equator ("Southernness") and Crime/Delinquency Rates.**

| Nature of the relationship | Officially detected offenses | | |
|---|---|---|---|
| | Violent offenses | Property offenses | General & adult offenses |
| Positive (closer) | **EUROPE** *France*: Guerry cited by Brearley 1932:161 (nineteenth century); *Italy*: Lombroso cited by Brearley 1932:162 (nineteenth century); Reinhardt 1982; Savona 1993:106 **NORTH AMERICA** *United States*: Brearley 1934; Lottier 1938; Shannon 1954; Langberg 1967:6; Hackney 1969; Gastil 1971; Harries 1974:16; GF Pyle 1976; D Smith & Parker 1980; JR Blau & Blau 1982; Messner 1983a; Light 1984; Huff-Corzine 1986; Rosenfeld 1986 (SMSA's, population size, unemployment & Gini Index controlled); D Lester 1988; Browne & Williams 1989:84; Land et al. 1990b:941; Kowalski & Petee 1991; McCall et al. 1992; Weisheit 1993:195; D Lester 1994:8; Kposowa et al. 1995* (counties); D Lester & Shephard 1998; LW Reid et al. 2005:769* (metropolitan areas, no controls); J Schwartz 2006:268* (counties) | **EUROPE** *Slovokia*: A Michalek 1996 **NORTH AMERICA** *United States*: LW Reid et al. 2005:769* (metropolitan areas, no controls) | **NORTH AMERICA** *United States*: Porterfield 1948:50; ME Wolfgang & Ferracuti 1967 (states); Loftin & Hill 1974; PI Jackson 1984:179 |
| Not signif. | **NORTH AMERICA** *United States*: Balkwell 1990:66; Harer & Steffensmeier 1992:1041; SF Messner & Golden 1992 (race controlled); Unnithan et al. 1994;Kovandzic et al. 1998:586; Kposowa et al. 1995:93*; JA Phillips 1997:550; J Schwartz 2006:268* (counties, with female headed households controlled) | **NORTH AMERICA** *United States*: Kposowa et al. 1995* (counties) | |
| Negative (more distant) | **NORTH AMERICA** *Canada*: Gartner 1995:196 | | |

**TABLE 3.7.4 Geographic Diffusion of Crime and Crime/Delinquency Rates.**

| Nature of the relationship | Officially detected offenses | |
|---|---|---|
| | Violent offenses | General & adult offenses |
| Positive | **NORTH AMERICA** *United States*: J Cohen & Tita 1999 (neighborhoods, homicide) | **NORTH AMERICA** *United States*: WR Smith et al. 2000 (neighborhoods) |
| Not signif. | | |
| Negative | | |

**TABLE 3.7.5 Political Participation and Crime/Delinquency Rates.**

| Nature of the relationship | Officially detected offenses |
|---|---|
| | General & adult offenses |
| Positive | |
| Not signif. | |
| Negative | **NORTH AMERICA** *United States*: Chamlin & Cochran 1997 (eligible voters who voted) |

consistent with the association found between proximity to the equator and crime discussed below.

### 3.7.3 Distance from the Equator ("Southernness")

Over the years, many studies have investigated how crime rates vary in relationship with residing close to (versus away from) the earth's equator. Because most habitable land masses are north of the equator, this phenomenon is sometimes referred to as the *southernness factor*. Table 3.7.3 shows that in most countries the further south one lives, the

**TABLE 3.7.6 Precipitation Rate and Crime/Delinquency Rates.**

| Nature of the relationship | Officially detected offenses | |
|---|---|---|
| | Violent offenses | General & adult offenses |
| Positive | **NORTH AMERICA** *United States*: PJ Perry & Simpson 1987:84 (assault, monthly precipitation) | **ASIA** *Korea*: Chang 1972 (monthly precipitation) |
| Not signif. | | |
| Negative | | |

**TABLE 3.7.7 Seasonality and Crime/Delinquency Rates.**

| Nature of the relationship | Officially detected offenses | | | |
|---|---|---|---|---|
| | Violent offenses | Property offenses | Sex offenses | General & adult offenses |
| Highest in summer and/or spring | **ASIA** *Korea*: Chang 1972 (aggravated assaults) **EUROPE** *Britain*: Bonger 1936:112 **NORTH AMERICA** *United States*: Dexter 1904; Brearley 1932:176; Cohen 1941 (aggravated assault); Voss & Hepburn 1968:504; U.S. Department of Justice 1969; Carol 1973; ME Wolfgang 1975:99; PJ Perry & Simpson 1987:84* (assault, warmer temperature) **INTERNATIONAL** *Multiple Countries*: Brearley 1932:166 | **NORTH AMERICA** *United States*: RW Dodge & Lentzner 1980 | **NORTH AMERICA** *United States*: Perry & Simpson 1987:84* (rapes) | **NORTH AMERICA** *United States*: EG Cohen 1996 |
| Highest in winter and/or fall | **EUROPE** *Germany*: Bonger 1936:114 (nineteenth century, fall) | **EUROPE** *Britain*: Burt 1925; *France*: Bonger 1936:109 (nineteenth century); Quetelet 1969; *Germany*: Bonger 1936:109* (nineteenth century) | | **EUROPE** *Britain*: Samaha 1974:170 (fourteenth century) |
| No signif. diff. | **NORTH AMERICA** *United States*: Dublin & Bunzel 1935:130 | | | |

higher the crime rate becomes. The one documented exception is Canada, where one study reported the opposite pattern.

### 3.7.4 Geographic Diffusion of Crime

Geographic diffusion of crime refers to the tendency for crimes in a nearby area, such as a neighborhood, to "spill over" into adjacent areas. Two studies have documented that such a phenomenon occurs (Table 3.7.4).

### 3.7.5 Political Participation within a Geographic Area

According to one study, parts of the country which had the heaviest rate of voting in political elections tended to exhibit lower crime rates than those areas where voting was the lightest (Table 3.7.5).

### 3.7.6 Precipitation Rate

Two studies have suggested that crime rates tend to be the highest during months when precipitation is greatest (Table 3.7.6).

### 3.7.7 Seasonality

Regarding seasonality, Table 3.7.7 indicates that violent crimes tend to be most common in the spring and summer. Other crimes seem to exhibit less consistent patterns.

Chapter 4

# Family and Peer Factors

Contents



Without a doubt, the family encompasses the most important factor for socializing each new generation of humans into the society within which they will live. This chapter will examine the criminological research surrounding the family, including issues such as its formation, stability, and functioning. Intragenerational aspects of criminality will also be reviewed. At the end of the chapter, links between peer relationships and offending are given consideration.

## 4.1 FAMILY FORMATION

Considerable research has investigated how marriage, and at what age it occurs, is related to involvement in crime and delinquency. Results from these investigations are summarized in the following two tables.

### 4.1.1 Married versus Unmarried

Several studies have sought to determine how married people compared with those who are single or divorced regarding criminal tendencies. As shown in Table 4.1.1a, most of these studies have concluded that married people are less involved in criminal/delinquent behavior than their unmarried counterparts.

Table 4.1.1b cites the only study linking antisocial behavior to marital status. This study was able to include a significant sample of male widowers, as well as single, married and divorced men, all of approximately the same age. According to this study, widowers and married men had comparably low rates of psychopathy; divorced men had the highest rates, and the rates among single (never married) men were intermediate.

**TABLE 4.1.1a** Married versus Unmarried and Criminal/Delinquent Behavior.

| Nature of the relationship | Officially detected offenses | | | | Self-reported offenses | |
|---|---|---|---|---|---|---|
| | Violent offenses | Delinquency | General & adult offenses | Recidivism | Overall offenses | Illegal drugs |
| Higher among married persons | | | **MIDDLE EAST** *Israel*: Shavit & Rattner 1988:1465 (age controlled) | | | |
| Not signif. | | **EUROPE** *Britain*: Knight et al. 1977 | **NORTH AMERICA** *United States*: Thornberry et al. 1985 | **EUROPE** *Britain*: FH Simon 1971; DJ West 1982 **NORTH AMERICA** *United States*: Roundtree et al. 1984 | | |
| Lower among married persons | **NORTH AMERICA** *United States*: M Wilson & Daly 1985 | **EUROPE** *Britain*: DP Farrington 1989:229 **NORTH AMERICA** *United States*: Laub & Sampson 1994:245*; Warr 1998:209 | **EUROPE** *Netherlands*: Blokland 2005:111* **NORTH AMERICA** *United States*: Grigsby 1963:297; Farrington & West 1995 (in males); Horney et al. 1995 (in males); Laub et al. 1998; Laub & Sampson 2003 (in males); Sampson et al. 2006 | **EUROPE** *Netherlands*: Buikhuisen & Hoekstra 1974 **NORTH AMERICA** *United States*: Burgess 1928; Vold 1931; RL Martin et al. 1978 (females); SD Gottfredson & Gottfredson 1979; R Moos et al. 1994 (substance abuse, within four years) | **EUROPE** *Netherlands*: Blokland 2005:111* **NORTH AMERICA** *United States*: Laub & Sampson 1994:245* | **NORTH AMERICA** *United States*: Yamaguchi & Knadel 1985; Kaestner 1997; Maume et al. 2005 (marijuana use) |

**TABLE 4.1.1b** Married versus Unmarried and Clinical or Personality Traits Associated with Criminality.

| Nature of the relationship | Antisocial behavior |
|---|---|
| | Late adol. & adulthood |
| Higher among married/ widowed persons | |
| Not signif. | |
| Lower among married/ widowed persons | **NORTH AMERICA** *United States*: LN Robins et al. 1991:283 |

## 4.1.2 Age at Marriage

According to the studies cited in Table 4.1.2, delinquents who marry do so at significantly earlier ages than is the case for non-delinquents. Overall, while *being* married, and *staying* married, appears to be associated with low rates of criminal/delinquent behavior, getting married at an early age is more common among offenders than non-offenders.

# 4.2 REPRODUCTIVE FACTORS

Reproductive factors are those having to do with fertility and birth. Most of the research regarding the possible relationship between reproduction and criminality has been rare until the mid twentieth century.

## 4.2.1 Out-of-Wedlock Births

Since 1990, over one-fourth of all births in the United States were to women who were not married (Gress-Wright 1993). Table 4.2.1a summarizes the results of research that compared offending probabilities for persons born out-of-wedlock as opposed to those whose parents were married at the time of the birth. Most of these studies show that children born out-of-wedlock are more likely than children in general to exhibit criminal/delinquent behavior.

One study of childhood conduct disorder indicated that this condition also was more common among children who were born out-of-wedlock (Table 4.2.1b).

## 4.2.2 Unwanted Births

There are many reasons women who are pregnant may not want to be so. A few studies have sought to determine if the offspring resulting from these pregnancies are more likely than other offspring to engage in crime and delinquency. As shown in Table 4.2.2a, most of the studies have concluded that children resulting from unwanted pregnancies are more prone toward offending than are children in general.

**TABLE 4.1.2** Age at Marriage and Criminal/Delinquent Behavior.

| Nature of the relationship | Officially detected offenses | | Self-reported offenses |
|---|---|---|---|
| | Delinquency | General & adult offenses | Illegal drugs |
| Positive | **EUROPE** *Britain*: Knight et al. 1977; Kolvin et al. 1990<br>**MIDDLE EAST** *Israel*: Shavit & Rattner 1988 | **EUROPE** *Germany*: Aschaffenburg 1913:166 | **NORTH AMERICA** *United States*: Bachman et al. 1978 |
| Not signif. | | | |
| Negative | | | |

**TABLE 4.2.1a** Out-of-Wedlock Births and Criminal/Delinquent Behavior.

| Nature of the relationship | Officially detected offenses | | Self-reports | |
|---|---|---|---|---|
| | Violent offenses | Delinquency | Offenses in general | Drug offenses |
| Positive | **NORTH AMERICA** *United States*: A Walsh 1990b; Leyton 1986:316 | **EUROPE** *Britain*: DJ West & Farrington, 1977:197; *Sweden*: Jonsson 1967: 209 | **EUROPE** *Sweden*: Ekeus & Christiansson 2003:76* (males, violent & property offenses) | |
| Not signif. | | | | **EUROPE** *Sweden*: Ekeus & Christiansson 2003:76* (males) |
| Negative | | | | |

**TABLE 4.2.1b Parental Out-of-Wedlock Births and Clinical or Personality Traits Associated with Criminality.**

| Nature of the relationship | Antisocial behavior |
|---|---|
| | Childhood & early adol. |
| Positive | **NORTH AMERICA** *United States*: Elster et al. 1987 |
| Not signif. | |
| Negative | |

**TABLE 4.2.2b Parental Unwanted Births and Clinical or Personality Traits Associated with Criminality.**

| Nature of the relationship | Antisocial behavior |
|---|---|
| | Childhood & early adol. |
| Positive | **EUROPE** *Czech Republic*: Kubicka et al. 1995; *Sweden*: Hook 1963 |
| Not signif. | |
| Negative | |

According to two studies, children who were the result of unwanted pregnancies were also more likely to exhibit conduct disorders (Table 4.2.2b).

## 4.2.3 Age at Parenthood

Some studies have assessed the association between an individual's age at parenthood and offending behavior by his or her offspring. The relevant studies are presented in Table 4.2.3a. Most of the research indicates that offspring who have relatively young parents are more often involved in crime and delinquency than offspring of older parents.

Two studies regarding the association between parental age and the antisocial behavior of offspring were found. Both concluded that younger parents are more likely than older parents to have conduct disordered children (Table 4.2.3b).

**TABLE 4.2.3a Age at Parenthood and Offspring Involvement in Criminal/Delinquent Behavior.**

| Nature of the relationship | Officially detected offenses | |
|---|---|---|
| | Delinquency | General & adult offenses |
| More crime when younger | **EUROPE** *Britain*: Nagin et al. 1997; DP Farrington & Painter 2002:50 (males); *Finland*: Rantakallio et al. 1995* (male offspring) **NORTH AMERICA** *United States*: Morash & Rucker 1989* | **NORTH AMERICA** *United States*: Morash & Rucker 1989* |
| Not signif. | **EUROPE** *Finland*: Rantakallio et al. 1995* (female offspring) | |
| More crime when older | | |

## 4.2.4 Family Size

Family size (or sibship size) refers to the number of children born to a couple and living in a household. Measuring this is almost always accomplished by simply asking subjects how many brothers and sisters they have. Because families are fairly often composed of biological children along with half-siblings and/or adopted siblings, a variety of ways are used to determine family size.

As shown in Table 4.2.4a, despite difficulties in measuring family size, the results for official statistics are

**TABLE 4.2.2a Unwanted Births and Criminal/Delinquent Behavior in the Offspring.**

| Nature of the relationship | Officially detected offenses | | Self-reported offenses | |
|---|---|---|---|---|
| | Delinquency | General & adult offenses | Overall offenses | Illegal drugs |
| Positive | **EUROPE** *Sweden*: Jonsson 1967: 209 | **EUROPE** *Czech Republic*: Kubicka et al. 1995:363; *Sweden*: Forssman & Thuwe 1966* | **NORTH AMERICA** *United States*: Friedman et al. 1991 | **EUROPE** *Sweden*: Forssman & Thuwe 1966* |
| Not signif. | | **EUROPE** *Sweden*: Forssman & Thuwe 1981 | | **NORTH AMERICA** *United States*: Brook et al. 1989 |
| Negative | | | | |

**TABLE 4.2.3b Age at Parenthood and Clinical or Personality Traits Associated with Criminality.**

| Nature of the relationship | Antisocial behavior |
|---|---|
| | Childhood & early adol. |
| More crime when younger | **OCEANIA** *New Zealand*: Moffitt et al. 2001; Jaffee 2002 |
| Not signif. | |
| More crime when older | |

very clear in indicating that large families have offspring with greater average involvement in crime than do smaller families. One study found that the crime–family size relationship is particularly strong when the spacing between the births of each child is relatively short (Friedman et al. 1991).

With respect to self-reported delinquency and criminality, one must describe the findings regarding any significant relationship with family size as inconsistent (Table 4.2.4b).

The evidence concerning a possible relationship between family size and antisocial behavior supports the view that a positive link exists, at least for childhood forms of the disorder (Table 4.2.4c).

### 4.2.5 Birth Order

Researchers have studied for over a century birth order as it relates to human behavior and personality. The studies that have sought to link birth order with crime and delinquency are summarized in Table 4.2.5. One can see that nearly all of the studies suggest that later born children tend to be more criminal than their earlier born siblings. It can be added that nearly all of these differences appear to be largely confined to the first born versus all subsequent children (Wilkinson et al. 1982:224).

**TABLE 4.2.4a Family Size and Officially Detected Criminal/Delinquent Behavior.**

| Nature of the relationship | Officially detected offenses | | | |
|---|---|---|---|---|
| | Drug offenses | Delinquency | General & adult offenses | Recidivism |
| Positive | **NORTH AMERICA** *United States*: Barker & Adams 1962 | **EUROPE** *Britain*: Berg et al. 1967; Rutter et al. 1970:223; DP Farrington & West 1971*; PJ West & Farrington 1973; McKissack 1974; Miller et al. 1974; Osborn & West 1978; MB Jones et al. 1980; West 1982; Farrington 1987a:32; Kolvin et al. 1988; Farrington 1993a:16*; Farrington & Painter 2002:50* (males); *Yugoslavia*: Todorovich 1970 **NORTH AMERICA** *Canada*: Offord 1982; *United States*: Slawson 1926; Reinhardt & Harper 1936; Maller 1937a; Middleton & Wright 1941:142; Kvaraceus 1945:78; Merrill 1947; Glueck & Glueck 1950; Ferguson 1952; Glueck & Glueck 1968; Hirschi 1969:240; Ostapiuk et al. 1974; Ryan 1974; Robins et al. 1975; Hennessy et al. 1978; Wadsworth 1979:43; Murrell & Lester 1981:76; Rosen 1985:569; Walsh & Petee 1987; LeFlore 1988 **OCEANIA** *Australia*: Cullen & Boundy 1966; Biles 1971; Ogden et al. 1976 | **ASIA** *Japan*: Clifford 1976:114 **EUROPE** *Britain*: Bagot 1944:44; Farrington & West 1971*; Farrington 1993a:16*; R1 Lynn 1995; Farrington 1997b:97* **NORTH AMERICA** *United States*: Wootten 1959:85; Mannheim 1965:610; Sutker & Moan 1973; Wagner et al. 1979 | |
| Not signif. | | **NORTH AMERICA** *United States*: Hathaway & Monachesi 1963; Calhoun et al. 1984 | | **NORTH AMERICA** *United States*: Horton & Medley 1978 |
| Negative | | | | **NORTH AMERICA** *United States*: Kirkpatrick 1937 |

**TABLE 4.2.4b** Family Size and Self-Reported Criminal/Delinquent Behavior.

| Nature of the relationship | Self-reported offenses | |
|---|---|---|
| | Overall offenses | Illegal drugs |
| Positive | **AFRICA** *Nigeria* Ojile 1993<br>**EUROPE** *Britain*: Farrington 1997b:100*; Farrington & Painter 2002:50*<br>**NORTH AMERICA** *United States*: Nye 1958; Tygart 1991; Hirschi 1994:62 | **NORTH AMERICA** *United States*: Bogg & Hughes 1973; Craig & Brown 1975 |
| Not signif. | **AFRICA** *Nigeria* Madaki 1985<br>**NORTH AMERICA** *United States*: Broidy 1995:551 | |
| Negative | **EUROPE** *Britain*: Riley & Shaw 1985; J Graham & Bowling 1995<br>**NORTH AMERICA** *United States*: Martens 1997 | |

**TABLE 4.2.4c** Family Size and Clinical or Personality Traits Associated with Criminality.

| Nature of the relationship | Antisocial behavior | |
|---|---|---|
| | Childhood & early adol. | Late adol. & adulthood |
| Positive | **EUROPE** *Britain*: PJ West & Farrington 1973; Rutter et al. 1981; Farrington et al. 1990 | |
| Not signif. | | **NORTH AMERICA** *United States*: Robins 1966:176 |
| Negative | | |

## 4.2.6 Adopted–Nonadopted Child Comparisons

In two studies, adopted children were compared with nonadopted children. Both concluded that the adopted children were more involved in crime and delinquency (Table 4.2.6).

## 4.2.7 Singleton–Twin Comparisons

No research was located regarding any relationship between criminality of a child of a single birth versus twin births. However, there was research found pertaining to antisocial behavior, all of which concluded that singletons were just as likely to exhibit criminal behavior as were twins (Table 4.2.7).

**TABLE 4.2.5** Birth Order and Criminal/Delinquent Behavior.

| Nature of the relationship | Officially detected offenses | | Self-reported offenses |
|---|---|---|---|
| | Violent offenses | Delinquency | Overall offenses |
| Positive (latter born more criminal) | **ASIA** *India*: Jeyasingh 1983 | **ASIA** *India*: A Singh 1978<br>**EUROPE** *Britain*: McKissack 1974<br>**NORTH AMERICA** *United States*: Sletto 1934; Dentler & Monroe 1961; Nield 1976; Wilkinson et al. 1982:228; Calhoun et al. 1984:326; LeFlore 1988:637; Cowie et al. 1968 | **NORTH AMERICA** *United States*: Hogan & Mookherjee 1981:54 |
| Not signif. | | | **NORTH AMERICA** *United States*: Hirschi 1969 |
| Negative (first born more criminal) | | | |

TABLE 4.2.6 Adopted–Nonadopted Child Comparisons Regarding Criminal/Delinquent Behavior.

| Nature of the relationship | Officially detected offenses | |
|---|---|---|
| | Delinquency | Adult or general criminality |
| Adopted more | **NORTH AMERICA** *United States*: Sharma et al. 1998 | **EUROPE** *Denmark*: Hutchings & Mednick 1973a |
| Not signif. | | |
| Nonadopted more | | |

TABLE 4.2.7 Singleton–Twin Comparisons and Clinical or Personality Traits Associated with Criminality.

| Nature of the relationship | Antisocial behavior | |
|---|---|---|
| | Childhood & early adol. | Late adol. & adulthood |
| Positive | | |
| Not signif. | **EUROPE** *Netherlands*: van den Oord et al. 1995; *Sweden*: Moilanen et al. 1999 **NORTH AMERICA** *United States*: F Levy et al. 1996; G Jone & Novik 1995 | **NORTH AMERICA** *United States*: W Johnson et al. 2002 |
| Negative | | |

## 4.3 INTRA-FAMILY COMPARISONS

Are there any traits of family members that can be linked to an individual's tendencies to be criminal? The findings are presented in the tables below. The main traits to be considered are parental criminality itself, parental alcoholism and illegal drug use, and parental employment/unemployment.

### 4.3.1 Concordance between Parents and Offspring (Excluding Adoptees)

*Concordance* refers to similarities. Since the 1930s, studies have sought to determine whether crime "runs in families". In other words, do children have a higher probability of becoming involved in crime and delinquency if either parent has also been an offender? And, what about other family members, particularly brothers and sisters?

Results from research on concordance for parents and offspring are shown in Table 4.3.1a. These studies are very consistent in indicating that persons who engage in officially measured delinquent and criminal behavior are significantly more likely to have one or both parents who have been criminally involved than is true for persons in general.

Some researchers have concluded that criminality in a parent is, in fact, the strongest family-related variable yet identified for predicting a child's probability of serious delinquency or crime (Ferguson 1952:67; Rutter & Giller 1984:182). As one would expect, if both parents happen to have a criminal record, the likelihood of their children being involved in legal trouble appears to be elevated even more than with just one offending parent (Robins et al. 1975).

As with research based on official data, most self-report studies have concluded that children who have parents with a criminal record are more likely to offend than are offspring of parents who have no such record (Table 4.3.1b).

Numerous studies of parent–child concordance surrounding antisocial behavior have also been conducted. As shown in Table 4.3.1c, all of these studies have concluded that antisocial behavior tends to run in families (for an earlier review see Dinwiddie 1994).

### 4.3.2 Concordance between Parents and Offspring among Adopted Offspring

While studies clearly show that criminal behavior "runs in the family", these studies have not been very useful for determining if the main causes are genetic or environmental. Adoption studies shed light on the etiology by examining whether adoptees more closely resemble their genetic parents (whom they have rarely if ever seen) or their rearing parents.

According to Table 4.3.2a, nearly all of the available findings point toward greater parent–offspring concordance when adoptees are compared with their genetic parents than with their rearing parents. These findings are consistent across various types of criminality except for one study of violent crime and have lead researchers to conclude that genetic factors must be contributing to variations in criminal behavior.

As shown in Table 4.3.2b, studies of adoptees have consistently shown that several traits are frequently linked to criminality, including both childhood and adult forms of antisocial behavior, and exhibit greater parent–child concordance when adoptees are compared with their biological parents than when they are compared with their rearing parents. Even one study among rhesus macaques indicated that offspring more closely resembled their genetic parents than their rearing parents for physical aggression. The weight of this evidence provides considerable support for the view that some type of genetic factors are operating on these traits, although certainly not to the exclusion of environmental influences.

**TABLE 4.3.1a** Concordance between Parent and Offspring (Excluding Adoptees) and Officially Detected Criminal/Delinquent Behavior.

| Nature of the relationship | Officially detected offenses | | | |
|---|---|---|---|---|
| | Violent offenses | Delinquency | General & adult offenses | Recidivism |
| Positive | **EUROPE** *Britain*: Farrington 1989a | **ASIA** *Japan*: Takahashi 1986 **EUROPE** *Britain*: Ferguson 1952:67; H Wilson 1975; West & Farrington 1977:11 & 125; Osborn & West 1979*; Farrington 1987a:32; Rutter & Giller 1984:182; Farrington & Hawkins 1991; Farrington 1993a:16; Farrington & Painter 2002:50* (males); *Norway*: Jonsson 1967; *Sweden*: Jonsson 1967:209 **NORTH AMERICA** *United States*: Glueck & Glueck 1950; McCord & McCord 1958; Robins et al. 1975; Robins 1966; Glueck & Glueck 1968; Ahlstrom & Havinghurst 1971:137; Heatherington et al. 1971; Glueck & Glueck 1974:50; Robins et al. 1975:131; McCord 1977; Offord et al. 1978; Loeber & Dishion 1983; Tarter et al. 1984; Loeber 1990; Biederman et al. 1996a:1198 **OCEANIA** *Hawaii*: Werner 1977 | **EUROPE** *Denmark*: Mednick & Christiansen 1977; Mednick et al. 1984; B. Mednick et al. 1987, 1990; Kandel et al. 1988; *Britain*: Farrington et al. 1975; Osborn & West 1979*; H. Wilson 1987; Nagin & Farrington 1992:254, 1993a:15; Nagin & Land 1993:352; Nagin et al. 1997; Rowe & Farrington 1997; *Sweden*: Cloninger et al. 1982 **NORTH AMERICA** *United States*: Cloninger & Guze 1970a; L Robins 1975; LN Robins 1979; Jones et al. 1980; Blumstein et al. 1985:143; McCord 1990:130 | **EUROPE** *Britain*: Knight & West 1975; Osborn & West 1978 *Netherlands*: Buikhuisen & Hoekstra 1974:68; *Sweden*: Johansson 1981 **NORTH AMERICA** *United States*: LN Robins et al. 1975; Hanson et al. 1984:533 |
| Not signif. | | | | **EUROPE** *Britain*: Mannheim & Wilkins 1955 |
| Negative | | | | |

## 4.3.3 Concordance between Siblings (Excluding Twins)

Another way to assess the extent to which crime "runs in families" is to assess the concordance rates for siblings. As shown in Table 4.3.3a, nearly all of these studies have determined that if one child in a family is involved in crime/delinquency, there is an elevated probability of other children in the family also having been involved in this type of behavior. In addition, one study looked beyond the nuclear

**TABLE 4.3.1b** Concordance between Parent and Offspring (Excluding Adoptees) and Self-Reported Criminal/Delinquent Behavior.

| Nature of the relationship | Self-reported offenses | |
|---|---|---|
| | Overall offenses | Illegal drugs |
| Positive | **EUROPE** *Britain*: Farrington 1979; Farrington & Painter 2002* (adol.) **NORTH AMERICA** *United States*: McCord 1979; Herrenkohl et al. 2000 (violent offenses, teens) | **NORTH AMERICA** *United States*: Tolone & McDermott 1975; Nyberg & McIntosh 1979; McIntosh et al. 1981; Brook et al. 1984a, 1984b; Brody 1987 |
| Not signif. | **NORTH AMERICA** *United States*: Kruttschnitt et al. 1987:509; Polakowski 1994:70 | |
| Negative | | |

TABLE 4.3.1c Concordance between Parent and Offspring (Excluding Adoptees) and Clinical or Personality Traits Associated with Criminality.

| Nature of the relationship | Antisocial behavior | | Mental disorder | Physiological factors |
|---|---|---|---|---|
| | Childhood & early adol. | Late adol. & adulthood | | |
| Positive | **EUROPE** *Britain*: Farrington et al. 1990; Farrington 1993a:15 **NORTH AMERICA** *United States*: Stewart & Leone 1978; Robins & Ratcliff 1979; Lahey et al. 1988; Velez et al. 1989:864; Eron & Huesmann 1990; Perry et al. 1990; LN Robins 1991; Frick 1994; Cadoret et al. 1996; Faraone et al. 1997; Lahey et al. 1998; McCabe et al. 2004; Merikangas et al. 1998:716 **OCEANIA** *New Zealand*: Moffitt et al. 2001 | **NORTH AMERICA** *United States*: O'Neil et al. 1962; Robins 1966:164; LN Roberts 1978; Cadoret et al. 1983; McCord 1986; Frick et al. 1992; Lahey et al. 1995; Dinwiddie 1996 (father–son) | **NORTH AMERICA** *United States*: Biederman et al. 1991 (ADHD) | **EUROPE** *Britain*: Farrington 1987c (lower resting heart rate) **NORTH AMERICA** *United States*: Venables 1987 (lower resting heart rate) |
| Not signif. | | | | |
| Negative | | | | |

TABLE 4.3.2a Concordance between Parents and Offspring among Adoptees and Criminal/Delinquent Behavior.

| Nature of the relationship | Officially detected offenses | | |
|---|---|---|---|
| | Violent offenses | Property offenses | General & adult offenses |
| Concordance higher with genetic parents | | **EUROPE** *Demark*: Brennan et al. 1996* (males) | **EUROPE** *Demark*: Mednick et al. 1987 (males); *Sweden*: Bohman 1996 **NORTH AMERICA** *United States*: Crowe 1974; Cadoret 1995; Lyons et al. 1995 **OCEANIA** *New Zealand*: Moffitt 1987 |
| Not signif. | **EUROPE** *Demark*: Brennan et al. 1996* (males) | | |
| Concordance higher with rearing parents | | | |

family and found that even an aunt or uncle with a criminal record increased the probability of a child being criminal (Stewart & Leone 1978).

Table 4.3.3b shows that sibling comparison studies support the view that factors closely related to involvement in criminality tends to "run in families" just as criminality itself does.

## 4.3.4 Concordance among Twins

The family (or pedigree) studies reviewed above demonstrate that criminality tends to run in "genetically intact" families. In order to assess whether genetics has a significant influence on criminal and antisocial behavior, twin studies have been conducted. There are two types of twins: monozygotic (i.e., identical) and dizygotic (i.e., fraternal). Except for a rare mutation, monozygotic twins share 100% of their DNA in common while same-sex dizygotic twins share on average only 50% of their DNA. If genetics plays a significant role in criminal and antisocial behavior, the concordance rate between monozygotic twins should be higher than that between dizygotic twins.

The majority of the twin studies presented in Table 4.3.4a reveal that identical twins are more concordant for criminality than are fraternal twins. These results have been obtained across various continents using diverse (albeit, usually male) samples.

With regard to antisocial behavior and various other traits that are unquestionably associated with criminality,

**TABLE 4.3.2b** Concordance between Parents and Offspring among Adoptees and Clinical or Personality Traits Associated with Criminality.

| Nature of the relationship | Antisocial behavior | | Physical aggression | Alcoholism | Drug abuse | Mental disorder |
|---|---|---|---|---|---|---|
| | Childhood & early adol. | Late adol. & adulthood | | | | |
| Concordance higher with genetic parents | **NORTH AMERICA** *United States*: Cadoret 1978 (males) | **NORTH AMERICA** *United States*: Crowe 1974 (males); Bohman et al. 1984; Cadoret et al.1986; Grove et al. 1990* (clinical diagnosis) | **NORTH AMERICA** *United States*: Ge et al. 1996; TG O'Connor et al. 1998; Riggins-Caspero et al. 2003 **PRIMATE** *Rhesus macaques*: Maestripieri 2003 (compared with mothers, cross-foster experiment) | **NORTH AMERICA** *United States*: Cloninger et al. 1981 (adult males, adoption study) | **NORTH AMERICA** *United States*: Grove et al. 1990* (clinical diagnosis) | **INTERNATIONAL** *Multiple Countries*: van der Valk et al. 1998 (attention problems, adoption study) |
| Not signif. | | | | | | |
| Concordance higher with rearing parents | | | | | | |

Table 4.3.4b shows that they too are more concordant among identical twins than among fraternal twins.

## 4.3.5 Alcoholism within the Family

Over the years, quite a number of studies have investigated the link between alcoholism among parents and criminality among offspring. Even though the precise definition of *alcoholism* varies from one study to another, the research summarized in Table 4.3.5a shows that the findings have consistently concluded that familial alcoholism (especially by the father) is more common among persons with serious criminal histories than those without such histories.

**TABLE 4.3.3a** Concordance between Siblings (Excluding Twins) and Criminal/Delinquent Behavior.

| Nature of the relationship | Officially detected offenses | | | Self-reported offenses |
|---|---|---|---|---|
| | Drug offenses | Delinquency | General & adult offenses | Overall offenses |
| Positive | **NORTH AMERICA** *United States*: Cadoret 1991 | **EUROPE** *Britain*: Ferguson 1952:60; Farrington 1979, 1983a:15, 1987a:32; Farrington & Painter 2002* **OCEANIA** *Hawaii*: Werner 1987:25 | **EUROPE** *Britain*: Farrington et al. 1996, 2001 **NORTH AMERICA** *United States*: Rowe & Farrington 1997:177; Polakowski 1994:66 | **EUROPE** *Britain*: J Graham & Bowling 1995 (delinquency); Farrington & Painter 2002*; *Netherlands*: Buikhuisen & Hoekstra 1974:65 **NORTH AMERICA** *United States*: Jones et al. 1980; Patterson 1984; Kruttschnitt et al. 1987:511; Rowe & Britt 1991; DR Jones & Jones 1992; Rowe & Gulley 1992; Rowe et al. 1992; Lauritsen 1993; MB Jones & Jones 1994, 1995; Herrenkohl et al. 2000 (violent delinquency, teens) |
| Not signif. | | | | **NORTH AMERICA** *United States*: Polakowski 1994:70 |
| Negative | | | | |

**TABLE 4.3.3b** Concordance between Siblings (Excluding Twins) and Clinical or Personality Traits Associated with Criminality.

| Nature of the relationship | Antisocial behavior | Alcoholism | Mental illness |
|---|---|---|---|
| | Childhood & early adol. | | |
| Positive | **NORTH AMERICA** *Canada*: Szatmari et al. 1993; *United States*: McGuffin & Gottesman 1985; Lytton 1990 | **EUROPE** *Sweden*: Allgulander et al. 1991; Kendler et al. 1997 | **NORTH AMERICA** *United States*: Merikangas et al. 1985* (clinical diagnosis, depression) |
| Not signif. | | **NORTH AMERICA** *United States*: Merikangas et al. 1985* (clinical diagnosis); Romanov et al. 1991; CA Prescott et al. 1994; Heath et al. 1997 | |
| Negative | | | |

As with criminality itself, studies have repeatedly shown that familial alcoholism is statistically associated with antisocial behavior and with other established factors associated with criminality (Table 4.3.5b).

## 4.3.6 Drug Use within the Family

Is illegal drug use among family members correlated with an individual's tendency to engage in criminal behavior? The evidence is summarized in Table 4.3.6a. Nearly all of these studies have concluded that parental use of illegal drugs is positively associated with an offspring's illegal drug use as well as with other forms of criminality. This conclusion is consistent with an earlier literature review (JL Johnson & Jeff 1999).

A few studies have looked at how antisocial behavior of individuals relates to their parents' use of illegal drugs. These studies have indicated that both conduct disorders and adult antisocial personality disorder are positively correlated with the parental use of illegal drugs (Table 4.3.6b).

## 4.3.7 Ill-Health within the Family

Only one study was found to have assessed the association between ill health in an individual's family and his/her involvement in criminal or antisocial behavior. Table 4.3.7

**TABLE 4.3.4a** Concordance among Twins and Criminal/Delinquent Behavior.

| Nature of the relationship | Officially detected offenses | | Self-reported offenses |
|---|---|---|---|
| | Delinquency | General & adult offenses | Overall offenses |
| Concordance for MZ twins higher | **EUROPE** *Netherlands*: Van der Oord et al. 1994 **NORTH AMERICA** *United States*: Taylor et al. 2000 (males) | **ASIA** *Japan*: Yoshimashu 1961 (males) **EUROPE** *Bavaria*: Lange 1929 (males); *Britain*: Slater 1953 (males); *Denmark*: KO Christiansen 1968a (males); KO Christiansen 1968b (males); Christiansen 1977a; *Finland*: Borgstrom 1939 (males); *Germany*: Stumpfl 1936; *Netherlands*: Legras 1932 (males); *Norway*: Dalgaard & Kringlen 1976 (males); *Prussia*: Kranze 1935 (males) **NORTH AMERICA** *United States*: Rosanoff et al. 1934b* (males); RR Crowe 1974 (twins reared apart); | **NORTH AMERICA** *United States*: Lyons 1996 (males); Arsenault et al. 2003 (parent–teacher reports) |
| Not signif. | | **EUROPE** *Norway*: Dalgard and Kringlen 1976 **NORTH AMERICA** *United States*: Rosanoff et al. 1934b* (females) | |
| Concordance for DZ twins higher | | | |

**TABLE 4.3.4b** Concordance among Twins and Clinical or Personality Traits Associated with Criminality.

| Nature of the relationship | Antisocial behavior | | Physical aggression | Cognitive & personality factors | Alcoholism | Drug abuse | Mental illness | Mental disorder |
|---|---|---|---|---|---|---|---|---|
| | Childhood & early adol. | Late adol. & adulthood | | | | | | |
| Concordance higher for MZ twins | **EUROPE** *Britain*: Meyer et al. 2000 **NORTH AMERICA** *United States*: RR Crowe 1974* (twins reared apart); Ghodsian-Carpey & Baker 1987; Edelbrock et al. 1995* (clinical assessment); Schmitz et al. 1995* (clinical assessment); True et al. 1999*; KC Jacobson et al. 2000 (males); Coolidge et al. 2001; Arseneault et al. 2003*; Viding et al. 2005; Button et al. 2006* **OCEANIA** *Australia*: Slutske et al. 1997; Arseneault et al. 2003* | **EUROPE** *Sweden*: H Larsson et al. 2006 **NORTH AMERICA** *United States*: RR Crowe 1974* (twins reared apart); Krueger et al. 2002* (multiple measures); Blonigen et al. 2003; J Taylor et al. 2003 | **EUROPE** *Netherlands*: Van den Oord et al. 1994 (observer rated) **NORTH AMERICA** *United States*: Edelbrock et al. 1995* (twin study, clinical assessment); Schmitz et al. 1995* (clinical assessment, childhood); Coccaro et al. 1997 (Buss-Durkee scale, males); Miles & Carey 1997; Vernon et al. 1999 (multiple observer measures) **INTERNATIONAL** *Multiple Countries*: Eley et al. 1999 | **NORTH AMERICA** *United States*: Grove et al. 1990* (antisocial personality, clinical diagnosis); Kim-Cohen et al. 2004 (IQ) | **EUROPE** *Finland*: Kaprio et al. 1987; *Sweden*: Kendler et al. 1997 **NORTH AMERICA** *United States*: Pickens et al. 1991* (males, clinical diagnosis); McGue et al. 1992 | **EUROPE** *Britain*: Silberg et al. 2003 (tobacco use) **NORTH AMERICA** *United States*: Grove et al. 1990* (clinical diagnosis); Pickens et al. 1991* (males, clinical diagnosis); Pickens et al. 1995; EO Johnson et al. 1996; Tsuang et al. 1996 (clinical diagnosis); Tsuang et al. 1998 (males); PF Sullivan & Kendler 1999 (tobacco use); True et al. 1999*; Krueger et al. 2002* (multiple measures); Miles et al. 2002 (marijuana); Kendler et al. 2003 (males, clinical diagnosis); Button et al. 2006* | **EUROPE** *Finland*: Cannon et al. 1998 (schizophrenia) | **NORTH AMERICA** *United States*: Edelbrock et al. 1994 (ADHD); Gillis et al. 1992 (ADHD); Boomsma & Koopmans 1994 (attention problems); R Goodman et al. 1995 (ADHD) |
| Not signif. | | | | | | | | |
| Concordance higher for DZ twins | | | | | | | | |

**TABLE 4.3.5a** Alcoholism within the Family and Offspring Involvement in Criminal/Delinquent Behavior.

| Nature of the relationship | Officially detected offenses | | | | Self-reported offenses | |
|---|---|---|---|---|---|---|
| | Drug offenses | Delinquency | General & adult offenses | Recidivism | Overall offenses | Illegal drugs |
| Positive | **EUROPE** *Britain*: West & Farrington 1973 (parents) **NORTH AMERICA** *United States*: Glueck & Glueck 1950 (parents) | **ASIA** *Japan*: Takahashi 1986 (parents) **EUROPE** *Sweden*: Jonsson 1967:209 (parents); Stattin et al. 1997:204* (parents); Bohman 1996 (alcoholic biological fathers, male adoptees) **NORTH AMERICA** *United States*: Channing 1927 (parents); Robins 1966* (parents), Guze et al. 1968* (parents); Robins 1979* (parents); McCord 1990:130 (parents) | **NORTH AMERICA** *United States*: Robins 1966*; Robins 1979 (parents); Guze et al. 1968* (parents) | **EUROPE** *Sweden*: Stattin et al. 1997:204* (parents) | **NORTH AMERICA** *United States*: Widom 1991c (alcoholic fathers); Greenfield et al. 1993; Giancola et al. 1996; Alterman et al. 1998 | **NORTH AMERICA** *United States*: Chassin et al. 1993 (parents); McKillip et al. 1973 (parents); Chassin et al. 1996 (parents) |
| Not signif. | | | | | | |
| Negative | | | | | | |

**TABLE 4.3.5b** Alcoholism within the Family and Offspring Clinical or Personality Traits Associated with Criminality.

| Nature of the relationship | Antisocial behavior | | Physical aggression | Cognitive & personality factors | Alcoholism |
|---|---|---|---|---|---|
| | Childhood & early adol. | Late adol. & adulthood | | | |
| Positive | **NORTH AMERICA** *United States*: MA Stewart et al. 1980 (parents); Steinhausen et al. 1984; Merikangas et al. 1985 (parents); Earls et al. 1988 (parents); Welner & Rice 1988 (parents); LN Robins 1991 (parents); Weintraub 1990–91 (parents); Reich et al. 1993; Faraone et al. 1997 (parents) | **NORTH AMERICA** *United States*: LN Robins 1966:164 (parents); Pollock et al. 1990 (parents) | **NORTH AMERICA** *United States*: Greenfield et al. 1993 (adol.); Giancola et al. 1996 (adol.); Alterman et al. 1998 (adol.) | **NORTH AMERICA** *United States*: Chassin et al. 1999 (externalizing behavior); Chassin et al. 2002 (externalizing behavior) | **NORTH AMERICA** *United States*: Ohannessian et al. 2004 |
| Not signif. | **OCEANIA** *New Zealand*: Connolly et al. 1993 (parents) | | | | |
| Negative | | | | | |

**TABLE 4.3.6a** Drug use within the Family and Offspring Involvement in Criminal/Delinquent Behavior.

| Nature of the relationship | Officially detected offenses | | | Self-reported offenses | |
|---|---|---|---|---|---|
| | Drug offenses | Delinquency | Recidivism | Overall offenses | Illegal drugs |
| Positive | **NORTH AMERICA** *United States*: Luthar et al. 1992 (siblings) | **NORTH AMERICA** *United States*: DJ Hawkins et al. 1988:261 (parents) | **NORTH AMERICA** *United States*: Benda et al. 2000:95 | **NORTH AMERICA** *United States*: Blackson & Tarter 1994:818 (parents) **OCEANIA** *New Zealand*: DM Fergusson et al. 2002 | **NORTH AMERICA** *Canada*: RG Smart et al. 1970 (parents and siblings); Currie et al. 1977 (parents and siblings); *United States*: RG Smart & Fejer 1972 (parents); McKillip et al. 1973 (siblings); Kandel 1974 (parents); Tolone & McDermott 1975 (parents); Brook et al. 1977 (parents); Fontane & Norman 1979 (parents); Huba & Bentler 1980 (parents); Brook et al. 1983 (parents); Newcomb et al. 1983 (parents); GM Johnson et al. 1984 (parents); Kandel et al. 1984 (parents); McDermott 1984 (parents); Donovan & Jessor 1985 (parents); Needle et al. 1986 (parents & siblings); Halebsky 1987 (parents); Hundleby & Mercer 1987 (parents); Kandel & Andrews 1987 (parents); Kumpfer 1987 (parents); Hawkins et al. 1988:261 (parents); Pandina & Johnson 1989 (parents); Brook et al. 1990 (parents); Menon et al. 1990 (Hispanics, parents); Brook et al. 1991 (parents); Toray et al. 1991 (parents); Rowe & Gulley 1992 (siblings); Dielman et al. 1993 (parents); Orenstein & Uhlman 1996 (parents); Stephenson et al. 1996 (parents); Lopez 1997 (siblings); Prochnow & DeFronzo 1997:122 (parents); Brook et al. 1998:247 (Hispanics, parents & siblings)) |
| Not signif. | | **NORTH AMERICA** *United States*: Prochnow & DeFronzo 1997:122* (parents) | | | **NORTH AMERICA** *United States:* Kandel et al. 1978 (parents); Barnes et al. 1986 (parents); Schulsinger et al. 1986 (parents); Simons & Robertson 1989 (parents) |
| Negative | | | | | |

**TABLE 4.3.6b** Drug Use by Parents and Other Family Members and Offspring Antisocial Behavior or Other Factors Frequently Linked to Criminality.

| Nature of the relationship | Antisocial behavior | |
|---|---|---|
| | Childhood & early adol. | Late adol. & adulthood |
| Positive | **NORTH AMERICA** *United States*: Moss et al. 1994 (parents); Moss et al. 1995 (parents); Moss et al. 1997 (parents) | **NORTH AMERICA** *United States*: Rounsaville et al. 1991b (parents) |
| Not signif. | | |
| Negative | | |

**TABLE 4.3.7** Ill-Health within the Family and Offspring Involvement in Criminal/Delinquent Behavior.

| Nature of the relationship | Officially detected offenses |
|---|---|
| | General & adult offenses |
| Positive | **EUROPE** *Britain*: Kolvin et al. 1988 (parental illness) |
| Not signif. | |
| Negative | |

**TABLE 4.3.8a** Mental Illness in General within the Family and Offspring Involvement in Criminal/Delinquent Behavior.

| Nature of the relationship | Officially detected offenses |
|---|---|
| | Delinquency |
| Positive | **EUROPE** *Sweden*: Jonsson 1967<br>**NORTH AMERICA** *United States*: Glueck & Glueck 1950; Prochnow & DeFronzo 1997<br>**OCEANIA** Hawaii: Werner 1987:25 |
| Not signif. | |
| Negative | |

**TABLE 4.3.8b** Mental Illness in General within the Family and Offspring Clinical or Personality Traits Associated with Criminality.

| Nature of the relationship | Antisocial behavior |
|---|---|
| | Late adol. & adulthood |
| Positive | **NORTH AMERICA** *United States*: Heston & Denny 1968 (mental illness) |
| Not signif. | **EUROPE** *Denmark*: Rimmer & Jacobson 1980 (mental illness)<br>**NORTH AMERICA** *United States*: Kety et al. 1968 (mental illness) |
| Negative | |

suggests that there is a positive association between these two factors.

## 4.3.8 Mental Illness in General within the Family

Another type of family trait that has been investigated in relation to criminal/antisocial behavior is mental illness, including depression, whether formally diagnosed or simply self-reported. The results of these studies are shown in Table 4.3.8a and all are consistent with the conclusion that mental illness is more common among family members of delinquents than among those of non-delinquents.

Research findings concerning the possibility that familial mental illness is statistically associated with offspring antisocial behavior is currently mixed (Table 4.3.8b).

## 4.3.9 Depression within the Family

Depression within the family is a trait that has been investigated frequently regarding its possible association with antisocial behavior in offspring. As shown in Table 4.3.9, most of the studies have found that individuals with family members suffering from depression tend to exhibit significantly more antisocial behavior than persons with little or no depressed family members. Surprisingly, no research specifically linking depression in the family with criminality per se was located.

## 4.3.10 Schizophrenia within the Family

A few studies have sought to determine if high rates of schizophrenia in families is more common among offenders than nonoffenders. All of these studies, presented in Table

**TABLE 4.3.9** Depression within the Family and Offspring Clinical or Personality Traits Associated with Criminality.

| Nature of the relationship | Antisocial behavior | Cognitive and personality disorder | Alcoholism |
|---|---|---|---|
| | Childhood & early adol. | | |
| Positive | **NORTH AMERICA** *United States*: Connors et al. 1979 (depression); Merikangas et al. 1985 (depression); Lahey et al. 1988 (depression); Welner & Rice 1988 (depression); Fendrich et al. 1990; Frick et al. 1992; Weissman et al. 1992 (depression); Ohannessian et al. 2005 (parental depression)<br>**OCEANIA** *New Zealand*: Kim-Cohen et al. 2006 (depression by mother) | **NORTH AMERICA** *United States*: Downey & Coyne 1990 (parents); Fergusson & Lynsky 1993 (parents) | **NORTH AMERICA** *United States*: Ohannessian et al. 2004 (depressed fathers) |
| Not signif. | **NORTH AMERICA** *United States*: Fendrich et al. 1990 (depression) | | |
| Negative | | | |

**TABLE 4.3.10** Schizophrenia within the Family and Offspring Involvement in Criminal/Delinquent Behavior.

| Nature of the relationship | Officially detected offenses | |
|---|---|---|
| | Violent crime | Crime in general |
| Positive | **EUROPE** *Sweden*: Bohman 1996 (in adopted offspring, related to violent crime in biological fathers) | **NORTH AMERICA** *United States*: Heston 1970; Mednick et al. 1987a; Asnorow 1988; Silverton 1988a (among parents); Kay 1990 |
| Not signif. | | |
| Negative | | |

4.3.10, concluded that close genetic relatives of offenders are more likely to exhibit higher rates of schizophrenia than is true for the population at large.

### 4.3.11 Parent–Child Agreement on Issues

One study was located which sought to determine if parent–child agreement on religious issues was associated with the child's involvement in delinquent and or criminal behavior. As shown in Table 4.3.11, a negative relationship was found, with agreement between parent and child being lower when delinquent involvement was higher.

## 4.4 INTRA-FAMILIAL FACTORS

Given centrality of the family to human existence, it is not surprising to find that criminologists and other social scientists have been very interested in how the structuring and functioning of families are related to delinquent and criminal behavior. Findings from these studies are presented below.

### 4.4.1 One-Parent versus Two-Parent Families

Whether children are reared by a single parent or by both parents living together in the same household inticates the intactness of the parent's marital bond. Nonintact families (or broken homes) are most often the result of divorce or separation, although the death of one parent is also a cause. Research concerned with links between broken homes and officially identified offending is summarized in Table 4.4.1a. The vast majority of these studies reveal that crime and delinquency are higher among persons who come from broken homes than those from intact families.

**TABLE 4.3.11** Parent–Child Agreement on Issues and Offspring Involvement in Criminal/Delinquent Behavior.

| Nature of the relationship | Self-reported offenses |
|---|---|
| | Overall offenses |
| Positive | |
| Not signif. | |
| Negative | **NORTH AMERICA** *United States*: Pearce & Haynie 2004 (religious beliefs, delinquents) |

Table 4.4.1b summarizes the findings surrounding the relationship between one- versus two- parent families and self-reported offending by offspring. For this type of data, almost equal numbers of studies have concluded that either one-parent families have higher offending rates or that there are no significant links between offending and family composition. The studies are especially divided regarding overall offending, as opposed to those pertaining strictly to illegal drug use.

Given the large number of studies on basic family structure, it is not surprising that several reviews and meta-analyses have been conducted. All of these studies have concluded that broken homes appear to have at least slightly higher rates of offending than do intact homes, especially regarding serious and persistent offending (Geismar & Wood 1986; Loeber & Stouthamer-Loeber 1986; McLanahan & Booth 1991; LE Wells & Rankin 1991).

In Table 4.4.1c, one finds a summary of the links between family intactness and antisocial behavior among offspring. This table's findings are predominantly consistent with the view that one-parent families have higher rates of childhood conduct disorders and other behaviors associated with frequent offending than do two-parent families.

### 4.4.2 Living with Neither Parent

An issue related to the intactness of parental marital bonds is whether children living without either parent have higher rates of offending than do children from intact families. Only one pertinent study was located. As shown in Table 4.4.2, this study concluded that persons who grew up with neither parent self-reported higher offending rates.

### 4.4.3 Marital/Family Discord

All married couples have disagreements. However, in some marriages, the parents argue much more often than in others, often leading other family members to become embroiled in the disputes as well. Persistent conflicts of this sort are referred to as *marital/family discord.*

Numerous studies have examined the possibility of a relationship between marital/family discord and delinquent/criminal behavior among offspring. As shown in Table 4.4.3a, these studies have consistently shown that children who are reared in families with the greatest degree of discord are significantly more likely to engage in

**TABLE 4.4.11a** One-Parent versus two-Parent Families and Offspring Involvement in Criminal/Delinquent Behavior (Official Data).

| Nature of the relationship | Officially detected offenses | | | | | |
|---|---|---|---|---|---|---|
| | Violent offenses | Property offenses | Drug offenses | Delinquency | General & adult offenses | Recidivism |
| Positive | **AFRICA** *Egypt*: Okasha et al. 1975:35 **ASIA** *Japan*: Clifford 1976:116 **EUROPE** *Britain*: Wadsworth 1979* (from divorced couples); *Finland*: Sauvola et al. 2002* (parent death before age 14, males) **NORTH AMERICA** *United States*: Goetting 1989; Amato 1995 (father absence); Juon et al. 2006* (Blacks, SES controlled, father absent) | **NORTH AMERICA** *United States*: Juon et al. 2006* (blacks, SES controlled, mother only) | **NORTH AMERICA** *United States*: Hennessey et al. 1978 | **AFRICA** *Ghana*: Weinberg 1964; *Nigeria*: Asuni 1963:189 **ASIA** *Former Soviet Union*: Connor 1970:289; *Japan*: Takahashi 1986 **EUROPE** *Britain*: Burt 1925; Lees & Newson 1954; Burt 1957:64; Douglas 1970; Rutter et al. 1970; Koller 1971; Rutter 1971; Reige 1972; West & Farrington 1973*(males); Power et al. 1974; Wadsworth 1976:253; Farrington 1979; Wadsworth 1979*; Kolvin et al. 1988; J Graham & Bowling 1995; Juby & Farrington 2001; *Denmark*: Jonsson 1967*; Hurwitz & Christiansen 1983:298; *Finland*: Rantakallio et al. 1995; *Germany*: J Thomas et al. 1998 (males); *Norway*: Bodal 1962; *Sweden*: Jonsson 1967:165*, 1975:183; *Switzerland*: Haas et al. 2004 (males) **NORTH AMERICA** *United States*: Shideler 1918; Slawson 1923; Slawson 1926:359; Shaw & McKay 1931; Shaw & McKay 1932:521*; Hodgkiss 1933; Aichhorn 1935; Hodgkiss 1935; Sullenger 1936; Maller 1937b*; Weeks 1940; Middleton & Fay 1941:556; Gardner & Goldman 1945; Glueck & Glueck 1950, 1968; Block & Flynn 1956; Monahan 1957:35; Toby 1957; Miller 1958; Nye 1958, 1974; Browning 1960; McCord et al. 1962; Goode 1964:101; Chein et al. 1964; Morris 1964; Gregory 1965; Peterson & Becker 1965; Slocum & Stone 1965; Robins & Hill 1966; Koval & Polk 1967:135; Willie 1967; Anderson 1968; Douglas & Ross 1968; Rosen | **ASIA** *Japan*: Tamura 1980 **EUROPE** *Britain*: Kolvin et al. 1988a; Nagin et al. 1997; *Denmark*: B. Mednick et al. 1987; *Finland*: Kemppainen et al. 2002 (from divorced couples); *France*: Joly 1889 (nineteenth century); Corre 1891 (nineteenth century); *Slovakia*: Lubelcova 1996; *Sweden*: Sigvardsson et al. 1982 **LATIN AMERICA** *Chile*: Friedman 1966 **NORTH AMERICA** *United States*: Bonger 1905:545; Wood & Waite 1941:159; Robins & Hill 1966; Newman & Denman 1970; Andrew 1978; Austin 1980; Mednick & Finello 1983:9; Elliott et al. 1986:487; Rothman | **EUROPE** *Finland*: Virkkuenen 1976; Virkkunen et al. 1996 (violent alcoholic males); Sauvola et al. 2002* (offspring of divorced couples); *Netherlands*: Buikhuisen & Hoekstra 1974; *Sweden*: Stattin et al. 1997:204 **NORTH AMERICA** *United States*: Reiss 1951:198; Kelly & Baer 1969; Ganzer & Sarason 1973; Henson et al. 1984; Minor 1997:337 **OCEANIA** *Hawaii*: Werner & Smith 1992:114 |

| | | | | | | |
|---|---|---|---|---|---|---|
| | | | | 1968, 1985:569; Gibson 1969; Mosher 1969; Biller 1970; Herzog & Sudia 1970; Gannon 1970:501; Ahlstrom & Havinghurt 1971; Chilton & Markel 1972; Cortes & Gatti 1972:152; Berger & Simon 1974; Wiener & Egan 1973; Blakely et al. 1974; Datesman & Scarpitti 1975, 1980; Austin 1978; Rosen & Neilson 1978; Smith & Walters 1978; Norland et al. 1979; California Youth Authority 1982; Canter 1982a:161; Gove & Crutchfield 1982; Karniski et al. 1982:157; Kellam et al. 1982; McCord 1982 (males); Kiyonaga 1983; Rankin 1983; Goldstein 1984; Stern et al. 1984; Denno 1985:733; Dornbusch et al. 1985; Kalter et al. 1985; Rickel & Langner 1985; Wallerstein 1985; Rosen 1985; R Johnson 1986; Elster et al. 1987; Steinberg 1987; Le Flore 1988:637; Rosenbaum 1989; Dryfoos 1990; Fergusson et al. 1992; Rantakallio et al. 1992b; RJ Sampson & Laub 1993; Coughlin & Vuchinich 1996; Prochnow & DeFronzo 1997:122; Thornberry et al. 1999; DeMuth & Brown 2004<br>**OCEANIA** *Hawaii*: Werner & Smith 1992:104; *New Zealand:* Henry et al. 1996 | 1990:65; Huesmann et al. 2002<br>**INTERNATIONAL** *Multiple Countries*: Bacon et al. 1963 | |
| Not signif. | | **NORTH AMERICA** *United States*: Baker et al. 1929; Belson 1975; Austin 1978 | | **EUROPE** *Britain:* Ferguson 1952; West & Farrington 1973* (males, due to death of a parent); Wadsworth 1979* (males, due to death of a parent)<br>**NORTH AMERICA** *United States*: Shaw & McKay 1932*; RJ Sampson & Laub 1993b* (family SES controlled); Zingraff et al. 1993 (court referrals, family SES controlled); Polakowski 1994:66; Cao et al. 2004 (controlling for school attachment & family SES) | **NORTH AMERICA** *United States*: Van Voorhis et al. 1988 (delinquency, controlling for family SES) | **EUROPE** *Britain*: Mannheim & Wilkins 1955; *Finland*: Sauvola et al. 2002* (one parent deceased) |
| Negative | | | | **NORTH AMERICA** *United States*: Parsley 1933 | | |

TABLE 4.4.11b One-Parent versus Two-Parent Families and Offspring Involvement in Criminal/Delinquent Behavior (Self-Reports).

| Nature of the relationship | Self-reported offenses | |
|---|---|---|
| | Overall offenses | Illegal drugs |
| Positive | **EUROPE** *Britain:* Wadsworth et al. 1990 **NORTH AMERICA** *Canada:* Hetherington 1989; Pagani et al. 1998a; Kierkus & Baer 2002; *United States*: Slocum & Stone 1963; Gregory 1965; Stiegman 1966; Clarke & Koch 1975; Canter 1983 (adol., delinquency); Ensminger et al. 1983; R Johnson 1986; Peterson & Zill 1986; Matsueda & Heimer 1987; Tygart 1990; R Loeber et al. 1991; Lindner et al. 1992; Benson & Roehlepartain 1993; Goetting 1994; Rankin & Kern 1994; Chen & Kaplan 1997; K. Klein et al. 1997; Martens 1997a; Storvoll & Wichstrom 2002 (delinquency) | **EUROPE** *Britain*: Brook et al. 1985a*; *Spain*: Calafat et al. 1997:17; *Switzerland*: Killias et al. 1994:201 **NORTH AMERICA** *Canada*: Smart et al. 1970; Mercer & Smart 1974; Currie et al. 1977; *United States*: Frumkin et al. 1969; Tec 1970; Cowan & Roth 1972; Wechsler & Thum 1973; Craig & Brown 1975; Tolone & McDermott 1975; Anhalt & Klein 1976; Blechman et al. 1977; Dembo et al. 1979b; Martinez et al. 1979; Blechman 1982; Fors & Rojek 1983; Stern et al. 1984; Brook et al. 1985a*; Donnermeyer et al. 1987; Flewelling & Bauman 1990; Needle et al. 1990; Wallace & Bachman 1991; Hoffmann 1995; Amey & Albrecht 1998* (except blacks); Neher & Short 1998 |
| Not signif. | **EUROPE** *Switzerland*: Killias et al. 1994:201 **NORTH AMERICA** *United States*: Short & Nye 1957; Nye 1958; Dentler & Monrow 1961; McCord et al. 1962; Hirschi 1969; Gold 1970:128; Austin 1978; Hennessy et al. 1978; Grinnell & Chambers 1979; Wadsworth 1979; Wilkinson 1980; Farnworth 1984; RE Johnson 1986 (female, adol.); Sampson 1986d:881; White et al. 1987; Van Voorhis et al. 1988*; Gray-Ray & Ray 1990; Haurin 1992; Peeples & Loeber 1994; Polakowski 1994:70; Broidy 1995:551; Heimer 1997:814 | **NORTH AMERICA** *United States*: Kandel et al. 1978; Kirk 1979; Nyberg & McIntosh 1979; White et al. 1987; Hundleby & Mercer 1987; Van Voorhis et al. 1988; Needle et al. 1990; Bailey et al. 1992; Haurin 1992 |
| Negative | **NORTH AMERICA** *United States*: Friedman et al. 1998 (blacks, numerous family background variables controlled, father absent) | **NORTH AMERICA** *United States*: Amey & Albrecht 1998* (blacks only) |

TABLE 4.4.1c One Parent versus Two Parent Families and Offspring Clinical or Personality Traits Associated with Criminality.

| Nature of the relationship | Antisocial behavior | | Physical aggression | Drug abuse |
|---|---|---|---|---|
| | Childhood & early adol. | Late adol. & adulthood | | |
| Positive | **EUROPE** *Sweden*: Behar & Stewart 1982 **NORTH AMERICA** *Canada*: Offord et al. 1986:276; *United States*: Stewart & Leone 1978; Hetherington et al. 1982; Dornbusch et al. 1985; Heatherington 1985; Peterson & Zill 1986; Steinberg 1987; Capaldi & Patterson 1991; Mason et al. 1994; Pearson et al. 1994; Vaden-Kiernan et al. 1995; Neher & Short 1998 **OCEANIA** *New Zealand*: Moffitt et al. 2001 | **OCEANIA** *New Zealand*: Mulder et al. 1994:281 | **NORTH AMERICA** *United States*: Hetherington & Clingempeel 1992 | **NORTH AMERICA** *United States*: Nurco et al. 1996 (female headed household) |
| Not signif. | **OCEANIA** *New Zealand*: Jaffee et al. 2003 (parental criminality controlled, father absent) | | | |
| Negative | | | | |

**TABLE 4.4.2 Living with Neither Parent and Offspring Involvement in Delinquent/Criminal Behavior.**

| Nature of the relationship | Self-reported offenses |
|---|---|
| | Overall offenses |
| Positive | **OCEANIA** *New Zealand*: Wright et al. 1999a (at age 21) |
| Not signif. | |
| Negative | |

delinquent/criminal behavior than children reared in families with less conflict. At least one study indicated that family discord may be even more strongly associated with delinquency than is parental divorce (Yoshikawa 1994:35).

As with crime and delinquency per se, Table 4.4.3b shows that nearly all studies have found that antisocial behavior is relatively high among offspring whose parents often argued or otherwise failed to get along in a loving and respectful manner with one another.

### 4.4.4 Intra-Family Cohesion

While research shows a strong association between marital/family discord and criminal/antisocial behavior in offspring, could the opposite also be true? Does strong intra-family cohesion result in less delinquent involvement by offspring? As shown in Table 4.4.4a, studies have found that families that are cohesive tend to have offspring that are less involved in delinquent/criminal behavior than non-cohesive families.

According to one study, family cohesion is negatively correlated with physical aggression by offspring, similar to what has been documented with respect to crime and delinquency (Table 4.4.4b).

### 4.4.5 Intra-Family Respect

While intra-family cohesion appears to be a protective factor against delinquent/criminal involvement (discussed above), studies have also examined the influence of intra-family respect on the behavior of offspring. As shown in Tables 4.4.5a, these investigations have revealed that intra-family respect is negatively associated with offspring criminal involvement. In other words, the offspring living with family members who express high levels of respect towards one another tend to exhibit relatively low rates of delinquent and criminal behavior.

According to one study, greater self-control is found in children reared in families exhibiting high levels of respect for all family members (Table 4.4.5b). As will be documented in Chapter 6, self-control is negatively correlated with involvement in crime and delinquency.

### 4.4.6 Parent–Child Attachment

The extent to which parents and children feel close to one another has been investigated frequently as a possible correlate of crime. As shown in Table 4.4.6a, most research has revealed a tendency for strong parent–child bonds to be associated with low rates of delinquent and criminal behavior by offspring. Most of the exceptions involve the self-reported use of illegal drugs.

Studies of possible links between parent–child attachment and offspring factors associated with criminality have revealed that the relationship is negative (Table 4.4.6b).

### 4.4.7 Parent–Child/Family Interaction

One study reported that as the amount of parent–child interaction increased, the later involvement of the offspring in self-reported offending decreased (Table 4.4.7a).

According to one study, the amount of parent–child interaction was inversely correlated with childhood conduct disorder symptoms in the offspring (Table 4.4.7b).

### 4.4.8 Rearing by the Mother versus by the Father

From the standpoint of preventing crime and delinquency, would it be better in one-parent households for the father or the mother to be the primary parent? The limited research on whether father-reared offspring or mother-reared offspring are more involved in offending has not been consistent (Table 4.4.8).

## 4.5 PARENTING PRACTICES

Findings from research pertaining to possible connections between various parenting practices and offending probabilities will be reviewed in this section.

### 4.5.1 Child Maltreatment by Parents

The concept of child maltreatment encompasses both child abuse and child neglect (Zingraff et al. 1993:175). Whereas abuse describes active attempts to injure a child, neglect refers to more passive activities that cause physical or psychological harm to a child. Obviously, the dividing line between them is fuzzy, as is the dividing line between child abuse and "mere" harsh physical discipline (Besharov 1981). Most studies of child maltreatment have been concerned with physical abuse, and have been based on reports from social workers of medical personnel, or on reports by victims themselves, often years after the abuse took place.

Table 4.5.1a summarizes the evidence linking child maltreatment with offspring offending. The findings from these studies are largely consistent with the conclusion that

TABLE 4.4.3a Marital/Family Discord and Offspring Involvement in Delinquent/Criminal Behavior in the Offspring.

| Nature of the relationship | Officially detected offenses | | | | Self-reported offenses | |
|---|---|---|---|---|---|---|
| | Violent offenses | Delinquency | General & adult offenses | Recidivism | Overall offenses | Illegal drugs |
| Positive | **NORTH AMERICA** *United States*: Sendi & Blomgren 1975 | **ASIA** *China*: Zhang & Messner 1995:377 **EUROPE** *Britain*: West & Farrington 1977:58 **NORTH AMERICA** *United States*: Glueck & Glueck 1956:193; Ferreira & Winter 1968; Riskin & Faunce 1970; Hetherington et al. 1971*; Glick 1972; Wolfgang et al. 1972 (juvenile); Alexander 1973; McCord 1982 (males); Loeber & Dishion 1983; Levine et al. 1985; Borduin et al. 1986; Tolan & Mitchell 1989; Allen et al. 1990; Veneziano & Veneziano 1992; Fergusson et al. 1994a; Matlack et al. 1994 **OCEANIA** *Hawaii*: Werner 1987:25; Werner & Smith 1992:104 | **EUROPE** *Denmark*: Raine et al. 1996 **NORTH AMERICA** *United States*: McCord 1979; Henggeler et al. 1985 | **EUROPE** *Britain*: Power et al. 1974 **NORTH AMERICA** *United States*: Hanson et al. 1984; Cox 1996:21 | **EUROPE** *Britain*: Farrington 1995; Loeber et al. 1999 **NORTH AMERICA** *United States*: Hetherington et al. 1971*; Bane 1976; Snyder 1977; Krohn & Massey 1980; Massey & Krohn 1986; Tolan 1988; Tolan & Lorion 1988; Agnew & White 1992:486; Weber et al. 1995; Clark & Shields 1997; Davies & Windle 1997 (females, delinquency); Harold et al. 1997; K Klein et al. 1997; JH Williams et al. 1998:9 **OCEANIA** *New Zealand*: DM Fergusson et al. 2002 | **EUROPE** *Britain*: Power & Estaugh 1990 **NORTH AMERICA** *Canada*: Boggs & Hughes 1973; Boyle et al. 1993; *United States*: Blumenfield et al. 1972; Bachman et al. 1984; Jurich et al. 1985; Yamaguchi & Kandel 1985; Newcomb & Bentler 1988a; Brook et al. 1990; Agnew & White 1992:486; Stephenson et al. 1996:70 |
| Not signif. | | | | | | |
| Negative | | | | | | |

**TABLE 4.4.3b** Marital/Family Discord and Offspring Clinical or Personality Traits Associated with Criminality.

| Nature of the relationship | Antisocial behavior | Cognitive & personality factors | |
|---|---|---|---|
| | Childhood & early adol. | Late adol. & adulthood | |
| Positive | **EUROPE** *Britain*: Rutter 1978; Farrington et al. 1990; *Sweden*: Stattin & Magnusson 1996:621 **NORTH AMERICA** *United States*: Robins 1986; Shaw & Emery 1987; Holden & Ritchie 1991; Jouriles et al. 1991; Robins & Price 1991; Fincham & Osborne 1993; Carlo et al. 1998 **OCEANIA** *New Zealand*: Moffitt et al. 2001 | **OCEANIA** *New Zealand*: Mulder et al. 1994:282 | **NORTH AMERICA** *United States*: Crawford et al. 2001 (males) |
| Not signif. | **EUROPE** *Britain*: Meyer et al. 2000 (among twins) | | |
| Negative | | | |

**TABLE 4.4.4a** Intra-Family Cohesion and Offspring Involvement in Criminal/Delinquent Behavior.

| Nature of the relationship | Officially detected offenses | Self-reported offenses |
|---|---|---|
| | Delinquency | Overall offenses |
| Positive | | |
| Not signif. | | |
| Negative | **NORTH AMERICA** *United States*: Wolfgang et al. 1972 | **EUROPE** *Britain*: Farrington 1995b (juvenile); Loeber et al. 1999 (juvenile); Herrenkohl et al. 2000 (violent delinquency, teens) |

**TABLE 4.4.5a** Intra-Family Respect and Offspring Involvement in Criminal/Delinquent Behavior.

| Nature of the relationship | Officially detected offenses | Self-reported offenses |
|---|---|---|
| | Delinquency | Overall offenses |
| Positive | | |
| Not signif. | | |
| Negative | **NORTH AMERICA** *United States*: Wolfgang et al. 1972 (juvenile) | **EUROPE** *Britain*: Farrington 1995b (juvenile); Loeber et al. 1999 (juvenile) |

**TABLE 4.4.4b** Intra-Family Cohesion and Offspring Clinical or Personality Traits Associated with Criminality.

| Nature of the relationship | Physical aggression |
|---|---|
| Positive | |
| Not signif. | |
| Negative | **NORTH AMERICA** *United States*: KA Dodge et al. 1990 |

**TABLE 4.4.5b** Intra-Family Respect and Offspring Clinical or Personality Traits Associated with Criminality.

| Nature of the relationship | Cognitive & personality factors |
|---|---|
| Positive | |
| Not signif. | |
| Negative | **NORTH AMERICA** *United States*: Hay 2001 (self-control – *reverse scored*) |

TABLE 4.4.6a Parent–Child Attachment and Offspring Involvement in Criminal/Delinquent Behavior.

| Nature of the relationship | Officially detected offenses | | | Self-reported offenses | |
|---|---|---|---|---|---|
| | Violent offenses | Delinquency | General & adult offenses | Overall offenses | Illegal drugs |
| Positive | | | | | |
| Not signif. | **EUROPE** *Denmark*: Raine et al. 1994 | | | **NORTH AMERICA** *United States*: R Johnson 1986* (closeness to father, females) | **NORTH AMERICA** *United States*: Nyberg & McIntosh 1979; Krohn et al. 1984; Gardner & Shoemaker 1989; Donnermeyer & Huang 1991; Ousey & Maume 1997 (family attachment, marijuana use) |
| Negative | **EUROPE** *Denmark*: Raine et al. 1996 (males, maternal attachment combined with birth complications) | **ASIA** *China*: Zhang & Messner 1995:377; *Russia*: Ruchkin et al. 1997 **NORTH AMERICA** *Canada*: LeBlanc 1992; *United States*: Newell 1934, 1936; Goldfarb 1945; Bowlby 1951; Venezia 1968; Sumpter 1972; McCord 1982 (males, loving mother relationship); Truckenmiller 1982; McCord 1983a, McCord 1986:352; Edwards 1996:981; Wasserman et al. 1996:1233 | **EUROPE** *Finland*: Viemero 1996:94; *Portugal*: Gersao & Lisboa 1994:225 **NORTH AMERICA** *United States*: McCord 1979, 1991 | **EUROPE** *Britain*: Biron & LeBlanc 1977; Bowling et al. 1994:57; Otero-Lopez et al. 1994:472; J Graham & Bowling 1995 **NORTH AMERICA** *Canada*: Kierkus & Baer 2002; *United States*: Nye 1958; Hirschi 1969; Hindelang 1973; Jensen 1972; Offer et al. 1979; Poole & Regoli 1979; Krohn & Massey 1980; Simons et al. 1980; Wiatrowski et al. 1981; Hogan & Jones 1983:17; LaGrange & White 1985; Rowe 1985; R Johnson 1986* (closeness to father, females) Massey & Krohn 1986; Cernkovich & Giordano 1987; Loeber 1990:16; Rankin & Wells 1990; Fuligni & Eccles 1993; Warr 1993b; Rankin & Kern 1994; RJ Sampson & Laub 1994; Simons et al. 1994a; D Rowe et al. 1995; Adlaf & Ivis 1997; Sokol-Katz et al. 1997; Alarid et al. 2000 (among prisoners); Storvoll & Wichstrom 2002 **OCEANIA** *New Zealand*: Wright et al. 1999 (at age 21) | **EUROPE** *Norway*: Clausen 1996 **NORTH AMERICA** *United States*: Globetti & Windham 1967; Lassey & Carlson 1980; McIntosh et al. 1981; Brook et al. 1984a; Goe & Bachtel 1985; Marcos et al. 1986; Donnermeyer et al. 1987; White et al. 1987:729; Brook et al. 1989; Shedler & Block 1990; Friedman et al. 1991:328 |

TABLE 4.4.6b Parent–child Attachment and Offspring Clinical or Personality Traits Associated with Criminality.

| Nature of the relationship | Antisocial behavior | Physical aggression | Cognitive & personality factors |
|---|---|---|---|
| | Childhood & early adol. | | |
| Positive | | | |
| Not signif. | | | |
| Negative | **EUROPE** *Britain*: Rutter 1979; Riley & Shaw 1985; Flood-Page et al. 2000 **NORTH AMERICA** *United States*: R Johnson 1986 (males) | **EUROPE** *Germany*: Barnow et al. 2005* | **EUROPE** *Germany*: Barnow et al. 2005* (self-control – *reverse scored*) |

**TABLE 4.4.7a Parent–Child/Family Interaction and Offspring Involvement in Criminal/Delinquent Behavior.**

| Nature of the relationship | Self-reported offenses |
|---|---|
| | Overall offenses |
| Positive | |
| Not signif. | |
| Negative | **OCEANIA** *New Zealand*: Wright et al. 1999 (at age 21) |

**TABLE 4.4.7b Parent–Child/Family Interaction and Offspring Clinical or Personality Traits Associated with Criminality.**

| Nature of the relationship | Antisocial behavior |
|---|---|
| | Childhood & early adol. |
| Positive | |
| Not signif. | |
| Negative | **EUROPE** *Britain*: Flood-Page et al. 2000 |

**TABLE 4.4.8a Rearing by the Mother versus by the Father and Offspring Involvement in Criminal/Delinquent Behavior.**

| Nature of the relationship | Self-reported offenses | |
|---|---|---|
| | Delinquency | Offending in general |
| Father-reared offspring more involved | | **NORTH AMERICA** *United States*: Pederson 1994 (delinquency) |
| Not signif. | | |
| Mother-reared offspring more involved | **EUROPE** *Switzerland*: Haas et al. 2004 | |

such abuse and neglect are positively associated with elevated offending probabilities.

One research team compared the delinquency rates of abused children with siblings who had not been abused (Bolton et al. 1977). The conclusion was that the abused children were found to be more delinquent than their non-abused siblings. As a qualifying comment, one study separated their sample by race and concluded that a significant

**TABLE 4.5.1a Child Maltreatment by Parents and Offspring Involvement in Criminal/Delinquent Behavior.**

| Nature of the relationship | Officially detected offenses | | | Self-reported offenses | |
|---|---|---|---|---|---|
| | Violent offenses | Drug offenses | Delinquency | General & adult offenses | Overall offenses |
| Positive | **EUROPE** *Britain*: Browne 1993 **NORTH AMERICA** *United States*: Geller & Ford-Somma 1984; Kruttschnitt et al. 1986; Egeland et al. 1988; Lewis et al. 1988a, 1989a; Rivera & Widom 1990* (males, adol.); Maxfield & Widom 1996 (both sexes); Foley et al. 2004 | **NORTH AMERICA** *United States*: Burgess et al. 1987; Dembo et al. 1987; Regan et al. 1987; Dembo et al. 1989; Bays 1990; Kelley 1992; Boyd 1993 (among females who were sexually abused); Boyd et al. 1994 (among black females who were sexually abused); Kakar 1996; Bensley et al. 1999b; R Freeman et al. 2002 (among females who were sexually abused), Brems et al. 2004 (among persons in drug abuse treatment) | **NORTH AMERICA** *United States*:Lewis & Shanok 1977:1021; Alfaro 1981; Kratcoski & Kratcoski 1982b; McCord 1983a; AW Burgess et al. 1987; DO Lewis et al. 1987:749; Kruttschnitt et al. 1987; Henggeler et al. 1989; Rosenbaum 1989; Widom 1989a, 1989b, 1989c, 1989d; Pollock et al. 1990; Kruttschnitt & Dornfeld 1991; Truscott 1992; Kruttschnitt & Dornfeld 1993; Scudder et al. 1993; Zingraff et al. 1993; Prino & Peyrot 1994; Zingraff et al. 1994; C Smith & Thornberry 1995 | **NORTH AMERICA** *United States*: Hotaling et al. 1989 | **NORTH AMERICA** *United States*: Geller et al. 1984; Doerner 1987; Widom 1989b, 1991b (females only, no difference for males); Widom 1994; C Smith & Thornberry 1995; Maxfield & Widom 1996; Ireland et al. 2002 |
| Not signif. | **NORTH AMERICA** *United States*: Rivera & Widom 1990* (females, adol.) | | | | **NORTH AMERICA** *United States*: SE Brown 1984 |
| Negative | | | | | |

**TABLE 4.5.1b** Child Maltreatment by Parents and Offspring Clinical or Personality Traits Associated with Criminality.

| Nature of the relationship | Antisocial behavior | | Physical aggression |
|---|---|---|---|
| | Childhood & early adol. | Late adol. & adulthood | |
| Positive | **NORTH AMERICA** *United States*: Reidy 1977; Reid et al. 1981; Main & George 1985; Jaffee et al. 1986; Rogeness et al. 1986; Klimes-Dougan & Kistner 1990; Fergusson et al. 1994a; Frick et al. 2003; Foley et al. 2004 **OCEANIA** *New Zealand*: Caspi et al. 2002* | **EUROPE** *Britain*: Ertem et al. 2000 **NORTH AMERICA** *United States*: Luntz & Widom 1994 **OCEANIA** *New Zealand*: Caspi et al. 2002* (males) | **EUROPE** *Britain*: Jaffee et al. 2004 (among twins, physical maltreatment) **NORTH AMERICA** *United States*: George & Main 1979; Herrenkohl & Harrenkoho 1981; Hoffman-Plotkin & Twentyman 1984) |
| Not signif. | **NORTH AMERICA** *United States*: Friedreich et al. 1983 | | |
| Negative | | | |

abuse–crime relationship held for their predominantly white sample, but not for blacks, where the connection was not statistically significant (Kruttschnitt & Dornfeld 1991).

A few studies have given special attention to a specific type of child abuse, that of a sexual nature. Sexual abuse may involve not only a parent, a step-parent, but also a siblings or some other family member, as well as an acquaintance or even a stranger. Also, girls appear to be more likely than boys to be the victims of sexual abuse (Finkelhor et al. 1990). The evidence on sexual abuse is still fragmentary, but points toward the conclusion that sexual abuse victimization in childhood is associated with an increased risk of crime and delinquency later in life, both in terms of offenses in general (Benward & Densen-Gerber 1975) and in the case of illegal drug use (Glover et al. 1996). Nonetheless, the abuse–crime link does not appear to be as strong in the case of sexual abuse as it is for abuse of a more general nature (Zingraff et al. 1993:195).

Nearly all of the available studies of links between child maltreatment and factors associated with criminality have concluded that the two are positively correlated (Table 4.5.1b).

## 4.5.2 Degree of Parental Supervision/ Monitoring

Parents vary in the degree to which they monitor and supervise their children. Many researchers have sought to determine if the degree of monitoring and supervising is associated with offending. As shown in Table 4.5.2a, nearly all of these studies have concluded that as the degree of supervision monitoring increases, involvement of offspring in crime and delinquency decreases.

The few available studies of links between parental supervision monitoring and offspring exhibiting traits associated with criminality concluded that as supervising and monitoring increased, the probability that the offspring would exhibit delinquent/criminal traits decreased (Table 4.5.2b).

## 4.5.3 Authoritarian Parental Discipline

No studies were found directly linking authoritarian parental discipline with criminality. However, as shown in Table 4.5.3, one study of this type of discipline found it to be positively correlated with childhood conduct disorders.

## 4.5.4 Firm But Loving Parental Discipline

According to a few studies, parents whose disciplinary style tends to be firm but loving have children who self-report engaging in less crime than parents who use other disciplinary styles (Table 4.5.4a).

A firm but loving disciplinary style has been statistically associated with relatively low antisocial behavior and with greater self-control (Table 4.5.4b).

## 4.5.5 Inconsistent Parental Discipline

As noted above, most research has shown that harsh and erratic discipline is positively associated with delinquent/criminal involvement while firm yet loving parental discipline is negatively related. What about inconsistent parental discipline patterns? Such discipline occurs when a parent punishes a child for misbehaving one day then overlooks it the next. The few studies that have examined this issue have revealed that inconsistent parental discipline is positively associated with delinquency in youth (Tables 4.5.4a).

According to the limited evidence, inconsistent discipline patterns by parents appear to also be positively associated with childhood conduct disorders in offspring (Table 4.5.5b).

**TABLE 4.5.2a** Degree of Parental Supervision/Monitoring and Offspring Involvement in Criminal/Delinquent Behavior.

| Nature of the relationship | Officially detected offenses | | | | Self-reported offenses | |
|---|---|---|---|---|---|---|
| | Violent offenses | Drug offenses | Delinquency | General & adult offenses | Overall offenses | Illegal drugs |
| Positive | | | **EUROPE** *Britain*: Palmer & Hollin 1996:180 **OCEANIA** *Australia*: Mak 1994 | | | |
| Not signif. | | | | | **NORTH AMERICA** *United States*: Weintraub & Gold 1991 (females) | |
| Negative | **NORTH AMERICA** *United States*: Kruttschnitt & Dornfeld 1991 | **NORTH AMERICA** *United States*: Dishion et al. 1988 | **EUROPE** *Britain:* H Wilson 1980*; Riley & Shaw 1985*; Farrington 1993a:32 **NORTH AMERICA** *United States*: Glueck & Glueck 1956:190; Blakely et al. 1974; McCord 1979, 1980, 1990:130; Marshall & Webb 1994:334; Peeples & Loeber 1994; Wasserman et al. 1996:1234; DC Rowe 1997:150 | **EUROPE** *Britain*: Farrington 1986a, 1990 (males); Farrington 1993:15 **NORTH AMERICA** *United States*: McCord 1979; Robins 1979a; McCord 1995 | **ASIA** *China*: Chen et al. 1998:776 **EUROPE** *Britain*: Andry 1960; Biron & LeBlanc 1977; H Wilson 1980*; Riley & Shaw 1985*; Farrington 1986; H Wilson, 1987; Graham & Bowling 1995; Flood-Page et al. 2000; *Netherlands*: Terlouw & Bruinsma 1994:119; *Switzerland*: Vazsonyi 1997 **NORTH AMERICA** *Canada*: LeBlanc 1992:343; Avakame 1997; *United States*: Slocum & Stone 1963; Medinnus 1965; Jensen 1972a; Levine & Bartz 1979; Patterson & Stouthamer-Loeber 1984; Patterson & Dishion 1985; Cernkovich & Giordano 1987; Van Voorhis et al. 1988; Wells & Rankin 1988; Larzelere & Patterson 1990; Rankin & Wells 1990; Weintraub & Gold 1991* (males); Barnes & Farrell 1992; Warr 1993b; Hirschi 1994:56; Rowe et al. 1995; Jang & Smith 1997; Martens 1997a; Rowe 1997:150; Vazsonyi 1997; Vazsonyi & Flannery 1997; Gibbs et al. 1998 (barely significant); Hay 2001*; Storvoll & Wichstrom 2002 (delinquency); RL Simons et al. 2007 (blacks) | **NORTH AMERICA** *United States*: Hunt 1974a; Fors & Rojek 1983:213;DA Smith & Paternoster 1987; JL Richardson et al. 1989; Barnes & Farrell 1992; Chilcoat et al. 1995; Chilcoat & Anthony 1996; SC Duncan et al. 1998; Hay 2001* |

## 4.5.6 Parental Competence

Even though people will disagree about exactly what constitutes competent parenting, several studies have sought to determine if it is associated with offending in offspring. Table 4.5.6a shows that as parental competence increases, the involvement in offspring offending decreases (for an earlier literature review, see Loeber & Stouthamer-Loeber 1986).

According to several studies, children and adults exhibiting antisocial behavior were reared by parents whose parental skills were inferior to that of children and adults not exhibiting such behavior (Table 4.5.6b). Worth noting, however, is that

**TABLE 4.5.2b** Degree of Parental Supervision/Monitoring and Offspring Clinical or Personality Traits Associated with Criminality.

| Nature of the relationship | Antisocial behavior | Cognitive & personality factors |
|---|---|---|
| | Childhood & early adol. | |
| Positive | | |
| Not signif. | | |
| Negative | **EUROPE** *Britain*: Farrington et al. 1990; Farrington 1993a:15 **NORTH AMERICA** *United States*: Goldstein 1984; Dishion et al. 1991; Frick et al. 1992 | **NORTH AMERICA** *United States*: Hay 2001 (self-control – *reverse scored*) |

**TABLE 4.5.4b** Firm But Loving Parental Discipline and Offspring Clinical or Personality Traits Associated with Criminality.

| Nature of the relationship | Antisocial behavior | Cognitive & personality factors |
|---|---|---|
| | Childhood & early adol. | |
| Positive | | |
| Not signif. | | |
| Negative | **NORTH AMERICA** *United States*: Barber et al. 1994 **OCEANIA** *Australia*: Russell & Russell 1996 | **NORTH AMERICA** *United States*: Hay 2001 (self-control – *reverse scored*) |

**TABLE 4.5.3** Authoritarian Parental Discipline and Offspring Clinical or Personality Traits Associated with Criminality.

| Nature of the relationship | Antisocial behavior |
|---|---|
| | Childhood & early adol. |
| Positive | **NORTH AMERICA** *United States*: GR Patterson et al. 1989 |
| Not signif. | |
| Negative | |

**TABLE 4.5.5a** Inconsistent Parental Discipline and Offspring Involvement in Criminal/Delinquent Behavior.

| Nature of the relationship | Official |
|---|---|
| | Delinquency |
| Positive | **NORTH AMERICA** *United States*: Patterson et al. 1989, 1991; Patterson 1995 |
| Not signif. | |
| Negative | |

**TABLE 4.5.4a** Firm But Loving Parental Discipline and Offspring Involvement in Criminal/Delinquent Behavior.

| Nature of the relationship | Self-reported offenses | |
|---|---|---|
| | Overall offenses | Illegal drugs |
| Positive | | |
| Not signif. | | |
| Negative | **NORTH AMERICA** *United States*: Patterson & Stouthamer-Loeber 1984 | **NORTH AMERICA** *United States*: Kandel 1982; Dishion & Loeber 1985 |

**TABLE 4.5.5b** Inconsistent Parental Discipline and Offspring Clinical or Personality Traits Associated with Criminality.

| Nature of the relationship | Antisocial behavior |
|---|---|
| | Childhood & early adol. |
| Positive | **NORTH AMERICA** *United States*: GR Patterson et al. 198 **OCEANIA** *New Zealand*: Moffitt et al. 2001 (harsh & inconsistent) |
| Not signif. | |
| Negative | |

**TABLE 4.5.6a** Parental Competence and Offspring Involvement in Criminal/Delinquent Behavior.

| Nature of the relationship | Officially detected offenses | | Self-reported offenses | |
|---|---|---|---|---|
| | Delinquency | General & adult offenses | Overall offenses | Illegal drugs |
| Positive | | | | |
| Not signif. | | | | |
| Negative | **EUROPE** *Britain*: Farrington 1987a:32 **NORTH AMERICA** *United States*: Blakely et al. 1974 | **EUROPE** *Britain*: Kolvin et al. 1988 (parenting by mother) | **NORTH AMERICA** *United States*: Simons et al. 1991:658, 1994b; Brezina 1998; RL Simons et al. 2001; Reid et al. 2002 | **NORTH AMERICA** *United States*: Kandel & Andrews 1987 |

**TABLE 4.5.6b** Parental Competence and Offspring Clinical or Personality Traits Associated with Criminality.

| Nature of the relationship | Antisocial Behavior | | Physical aggression |
|---|---|---|---|
| | Childhood & early adol. | Late adol. & adulthood | |
| Positive | | | |
| Not signif. | **EUROPE** *Netherlands*: Dekovic et al. 2003:231* (offspring behavior controlled) | | |
| Negative | **EUROPE** *Netherlands*: Dekovic et al. 2003:231* (offspring behavior not controlled) **NORTH AMERICA** *United States*: Bierman & Smoot 1991; Campbell et al. 1991; Patterson et al. 1992 | **EUROPE** *Britain*: S Scott 1998; *Germany*: Salter et al. 2003 **NORTH AMERICA** *United States*: LA Marshall & Cooke 1999; McBride 1999 | **OCEANIA** *New Zealand*: Jaffee et al. 2003 (by the father) |

**TABLE 4.5.7a** Parental use of Physical Discipline and Offspring Involvement in Criminal/Delinquent Behavior.

| Nature of the relationship | Officially detected offenses | | Self-reported offenses | |
|---|---|---|---|---|
| | Delinquency | General & adult offenses | Overall offenses | Illegal drugs |
| Positive | **ASIA** *China*: Zhang & Messner 1995:377; *Russia*: Ruchkin et al. 1998b:229 **EUROPE** *Britain*: West & Farrington 1973; Newson & Newson 1989 **NORTH AMERICA** *United States*: Andrew 1981; McCord 1983a; E Gray 1988 | **EUROPE** *Britain*: Farrington 1986b | **OCEANIA** *Australia*: Shaw & Scott 1991; Peiser & Heaven 1996 **NORTH AMERICA** *United States*: Bryan & Freed 1982; Herrenkohl et al. 2000 (violent delinquency, teens) | **NORTH AMERICA** *United States*: Brook et al. 1985b; Baer & Corrado 1974 |
| Not signif. | **EUROPE** *Sweden*: Jonsson 1967:210 | | **NORTH AMERICA** *United States*: Kruttschnitt et al. 1987:509 | |
| Negative | | | | |

one study of conduct disorders statistically controlled the behavior of the offspring and concluded that once this was done, no significant link between parenting skills and conduct disorder remained. The implication of this study was that the negative correlation was largely due to seemingly poor parental skills which actually reflected the difficulty parents had in dealing with the behavior of their children.

### 4.5.7 Parental Use of Physical Discipline

When children disobey their parents, corrective measures are often taken by the parents. Among these corrective measures is the use of punishment that inflicts some degree of physical pain. Several criminological studies have sought to determine if the use of such punishment is associated with later offending by the offspring. As shown in Table 4.5.7a, the findings have generally indicated that there is a positive relationship between the use of physical forms of discipline and offending by offspring later in life.

In considering the above evidence, one should avoid the conclusion that physical punishment causes children to become delinquent and criminal. That may be true in some cases, but another possibility is that some children appear to be inherently less likely to "pay attention" to mild forms of punishment (RQ Bell 1968; Thomas & Chess 1980; Chess & Thomas 1984) and these children may grow up to be unusually inclined to ignore legal boundaries and the penalties associated with crossing those boundaries later in life.

According to a few studies, conduct disorders are more common among children whose parents use physical punishment most often (Table 4.5.7b).

## 4.6 INVOLVEMENT WITH PEERS

How much and what kinds of interactions do delinquents and criminals have with their peers? In this section, these along with related issues are addressed.

### 4.6.1 Involvement in Extracurricular Activities

Extracurricular activities refer to school sponsored athletic activities, drama and music programs, and debate and civic clubs. Table 4.6.1 shows that most studies have indicated

**TABLE 4.5.7b** Parental use of Physical Discipline and Offspring Clinical or Personality Traits Associated with Criminality.

| Nature of the relationship | Antisocial behavior |
|---|---|
| | Childhood & early adol. |
| Positive | **EUROPE** *Sweden*: Olweus 1980<br>**NORTH AMERICA** *United States*: Larzelere 1986; Weiss et al. 1992; Strassberg et al. 1994; Straus et al. 1997 |
| Not signif. | |
| Negative | |

**TABLE 4.6.1** Involvement in Extracurricular Activities and Criminal/Delinquent Behavior.

| Nature of the relationship | Officially detected offenses | Self-reported offenses | |
|---|---|---|---|
| | Delinquency | Overall offenses | Illegal drugs |
| Positive | | | **NORTH AMERICA** *Canada*: Paetsch & Bertrand 1997 (athletics); *United States*: Ewing 1998* (athletics, males only) |
| Not signif. | | **NORTH AMERICA** *United States*: Hirschi 1969:190 (in general) | **NORTH AMERICA** *United States*: Goe & Bachtel 1985 (in general); Gibbons et al. 1986 (in general); Wolford & Swisher 1986* (in general); Gardner & Shoemaker 1989 (in general) |
| Negative | **EUROPE** *Britain*: Chinn 1938 | **NORTH AMERICA** *Canada*: Paetsch & Bertrand 1997 (cultural/civic activities) | **NORTH AMERICA** *Canada*: Smart et al. 1970 (in general); *United States*: Frumkin et al. 1969 (in general); Krohn et al. 1984 (in general); Wolford & Swisher 1986* (athletics); JE Jenkins 1996 (in general); Downs et al. 1997 (in general); Ewing 1998* (athletics, females only) |

TABLE 4.6.2a Number of Friends (Popularity among Peers) and Criminal/Delinquent Behavior.

| Nature of the relationship | Officially detected offenses | | Self-reported offenses | |
|---|---|---|---|---|
| | Delinquency | General & adult offenses | Overall offenses | Illegal drugs |
| Positive | | | | |
| Not signif. | | | **EUROPE** *Britain*: Farrington 1997a:97 | |
| Negative | **EUROPE** *Britain*: Farrington 1987a:32; Nagin & Land 1993:352 **NORTH AMERICA** *United States*: Conger & Miller 1966*; Cowen et al. 1973; Gaffney 1984; Lawrence 1991; Simons et al. 1991; Claes & Simard 1992; Coughlin & Vuchinich 1996:497 | **EUROPE** *Britain*: Farrington 1993a:15 | **NORTH AMERICA** *Canada*: Tremblay et al. 1995a; *United States*: Conger & Miller 1966*; Roff & Sells 1968:17 Hirschi 1969; Roff et al. 1972; Offer et al. 1979; Hartup 1983; Menard & Morse 1984:1371; Giordano et al. 1986; Parker & Asher 1987; Cairns et al. 1988b; Dishon 2000 (delinquency); Barnow et al. 2005 | **NORTH AMERICA** *United States*: Hurd et al. 1980; Kandel 1985; Hundleby & Mercer 1987; O'Donnell et al. 1995b:534 |

that as involvement in such activities increases, offending behavior tends to decrease. Nevertheless, quite a few studies indicate an opposite pattern or no significant relationship. Researchers may eventually find that the relationship is positive depending on the exact type of extracurricular activities being considered.

## 4.6.2 Number of Friends (Popularity among Peers)

Over the years, quite a number of studies have sought to determine if popularity among peers is related to involvement in crime and delinquency. As shown in Table 4.6.2a, these studies have unanimously concluded that delinquents have fewer friends than do their relatively nondelinquent peers.

Do people who exhibit antisocial or other offending behavior have more or fewer friends than persons in general? Table 4.6.2b is very consistent in indicating that as with criminality per se, both childhood conduct disorders and physical aggression have been shown to be negatively related to the number of friends an individual has. One study of drug abusers also suggested that they have relatively few friends.

## 4.6.3 Associating with Delinquent Peers

A very large number of studies have investigated the link between having friends who are delinquent and one's own involvement in crime and delinquency. The vast majority of these studies have been based on self-reported offending. Table 4.6.3a clearly documents that "birds of a feather flock together" when it comes to delinquency and criminality.

TABLE 4.6.2b Number of Friends (Popularity among Peers) and Clinical or Personality Traits Associated with Criminality.

| Nature of the relationship | Antisocial behavior | Physical aggression | Drug abuse |
|---|---|---|---|
| | Childhood & early adol. | | |
| Positive | | | |
| Not signif. | | | |
| Negative | **EUROPE** *Britain*: Farrington 1993a:15 **NORTH AMERICA** *United States*: Janes et al. 1979; Roff & Wirt 1984; Cantrell & Prinz 1985; Conger et al. 1991; Dishion et al. 1991; Biernman & Smoot 1991; Pope et al. 1991; LM Lewin et al. 1999 | **EUROPE** *Germany*: Barnow et al. 2005 **NORTH AMERICA** *Canada*: Hymel et al. 1990; *United States*: Hektner et al. 2000; D Schwartz 2000 (children); Haselager et al. 2002 (male children) | **NORTH AMERICA** *United States*: Dishion 2000 |

**TABLE 4.6.3a** Associating with Delinquent Peers and Criminal/Delinquent Behavior.

| Nature of the relationship | Officially detected offenses | | | Self-reported offenses | |
|---|---|---|---|---|---|
| | General delinquency | General & adult offenses | Recidivism | Overall offenses | Illegal drugs |
| Positive | **NORTH AMERICA** *United States*: Glueck & Glueck 1950:164; Scarpitti et al. 1960; Truckenmiller 1982; Patterson et al. 1992 Marcos et al. 1986* | **NORTH AMERICA** *Canada:* Brownfield & Thompson 1991 | **NORTH AMERICA** *United States*: Hanson et al. 1984; Grenier & Roundtree 1987 | **ASIA** *China*: Cheung & Ng 1988; Ma et al. 1996 **EUROPE** *Britain*: Otero-Lopez et al. 1994:472 **NORTH AMERICA** *Canada*: Avakame 1997:491; Paetsch & Bertrand 1997; *United States*: Short 1957, 1960; Reiss & Rhodes 1964; Voss 1964; Erickson & Empey 1965; Hirschi 1969; Jensen 1972b; Elliott & Voss 1974; Farrell & Nelson 1978; Akers et al. 1979; Johnson 1979:99; Poole & Regoli 1979; Matsueda 1982; Morash 1983:318; Hanson et al. 1984; Menard & Morse 1984:1371; Elliott et al. 1985:71*; LaGrange & White 1985; Patterson & Dishion 1985; White et al. 1985; Marcos et al. 1986*; Sampson 1986d:881; Tittle et al. 1986; Fagan & Wexler 1987; Johnson, Marco & Bahr 1987; Matsueda & Heimer 1987; Henggeler 1989:50; Agnew 1991; Barrett et al. 1991; Dishion et al. 1991; Nagin & Paternoster 1991; Warr & Stafford 1991; Agnew & White 1992:486; Pabon et al. 1992; Rowe & Gulley 1992; Fuligni & Eccles 1993; Warr 1993a:33; Thornberry et al. 1994; Dishion et al. 1995; Fernquist 1995:173; Keenan et al. 1995; Tolan & Thomas 1995; Warr 1996; Dishio et al. 1997; Zhang et al. 1997; Matsueda & Anderson 1998; Herrenkohl et al. 2000 (violent delinquency, teens); Haynie 2001; Wright et al. 2001; Haynie 2002; Shortt et al. 2003; McGloin et al. 2004:621; Perrone et al. 2004; Barnow et al. 2005 (delinquency); Warr 2005; Haynie & Payne 2006 (violent delinquency) **OCEANIA** *New Zealand*: Wright et al. 1999b (at age 21); DM Fergusson et al. 2002; Woodward et al. 2002 | **ASIA** *China*: Wong et al. 1997 **MIDDLE EAST** *Israel*: Barnea et al. 1992, 1993 **NORTH AMERICA** *Canada*: SW Baron 2003 (self-control statistically controlled); *United States*: Alexander & Campbell 1968; Preston 1968; Goode 1970; Kane & Patterson 1972; Tec 1972; Kandel 1973; McKillip et al. 1973; Wechsler & Thum 1973; Krohn 1974a; Goldstein 1975; Tolone & Dermott 1975; O'Donnell et al. 1976; Brook et al. 1977; Globetti et al. 1978; Kleinman & Lukoff 1978; Akers et al. 1979; Beachy et al. 1979; Dembo et al. 1979a; GJ Ellis & Stone 1979; Hurd et al. 1980; Jessor et al. 1980; Lassey & Carlson 1980; Radosevich et al. 1980; Gleaton & Smith 1981; Glynn 1981; Jaquith 1981; McIntosh et al. 1981; Elliott et al. 1982; Fors & Rojeck 1983:213;Sarvela & McClendon 1983; Winfree & Griffiths 1983; Kaplan et al. 1984; Napier et al. 1984; Clayton & Ritter 1985; Elliott et al. 1985; Goe & Bachtel 1985; Kandel 1985; Barnes & Welte 1986; Marcos et al. 1986; Simcha-Fagan & Schwartz 1986:691; Burkett & Warren 1987; Dielman et al. 1987; Johnson et al. 1987; Kandel & Andrews 1987; Oetting & Beauvais 1987; Orcutt 1987; Smith & Paternoster 1987; White et al. 1987:729; Singer & Levine 1988; Gardner & Shoemaker 1989; Joe et al. 1991; Pruitt et al. 1991; Simons et al. 1991; Agnew & White 1992:486; Boyle et al. 1992; Iannotti & Bush 1992; Newcomb & Felix-Ortiz 1992; Dinges & Oetting 1993; Fernquist 1995:173; Mounts & Steinberg 1995; Catalano et al. 1996:442; Elliott & Menard 1996 (delinquency); Jenkins 1996; Liu & Kaplan 1996; Brook et al. 1997; Lopez 1997; Ousey & Maume 1997 (marijuana use); Ploeger 1997 (marijuana use); Reed & Roundtree 1997; Brook et al. 1998:247; C Chen et al. 1998*; Duncan et al. 1998; Curran et al. 2000 (illegal drug use by peers); JA Andrews et al. 2002; Guo & Hill 2002; Warr 2002 (delinquency); Neff & Waite 2007 (alcohol, marijuana and hard drugs) |
| Not signif. | | | | | |
| Negative | | | | | |

TABLE 4.6.3b Associating with Delinquent Friends and Clinical or Personality Traits Associated with Criminality.

| Nature of the relationship | Antisocial behavior | Physical aggression |
|---|---|---|
| | Childhood & early adol. | |
| Positive | **ASIA** *China*: C Chen et al. 1998 **NORTH AMERICA** *United States*: Dishion et al. 1991 | **EUROPE** *Germany*: Barnow et al. 2005 **NORTH AMERICA** *United States*: Coie et al. 1995; Bagwell et al. 2000; Liu & Kaplan 2004 (adult females) |
| Not signif. | | |
| Negative | | |

TABLE 4.6.4a Gang Membership and Criminal/Delinquent Behavior.

| Nature of the relationship | Officially detected offenses | | | Self-reported offenses | |
|---|---|---|---|---|---|
| | Delinquency | General & adult offenses | Recidivism | Overall offenses | Illegal drugs |
| Positive | **NORTH AMERICA** *United States*: Robin 1964; Short et al. 1965; JH Johnson & Fennell 1992; Esbensen & Huizinga 1993; Esbensen et al. 1993; Thornberry et al. 1993; Cox 1996:22 | **NORTH AMERICA** *United States*: Hagedorn 1988 | **EUROPE** *Britain*: Simon 1971 **NORTH AMERICA** *United States*: Benda et al. 2000:95 | **EUROPE** *Britain*: O'Hagan 1976; *Sweden*: Sarnecki 1986 **NORTH AMERICA** *United States*: Klein 1971; Napp 1977; Tracy 1978; Morash 1983:317; Curry & Spergel 1992; Lyon et al. 1992; Esbensen & Huizinga 1993; Thornberry & Burch 1997:3*; Battin et al. 1998; Esbensen & Winfree 1998; Office of Juvenile Justice 1999:47; Herrenkohl et al. 2000 (violent delinquency, teens); Whitbeck et al. 2002* (Native Americans) | **NORTH AMERICA** *United States*: Vigil 1988; Fagan 1989; Thornberry & Burch 1997:3*; Whitbeck et al. 2002* (Native Americans) |
| Not signif. | | | | **NORTH AMERICA** *United States*: Sampson 1986:881; Winfree et al. 1994:163*; Cox 1996:22 | **NORTH AMERICA** *United States*: Winfree et al. 1994:163* |
| Negative | | | | | |

A few studies of conduct disorders and tendencies toward physical aggression have found these traits to be positively correlated with the tendency to associate with delinquent friends (Table 4.6.3b).

## 4.6.4 Gang Membership

Historic accounts of adolescent males being involved in gang activities can be traced back far into antiquity (Puffer 1912), bringing at least one researcher to suggest that many boys seem to have a "gang instinct" (Staub 1965). Pushing back the roots of gangs even further, Ellis (1990:88) hypothesized that human gangs are a form of what is known as *peripheralization* among many species of primates. Peripheralization involves juvenile males leaving their natal troop during adolescence and residing on the periphery in small bachelor bands, usually for several years. These peripheralized males often harass and challenge the authority and social order being maintained by fully-adult alpha males. Eventually, the peripheralized males take over the troop and the process begins anew. Among humans, gangs are nearly always comprised of youngsters residing in the same neighborhood and belonging to the same ethnic/racial group (Moore 1978; Vigil 1988).

Many studies have sought to determine if gang membership is associated with involvement in crime and delinquency. The findings in this regard are summarized in Table 4.6.4a and have nearly always found the relationship to be positive and statistically significant. Only a few studies – all based on self-reports – have failed to find a statistically significant relationship.

As an aside, a few studies have sought to determine whether gang membership usually precedes offending or vice versa. The conclusion has been that some degree of delinquency usually occurs prior to participation in juvenile

TABLE 4.6.4b Gang Membership and Clinical or Personality Traits Associated with Criminality.

| Nature of the relationship | Antisocial behavior | Physical aggression | Drug abuse | Family factors |
|---|---|---|---|---|
| | Childhood & early adol. | | | |
| Positive | **NORTH AMERICA** *United States*: KG Hill et al. 1999* (ages 10–12) | **NORTH AMERICA** *United States*: Griffin & Hepburn 2006 (male prison inmates) | | **NORTH AMERICA** *United States*: KG Hill et al. 1999* (with parental violence, age 10–12) |
| Not signif. | | | **NORTH AMERICA** *United States*: Neff & Waite 2007 (alcohol, marijuana & hard drugs) | |
| Negative | | | | |

gangs (Glueck & Glueck 1950; Short 1957; Short & Strodtbeck 1965; Zhang et al. 1999).

A relatively small number of studies have sought to determine if gang members were more likely to be antisocial or physically aggressive than their age-peers. These studies have shown them to be so. However, one study of drug and alcohol abuse failed to find a significant link between such abuse and gang membership (Table 4.6.4b).

Chapter 5

# Institutional Factors

**Contents**



The focus of this chapter will be on relationships between criminality and the affiliation in one way or another with various types of institutions. The main focus will be on the institutions of education, work (commerce), and religion.

## 5.1 SCHOOL FACTORS

A number of school-related factors have been investigated with reference to the way in which they might be associated with criminality. All but one of these – years of education (which was addressed in Chapter 2 as an aspect of social stratification) – are covered here.

### 5.1.1 Dropping Out of High School (versus Graduating)

As one might suspect, nearly all of the available research has shown that high school drop-outs exhibit higher rates of offending than do their stay-in-school peers (Table 5.1.1a).

As with criminal and delinquent behavior, nearly all of the studies of the links between dropping out of high school before completion and being diagnosed as antisocial or being unusually physically aggressive have concluded that drop-outs exhibit these characteristics more than nondrop-outs (Table 5.1.1b).

### 5.1.2 Dropping Out of High School Time Sequence

An interesting qualification to the link between completion of high school and delinquency is a phenomenon that is dubbed the *dropout dip*. While there is little doubt that dropouts are more involved in offending than high school graduates, the dropout dip refers to a decline in the extent of delinquency by dropouts in the months immediately following their leaving school, especially if fulltime employment follows their leaving school (Pronovost & LeBlanc 1980; Farrington et al. 1986). As shown in Table 5.1.2, while most studies have documented a dropout dip, beyond the second year after dropping out, the offending rates for dropouts seem to rise again.

### 5.1.3 Single-Sex Education

According to one study, girls who attend all-girl schools engage in less delinquency than do their co-educated female counterparts (Table 5.1.3).

**TABLE 5.1.1a Dropping out of High School (versus Graduating) and Criminal/Delinquent Behavior.**

| Nature of the relationship | Officially detected offenses | | Self-reported offenses | |
|---|---|---|---|---|
| | Delinquency | General & adult offenses | Overall offenses | Illegal drugs |
| Positive | **EUROPE** *Britain*: Farrington et al. 1986 **NORTH AMERICA** *United States*: Glueck & Glueck 1934b:87; Robins & Lewis 1966; Hathaway et al. 1969; Bachman & O'Malley 1978:176; Polk et al. 1981:300; Thornberry et al. 1985; Wehlage & Rutter 1986; Pallas 1987; Lynam et al. 1993; Laub & Sampson 1994:245* | **EUROPE** *Britain*: Farrington 1997b:97 **MIDDLE EAST** *Israel*: Shavit & Rattner 1988:1468 **NORTH AMERICA** *United States*: Jarjoura 1996* | **EUROPE** *Britain*: Farrington 1997a:100 **NORTH AMERICA** *Canada*: WG West 1984; *United States*: Fagan et al. 1986:453*; Jarjoura 1993; Laub & Sampson 1994:245*; Jarjoura 1996*; Voelkl et al. 1999:82* (black students) **OCEANIA** *New Zealand*: Wright et al. 1999b (at age 21) | **NORTH AMERICA** *Canada*: Annis & Watson 1975; *United States*: Kandel 1975; Bruno & Doscher 1979; Harris 1983; Friedman et al. 1985; Fagan et al. 1986:453*; Mensch & Kandel 1986b; Mensch & Kandel 1988b; Chavez et al. 1989; Brennan & Anderson 1990; Fagan & Pabon 1990; Kaplan & Liu 1994; Swaim et al. 1997 |
| Not signif. | | | **NORTH AMERICA** *United States*: Voelkl et al. 1999:82* (white students) | |
| Negative | | | | |

**TABLE 5.1.1b Dropping Out of High School (versus Graduating) and Clinical or Personality Traits Associated with Criminality.**

| Nature of the relationship | Antisocial behavior | | Physical aggression |
|---|---|---|---|
| | Childhood & early adol. | Late adol. & adulthood | |
| Positive | **NORTH AMERICA** *United States*: Franklin 1989; Ellickson et al. 1997 **OCEANIA** *New Zealand*: Fergusson & Horwood 1998* (childhood) | **NORTH AMERICA** *United States*: Robins et al. 1991:277 | **NORTH AMERICA** *Canada*: Kokko et al. 2006 (childhood); *United States*: Cairns et al. 1989 (childhood); Ensminger & Slusarcick 1992 (childhood) **OCEANIA** *New Zealand*: Fergusson & Horwood 1998* (childhood) |
| Not Signif. | | | **EUROPE** *Italy*: Caprara et al. 2000 (childhood) |
| Negative | | | |

**TABLE 5.1.2 Dropping out of High School Time Sequence and Criminal/Delinquent Behavior.**

| Nature of the relationship | Time lapsing after dropping out | |
|---|---|---|
| | Short-term effects (within the first year or two) | Long-term effects (beyond the second year) |
| Offending decreases | **NORTH AMERICA** *Canada*: LeBlanc et al. 1979; *United States*: Elliott 1966; Mukherjee 1971:87; Elliott & Voss 1974; Thornberry et al. 1985* | |
| Not signif. | **EUROPE** *Britain*: Farrington et al. 1986:349 | |
| Offending increases | | **MIDDLE EAST** *Israel*: Shavit & Rattner 1988:1468 (among eventual dropouts) **NORTH AMERICA** *United States*: Hathaway et al. 1969; Bachman et al. 1978; Polk et al. 1981; Thornberry et al. 1985:3* |

**TABLE 5.1.3** Single-Sex education and Criminal/ Delinquent Behavior.

| Nature of the relationship | Officially detected offenses |
|---|---|
| | Delinquency |
| Positive | |
| Not signif. | |
| Negative | **OCEANIA** *New Zealand*: Caspi et al. 1993 (females, all girls school) |

**TABLE 5.1.4b** Truancy and Clinical or Personality Traits Associated with Criminality.

| Nature of the relationship | Antisocial behavior |
|---|---|
| | Childhood & early adol. |
| Positive | **NORTH AMERICA** *United States*: Russo et al. 1994 |
| Not signif. | |
| Negative | |

## 5.1.4 Truancy

*Truancy* refers to an unexcused absence from school by those who have not yet graduated from high school. The available research findings clearly show that truancy and delinquency/criminality are positively correlated (Table 5.1.4a). It should be noted, however, that because truancy is a status offense in most industrialized countries, part of the strength of its positive correlation with delinquency may be that it is a delinquent act. Nevertheless, the strength of the relationship appears to be strong. To illustrate the strength of this connection, one Canadian study found chronic truants self-reported three times as many delinquent acts as did their peers who attended school regularly (Paetsch & Betrand 1997:29).

One study was located which found truancy to be more common among conduct disordered children than among children in general (Table 5.1.4b).

## 5.1.5 School Discipline Problems

School discipline problems encompass a wide variety of activities, ranging from talking and acting up in class to smoking and engaging in vandalism on school property. Table 5.1.5a indicates that several studies over the years have shown that school discipline problems are positively associated with delinquent and criminal behavior.

As one would expect, the available evidence suggests that individuals who exhibit conduct disorders as children are more likely than other children to be troublesome in school settings (Table 5.1.5b).

## 5.2 WORK FACTORS

Reviewed below are the findings from studies of various factors related to gainful employment, both by individuals and by their parents.

**TABLE 5.1.4a** Truancy and Criminal/Delinquent Behavior.

| Nature of the relationship | Officially detected offenses | | | Self-reported offenses | |
|---|---|---|---|---|---|
| | Delinquency | General & adult offenses | Recidivism | Overall offenses | Illegal drugs |
| Positive | **AFRICA** *Ghana*: Weinberg 1964 **EUROPE** *Britain*: Ferguson 1952:30; Burt 1957:455; *Netherlands*: Garnefski & Okma 1996; *Sweden*: Jonsson 1967:206; 1975:184; Stattin et al. 1997:204* **NORTH AMERICA** *United States*: Glueck & Glueck 1934b:87; Robins & Hill 1966; Silberberg & Silberberg 1971 | **EUROPE** *Finland*: Pulkkinen 1983; *Sweden*: Nylander 1979* **NORTH AMERICA** *United States*: Robins 1979 | **EUROPE** *Britain*: Mannheim & Wilkins 1955; *Sweden*: Stattin et al. 1997:204* **NORTH AMERICA** *United States*: Reiss 1951:20; Black & Glick 1952; Cymbalisty et al. 1975; Wooldredge 1994 | **EUROPE** *Britain*: Farrington 1979 **NORTH AMERICA** *Canada*: Paetsch & Bertrand 1997*; T Peter et al. 2003; *United States*: Voelkl et al. 1999:82 | **EUROPE** *Sweden*: Holmberg 1985:133 **NORTH AMERICA** *Canada*: Paetsch & Bertrand 1997:30* *United States*: Galli 1974; Kandel 1975; Brooks et al. 1977; Newcomb et al. 1987:418; Van Kammen et al. 1991:406 |
| Not signif. | | | | | |
| Negative | | | | | |

**TABLE 5.1.5a School Discipline Problems and Criminal/Delinquent Behavior.**

| Nature of the relationship | Officially detected offenses | | | Self-reported offenses | |
|---|---|---|---|---|---|
| | Delinquency | General & adult offenses | Recidivism | Overall offenses | Illegal drugs |
| Positive | **EUROPE** *Britain*: *Netherlands*: Garnefski & Okma 1996; *Sweden*: Stattin et al. 1997:204* **NORTH AMERICA** *United States*: Khleif 1964; Craig & Glick 1968; Polk & Schafer 1972:178; Elster et al. 1987a | **EUROPE** *Finland*: Pulkkinen 1983; *Sweden*: Kirkegaard-Sarenson & Mednick 1977; Nylander 1979* | **NORTH AMERICA** *United States*: Kirkpatrick 1937 | **EUROPE** *Britain*: Farrington 1979 **NORTH AMERICA** *Canada*: Paetsch & Bertrand 1997*; Peter et al. 2003; *United States*: Hundleby 1982 | **EUROPE** *Sweden*: Nylander 1979* **NORTH AMERICA** *United States*: Blumenfield et al. 1972:607; Jessor & Jessor 1977; Barnes & Welte 1986 |
| Not signif. | | | | | |
| Negative | | | | | |

**TABLE 5.1.5b School Discipline Problems and Clinical or Personality Traits Associated with Criminality.**

| Nature of the relationship | Antisocial behavior |
|---|---|
| | Childhood & early adol. |
| Positive | **NORTH AMERICA** *United States*: Cox & Gunn 1980; Gittelman et al. 1985; Kupersmidt & Coie 1990 |
| Not signif. | |
| Negative | |

## 5.2.1 Employment During Adolescence

Are teenagers who are gainfully employed while maintaining their schooling more or less likely than their unemployed classmates to be involved in crime and delinquency? This question was first investigated by Willim Bonger (1916:419). His study concluded that working teenagers exhibited higher rates of offending than did their nonworking peers. As shown in Table 5.2.1 that conclusion has been reconfirmed by a substantial majority of subsequent studies.

## 5.2.2 Employment by the Father Outside the Home

One study concluded that whether the father was gainfully employed outside the home was not significantly related to the involvement in delinquency by children in the home (Table 5.2.2).

## 5.2.3 Employment by the Mother Outside the Home

In traditional families, it is most common for the father to work full time outside the home, and for the mother to

**TABLE 5.2.1 Employment during Adolescence and Criminal/Delinquent Behavior.**

| Nature of the relationship | Officially detected offenses | Self-reported offenses | |
|---|---|---|---|
| | Delinquency | Overall offenses | Illegal drugs |
| Positive | **EUROPE** *Britain*: Ferguson 1952:31 | **NORTH AMERICA** *United States*: Agnew 1986; Bachman et al. 1986*; Mortimer et al. 1992; Steinberg et al. 1993; Cullen et al. 1997; Ploeger 1997:664; Wright et al. 1997; Brame et al. 2004:252 | **NORTH AMERICA** *United States*: Greenberger et al. 1980; Greenberger & Steinberg 1981; Ruggiero et al. 1982; Bachman et al. 1986*; Greenberger & Steinberg 1986; Bachman & Schulenberg 1993; Johanson et al. 1996; Ploeger 1997 (marijuana use) |
| Not signif. | | **NORTH AMERICA** *United States*: Crowley 1984; DC Gottfredson 1985 | |
| Negative | | | |

**TABLE 5.2.2** Employment by the Father outside the Home and Offspring Criminal/Delinquent Behavior.

| Nature of the relationship | Officially detected offenses |
|---|---|
| | Delinquency |
| Positive | |
| Not signif. | **NORTH AMERICA** *United States*: Vander Ven & Cullen 2004:285 |
| Negative | |

**TABLE 5.2.3b** Employment by the Mother outside the Home and Offspring Clinical or Personality Traits Associated with Criminality.

| Nature of the relationship | Antisocial behavior |
|---|---|
| | Childhood & early adol. |
| Positive | **NORTH AMERICA** *United States*: Hoffman 1989 |
| Not signif. | |
| Negative | |

maintain the home and assume primary responsibility for routine child care. In recent decades, most industrialized societies have witnessed a gradual shift toward greater involvement of mothers in employment outside the home. Children of parents who both work outside the home have sometimes been labeled "latchkey kids", since they are often responsible for their own activities between the time the school day is over and their parents' arrival home from work (Steinberg 1986).

Over the years, researchers have investigated the possibility that having a mother who works outside the home might be associated with offending by the offspring. The research results are summarized in Table 5.2.3a. Basically, the findings have been nearly evenly divided between those reporting no significant differences and those suggesting that children of working mothers are more prone toward offending than children of stay-at-home mothers.

One study found that mothers employed outside the home were more likely than stay-at-home mothers to have children who exhibited conduct disorders (Table 5.2.3b).

## 5.2.4 Frequently Changing Jobs

As shown in Table 5.2.4a, nearly all pertinent studies have shown that persons who change jobs frequently are more involved in criminal activity.

According to Table 5.2.4b, persons who exhibit adult antisocial behavior are more likely than adults in general to change jobs frequently.

## 5.2.5 Being or Frequently Being Unemployed

Regarding the frequency of unemployment, numerous studies have been conducted with respect to criminality primarily among adult males. As shown in Table 5.2.5a, the majority of these studies have indicated that frequently unemployed persons are more likely to have a criminal record.

All of the available evidence suggests that antisocial behavior and high rates of physical aggression are positively correlated with being frequently unemployed (Table 5.2.5b).

**TABLE 5.2.3a** Employment by the Mother outside the Home and Offspring Criminal/Delinquent Behavior.

| Nature of the relationship | Officially detected offenses | | Self-reported offenses | |
|---|---|---|---|---|
| | Delinquency | Recidivism | Overall offenses | Illegal drugs |
| Positive | **EUROPE** *Finland*: Rantakallio et al. 1996:116* **NORTH AMERICA** *United States*: Hodgkiss 1935; S Glueck & Glueck 1950, 1956:178; Vander Ven & Cullen 2004:285 (coerced employment) | **EUROPE** *Netherlands*: Buikhuisen & Hoekstra 1974:68 | **NORTH AMERICA** *United States*: Nye 1958; Hirschi 1969 | **NORTH AMERICA** *United States*: Bachman et al. 1986; Greenberger & Steinberg 1986; Bachman & Schulenberg 1993; Johanson et al. 1996 |
| Not signif. | **AFRICA** *Ghana*: Weinberg 1964 **EUROPE** *Britain*: Ferguson 1952:24; Reige 1972; Farrington & Painter 2002:50 (males); *Finland*: Rantakallio et al. 1995; *Sweden*: Jonsson 1967:173 **NORTH AMERICA** *United States*: Laub & Sampson 1988; La Flone 1988:637 | | **EUROPE** *Britain*: Riley & Shaw 1985 **NORTH AMERICA** *United States*: Broidy 1995:551 | **NORTH AMERICA** *United States*: Fors & Rojek 1983:218 |
| Negative | | | | |

**TABLE 5.2.4a Frequently Changing Jobs and Criminal/Delinquent Behavior.**

| Nature of the relationship | Officially detected offenses | | | Self-reported offenses |
|---|---|---|---|---|
| | Delinquency | General & adult offenses | Recidivism | Overall offenses |
| Positive | **EUROPE** *Britain*: Ferguson 1952:35; West & Farrington 1977:65; Farrington 1987a:32; Nagin & Land 1993:352 **NORTH AMERICA** *United States*: Laub & Sampson 1994:245 | **EUROPE** *Britain*: Farrington 1983, 1997a:97* | **EUROPE** *Britain*: Mannheim & Wilkins 1955; Simon 1971; *Germany*: Richter et al. 1996 **NORTH AMERICA** *United States*: Borden 1928; Vold 1931; Kirby 1954; Glaser 1954; DM Gottfredson et al. 1978; SD Gottfredson & DM Gottfredson 1979 | **EUROPE** *Britain*: Farrington 1997a:100* **NORTH AMERICA** *United States*: Dishion et al. 1984; Laub & Sampson 1994:245 |
| Not signif. | | | **NORTH AMERICA** *United States*: Tibbitts 1931 | |
| Negative | | | | |

## 5.2.6 Welfare Dependency

Over the years, studies have been undertaken to determine if welfare dependency is associated with involvement in delinquent/criminal behavior (usually by offspring). As shown in Table 5.2.6a, the evidence is largely consistent with the view that the utilization of welfare services is positively correlated with criminal involvement, although some studies report no significant relationship, and one study concluded that there was actually a negative relationship.

All of the available evidence suggests that antisocial behavior is positively correlated with criminality among family members (Table 5.2.6b).

## 5.3 RELIGIOUS FACTORS

Since the early part of the twentieth century, there has been a great deal of research regarding the relationship between religious factors and criminal behavior. Nevertheless, the findings from these studies are barely mentioned in most criminology textbooks, bringing one researcher to declare the connection between religion and crime "criminology's lost relationship" (Stark et al. 1982). Part of the reason that criminologists have avoided discussing relationships between religion and crime is that not all of the evidence has been consistent. Another has to do with the emotional sentiments people feel toward religious issues, and especially toward their own religious affiliations.

**TABLE 5.2.4b Frequently Changing Jobs and Clinical or Personality Traits Associated with Criminality.**

| Nature of the relationship | Antisocial behavior | |
|---|---|---|
| | Childhood & early adol. | Late adol. & adulthood |
| Positive | | **NORTH AMERICA** *United States*: Robins et al. 1991:286 **OCEANIA** *New Zealand*: Mulder et al. 1994:282 |
| Not signif. | | |
| Negative | | |

### 5.3.1 Religious Involvement

Because there are many aspects to religion, researchers have devised several measures of people's religiosity. The most widely used measure has been to simply ask people to report how often they attend religious services (i.e., attending church, synagogue, or mosque). Results from this measure for officially detected offenses are shown in Table 5.3.1a. It indicates that as involvement in religious services increases, criminal behavior tends to decrease, with the main possible exception of property crime.

As with offending that is officially identified, research based on self-reports have predominantly indicated that those who attend religious services most often are less involved in crime and delinquency than those who attend little or not at all (Table 5.3.1b). This is especially well documented with regard to the use of illegal drugs.

### 5.3.2 Religious Saliency (Importance of Religion to One's Life)

Religious saliency refers to the extent to which one's religious faith is central to his/her life. As can be seen from viewing Table 5.3.2, most studies have concluded that the more salient religion is to one's life, the less involved in criminal activities the individual tends to be.

**TABLE 5.2.5a** Being or Frequently Being Unemployed and Criminal/Delinquent Behavior.

| Nature of the relationship | Officially detected offenses | | | | | Self-reports |
|---|---|---|---|---|---|---|
| | Violent offenses | Property offenses | Delinquency | General & adult offenses | Recidivism | Offending in general |
| Positive | **NORTH AMERICA** *United States*: Joong-Hwan Oh 2005:579 (aggravated assault and robbery) | **NORTH AMERICA** *United States*: Phillips et al. 1972 | **ASIA** *Japan*: Takahashi 1986 (parental unemployment) **EUROPE** *Britain*: Ferguson 1952:23 (parental unemployment); *Finland*: Rantakallio et al. 1992b (parental unemployment) **NORTH AMERICA** *Canada*: SW Baron 2003 (self-control statistically controlled); *United States*: Brownfield 1986:427 | **EUROPE** *Britain*: Farrington et al. 1986:342 **NORTH AMERICA** *United States*: Thornberry & Farnsworth 1982; Thornberry & Christenson 1984; Thornberry et al. 1985:16; Horney et al. 1995 (males); Shouer 1996 (males); J Tanner et al. 1999; Uggen 2000 (males); Bernburg & Krohn 2003; Laub & Sampson 2003 (males) **OCEANIA** *Australia*: Kraus 1978 | **EUROPE** *Scotland*: Cormack 1976:100 **NORTH AMERICA** *United States*: Sickles et al. 1979; Eisenberg 1985 | **OCEANIA** *New Zealand*: Wright et al. 1999 (at age 21, 6 months without work & less full-time employment) |
| Not signif. | | | **EUROPE** *Netherlands*: Junger & Polder 1992:61 (parental unemployment) | | **NORTH AMERICA** *United States*: Roundtree et al. 1984 | |
| Negative | | | | | | |

**TABLE 5.2.5b** Being or Frequently Being Unemployed and Clinical or Personality Traits Associated with Criminality.

| Nature of the relationship | Antisocial behavior | Physical aggression |
|---|---|---|
| | Late adol. & adulthood | |
| Positive | **OCEANIA** *New Zealand*: Mulder et al. 1994:281 | **EUROPE** *Finland*: Kokko & Pukkinen 2000 (childhood); Kokko et al. 2003 (childhood)<br>**NORTH AMERICA** *United States*: Caspi et al. 1987 (childhood); Brook & Newcomb 1995 (childhood); Caspi et al. 1998 (childhood)<br>**OCEANIA** *New Zealand*: Fergusson & Horwood 1998 (childhood) |
| Not signif. | | |
| Negative | | |

**TABLE 5.2.6a** Welfare Dependency and Family Involvement in Criminal/Delinquent Behavior.

| Nature of the relationship | Officially detected offenses | | | | Self-reported offenses | |
|---|---|---|---|---|---|---|
| | Violent offenses | Property offenses | Delinquency | General & adult offenses | Overall offenses | Illegal drugs |
| Positive | **EUROPE** *Britain*: MJ Brown et al. 1972:259* | **EUROPE** *Britain*: MJ Brown et al. 1972:259* | **EUROPE** *Britain*: Kolvin et al. 1988<br>**NORTH AMERICA** *United States*: Brown 1984 (welfare dependency) | **EUROPE** *Britain*: Kolvin et al. 1988 | **NORTH AMERICA** *United States*: Longmoor & Young 1936; Brownfield 1986:427; Furstenberg et al. 1987 (welfare dependency) | |
| Not signif. | | | **NORTH AMERICA** *United States*: Cao et al. 2004 (control for single-parent household & school attachment) | | **NORTH AMERICA** *United States*: Peeples & Loeber 1994; Polakowski 1994:70 | **NORTH AMERICA** *United States*: Fors & Rojek 1983:213 |
| Negative | **NORTH AMERICA** *United States*: Chamlin et al. 2002 (receiving AFDC, familial homicide, Oklahoma) | | | | | |

**TABLE 5.2.6b** Welfare Dependency and Family Clinical or Personality Traits Associated with Criminality.

| Nature of the relationship | Antisocial behavior | |
|---|---|---|
| | Childhood & early adol. | Late adol. & adulthood |
| Positive | **NORTH AMERICA** *United States*: Robins & Price 1991<br>**OCEANIA** *New Zealand*: Bardone et al. 1996:821 | **OCEANIA** *New Zealand*: Mulder et al. 1994:281 |
| Not signif. | | |
| Negative | | |

**TABLE 5.3.1a Religious Involvement and Officially Detected Criminal/Delinquent Behavior.**

| Nature of the relationship | Officially detected offenses | | |
|---|---|---|---|
| | Property offenses | Delinquency | General & adult offenses |
| Positive | | | |
| Not signif. | **NORTH AMERICA** *United States*: Baker et al. 1929; Dentler & Monroe 1961 | **NORTH AMERICA** *United States*: Allen & Sandhu 1968:264 | |
| Negative | | **NORTH AMERICA** *United States*: Reinhardt & Harper 1936; Middleton & Wright 1941:144; Carr-Saunders et al. 1942, 1944; Kvaraceus 1944a:288; Glueck & Glueck 1950:166; Wattenberg 1950; Ferguson 1952:38; Argyle 1959:100; Cortes 1965:123; Rosenquist & Megaree 1969; Glueck & Glueck 1974:164 | **NORTH AMERICA** *United States*: Miner 1931; Healy & Bronner 1936:70 |

**TABLE 5.3.1b Religious Involvement and Self-Reported Criminal/Delinquent Behavior.**

| Nature of the relationship | Self-reported offenses | |
|---|---|---|
| | Overall offenses | Illegal drugs |
| Positive | | |
| Not signif. | **NORTH AMERICA** *United States*: Hirschi & Stark 1969:211; Burkett & White 1974; Farrell et al. 1992:708 (Blacks); Bainbridge 1992:201; Ross 1994:76 | **EUROPE** *Sweden*: Pettersson 1991 **NORTH AMERICA** *United States*: Kane & Patterson 1972; Kandel et al. 1976b; Hundleby 1982; Baldinger et al. 1972; Farrell et al. 1992:708 (blacks); Kaestner 1997:168 |
| Negative | **NORTH AMERICA** *Canada*: Avakame 1997; *United States*: Nye 1958:35 & 155; Middleton & Putney 1962:150; Rhodes & Reiss 1970; Burkett & White 1974; Donovan 1977; Higgins & Albrecht 1977; Jensen & Erickson 1979:163; Stark et al. 1982:14; Elifson et al. 1983; Tittle & Welch 1983; Sloane & Potvin 1986; Ellis & Thompson 1989; Mitchell et al. 1990; Cochran et al. 1994; Ross 1996; Stark 1996:170* | **EUROPE** *Britain*: Kosviner et al. 1973; Adalf & Smart 1985*; *Ireland*: Parfey 1976:137 **NORTH AMERICA** *Canada*: Fejer 1971; Smart & Fejer 1971; Boggs & Hughes 1973; Moyer & Fejer 1972; Mercer & Smart 1974; Killeen 1977; Linden & Currie 1977; Adalf & Smart 1985*; Hundleby 1987; *United States*: Preston 1968; Blum et al. 1969; Frumkin et al. 1969; Greenwald & Luetgert 1971; Grupp et al. 1971; Blumenfield et al. 1972:605; Gergen et al. 1972; Steffenhagen et al. 1972; Baskett & Nyswander 1973; Henley & Adams 1973; Martino & Truss 1973; Strimbu & Schoenfeldt 1973; Burkett & White 1974:459; Rohrbaugh & Jessor 1975:147; Albrecht et al. 1977:270; Brook et al. 1977; Margulies et al. 1977; Guinn 1978; Kleinman & Lukoff 1978:195; Jensen & Erickson 1979:163; Oetting & Goldstein 1979; Burkett 1980; Bachman et al. 1981; Gersick et al. 1981; McIntosh et al. 1981; Khavari & Harmon 1982; NM Nelson & Rooney 1982; PL Benson et al. 1983; Fors & Rojek 1983:213; MacDonald & Luckett 1983; JS Brook et al. 1984b; Goe & Bachtel 1985; Lorch & Hughes 1985; HW Perkins 1985; Amoateng & Bahr 1986; PL Benson et al. 1986; Marcos et al. 1986; Burkett & Warren 1987; Dudley et al. 1987; PL Benson & Donahue 1989; JS Brook et al. 1989a; Cochran & Akers 1989; Brownfield & Sorenson 1991; Donnermeyer & Huang 1991; J Wallace & Bachman 1991; Bainbridge 1992:201; PL Benson 1992; J Cochran 1992; Hawks & Bahr 1992; JS Brook et al. 1995:1233; Amey et al. 1996; Johanson et al. 1996; S Moore et al. 1996:535*; Stark 1996:171 |

**TABLE 5.3.2** Religious Saliency (Importance of Religion to One's Life) and Criminal/Delinquent Behavior.

| Nature of the relationship | Officially detected offenses | Self-reported offenses | |
|---|---|---|---|
| | Delinquency | Overall offenses | Illegal drugs |
| Positive | | | |
| Not signif. | **OCEANIA** *Hawaii*: Werner & Smith 1992:221* (males) | **NORTH AMERICA** *United States*: Hirschi & Stark 1969*; Levine & Singer 1988:392* | **EUROPE** *Sweden*: Pettersson 1991 **NORTH AMERICA** *United States*: Gardner & Shoemaker 1989* |
| Negative | **OCEANIA** *Hawaii*: Werner & Smith 1992:221* (females) | **MIDDLE EAST** *Israel*: Shavit & Rattner 1988:1465 **NORTH AMERICA** *United States*: Nye 1958:147; Travers & Davis 1961; Allen & Sandhu 1968:264; Elifson et al. 1983; Sloane & Potvin 1986; Cochran 1989:157; Gardner & Shoemaker 1989:490*; Fernquist 1995* | **NORTH AMERICA** *Canada*: Adalf & Smart 1985; *United States*: Preston 1968; Blumenfield et al. 1972; Globetti et al. 1978; McInosh et al. 1979; Nyberg & McIntosh 1979; Oetting & Goldstein 1979; Khavari & Harmon 1982; Hadaway et al. 1984; Perkins 1985; Forliti & Benson 1986; Benson et al. 1987; Newcomb et al. 1987:418; Levine & Singer 1988:393*; McGee & Newcomb 1992; Fernquist 1995 |

## 5.3.3 Religious Membership

As shown in Table 5.3.3, the findings pertaining to a relationship between membership in a religious organization and involvement in crime or delinquency have been mixed. Regarding violent and property crime and the use of illegal drugs, evidence suggests that religious membership is associated with less criminality. However, for general delinquency and adult or general offending, most studies have found a positive relationship.

## 5.3.4 Orthodox Religious Beliefs

Most of the relevant research suggests that people who subscribe to various orthodox religious beliefs are less involved in crime and delinquency than are those who reject those beliefs (Table 5.3.4).

**TABLE 5.3.3** Religious Membership and Criminal/Delinquent Behavior.

| Nature of the relationship | Officially detected offenses | | | | Self-reported offenses |
|---|---|---|---|---|---|
| | Violent offenses | Property offenses | Delinquency | General & adult offenses | Illegal drugs |
| Positive | | | **NORTH AMERICA** *United States*: Middleton & Fay 1941; Middleton & Wright 1941 | **EUROPE** *Britain*: H. Ellis 1910:189 **NORTH AMERICA** *United States*: Murchison 1924; Miner 1931:431; Block & Flynn 1956:232 | |
| Not signif. | | | | **NORTH AMERICA** *United States*: Kvaraceus 1944a:288 | **NORTH AMERICA** *United States*: Kirk 1979; Amey et al. 1996:1321* (blacks) |
| Negative | **NORTH AMERICA** *United States*: Stark et al. 1980 | **NORTH AMERICA** *United States*: Baker et al. 1929 | | | **NORTH AMERICA** *Canada*: Whitehead 1970; Currie et al. 1977; *United States*: Mauss 1969; Gergen et al. 1972; Kane & Patterson 1972; Jensen & Erickson 1979:163*; McIntosh et al. 1981; Bock et al. 1987; Donnermeyer et al. 1987; Perkins 1987; Clark et al. 1992; Amey 1996:1321* (whites) |

**TABLE 5.3.4 Orthodox Religious Beliefs and Criminal/Delinquent Behavior.**

| Nature of the relationship | Officially detected offenses | Self-reported offenses | |
|---|---|---|---|
| | General & adult offenses | Overall offenses | Illegal drugs |
| Positive | | | |
| Not signif. | **NORTH AMERICA** *United States*: Middleton & Wright 1941:142 (belief in god) | **NORTH AMERICA** *United States*: Middleton & Putney 1962:149* (belief in god); Hirschi & Stark 1969:211 (belief in an afterlife) | |
| Negative | | **EUROPE** *Netherlands*: Junger & Palder 1993 (Christian orthodoxy) **NORTH AMERICA** *United States*: Burkett & White 1974:459* (belief in an afterlife); Jensen & Erickson 1979:163* (belief in an afterlife); Elifson et al. 1983 (belief in an afterlife); Benda 1995* (Christian orthodoxy); Evans et al. 1996:55 (Christian orthodoxy) | **EUROPE** *Britain*: Kosviner et al. 1973 (belief in god); *Ireland*: Parfey 1976:136 (belief in god) **NORTH AMERICA** *United States*: Middleton & Putney 1962:149* (belief in god); Blumenfield et al. 1972 (belief in god); Burkett & White 1974:459 (belief in an afterlife); Albrecht et al. 1977:270 (belief in god & an afterlife); Benda 1995* (Christian orthodoxy) |

### 5.3.5 Prayer

The small amount of research on the practice of prayer has reached somewhat inconsistent findings regarding any involvement in criminal and delinquent activities, suggesting that there may exist a sex difference (Table 5.3.5).

### 5.3.6 Religious Compared to Non-Religious

The first between-religion comparison to be made involved persons who affiliated with no religion relative to those who did. As shown in Table 5.3.6, the findings have been somewhat mixed. For officially detected offending, the non-religious are less involved than Christians but more involved

**TABLE 5.3.5 Prayer and Criminal/Delinquent Behavior.**

| Nature of the relationship | Officially detected offenses | Self-reported offenses |
|---|---|---|
| | Delinquency | Overall offenses |
| Positive | | |
| Not signif. | **OCEANIA** *Hawaii*: Werner & Smith 1992:221* (males) | |
| Negative | **OCEANIA** *Hawaii*: Werner & Smith 1992:221* (females) | LE Ross 1996 |

**TABLE 5.3.6 Nonreligious Compared with Religious and Criminal/Delinquent Behavior.**

| Nature of the relationship | Officially detected offenses | Self-reported offenses |
|---|---|---|
| | Crime in general | Illegal drugs |
| Nonreligious more | **EUROPE** *Netherlands*: Bonger 1936:131* (compared with Jews) **NORTH AMERICA** *United States*: Gillin 1946 (compared with Jews) | **NORTH AMERICA** *United States*: Smart et al. 1970* (compared with Christians) |
| Not signif. | | **NORTH AMERICA** *Canada*: Smart et al. 1970* (compared with Jews) |
| Nonreligious less | **EUROPE** *Netherlands*: Bonger 1936:131* (compared with Christians) **NORTH AMERICA** *United States*: Lunden 1942:130 (compared with Christians); Gillin 1946 (compared with Christians) | |

**TABLE 5.3.7** Christians Compared with Non-Christians and Criminal/Delinquent Behavior.

| Nature of the relationship | Officially detected offenses |
|---|---|
| | Delinquency |
| Christians more | **AFRICA** *Nigeria*: Asuni 1963:188 (compared with Muslims) |
| No signif. diff. | |
| Christians less | |

than Jews. For self-reported illegal drug use, however, the nonreligious tend to be more involved than Christians but on par with Jews.

## 5.3.7 Christians Compared with Non-Christians

The only study located which compared offending rates among Christians with a group of non-Christians involved Muslims. It concluded that Christians exhibited higher rates of delinquency (Table 5.3.7).

## 5.3.8 Catholic Compared with Non-Catholic

Nearly all of the available research specific to crime rates among Catholics has compared their rates with those of Protestants. As shown in Table 5.3.8, the majority of these studies have concluded that Catholics exhibit greater involvement in crime and delinquency than do Protestants, at least when the latter is considered as a single collective group. The most notable exception has to do with illegal drugs where the findings have been very inconsistent.

**TABLE 5.3.9** Fundamentalists Compared with Non-Fundamentalist Christians and Criminal/Delinquent Behavior.

| Nature of the relationship | Self-reported offenses |
|---|---|
| | Offenses in general |
| Fundamentals more | |
| No signif. diff. | **NORTH AMERICA** *United States*: Free 1994 (compared with non-fundamentalist Christians) |
| Fundamentalists less | |

## 5.3.9 Fundamentalists Compared-with Non-Fundamentalist Christians

Fundamentalist Christians believe in the literal interpretation of the Bible. According to the single available study, there is no significant difference between fundamentalist Christians and non-fundamentalist Christians regarding their self-reported offending (Table 5.3.9).

**TABLE 5.3.8** Catholic Compared with Non-Catholic and Criminal/Delinquent Behavior.

| Nature of the relationship | Officially detected offenses | | Self-reported offenses | |
|---|---|---|---|---|
| | Delinquency | Crime in general | Offenses in general | Illegal drugs |
| Catholics more | **EUROPE** *Multiple Eastern European Countries*: Hersch 1936:515 (compared with Protestants) **NORTH AMERICA** *United States*: Kvaraceus 1944a:288; Glueck & Glueck 1950:166 (compared with Protestants) | **EUROPE** *Germany*: Aschaffenberg 1933:58 (compared with Protestants); *Netherlands*: Bonger 1936:131 (compared with Protestants, Jews, & nonreligious) **NORTH AMERICA** *United States*: Lunden 1942:130 (compared with Protestants, Jews, & nonreligious); von Hentig 1948b:337 (compared with Protestants); Gillin 1946* (compared with Protestants, Jews, & nonreligious) | **NORTH AMERICA** *United States*: Jensen & Erickson 1979:165 (compared with Protestants) | **NORTH AMERICA** *Canada*: Adlaf & Smart 1985 (underage drinking, compared with Protestants) |
| No signif. diff. | | | | **NORTH AMERICA** *United States*: Sarvela & McClendon 1988 (compared with Protestants); Forthun et al. 1999:82 (compared with Protestants) |
| Catholics less | | | | **NORTH AMERICA** *Canada*: Fejer 1971 (compared with Protestants) |

TABLE 5.3.10 Mormons Compared with Non-Mormons and Criminal/Delinquent Behavior.

| Nature of the relationship | Self-reported offenses |
|---|---|
| | Offenses in general |
| Mormons more | |
| No signif. diff. | |
| Mormons less | **NORTH AMERICA** *United States*: Jensen & Erickson 1979:165 (compared with other Christians) |

## 5.3.10 Mormons Compared-with Non-Mormons

One study compared Mormons with other Christians. It concluded that Christians exhibited higher rates of delinquency (Table 5.3.10).

## 5.3.11 Jews Compared-with Non-Jews

Numerous studies have compared crime and delinquency among Jews relative to members of other religious groups. As shown in Table 5.3.11a, nearly all of these studies have concluded that Jews have lower rates. There are exceptions, the main one being that Jews have relatively high self-reported drug use.

Contrary to information derived from official delinquency data (see above), studies of self-reported acts of aggression by adolescents living in Israel have concluded that Jewish youth engage in more acts of aggression toward peers than do Arab (largely Muslim) youth (Table 5.3.11b).

# 5.4 OTHER INSTITUTIONAL FACTORS

Research findings on the relationship between criminality and two of other institutional factors are reviewed below.

TABLE 5.3.11a Jews Compared with Non-Jews and Criminal/Delinquent Behavior.

| Nature of the relationship | Officially detected offenses | | Self-reported offenses | |
|---|---|---|---|---|
| | Delinquency | Criminality in general | Offenses in general | Illegal drugs |
| Jews more | | **NORTH AMERICA** *United States*: Lunden 1942:130* (compared with the nonreligious); Gillin 1946* (compared with the nonreligious) | | **NORTH AMERICA** *Canada*: Smart et al. 1970* (compared with Christians) |
| No signif. diff. | | | | **NORTH AMERICA** *Canada*: Smart et al. 1970* (compared with the nonreligious) |
| Jews less | **EUROPE** *Poland*: Hersch 1937 (compared with the gen. pop.); Hersch 1945 (compared with the gen. pop.); *Multiple Countries in Eastern Europe*: Hersch 1936:515 (compared with Christians) **MIDDLE EAST** *Israel*: Sherer 1990 (compared with Arab Muslims); Hassin 1997 (compared with Arab Muslims) **NORTH AMERICA** *United States*: Maller 1932 (compared with Christians); Kvaraceus 1944a:288 (compared with Christians); Glueck & Glueck 1950:166 (compared with Christians); Goldberg 1950 (compared with the gen. pop.); Peck et al. 1955 (compared with the gen. pop.); Robinson 1958 (compared with the gen. pop.) | **EUROPE** *Austria*: Herz 1908; *Germany*: von Mayr 1917; Aschaffenberg 1933:58 (compared with Christians); Exner 1939:67 (compared with Christians); *Hungary*: Thon 1907 (compared with Christians); *Netherlands*: Bonger 1936:131 (compared with Christians & the nonreligious) **NORTH AMERICA** *United States*: Levinger 1940 (compared with the gen. pop.); Linfield 1940 (compared with the gen. pop.); Lunden 1942:130* (compared with Christians); Kvaraceus 1945:102 (compared with Protestants); Gillin 1946* (compared with the nonreligious) | **EUROPE** *Germany*: Belson et al. 1975:86 (compared with Christians) **NORTH AMERICA** *United States*: Milman & Su 1973 (compared with gen. pop.) | |

**TABLE 5.3.11b** Jews versus Non-Jews and Clinical or Personality Traits Associated with Criminality.

| Nature of the relationship | Physical aggression |
|---|---|
| Jews more | **MIDDLE EAST** *Israel*: Horowitz & Frenkel 1990 (adol., self-reported hit peers, compared with Arab Muslims); Iram 1997 (adol., self-reported, compared with Arab Muslims); Sherer & Karnieli-Miller 2004:104 (adol., self-report, hitting peers, compared with Arab Muslims) |
| No signif. diff. | |
| Jews less | |

**TABLE 5.4.1** Being in the Armed Forces and Criminal/Delinquent Behavior.

| Nature of the relationship | Officially detected offenses | | |
|---|---|---|---|
| | Violent offenses | General & adult offenses | Recidivism |
| Positive | | **NORTH AMERICA** *United States*: Galiani et al. 2006 | |
| Not signif. | **NORTH AMERICA** *United States*: Bouffard 2005 (white males); Bouffard 2006 | **NORTH AMERICA** *United States*: JP Wright et al. 2005 (males) | |
| Negative | **NORTH AMERICA** *United States*: Bouffard 2003 (black males) | **NORTH AMERICA** *United States*: Laub & Sampson 2003 (males) | **NORTH AMERICA** *United States*: Mattick 1960 (males) |

**TABLE 5.4.2** Involvement with the Mass Media and Criminal/Delinquent Behavior.

| Nature of the relationship | Officially detected offenses |
|---|---|
| | Delinquency |
| Positive | **NORTH AMERICA** *United States*: Mitchell 1929b:181 (movie attendance) |
| Not signif. | |
| Negative | |

## 5.4.1 Being in the Armed Forces

The possible association between being in the armed forces and becoming involved in crime and delinquency has been examined using a variety of different research designs. As one can see by viewing Table 5.4.1, the evidence has been quite mixed with regard to an association between military experience and involvement in criminal behavior.

## 5.4.2 Involvement with the Mass Media

According to one study (conducted in the 1930s), delinquency was higher among adolescents who attended movies most often relative to those who attended least often (Table 5.4.2).

# Personality and Behavioral Factors

**Contents**



This chapter considers the connections between criminality and numerous personality and behavioral traits. These traits range from broad-ranging patterns of temperament to some specific types of behavior such as those involving sexuality and the consumption of various drugs.

## 6.1 PERSONALITY/TEMPERAMENT TRAITS

Personality and temperamental variables are concerned with fairly consistent behavioral tendencies that vary from one person to another. Among the traits to be examined under this heading are those of aggression, impulsivity, sensation seeking, bullying, extroversion, and trustworthiness/deceptiveness.

### 6.1.1 Aggression in General, Except Childhood

Everyone exhibits aggression sometime in his/her life, but some people seem to be chronically aggressive. Table 6.1.1a indicates that most studies have found delinquents and criminals to be more aggressive than their relatively law abiding counterparts. The few exceptions have involved studies of illegal drug use.

Research on links between the frequency in the display of aggression and the tendency to exhibit antisocial behavior along with involvement in the abuse of drugs is consistent in indicating that positive relationships exist (Table 6.1.1b).

### 6.1.2 Aggression in Childhood

Childhood aggression refers to a child's tendency to become involved in physical fights. Most social science efforts to measure childhood aggression have relied on retrospective self-reports or upon ratings given by parents, teachers, or peers (Loeber & Stouthamer-Loeber 1987:332).

The results of the research published to date are summarized in Table 6.1.2a. This evidence supports the view that childhood aggression is positively associated with delinquent and criminal behavior later in life. In recent decades, long-term studies have concluded that persistent childhood aggression is in fact the single best childhood predictor of serious

**TABLE 6.1.1a** Aggression in General and Criminal/Delinquent Behavior.

| Nature of the relationship | Officially detected offenses | | | Self-reported offenses |
|---|---|---|---|---|
| | Violent offenses | Delinquency | Overall offenses | Illegal drugs |
| Positive | **NORTH AMERICA** *United States*: DT George et al. 2001 (domestic violence) | **NORTH AMERICA** *Canada*: Tremblay et al. 2003 | **EUROPE** *Britain*: P Smith & Waterman 2003 **NORTH AMERICA** *United States*: Ensminger et al. 1983 (teacher-rated aggression) | **NORTH AMERICA** *United States*: Yudofsky et al. 1993 (cocaine); Moeller et al. 1994 (cocaine); Berenson et al. 2001 (females, marijuana); Patkar et al. 2003 (blacks, cocaine use) **OCEANIA** *New Zealand*: Fergusson et al. 2002 (marijuana) |
| Not signif. | | | | |
| Negative | | | | **EUROPE** *Switzerland*: Schaub et al. 2006 (college students, marijuana) **NORTH AMERICA** *United States*: Hoaken & Stewart 2003 (marijuana) |

criminality yet found (Farrington 1986a; Viemero 1996), except in the case of illegal drug use (Stattin & Magnusson 1991).

As with criminality per se, studies of antisocial behavior and adult physical aggression have concluded that these phenomena are positively correlated (Table 6.1.2b).

## 6.1.3 Anxiety

Are criminals more or less anxious than persons in general? As shown in Table 6.1.3a, the evidence thus far has been mixed. Regarding officially detected offending, the research indicates that anxiety is unusually low, but for self-reported offending, there seems to be a tendency toward the opposite pattern.

As with criminality per se, the research on a statistical link between antisocial behavior and anxiety has been mixed (Table 6.1.3b).

## 6.1.4 Boredom Proneness

Boredom is a subjective feeling of dissatisfaction with one's environment as being too ordinary and lacking in sufficient variation as to maintain attention and interest. So far, the available studies indicate that criminals are more likely to feel bored than are persons in general.

**TABLE 6.1.1b** Aggression in General and Clinical or Personality Traits Associated with Criminality.

| Nature of the relationship | Antisocial behavior | | Drug abuse |
|---|---|---|---|
| | Childhood & early adol. | Late adol. & adulthood | |
| Positive | **NORTH AMERICA** *Canada*: Nagin & Tremblay 1999 (males); Broidy et al. 2003; Santesso et al. 2006 (externalizing behavior); *United States*: Maughan et al. 2000; Schaeffer et al. 2003:1028 (males) **OCEANIA** *New Zealand*: Ehrensaft et al. 2004 (domestic violence); Jaffee et al. 2006 (domestic violence) | **NORTH AMERICA** *United States*: Brandt et al. 1997 (adol. offenders); Loeber & Hay 1997; GM Vincent et al. 2003 (among offenders) | **NORTH AMERICA** *United States*: CS Martin et al. 1994 (adol. males); McCormick & Smith 1995; TJ Allen et al. 1997 |
| Not signif. | | | |
| Negative | | | |

**TABLE 6.1.2a Aggression in Childhood and Criminal/Delinquent Behavior.**

| Nature of the relationship | Officially detected offenses | | | | | Self-reported offenses | |
|---|---|---|---|---|---|---|---|
| | Violent offenses | Drug offenses | Delinquency | General & adult offenses | Recidivism | Overall offenses | Illegal drugs |
| Positive | **EUROPE** *Finland*: Pulkkinen 1983; Pulkkinen & Pitkanen 1993 **NORTH AMERICA** *United States*: Justice et al. 1974; Huesmann et al. 1984* (aggression at age 8, spouse abuse at age 30) | **NORTH AMERICA** *Canada*: Dobkin et al. 1995; *United States*: Kellam et al. 1983 | **EUROPE** *Britain*: Farrington 1979; Stattin & Magnusson 1989; Rutter et al. 1998; *Finland*: Viemero 1992; *Scotland*: Mulligan et al. 1963:1085* **NORTH AMERICA** *Canada*: Nagin & Tremblay 1999; *United States*: Havighurst et al. 1962; Feldhurst et al. 1973; Farley & Sewell 1976; Loney et al. 1981; Stattin & Magnusson 1989* (males, teacher rating of aggression); Pakiz et al. 1992; Cairns & Cairns 1994; Kellam et al. 1994; Pakiz et al. 1997; Bierman et al. 2002 **INTERNATIONAL** *Multiple Countries*: Broidy et al. 2003* (males) | **EUROPE** *Finland*: Viemero 1996; *Britain*: Magnusson et al. 1983; Farrington 1986b; Stattin & Magnusson 1991; *Sweden*: Kirkegaard-Sorensen & Mednick 1977; Olweus 1980 **NORTH AMERICA** *United States*: Kandel et al. 1976b; Huesmann et al. 1984 *(at age 30, DWIs & traffic violations); EM Cummings et al. 1989; Kupersmidt & Coie 1990; Brook et al. 1996; Huesmann et al. 2002; Juon et al. 2006 | **EUROPE** *Britain*: Mulligan et al. 1963*; *Finland*: Pulkkinen 1983 **NORTH AMERICA** *United States*: Wenk et al. 1972 | **EUROPE** *Britain*: Farrington 1986* **NORTH AMERICA** *Canada*: Haapasalo & Tremblay 1994; Tremblay et al. 1995b; *United States*: Huesmann et al. 1984*; Loeber 1988; Loeber & Hay 1997 (violent delinquency); Coie & Dodge 1998 (delinquency) | **NORTH AMERICA** *United States*: Robins et al. 1970; Kay et al. 1978; Kellam et al. 1980; Kellam & Brown 1982; Kellam et al. 1983*; Baumrind 1985; Block et al. 1988; Shedler & Block 1990; Brook et al. 1992; Dukarm et al. 1996; TJ Allen et al. 1997 |
| Not signif. | | | **NORTH AMERICA** *United States*: Stattin & Magnusson 1989* (females, teacher rating of aggression **INTERNATIONAL** *Multiple Countries*: Broidy et al. 2003* (females) | | | | |
| Negative | | | | | | | **EUROPE** *Sweden*: Stattin & Magnusson 1984 |

**TABLE 6.1.2b Aggression in Childhood and Clinical or Personality Traits Associated with Criminality.**

| Nature of the relationship | Antisocial behavior | | Physical aggression |
|---|---|---|---|
| | Childhood & early adol. | Late adol. & adulthood | |
| Positive | **NORTH AMERICA** *United States*: Stewart et al. 1981; Biederman et al. 1996a:1198 | **EUROPE** *Finland*: Viemero 1992 **NORTH AMERICA** *United States*: Cadoret & Stewart 1991; Robins et al. 1991 | **NORTH AMERICA** *United States*: Liu & Kaplan 2004 (self-reported, aggression in adulthood) |
| Not signif. | | | |
| Negative | | | |

**TABLE 6.1.3a Anxiety and Criminal/Delinquent Behavior.**

| Nature of the relationship | Officially detected offenses | | | Self-reported offenses |
|---|---|---|---|---|
| | Delinquency | Recidivism | Overall offenses | Illegal drugs |
| Positive | | | **EUROPE** *Belgium*: Vermeiren et al. 2004:572* | **OCEANIA** *New Zealand*: Woodward & Fergusson 2000 (females) |
| Not signif. | | | **NORTH AMERICA** *United States*: Vermeiren et al. 2004:572* | |
| Negative | **NORTH AMERICA** *Canada*: Tremblay et al. 2003; *United States*: LJ Walker et al. 1991 | **NORTH AMERICA** *United States*: Quay & Love 1977 (delinquency) | | |

One study of a possible link between boredom and antisocial behavior indicates that as with criminality, persons who exhibit antisocial traits are more often bored than is true for those in the general population (Table 6.1.4b).

## 6.1.5 Bullying

Bullying refers to the tendency to dominate others through intimidation and physical aggression. Most studies of bullying have involved children. To measure bullying, researchers have used ratings by teachers, counselors, parents, and peers (Jonsson 1967:205), as well as self-reports (Connell & Farrington 1997; Power et al. 1997:210). Table 6.1.5a shows that all studies have found a positive relationship between bullying and delinquent/criminal behavior.

**TABLE 6.1.3b Anxiety and Clinical or Personality Traits Associated with Criminality.**

| Nature of the relationship | Antisocial behavior Late adol. & adulthood |
|---|---|
| Positive | **NORTH AMERICA** *United States*: Robins et al. 1991; Levenson et al. 1995; Goodwin & Hamilton 2003; SR Ross et al. 2004; Sareen et al. 2004; BF Grant et al. 2005a; JP Newman et al. 2005* (secondary) |
| Not signif. | **EUROPE** *Sweden*: Skeem et al. 2007* (among prisoners, secondary) |
| Negative | **EUROPE** *Sweden*: Skeem et al. 2007* (among prisoners, primary) **NORTH AMERICA** *United States*: Frick et al. 2000; Verona et al. 2001 (especially primary psychopathy); JP Newman et al. 2005* (primary) |

According to Table 6.1.5b, bullies are more likely than non-bullies to exhibit antisocial behavior and physical aggression in general.

## 6.1.6 Callousness

Callousness is a temperamental attitude of insensitivity, indifference, and lack of sympathy or concern for the suffering of others. Table 6.1.6a shows that the one available study of callousness and criminality found these traits to be positively correlated.

The research pertaining to a possible relationship between callousness and both antisocial behavior and physical aggression has concluded that the relationship is positive (Table 6.1.6b).

## 6.1.7 Extroversion

*Extroversion* refers to people's varying tendencies to be spontaneous and outgoing in social circumstances. This personality trait is usually measured by asking subjects a series of questions about their preferences for being in lively social gatherings as opposed to being alone or in quiet company, and then combining the responses into a single extroversion measure (Francis & Pearson 1988:913).

**TABLE 6.1.4a Boredom Proneness and Delinquent/ Criminal Behavior.**

| Nature of the relationship | Self-reported offenses Overall offenses |
|---|---|
| Positive | **NORTH AMERICA** *Canada*: Wasson 1981; *United States*: Ellis & Thompson 1989; Cochran et al. 1994; Wood et al. 1995 |
| Not signif. | |
| Negative | |

TABLE 6.1.4b Boredom proneness and Clinical or Personality Traits Associated with Criminality.

| Nature of the relationship | Antisocial behavior Late adol. & adulthood |
|---|---|
| Positive | **NORTH AMERICA** *United States*: Levenson et al. 1995:153 |
| Not signif. | |
| Negative | |

TABLE 6.1.5b Bullying and Clinical or Personality Traits Associated with Criminality.

| Nature of the relationship | Antisocial behavior | Physical aggression |
|---|---|---|
| | Childhood & early adol. | |
| Positive | **NORTH AMERICA** *United States*: Russo et al. 1994:64; Biederman et al. 1996b:1199 | **ASIA** *Korea*: YS Kim et al. 2006 |
| Not Signif. | | |
| Negative | | |

As shown in Table 6.1.7a, most studies have found extroverts being more involved in crime than their introverted counterparts. Nevertheless, quite a few studies have failed to find significant correlations in this regard.

Most studies of persons exhibiting varying degrees of antisocial behavior have concluded that such behavior is positively correlated with tendencies to be extroverted (Table 6.1.7b).

TABLE 6.1.6a Callousness and Criminal/Delinquent Behavior.

| Nature of the relationship | Self-reported offenses |
|---|---|
| | Overall offenses |
| Positive | **NORTH AMERICA** *United States*: Frick et al. 2003 (in childhood) |
| Not signif. | |
| Negative | |

## 6.1.8 Gambling

Research findings having to do with compulsive gambling and criminality will be reviewed in Chapter 7. In Table 6.1.8, however, the results of one study of recreational gambling and criminality are reported. As one can see, this study found that adolescent drug offenders were more likely to engage in such gambling than the average individual.

## 6.1.9 Hostility/Easily Angered (Having a Quick Temper)

When challenged or subjected to stress, some people respond angrily, whereas others seem to control their emotions. Table 6.1.9a shows that there appears to be a consistent tendency for persons who "quickly fly off the handle" when irritated to be involved in crime to a greater degree than their more reserved counterparts.

As with criminality per se, persons who are antisocial or who are drug abusers seem to be unusually prone toward

TABLE 6.1.5a Bullying and Criminal/Delinquent Behavior.

| Nature of the relationship | Officially detected offenses | | | | Self-reported offenses |
|---|---|---|---|---|---|
| | Violent offenses | Delinquency | General & adult offenses | Recidivism | Overall offenses |
| Positive | **EUROPE** *Britain*: Farrington 1993c | **EUROPE** *Sweden*: Jonsson 1967:205; *Norway*: Olweus 1993 | **NORTH AMERICA** *United States*: Cairns & Cairns 1994:227 | **EUROPE** *Britain*: Farrington 1989a; *Scotland*: Beck 1994; Power et al. 1997 **OCEANIA** *Hawaii*: Werner & Smith 1992:113 | **EUROPE** *Switzerland*: Killias & Rabasa 1997 **PACIFIC** *Australia*: Rigby & Cox 1996 |
| Not signif. | | | | | |
| Negative | | | | | |

**TABLE 6.1.6b** Callousness and Clinical or Personality Traits Associated with Criminality.

| Nature of the relationship | Antisocial behavior | | Physical aggression |
|---|---|---|---|
| | Childhood & early adol. | Adult & late adol. | |
| Positive | **NORTH AMERICA** *United States*: RJ Blair 1999; Frick et al. 2003* | **NORTH AMERICA** *United States*: Burke et al. 2007 | **NORTH AMERICA** *United States*: Frick et al. 2003* |
| Not signif. | | | |
| Negative | | | |

exhibiting hostile responses to stressful circumstances (Table 6.1.9b).

## 6.1.10 Impulsivity/Disinhibited

The concept of *impulsivity* (or *impulsiveness*) refers to the varying tendencies of people to act quickly, without giving much forethought to the consequences (Jensen & Garfinkel 1988:111). One way this concept has been measured is to ask subjects to imagine hypothetical scenarios that could elicit impulsive responses and ask them how they think they would in fact respond (Arbuthnot et al. 1987:148). In the case of young children, researchers usually rely on assessments made by parents and teachers (Vitiello et al. 1990:112).

Studies have revealed that impulsivity is comprised of two fairly distinct dimensions. One area involves how quickly people come to decisions (e.g., "I make up my mind quickly"), and the other pertains to how persistent people are in carrying out long-term tasks (e.g., "I don't like work that always demands extreme patience and care") (Barratt 1994:63).

Nearly all of the research concerning impulsivity and delinquent/criminal behavior has yielded fairly consistent findings as shown in Table 6.1.10a. According to studies in many countries, impulsive individuals have a higher probability of committing crimes than is true for people in general (for an earlier review drawing the same conclusion see Bassarath 2001).

According to Table 6.1.10b, impulsive people also have been shown to have elevated probabilities of exhibiting conduct disorders, psychopathy, and externalizing behavior. One study also suggested that these individuals were unusually aggressive.

## 6.1.11 Lying/Deception

Everyone lies at least occasionally, but some do so habitually and in ways that often hurt others. According to Table 6.1.11a, lying is considerably more common among persons who engage in criminality most often when compared with those who are more law abiding.

As appears to be the case for criminality, lying and deception have been found to be more common among persons diagnosed as antisocial than among persons in general (Table 6.1.11b).

## 6.1.12 Neuroticism

Neuroticism is one of psychology's "big five" personality traits, and can be defined as a chronic tendency to experience negative emotional states such as depression, anxiety, and anger. People high on the neuroticism scale are emotionally volatile and gravitate toward negative emotions. The findings from various studies of how neuroticism might be associated with criminality are shown in Table 6.1.11a. Overall, about equal numbers of studies have found neurotics to be more criminal as have failed to find any significant association between neuroticism and offending.

Only a couple of studies have examined a possible connection between neuroticism and conduct disorders in children. Table 6.1.12b suggests that the relationship is either positive or nonexistent.

## 6.1.13 Novelty Seeking

Novelty seeking involves looking for unusual experiences and may be indicative of restlessness and boredom. This trait is considered a major type of sensation seeking (Zuckerman 1978). Table 6.1.13a indicates that novelty seeking is positively correlated with involvement in crime and delinquency, although the only evidence currently available is based on self-reported offending.

The one pertinent study linking novelty seeking with physical aggression suggested that the two are positively correlated (Table 6.1.13b).

## 6.1.14 Psychoticism

*Psychoticism* refers to a personality pattern typified by aggressiveness and interpersonal hostility, often to the point of mental instability (Eysenck & Nias 1978:239; Heath and Martin 1990:111). Studies of psychoticism and criminality are summarized in Table 6.1.14a. As the table clearly shows, there appears to be a positive connection between psychoticism and involvement in crime and delinquency.

TABLE 6.1.7a Extroversion and Delinquent/Criminal Behavior.

| Nature of the relationship | Officially detected offenses | | | | | | Self-reported offenses |
|---|---|---|---|---|---|---|---|
| | Property offenses | Drug offenses | Delinquency | General & adult offenses | Recidivism | Overall offenses | Illegal drugs |
| Positive | | **ASIA** *Russia*: Knyazev 2004 (adol.) | **ASIA** *India*: Shanmugam 1980; Singh 1980 **EUROPE** *Britain*: Price 1968; Eysenck & Eysenck 1978:207; Lane & Hymans 1982; Farrington 1997b:100* **NORTH AMERICA** *Canada*: Saklofske & Eysenck 1980; *United States*: McCord 1977; Ensminger et al. 1983 **OCEANIA** *Australia*: Bartholomew 1963 | **EUROPE** *Britain*: Burgess 1972; Eysenck & Eysenck 1973; G Wilson & MacLean 1974; *Poland*: Sanocki 1969 | **EUROPE** *Britain*: Eysenck & Eysenck 1970 | **ASIA** *China*: Ma et al. 1996:262 **EUROPE** *Britain*: Gibson 1967; Allsopp & Feldman 1974; Shapland & Rushton 1975; Allsopp & Feldman 1976; SB Eysenck 1981; Rushton & Chrisjohn 1981; Farrington 1992; Farrington 1997b:100* **NORTH AMERICA** *Canada*: Cote & Leblanc 1982; *United States*: Siegman 1963; Hindalang 1971:26; Hindalang & Weis 1972:272; Hogan & Jones 1983:17 **OCEANIA** *Australia*: Saklofske et al. 1978; Heaven 1996:748 | **EUROPE** *Spain*: Calafat et al. 1994 **NORTH AMERICA** *United States*: Kay et al. 1978; Shanmugan 1979; Wingard et al. 1979:140; Segal 1983; Chassin 1984 |
| Not signif. | **EUROPE** *Netherlands*: Buikhuisen & Hemmel 1972 | | **EUROPE** *Britain*: Bartholomew 1959; Hoghughi & Forrest 1970*; West & Farrington 1973; Allsopp 1975; Putins 1982; Lane 1987; *Portugal*: Fonseca & Yule 1995 **MIDDLE EAST** *Israel*: Addad & Leslau 1990 | **EUROPE** *Britain*: Eysenck & Eysenck 1970 **OCEANIA** *New Zealand*: Black & Gregson 1973 | | **EUROPE** *Britain*: DJ West & Farrington 1973:198; Furnham 1984:416 | **NORTH AMERICA** *United States*: Cookson 1994 |
| Negative | | | **EUROPE** *Scotland*: Hoghughi & Forrest 1970:247*; Forrest 1977 | | | | |

**TABLE 6.1.7b** Extroversion and Clinical or Personality Traits Associated with Criminality.

| Nature of the relationship | Antisocial behavior | |
|---|---|---|
| | Childhood & early adol. | Late adol. & adulthood |
| Positive | **EUROPE** *Britain*: Lane 1987 **NORTH AMERICA** *United States*: Gabry et al. 1988 | **NORTH AMERICA** *United States*: Stewart & Leone 1978 |
| Not signif. | **EUROPE** *Britain*: Tranah et al. 1998 | |
| Negative | | |

**TABLE 6.1.8** Gambling and Delinquent/Criminal Behavior.

| Nature of the relationship | Officially detected offenses |
|---|---|
| | Drug offenses |
| Positive | **EUROPE** *Britain*: Griffiths & Sutherland 1998 (adol.) |
| Not signif. | |
| Negative | |

**TABLE 6.1.9a** Hostility/Easy to Anger (Having a Quick Temper) and Delinquent/Criminal Behavior.

| Nature of the relationship | Self-reported offenses | |
|---|---|---|
| | Overall offenses | Illegal drugs |
| Positive | **NORTH AMERICA** *Canada*: LaGrange & Silverman 1999* (property & violent offenses); *United States*: Agnew 1985a (respond to stress with anger); Berkowitz 1990 (respond to stress with anger); Mazerolle & Piquero 1997 (respond to stress with anger); Mazerolle & Piquero 1998 (respond to stress with anger); Broidy 2001 (respond to stress with anger); RL Simons et al. 2004 (respond to stress with anger) | **NORTH AMERICA** *Canada*: LaGrange & Silverman 1999* |
| Not signif. | | |
| Negative | | |

**TABLE 6.1.9b** Hostility/Easy to Anger (Having a Quick Temper) and Clinical or Personality Traits Associated with Criminality.

| Nature of the relationship | Antisocial behavior | Drug abuse |
|---|---|---|
| | Late adol. & adulthood | |
| Positive | **OCEANIA** *New Zealand*: Krueger et al. 1996 | **NORTH AMERICA** *United States*: Yudofsky et al. 1993 (cocaine use); RA McCormick & Smith 1995; Patkar et al. 2003:438 (cocaine use, blacks) |
| Not signif. | | |
| Negative | | |

In addition to being positively associated with criminality (as indicated by the previous table), Table 6.1.14b suggests that psychoticism is positively correlated with childhood conduct disorder.

## 6.1.15 Risk Taking/Recklessness

Risk taking and reckless behavior refers to a willingness to sustain injury or even death in order to obtain some goal. Table 6.1.15 summarizes the research findings on the relationship between risk taking and recklessness and criminality and suggests that a substantial positive correlation exists.

## 6.1.16 Self-Control

In putting forth a well-known criminological theory, Gottfredson and Hirschi (1990:87) define *self-control* as "the extent to which [individuals] are vulnerable to the temptations of the moment". Elsewhere in their book, these authors note that low self-control also encompasses traits such as an orientation to the present, risk taking, self-centeredness, and lacking in patience.

If one examines most of the operational measures of self-control, nearly all of the indicators focus on issues of obedience, civility, and compliance with authority (Perrone et al. 2004:302). These aspects of behavior are almost by definition inversely correlated with violating criminal statutes.

As seen in Table 6.1.16a, self-control has attracted much criminological research interest. The evidence suggests overwhelmingly that criminals and delinquents have lower levels of self-control than people in general. According to a meta-analysis by Pratt and Cullen (2000), most studies indicate that self-control accounts for about 7% of the variance in delinquent and criminal behavior.

**TABLE 6.1.10a Impulsivity and Delinquent/Criminal Behavior.**

| Nature of the relationship | Officially detected offenses | | | | | Self-reported offenses | |
|---|---|---|---|---|---|---|---|
| | | Drug offenses | Delinquency | General & adult offenses | Recidivism | Overall offenses | Illegal drugs |
| Positive | **NORTH AMERICA** *United States*: Pallone & Hennessy 1996 | **NORTH AMERICA** *United States*: WR Miller & Brown 1991; WL Johnson et al. 1993; MS Stanford et al. 1996 | **ASIA** *India*: Misra 1983:35 **EUROPE** *Britain*: HB Gibson 1964; Eysenck & Eysenck 1971; Foggitt 1974; Eysenck & McGurk 1980; Osborn & West 1980; Farrington 1995b; *Finland*: Pulkkinen et al. 2000; *Germany*: Schwenkmezger 1983; *Spain*: Romero et al. 2001 **MIDDLE EAST** *Israel*: Rotenberg & Nachson 1979 **NORTH AMERICA** *Canada*: Tremblay et al. 1994*; Kerr et al. 1996; *United States*: Healy & Bronner 1936:62; Doctor & Winter 1954; Eisen 1956 (females); Gibbens 1958; Hathaway et al. 1960; Gough 1971; GF Jensen 1973:466; Curtiss et al. 1979; Oas 1983; Widom et al. 1983; Roff & Wirt 1984:115; Royse & Wiehe 1988; Mak 1990; Mak 1991; Feldman & Weinberger 1994; JL White et al. 1994*; Lynam et al. 2000* (males, living in poor neighborhoods); Vitacco & Rogers 2001; Vitacco et al. 2002 **OCEANIA** *Australia*: A Carroll et al. 2006 (males); *New Zealand*: Lynam et al. 1993:193; White et al. 1994; B Henry et al. 1996; Bartusch et al. 1997; Lynam et al. 2000*; Moffitt et al. 2002 | **EUROPE** *Britain*: Farrington 1993a:15 **NORTH AMERICA** *Canada*: Fedora & Reddon 1993:329; *United States*: Guze et al. 1969; Barratt 1994:64; Lynam et al. 2000* **OCEANIA** *New Zealand*: RF Krueger et al. 1994 | **NORTH AMERICA** *United States*: Erickson & Roberts 1966; AH Roberts et al. 1974; Tinklenberg et al. 1996 | **EUROPE** *Britain*: SB Eysenck 1981; *Spain*: Ortet et al. 1988; Luengo et al. 1994 **NORTH AMERICA** *Canada*: Tremblay et al. 1994*; Kerr et al. 1997; LaGrange & Silverman 1999* (males, property & violent offenses, under age 18); *United States*: Marohn et al. 1971; Hindelang 1972:77; DC Rowe 1986:523; Grasmick et al. 1993; Lynam et al. 1993:194; PB Wood et al. 1993; Caspi et al. 1994; JL White et al. 1994*; Longshore et al. 1996; Vazsonyi et al. 2006:527 (delinquency) **OCEANIA** *Australia*: Mak 1987; Heaven 1989; Rigby et al. 1989; Heaven 1993:71; *New Zealand*: White et al. 1994* (delinquency); Wright et al. 1999b (at age 15 & 21, teacher & parent rated) | **ASIA** *China*: Wong et al. 1997 **EUROPE** *Britain*: Bushnell et al. 1996 **NORTH AMERICA** *Canada*: LaGrange & Silverman 1999* (under age 18, females); PJ Conrod et al. 2000; *United States*: White et al. 1987:729; CS Martin et al. 1994 (adolescent males); Wood et al. 1995; KT Brady et al. 1998; Curran et al. 2000 (marijuana use); Kaplow et al. 2002; Patkar et al. 2003 (cocaine use, blacks) |
| Not signif. | | | **NORTH AMERICA** *United States*: Lynam et al. 2000* (males, living in good neighborhoods) | | | **NORTH AMERICA** *United States*: Saunders et al. 1973 | |
| Negative | | | | | | | |

**TABLE 6.1.10b** Impulsivity and Clinical or Personality Traits Associated with Criminality.

| Nature of the relationship | Antisocial behavior | | Physical aggression | Mental illness or disorder |
|---|---|---|---|---|
| | Childhood & early adol. | Late adol. & adulthood | | |
| Positive | **EUROPE** *Britain*: Sandberg et al. 1978; Farrington et al. 1990; Farrington 1997a:100; Tranah et al. 1998 **NORTH AMERICA** *Canada*: Tremblay et al. 1994 *United States*: Dodge & Newman 1981; McDermott 1993:422 | **EUROPE** *Britain*: Blackburn 1969; *Spain*: Silva et al. 1986 **NORTH AMERICA** *Canada*: Hare 1982:270; Belmore & Quinsey 1994; *United States*: Kipnis 1971; Schalling 1978:95; Heilbrun 1982:553; Oas 1985; Dickman 1990; DJ Miller et al. 2003 | **NORTH AMERICA** *United States*: Hollander & Stein 1995 | **NORTH AMERICA** *United States*: Bates et al. 1998 (externalizing behavior) **OCEANIA** *New Zealand*: Caspi et al. 1995 (externalizing behavior) |
| Not signif. | **EUROPE** *Britain*: Farrington 1993a:15 | | | |
| Negative | | | | |

**TABLE 6.1.11a** Lying/Deception and Criminal/Delinquent Behavior.

| Nature of the relationship | Officially detected offenses | | | Self-reported offenses | |
|---|---|---|---|---|---|
| | Property offenses | Delinquency | General & adult offenses | Overall offenses | Illegal drugs |
| Positive | **NORTH AMERICA** *United States*: McCord 1977 | **EUROPE** *Britain*: Farrington 1981; Farrington 1987a:31 **NORTH AMERICA** *United States*: Mitchell & Rosa 1981 (Lying and deception); Wiebe 2006:525 | **EUROPE** *Britain*: Farrington 1993a:15; *Finland*: Pulkkinen 1983 | **NORTH AMERICA** *United States*: Rowe 1986:523 | **NORTH AMERICA** *United States*: Catalano et al. 1996 (cheating in school) |
| Not signif. | | | | | |
| Negative | | | | | |

**TABLE 6.1.11b** Lying/Deception and Clinical or Personality Traits Associated with Criminality.

| Nature of the relationship | Antisocial behavior | |
|---|---|---|
| | Childhood & early adol. | Late adol. & adulthood |
| Positive | **NORTH AMERICA** *United States*: Rowe 1986 | **NORTH AMERICA** *Canada*: Seto et al. 1997 **OCEANIA** *New Zealand*: Mulder et al. 1994:282 |
| Not signif. | | |
| Negative | | |

As with delinquency and criminality per se, the evidence supporting a link between low self-control and factors frequently related to criminality is very supportive (Table 6.1.1.16b).

## 6.1.17 Sensation Seeking

Sensation seeking refers to the active desire for novel, varied, and extreme experiences often to the point of taking physical and social risks to obtain these experiences (Zuckerman et al. 1990). Because sensation – seeking is positively associated with impulsiveness and fearlessness (other correlates of crime) (Gatzke-Kopp et al. 2002), it is not surprising that the evidence supporting a positive link between sensation seeking and delinquent and

TABLE 6.1.12a Neuroticism and Criminal/Delinquent Behavior.

| Nature of the relationship | Officially detected offenses | | | Self-reported offenses |
|---|---|---|---|---|
| | Delinquency | General & adult offenses | Recidivism | Overall offenses |
| Positive | **ASIA** *India*: Singh (females) 1980 **EUROPE** *Britain*: Bartholomew 1959; Lane 1987; Farrington 1992 **MIDDLE EAST** *Israel*: Addad & Leslau 1990 **OCEANIA** *Australia*: Bartholomew 1963 | **ASIA** *Bangladesh*: Rahman & Husain 1984 **EUROPE** *Britain*: PK Burgess 1972; Farrington 1993a:16 | | **ASIA** *China*: Ma et al. 1996:262 **EUROPE** *Britain*: Shapland & Rushton 1975; Allsopp & Feldman 1976 |
| Not signif. | **EUROPE** *Britain*: Hoghughi & Forrest 1970; West & Farrington 1973; Putins 1982; *Scotland*: Forrest 1977 | **EUROPE** *Poland*: Sanocki 1969 | **EUROPE** *Britain*: Eysenck & Eysenck 1970 | **EUROPE** *Britain*: Rushton & Chrisjohn 1981; Furnham 1984:416 **OCEANIA** *New Zealand*: Saklofske et al. 1978 |
| Negative | | | | |

TABLE 6.1.12b Neuroticism and Clinical or Personality Traits Associated with Criminality.

| Nature of the relationship | Antisocial behavior |
|---|---|
| | Childhood & early adol. |
| Positive | **NORTH AMERICA** *United States*: Gabrys 1983 |
| Not signif. | **EUROPE** *Britain*: Tranah et al. 1998 |
| Negative | |

criminal behavior shown in Table 6.1.17a has been well documented.

As shown in Table 6.1.17b, all of the available research suggests that sensation seeking and other factors associated with criminality are positively correlated.

TABLE 6.1.13a Novelty Seeking and Criminal/Delinquent Behavior.

| Nature of the relationship | Self-reported offenses | |
|---|---|---|
| | Overall offenses | Illegal drugs |
| Positive | **EUROPE** *Germany*: Barnow et al. 2005 (delinquency) | **NORTH AMERICA** *United States*: Wills et al. 1994; Sher et al. 1995; Wills et al. 1995 |
| Not signif. | | |
| Negative | | |

TABLE 6.1.13b Novelty Seeking Clinical or Personality Traits Associated with Criminality.

| Nature of the Relationship | Physical aggression |
|---|---|
| Positive | **EUROPE** *Germany*: Barnow et al. 2005 |
| Not signif. | |
| Negative | |

## 6.1.18 Shyness

Only one study of a possible association between shyness and criminality was located (Table 6.1.18). Based on teacher ratings, the study concluded that aggressive forms of delinquency were positively correlated with shyness, but that the opposite was found for nonaggressive forms of delinquency.

## 6.1.19 Short Attention Span/Attention Problems

A short attention span is the inability to focus on a given task or activity for a substantial amount of time. The opposite of a short attention span is known as tenacity or task persistence. A short attention span is part of the wider syndrome of ADHD (attention deficit hyperactivity disorder), discussed in Chapter 7. The two available studies specific to a short attention span both indicate a positive correlation with offending (Table 6.1.19).

**TABLE 6.1.14a** Psychoticism and Criminal/Delinquent Behavior.

| Nature of the relationship | Officially detected offenses | | | Self-reported offenses |
|---|---|---|---|---|
| | Delinquency | General & adult offenses | Recidivism | Overall offenses |
| Positive | **EUROPE** *Britain*: Putins 1982; Lane 1987; *Scotland*: Forrest 1977<br>**OCEANIA** *Australia*: Heaven 1994; Heaven 1996:748 | **ASIA** *Bangladesh*: Rahman & Husain 1984<br>**EUROPE** *Britain*: Eysenck & Eysenck 1970*; PK Burgess 1972; GD Wilson & McLean 1974 | **EUROPE** *Britain*: DE Smith & Smith 1977 | **ASIA** *China*: Ma et al. 1996:262<br>**EUROPE** *Britain*: Allsopp & Feldman 1974; Allsopp & Feldman 1976; Rushton & Chrisjohn 1981; Furnham 1984:416<br>**NORTH AMERICA** *Canada*: Cote & Leblanc 1982<br>**OCEANIA** *Australia*: Heaven 1993:71; Heaven 1994:452; *New Zealand*: Saklofske et al. 1978 |
| Not signif. | | | **EUROPE** *Britain*: Eysenck & Eysenck 1970* | |
| Negative | | | | |

**TABLE 6.1.14b** Psychoticism and Clinical or Personality Traits Associated with Criminality.

| Nature of the relationship | Antisocial behavior |
|---|---|
| | Childhood & early adol. |
| Positive | **EUROPE** *Britain*: Tranah et al. 1998<br>**NORTH AMERICA** *United States*: Gabry 1983 |
| Not signif. | |
| Negative | |

## 6.1.20 Time Estimation

According to the single available study, when left in a room to wait for a specific amount of time, delinquents estimate the wait-time to be longer than did age peers (Table 6.1.20).

## 6.1.21 Trustworthiness

Trustworthiness refers to the extent to which people will do what they promise or what is reasonably expected of them. To measure such tendencies, social scientists usually rely on reports by parents, teachers, and peers (Loeber & Stouthhamer-Loeber 1987:337). Studies attempting to

**TABLE 6.1.15** Risk Taking/Recklessness and Criminal/Delinquent Behavior.

| Nature of the relationship | Officially detected offenses | Self-reported offenses | |
|---|---|---|---|
| | Delinquency | Overall offenses | Illegal drugs |
| Positive | **EUROPE** *Spain*: Luengo et al. 1994<br>**NORTH AMERICA** *United States*: Harano et al. 1973; Harano 1975; Lewis & Shanok 1977; Shanok & Lewis 1981; Arnett 1992<br>**OCEANIA** *Australia*: Carroll et al. 2006:524 (males) | **EUROPE** *Sweden*: Dahlback 1990a; Dahlback 1990b<br>**NORTH AMERICA** *Canada*: LaGrange & Silverman 1999* (violent & property offenses); *United States*: Levine & Singer 1988; Herrenkohl et al. 2000 (violent delinquency); Junger et al. 2001 (reckless driving); Wiebe 2006:525<br>**OCEANIA** *New Zealand*: Wright et al. 1999 (at age 21) | **NORTH AMERICA** *Canada*: LaGrange & Silverman 1999*; *United States*: Hogan & Jones 1983:17 |
| Not signif. | | | |
| Negative | | | |

**TABLE 6.1.16a Self-Control and Criminal/Delinquent Behavior.**

| Nature of the relationship | Officially detected offenses | Self-reported offenses | |
|---|---|---|---|
| | Delinquency | Overall offenses | Illegal drugs |
| Positive | | | |
| Not signif. | | **NORTH AMERICA** *United States*: McGloin et al. 2004:622* (when GPA and deviant peer pressure were controlled) | |
| Negative | **NORTH AMERICA** *Canada*: Junger & Tremblay 1999; *United States*: Paternoster & Brame 1998; LaGrange & Silverman 1999; Cauffman et al. 2005; Doherty 2006:815 | **NORTH AMERICA** *Canada*: Tremblay & Craig 1995; SW Baron 2003; *United States*: Menard & Morse 1984; Arneklev et al. 1993; Brownfield & Sorenson 1993 (delinquency); Grasmick et al. 1993; Keane et al. 1993 (drunk driving); Nagin & Paternoster 1993; Wood et al. 1993; Burton et al. 1994; Polakowski 1994; DA Ward & Tittle 1994; Gibbs & Giever 1995; Longshore et al. 1996; Piquero & Tibbetts 1996 (drunk driving, shoplifting); Tibbetts & Herz 1996 (shoplifting); Evans et al. 1997; Tibbetts 1997 (shoplifting); Avakame 1998; Burton et al. 1998; Deng & Zhang 1998; Gibbs et al. 1998; Longshore 1998; Longshore & Turner 1998 (fraud & force crimes, by offenders); Paternoster & Brame 1998; Piquero & Rosay 1998; Burton et al. 1999; Sellers 1999 (violent offending); Hay 2001; Wright et al. 2001; Wiebe 2003 McGloin et al. 2004:621*; Perrone et al. 2004; Burt et al. 2006; Felson & Staff 2006; Wiebe 2006; Piquero & Bouffard 2007<br>**OCEANIA** *New Zealand*: Wright et al. 1999 (at childhood related to crime at age 21) | **NORTH AMERICA** *United States*: Winfree & Bernat 1998 |

determine if trustworthiness is associated with delinquent/criminal behavior are summarized in Table 6.1.21a. These studies have consistently concluded that an inverse relationship exists.

A few studies of persons with antisocial personality indicate that they are less trustworthy than those without the disorder (Table 6.1.21b).

## 6.2 ALCOHOL AND DRUG USE

Next to be considered are how the use of alcohol and various other drugs is related to the involvement in criminal and related behavior. Readers will see that a great amount of research has sought answers to the questions surrounding such relationships.

### 6.2.1 Alcohol Use

Alcohol is a neurologically active drug that is the most often used "recreational" (or nontherapeutic) drug in the world. Table 6.2.1a summarizes the evidence regarding an association between alcohol and drug use and criminality. Setting aside the illegality of possessing and consuming alcohol itself (in several countries), the evidence overwhelmingly

**TABLE 6.1.16b Self-Control and Clinical or Personality Traits Associated with Criminality.**

| Nature of the relationship | Antisocial behavior | Physical aggression | Cognitive & personality factors | Drug abuse |
|---|---|---|---|---|
| | Childhood & early adol. | | | |
| Positive | | | | |
| Not signif. | | | | |
| Negative | **NORTH AMERICA** *United States*: Brownfield & Sorenson 1993 (delinquency); Polakowski 1994 (delinquency); Hay 2001*; Doherty 2006:815 (delinquency) | **NORTH AMERICA** *United States*: Avakame 1998; Unnever & Cornell 2003 (bullying); Liu & Kaplan 2004 (females, adults) | **NORTH AMERICA** *United States*: Gibbs & Giever 1995* (cheating); Cochran et al. 1998 (cheating); Tibbetts & Herz 1999 (cheating); Bichler-Robertson et al. 2003 (cheating); Muraven et al. 2006 (cheating) | **NORTH AMERICA** *United States*: Arneklev et al. 1993; Gibbs & Giever 1995*; Forde & Kennedy 1997; Winfree & Bernat 1998 (adol.); Hay 2001* |

**TABLE 6.1.17a** Sensation Seeking and Criminal/Delinquent Behavior.

| Nature of the relationship | Officially detected offenses | | | Self-reported offenses | |
|---|---|---|---|---|---|
| | Drug offenses | Delinquency | General & adult offenses | Overall offenses | Illegal drugs |
| Positive | **NORTH AMERICA** *United States*: Scourfield et al. 1996 | **ASIA** *Russia*: Ruchkin et al. 1998b (between neighborhoods) **EUROPE** *Belgium*: Vermeiren et al. 2004:572*; *Germany*: Losel 1975; Schwenkmezger 1983 **NORTH AMERICA** *United States*: Fadey & Farley 1972*; Farley & Sewell 1976; Whitehill et al. 1976; Donnelly 1981:426; Serok 1981; Perez & Torrubia 1985*; Tremblay et al. 1994; Vermeiren et al. 2004:572* | **EUROPE** *Britain*: Farrington 1993a:16; Farrington 1997b:97*; *Spain*: Perez 1983a; *Sweden*: Dahlback 1990a; Dahlback 1990b **NORTH AMERICA** *United States*: Horvath & Zuckerman 1993 | **ASIA** *Russia*: Ruchkin et al. 1998 **EUROPE** *Belgium*: Simo & Perez 1991; Vermeiren et al. 2004:572* (delinquency); *Britain*: Otero-Lopez et al. 1994:472; Farrington 1997b:97* (risk taking); *Spain*: Perez 1983a; Perez & Torrubia 1985*; Luengo et al. 1994 **NORTH AMERICA** *United States*: Fadey & Farley 1972*; White et al. 1985; Cloninger 1987 (delinquency); Young 1990; Newcomb & McGee 1991; Wood et al. 1993; Arnett et al. 1997*; Vermeiren et al. 2004:572* **OCEANIA** *New Zealand*: DM Fergusson et al. 2002 (novelty seeking) | **EUROPE** *Britain*: Kohn & Annis 1977; *Spain*: Luengo et al. 1994 **MIDDLE EAST** *Israel*: Teichmann et al. 1989 **NORTH AMERICA** *United States*: Zuckerman et al. 1972; Jessor & Jessor 1977; Sutker et al. 1978; Segal et al. 1980; Galizio & Stein 1983; Hobfall & Segal 1983; Satinder & Black 1984; Jaffe & Archer 1987; Brook et al. 1988:151; Andrucci et al. 1989; TR Simon et al. 1994; Wood et al. 1995; Liu & Kaplan 1996; CS Tang et al. 1996; Arnett et al. 1997*; Dervaux et al. 2001; Patkar et al. 2003 (blacks, cocaine use) **OCEANIA** *Australia*: Andrew & Cronin 1997 |
| Not signif. | | | | **NORTH AMERICA** *United States*: Karoly 1975 | |
| Negative | | | | | **NORTH AMERICA** *United States*: AW Stacy 1997 (marijuana use); Forthun et al. 1999 (marijuana use) |

supports the conclusion that alcohol use and criminality are positively correlated.

Table 6.2.1b complements the preceding table pertaining to criminality by showing that antisocial personality is positively associated with alcohol consumption.

## 6.2.2 Illegal Drug Use in General

Most illegal (non-therapeutic) drugs can be subsumed under the following three categories: depressants, stimulants, and hallucinogens (Fishbein & Pease 1996). The main effect of depressants is to slow down the functioning of the brain; stimulants help to speed up brain functioning, and hallucinogens cause distortions in the brain's processing of perceptual information.

Studies that have examined the possible recreational drug use-criminality relationship are shown in Table 6.2.2a. As one can see, nearly all of the research findings have suggested that a positive correlation exists. Even the use of nicotine (usually via cigarette smoking) has been found to be positively associated with involvement in delinquent/criminal behavior (Watts & Wright 1990:180).

**TABLE 6.1.17b** Sensation Seeking and Clinical or Personality Traits Associated with Criminality.

| Nature of the relationship | Antisocial behavior | | Physical aggression |
|---|---|---|---|
| | Childhood & early adol. | Late adol. & adulthood | |
| Positive | **EUROPE** *Norway*: Thuen & Bendixen 1996:54 **NORTH AMERICA** *United States*: Orris 1969; Whitehill et al. 1976; DeMyer-Gapin & Scott 1977; Frick et al. 1995 | **EUROPE** *Britain*: Blackburn 1969 **NORTH AMERICA** *United States*: Quay 1965b; Emmons & Webb 1974 | **AFRICA** *Mauritius*: Raine et al. 1998 (at age 11) |
| Not signif. | | | |
| Negative | | | |

**TABLE 6.1.18 Shyness and Criminal/Delinquent Behavior.**

| Nature of the relationship | Self-reported offenses |
|---|---|
| | Overall offenses |
| Positive | **NORTH AMERICA** *United States*: Ensminger et al. 1983* (teacher-rated, delinquency, with aggression) |
| Not signif. | |
| Negative | **NORTH AMERICA** *United States*: Ensminger et al. 1983* (teacher-rated, delinquency, without aggression) |

As shown in Table 6.2.2b, as with delinquency and criminality, the evidence of a positive association between illegal recreational drug use and factors frequently associated with criminality is extremely strong.

### 6.2.3 Cigarette Smoking

Cigarettes contain nicotine, a drug that is vaporized and transported to the lungs when tobacco is burnt and the vapor is inhaled. Table 6.2.3a shows that individuals who smoke cigarettes are more likely than nonsmokers to self-report involvement in delinquent and criminal offenses.

As with criminality itself, the available evidence on factors such as antisocial behavior that are frequently associated with criminality suggests that these factors are positively associated with smoking cigarettes (Table 6.2.3b).

### 6.2.4 Marijuana Use

Evidence directly linking marijuana use with offending in general was not found. However, as shown in Table 6.2.4, some studies suggest that such use is positively correlated with childhood conduct disorders and with physical aggression

**TABLE 6.1.19 Short Attention Span/Attention Problems and Criminal/Delinquent Behavior.**

| Nature of the relationship | Officially detected offenses | Self-reported offenses |
|---|---|---|
| | General & adult offenses | Overall offenses |
| Positive | **NORTH AMERICA** *United States*: Silverton 1988a | **OCEANIA** *New Zealand*: Wright et al. 1999b (delinquency at age 15 & crime at age 21, parent rated) |
| Not signif. | | |
| Negative | | |

**TABLE 6.1.20 Time Estimation and Criminal/Delinquent Behavior.**

| Nature of the relationship | Officially detected offenses |
|---|---|
| | Delinquency |
| Estimated longer time lapse | **OCEANIA** *Australia*: Carroll et al. 2006:524 (males) |
| Not signif. | |
| Estimated shorter time lapse | |

**TABLE 6.1.21a Trustworthiness and Criminality/Antisocial Behavior.**

| Nature of the relationship | Self-reported offenses | |
|---|---|---|
| | Overall offenses | Illegal drugs |
| Positive | | |
| Not signif. | | |
| Negative | **NORTH AMERICA** *United States*: Hogan & Jones 1983:17 | **NORTH AMERICA** *United States*: Smith & Fogg 1975; Gulas & King 1976; Goldstein & Sappington 1977; Kay et al. 1978; Janes et al. 1979; Wingard et al. 1979 |

### 6.2.5 Age of Onset of Marijuana Use (Early)

According to one study of young adults who had ever consumed marijuana, those with the earliest onset of use self-reported more delinquency and criminality in general than later onset users (Table 6.2.5).

**TABLE 6.1.21b Trustworthiness and Clinical or Personality Traits Associated with Criminality.**

| Nature of the relationship | Antisocial behavior |
|---|---|
| | Late adol. & adulthood |
| Positive | |
| Not signif. | |
| Negative | **NORTH AMERICA** *United States*: Costa & McCrae 1990; Clark & Livesley 1994; Harper et al. 1994 |

**TABLE 6.2.1a** Alcohol use and Criminal/Delinquent Behavior.

| Nature of the relationship | Officially detected offenses | | | | | Self-reported offenses | |
|---|---|---|---|---|---|---|---|
| | Violent offenses | Property offenses | Delinquency | General & adult offenses | Recidivism | Overall offenses | Illegal drugs |
| Positive | **EUROPE** *Finland*: Virkkunen 1974; Rasanen et al. 1999 (drunk driving); *Scotland*: Gillies 1965; *Sweden*: Roslund & Larson 1979; Wiklund & Lidberg 1990 **NORTH AMERICA** *United States*: Mayfield 1976; Mungas 1983:360; T Myers 1986; Kantor & Straus 1990 (domestic violence); Pernanen 1991; RN Parker 1995 (homicide); K Graham et al. 1998; S Wells et al. 2000 **OCEANIA** *Australia*: I Smith 1990 | **NORTH AMERICA** *United States*: Cordilia 1985 | **EUROPE** *Belgium*: Vermeiren et al. 2004:572*; *Britain*: Farrington 1982:190; Farrington 1988:72; *Finland*: Pulkkinen 1982:27; *Sweden*: Rydelius 1983; Stattin et al. 1997:204* **NORTH AMERICA** *Canada*: Smart et al. 1997; *United States*: Blacker et al. 1965; Pearce & Garrett 1970; Glueck & Glueck 1974:150; Vermeiren et al. 2004:572* | **EUROPE** *Britain*: Hore 1988; *Germany*: Kerner 1993; *Scotland*: Crawford et al. 1982 **NORTH AMERICA** *Canada*: Seltzer & Langford 1984; *United States*: Shupe 1954; Grigsby 1963:304; Collins & Schlenger 1988; Almog et al. 1993 | **EUROPE** *Germany*: Kerner et al. 1997:418; *Sweden*: Stattin et al. 1997:204* **NORTH AMERICA** *United States*: Heller & Ehrlich 1984; Klassman & O'Connor 1988 | **EUROPE** *Belgium*: Vermeiren et al. 2004:572*; *Britain*: McMurran & Hollin 1989; Farrington & West 1990 **NORTH AMERICA** *Canada*: LaGrange & Silverman 1999 (property & violent offenses, under age 18); *United States*: Globett & Windham 1967; Watts & Wright 1990; Harford & Parker 1994; Fergusson et al. 1996; Zhang et al. 1997 Vermeiren et al. 2004:572* (delinquency) | **NORTH AMERICA** *United States*: Cockerham et al. 1976; Globetti et al. 1978; Eisterhold et al. 1979; Kirk 1979; Gibbons et al. 1986; DS Miller & Miller 1997 |
| Not signif. | | | | | | | |
| Negative | | | | | **NORTH AMERICA** *United States*: Menzies & Webster 1995 | | |

TABLE 6.2.1b Alcohol Use and Clinical or Personality Traits Associated with Criminality.

| Nature of the relationship | Antisocial behavior | | Cognitive & personality factors |
|---|---|---|---|
| | Childhood & early adol. | Late adol. & adulthood | |
| Positive | **ASIA** *Russia*: Parker et al. 1996 **NORTH AMERICA** *United States*: Robins et al.1962; KM Thompson & Wilsnack 1984; Helzer & Pryzbeck 1988; Windle 1990; Conger et al. 1991; EO Johnson et al. 1995:666; Moss & Kirisci 1995:645; Biederman et al. 1996a | **NORTH AMERICA** *Canada*: Mailloux et al. 1997 **OCEANIA** *New Zealand*: Mulder et al. 1994:283 | **NORTH AMERICA** *United States*: La Grange et al. 1995 (college students, sensation seeking) |
| Not signif. | | | |
| Negative | | | |

## 6.3 SEXUAL BEHAVIOR

The research findings pertaining to relationships between various aspects of sexual behavior and criminality are reviewed in the present section.

### 6.3.1 Sexuality (Mating) in General

According to evolutionary reasoning, the purpose of life is to produce more life. In sexually-reproducing animals, this "ultimate purpose" is achieved by combining so-called *mating effort* with *parenting effort*. Some animals devote high proportions of their total reproductive time and energy to mating while others focus mainly on parenting. Of course, most of the variation is between species in this regard, but within-species variations are also observable. Two research studies asked human subjects various questions about their sexual interests and desires, and concluded from the responses that the most crime-prone individuals seemed to focus greater time and energy on mating (and less on parenting) than did those who were the least crime-prone (Table 6.3.1a).

No research involving humans was found linking antisocial behavior or other crime-related traits with an emphasis on mating effort as one's approach to reproduction. However, three studies of male mice concluded that there was a positive correlation between physical aggression and a tendency to devote greater time to seeking females with which to copulate (Table 6.3.1b).

### 6.3.2 Premarital Sexual Intercourse

All of the available evidence indicates that there is a positive correlation between involvement with illegal drugs and sexual intercourse prior to marriage (Table 6.3.2).

### 6.3.3 Number of Sex Partners

Table 6.3.3a presents the findings of research concerning the number of self-reported sex partners and involvement in criminal/delinquent behavior. These studies have consistently shown that delinquents and criminals report having had more sex partners than is true for persons in general.

Most of the available studies of antisocial behavior and the number of sex partners one has had indicates that persons who are diagnosed as having either conduct disorders or psychopathy self-report having had more sex partners than do the population in general (Table 6.3.3b).

### 6.3.4 Age of Onset of Sexual Intercourse (Early)

Numerous studies have been designed to determine if delinquents and criminals begin engaging in sexual intercourse earlier than do persons who are law abiding. Table 6.3.4a shows that all of these studies have reached the same affirmative answer.

Several studies of the age at which persons who are diagnosed as antisocial first experience sexual intercourse have all concluded that they begin earlier on average than do persons without such diagnoses (Table 6.3.4b).

### 6.3.5 Emotional Intimacy with Sex Partner

According to one study, people who were most emotionally intimate with their sex partners as young adults self-reported committing fewer offenses than did those who were least emotionally intimate (Table 6.3.5).

**TABLE 6.2.2a Illegal Drug Use in General and Criminal/Delinquent Behavior.**

| Nature of the relationship | Officially detected offenses | | | | | Self-reported offenses |
|---|---|---|---|---|---|---|
| | Violent offenses | Property offenses | Delinquency | General & adult offenses | Recidivism | Overall offenses |
| Positive | **NORTH AMERICA** *United States*: Gardner & Shoemaker 1989 | **EUROPE** *Britain*: Farrington 1977 **NORTH AMERICA** *United States*: Kane & Patterson 1972; Forslund 1977; Donnermeyer et al. 1987 | **EUROPE** *Britain*: Farrington 1979; Farrington 1988:72; Nagin & Land 1993:352; Hagell & Newburn 1996:14; *Finland*: Pulkkinen 1982:27; *Sweden*: Stattin & Magnusson 1996:619 **NORTH AMERICA** *Canada*: Smart et al. 1997; *United States*: Jacoby et al. 1973; O'Donnell et al.1976; Stephens & McBride 1976; Johnston et al.1978; Kandel et al. 1978; Jessor 1979; McGlothlin 1979; Nurco 1979; Clayton 1981; White et al. 1985; White et al. 1987:735; Brook et al. 1992; Laub & Sampson 1994:242 | **NORTH AMERICA** *United States*: McGlothlin 1979; McBride & McCoy 1981*; Clayton & Tuchfeld 1982; Anglin & Speckart 1988; Stacy & Newcomb 1995 | **EUROPE** *Britain*: Osborn & West 1980; Hagell & Newburn 1996:14; *Netherlands*: Blokland 2005:49 (than nonabusers) **NORTH AMERICA** *United States*: MR Gottfredson & Mitchell-Herzfelt 1982; Hoffman & Beck 1985; Dembo et al. 1987; Niarhos & Routh 1992; Dembo et al. 1995a:1444 | **NORTH AMERICA** *Canada*: Gillis & Hagan 1982:522; *United States*: Voss & Stephens 1973; Kratcoski & Kratcoski 1975; Elliott & Ageton 1976; McBride 1976; Block & Goodman 1978; Levine & Kozak 1979; Inciardi 1980 (females) Rathus et al. 1980; Bachman et al. 1981; McBride & McCoy 1981*; Wright & Moore 1982; Donovan & Jessor 1985; Hawkins et al. 1986; Kandel et al. 1986 (females); Herzog et al. 1987; Newcomb & Bentler 1988; Elliott et al. 1989; Kandel et al. 1986*; Hops et al. 1990; Watts & Wright 1990; van Kammen et al. 1991; Andrews et al. 1993; Huizinga et al. 1993; Laub & Sampson 1994:242; van Kammen & Loeber 1994 (adolescents); Dembo et al. 1995b:273; JP Allen et al. 1996; Brook et al. 1996; Saner & Ellickson 1996; Bankston & Zhou 1997:356; Herman et al. 1997; Vazsonyi & Flannery 1997; Zhang et al. 1997; Stice et al. 1998; Brook et al. 1999; WA Mason & Windle 2002 **OCEANIA** *New Zealand*: McGee et al. 2000; Fergusson et al. 2002 |
| Not signif. | | | | | **OCEANIA** *Australia*: Broadhurst et al. 1988 | **NORTH AMERICA** *United States*: DB Kandel et al. 1986* (males) |
| Negative | | | | | | |

TABLE 6.2.2b Illegal Drug Use in General and Clinical or Personality Traits Associated with Criminality.

| Nature of the relationship | Antisocial behavior | | Physical aggression | Cognitive & personality factors | Mental illness or disability | Family factors |
|---|---|---|---|---|---|---|
| | Childhood & early adol. | Late adol. & adulthood | | | | |
| Positive | **EUROPE** *Britain*: Rutter 1996:496; *Sweden*: Holmberg 1985 **NORTH AMERICA** *Canada*: Boyle et al. 1992; *United States*: Kellam et al. 1980; Kellam et al. 1982; Gittelman et al. 1985; Kandel et al. 1986; Simcha-Fagan et al. 1986; Hundleby 1987; Kellam et al. 1989; Robins & McEvoy 1990; Tomas et al. 1990; Windle 1990; Greenbaum et al. 1991 (psychiatric patients); Van Kammen et al. 1991; Brook et al. 1992; MB Keller et al. 1992; CS Martin et al. 1993; Gfellner & Hundleby 1994; Van Kammen & Loeber 1994; Brook & Newcomb 1995; Biederman et al. 1996a; Brook et al. 1996; Booth & Zhang 1997; Neumark & Anthony 1997; DG Stewart et al. 1997 **OCEANIA** *New Zealand*: Fergusson et al. 1993a | **NORTH AMERICA** *Canada*: Mailloux et al. 1997; *United States*: Hill et al. 1960; Regier et al. 1990b; SS Smith & Newman 1990; CA Martin et al. 1997 **OCEANIA** *New Zealand*: Mulder et al. 1994:283 | **NORTH AMERICA** *United States*: Kellam et al. 1983 (black males); Kingery et al. 1992; Moeller et al. 1994 (cocaine use, impulsive aggression); McCormick & Smith 1995; Herrenkohl et al. 2000 (drug selling in teens, self-report) | **NORTH AMERICA** *United States*: Moss et al. 1990 (cocaine use, sensation seeking) | **NORTH AMERICA** *United States*: JA Rich & Grey 2005 (black males) | **NORTH AMERICA** *United States*: Kaestner 1997 (divorce & unstable marriage) |
| Not signif. | | | | | | |
| Negative | | | | | | |

## 6.3.6 Sexual Orientation (Being Homosexual)

The available research on any connection between sexual orientation and involvement in crime and delinquency has indicated that gays and lesbians are more involved in illegal drug use than are their straight counterparts (Table 6.3.6).

TABLE 6.2.3a Cigarette Smoking and Criminal/Delinquent Behavior.

| Nature of the relationship | Self-reported offenses | |
|---|---|---|
| | Overall offenses | Illegal drugs |
| Positive | **NORTH AMERICA** *Canada*: LaGrange & Silverman 1999* (males, property & violent offenses); *United States*: Watts & Wright 1990:180 | **EUROPE** *Norway*: Pedersen et al. 2001 **NORTH AMERICA** *Canada*: LaGrange & Silverman 1999* (males); *United States*: Torabi et al. 1993; Schorling et al. 1994 (cocaine use); Milberger et al. 1997; Roll et al. 1997 (cocaine use) |
| Not signif. | | |
| Negative | | |

## 6.4 OTHER BEHAVIOR TENDENCIES

Three difficult-to-categorize behavioral tendencies are discussed regarding their possible association with criminality.

TABLE 6.2.3b Cigarette Smoking and Clinical or Personality Traits Associated with Criminality.

| Nature of the relationship | Antisocial behavior | Mental disorder |
|---|---|---|
| | Late adol. & adulthood | |
| Positive | **NORTH AMERICA** *United States*: Milberger et al. 1997 | **NORTH AMERICA** *United States*: Lambert & Hartsough 1998 (ADHD) |
| Not signif. | | |
| Negative | | |

**TABLE 6.2.4** Marijuana Use and Clinical or Personality Traits Associated with Criminality.

| Nature of the relationship | Antisocial behavior | Physical aggression |
|---|---|---|
| | Childhood & early adol. | |
| Positive | **EUROPE** *Norway*: Pedersen et al. 2001<br>**NORTH AMERICA** *Canada*: MH Boyle et al. 1992 | **NORTH AMERICA** *United States*: Beachy et al. 1979 |
| Not signif. | | |
| Negative | | |

**TABLE 6.3.1b** Sexuality (Mating) in General and Clinical or Personality Traits Associated with Criminality.

| Nature of the relationship | Physical aggression |
|---|---|
| Positive | **RODENT** *Mouse*: Beeman 1947 (adult males); MV Kahn 1961 (adult males); Korpela & Sandnabba 1994 (males) |
| Not signif. | |
| Negative | |

**TABLE 6.2.5a** Age of Onset of Marijuana Use (Early) and Criminal/Delinquent Behavior.

| Nature of the relationship | Self-reported offenses |
|---|---|
| | Overall offenses |
| Positive | **OCEANIA** *New Zealand*: Fergusson & Horwood 1997 (marijuana use) |
| Not signif. | |
| Negative | |

**TABLE 6.3.2** Premarital Sex and Criminal/Delinquent Behavior.

| Nature of the relationship | Self-reported offenses |
|---|---|
| | Illegal drugs |
| Positive | **NORTH AMERICA** *United States*: Yamaguchi & Kandel 1987 (females); Mott & Haurin 1988; Elliot & Morse 1989; Kandel 1989; Biglan et al. 1990; Ensminger 1990 (blacks); Rosenbaum & Kandel 1990; Orr et al. 1991; Shafer & Boyer 1991; Strunin & Hingson 1992; Leigh & Stall 1993; Shafer et al. 1993; Lowry et al. 1994; de Gaston et al. 1995; Graves & Leigh 1995; Harvey & Spigner 1995; Fortenberry et al. 1997 |
| Not signif. | |
| Negative | |

**TABLE 6.3.1a** Sexuality (Mating) in General and Criminal/Delinquent Behavior.

| Nature of the relationship | Self-reported offenses |
|---|---|
| | Overall offenses |
| Positive | **NORTH AMERICA** *United States*: DC Rowe et al. 1989 (mating effort); DC Rowe et al. 1997 (mating effort) |
| Not signif. | |
| Negative | |

## 6.4.1 Aggressive Driving

No research was found directly linking aggressive driving and criminality. However, one study reported that aggressive driving was statistically associated with physical aggression (Table 6.4.1).

## 6.4.2 Recreational Driving

Recreational driving refers to that done for pleasure rather than for the purpose of work or education. According to one study, those who engaged in the most recreational driving self-reported greater involvement in the commission of property crimes than those who drove less recreationally (Table 6.4.2).

## 6.4.3 Game Playing

No evidence was located directly linking the playing of computer or video games to involvement in criminal behavior. However, as shown in Table 6.4.3, two studies have found a positive association between the playing of electronic action games and engaging in physical aggression.

**TABLE 6.3.3a** Number of Sex Partners and Criminal/Delinquent Behavior.

| Nature of the relationship | Officially detected offenses | | | | Self-reported offenses | |
|---|---|---|---|---|---|---|
| | Violent offenses | Delinquency | General & adult offenses | Recidivism | Overall offenses | Illegal drugs |
| Positive | **NORTH AMERICA** *United States*: Kaplun & Reich 1977:656 | **EUROPE** *Britain*: West & Farrington 1973; Farrington 1988:72 **NORTH AMERICA** *Canada*: Bogaert 1993; *United States*: Gebhard et al. 1965:598; Cantwell 1981:22; Jessor et al. 1983; Figueira-McDonough 1984; Donovan & Jessor 1985; Donovan et al. 1988; Rowe et al. 1989 | **EUROPE** *Britain*: West & Farrington 1977; Farrington 1982:190 | **EUROPE** *Britain*: Osborn & West 1980 | **EUROPE** *Britain*: Schofield 1965:151 **NORTH AMERICA** *United States*: Elliott & Morse 1987; Elliott & Morse 1989; Weiher et al. 1991; Huizinga et al. 1993 | **EUROPE** *Britain*: Noble et al. 1972 **NORTH AMERICA** *United States*: Blumenfield et al. 1972:607; Arafat & Yorburg 1973; Vener & Stewart 1974; Murstein & Holden 1979; J Gibbs et al. 1984; Donovan & Jessor 1985; Bentler & Newcomb 1986; Zabin et al. 1986; Yamaguchi & Kandel 1987; Donovan et al. 1988; Mott & Haurin 1988; Farrell et al. 1992; McGee & Newcomb 1992:775; Strunin & Hingson 1992; Durbin et al. 1993; Huizinga et al. 1993; Tildesley et al. 1995; DuRant et al. 1998 **OCEANIA** *Australia*: Reynolds & Rob 1988 |
| Not signif. | | | | | | |
| Negative | | | | | | |

**TABLE 6.3.3b** Number of Sex Partners and Clinical or Personality Traits Associated with Criminality.

| Nature of the relationship | Antisocial behavior | |
|---|---|---|
| | Childhood & early adol. | Late adol. & adulthood |
| Positive | **EUROPE** *Sweden*: Stattin & Magnusson 1996:621 **NORTH AMERICA** *United States*: Robins 1966:139; Booth & Zhang 1997 **OCEANIA** *New Zealand*: Bardone et al. 1996 | **NORTH AMERICA** *United States*: Cantwell 1981:22 |
| Not signif. | | **NORTH AMERICA** *Canada*: Seto et al. 1997:305 |
| Negative | | |

**TABLE 6.3.4a** Age of Onset of Sexual Intercourse (Early) and Criminal/Delinquent Behavior.

| Nature of the relationship | Officially detected offenses | | Self-reported offenses | |
|---|---|---|---|---|
| | Delinquency | General & adult offenses | Overall offenses | Illegal drugs |
| Positive | **NORTH AMERICA** *United States*: Reitsma-Street et al. 1985:421; Condy et al. 1987 | **NORTH AMERICA** *United States*: Yochelson & Samenow 1976:178 | **NORTH AMERICA** *Canada*: Bogaert 1993; *United States*: Zucker & Devoe 1975; Bachman et al. 1981; Jessor et al. 1983*; Elliott et al. 1989; Newcomb & Bentler 1989:243; DC Rowe et al. 1989 | **NORTH AMERICA** *United States*: R Jessor & Jessor 1977; PY Miller & Simon 1974; Vener & Stewart 1974; Jessor et al. 1983*; Jessor 1987; Christopher & Cate 1988; Donovan et al. 1988; Mott & Haurin 1988; Rosenbaum & Kandel 1990; Cornelius et al. 1993; Dorius et al. 1993; Costa et al. 1995; Shrier et al. 1996 |
| Not signif. | | | | |
| Negative | | | | |

**TABLE 6.3.4b** Age of Onset of Sexual Intercourse (Early) and Clinical or Personality Traits Associated with Criminality.

| Nature of the relationship | Antisocial behavior | |
|---|---|---|
| | Childhood & early adol. | Late adol. & adulthood |
| Positive | **EUROPE** *Sweden*: Stattin & Magnusson 1996:621 **NORTH AMERICA** *United States*: LN Robins & Price 1991; Zoccollilo & Rogers 1991; Fergusson et al. 1994 | **NORTH AMERICA** *Canada*: Seto et al. 1997:305 |
| | **OCEANIA** *New Zealand*: Bardone et al. 1996:821; Bardone et al. 1998 (early pregnancy among females) | |
| Not signif. | | |
| Negative | | |

**TABLE 6.3.5** Emotional Intimacy with Sex Partner and Criminal/Delinquent Behavior.

| Nature of the relationship | Self-reported offenses |
|---|---|
| | Overall offenses |
| Positive | |
| Not signif. | |
| Negative | **OCEANIA** *New Zealand*: B Wright et al. 1999b (at age 21) |

**TABLE 6.3.6** Sexual Orientation (Being Homosexual) and Criminal/Delinquent Behavior.

| Nature of the relationship | Self-reported offenses |
|---|---|
| | Illegal drugs |
| Homosexual more involved | **NORTH AMERICA** *United States*: McKirnan & Peterson 1988 (males); Stall & Wiley 1988 (males); McKirnan & Peterson 1989b (both sexes); W Skinner 1994 (both sexes); Klitzman et al. 1998 (both sexes, psychiatrists) |
| Not signif. | |
| Heterosexual more involved | |

**TABLE 6.4.1** Aggressive Driving and Clinical or Personality Traits Associated with Criminality.

| Nature of the relationship | Physical aggression |
|---|---|
| Positive | **EUROPE** *Britain*: Lajunen & Parker 2001 |
| Not signif. | |
| Negative | |

**TABLE 6.4.2** Recreational Driving and Criminal/ Delinquent Behavior.

| Nature of the relationship | Self-reported offenses |
|---|---|
| | Overall offenses |
| Positive | **NORTH AMERICA** *Canada*: LaGrange & Silverman 1999 (property offenses) |
| Not signif. | |
| Negative | |

**TABLE 6.4.3** Game Playing and Clinical or Personality Traits Associated with Criminality.

| Nature of the relationship | Physical aggression |
|---|---|
| Positive | **NORTH AMERICA** *United States*: CA Anderson & Dill 2000 (violent video games) **INTERNATIONAL** *Online Sample*: Norris 2004(women, online games) |
| Not signif. | |
| Negative | |

Chapter 7

# Cognitive Factors

Contents



This chapter examines a wide variety of cognitive factors that have been investigated in connection with criminality. It begins by considering various attitudes, including those related to morality and self-esteem. Then attention is given to intelligence and learning ability along with grades received in formal education. The final variables to be considered are those concerned with mental illnesses, mental disorders, and drug addiction.

## 7.1 ATTITUDES

Numerous types of attitudes have been explored regarding their possible relationship with criminal and delinquent behavior. These include opinions about education, as well as cynicism and empathy. Other attitudinal variables to be examined in this section are those of present/future orientation and locus of control.

### 7.1.1 Commitment to Education

The extent to which people have a commitment to becoming educated or believe in the value of education is measured

**TABLE 7.1.1a Commitment to Education and criminal/Delinquent Behavior.**

| Nature of the relationship | Officially detected offenses | Self-reported offenses | |
|---|---|---|---|
| | Delinquency | Overall offenses | Illegal drugs |
| Positive | | | |
| Not signif. | | | **NORTH AMERICA** *United States*: Ginsberg & Greenley 1978; Goe & Bachtel 1985 |
| Negative | **ASIA** *China*: Zhang & Messner 1996 **EUROPE** *Britain*: Mitchell & Shepherd 1967; Wadsworth 1979; *Sweden*: Jonsson 1967:204 **NORTH AMERICA** *United States*: Healy & Bronner 1936:62; Merrill 1947:105; Polk & Halferty 1966; Rhodes & Reiss 1969; Sampson & Laub 1993b:111; Marshall & Webb 1994:334; Ward & Tittle 1994; Cao et al. 2004 (among low SES adol.) | **EUROPE** *Switzerland*: Vazsonyi 1997:92 **NORTH AMERICA** *United States*: Pine 1965; Epps 1967; GF Jensen 1969; Bachman et al. 1971; Kelly & Balch 1971; Elliott & Voss 1974; Figueira-McDonough 1983; LaGrange & White 1985; Fiqueira-McDonough 1986; DC Rowe 1986:523; Simcha-Fagan & Schwartz 1986:691; HR White et al. 1987:729; Wiatrowski & Anderson 1987; Grande 1988; Hawkins et al. 1988:263; Levine & Singer 1988:392; Gardner & Shoemaker 1989:490; DC Gottfredson et al. 1991:213; Agnew & White 1992:486; Joseph 1996; Katimas et al. 1996; Herrenkohl et al. 2000 (violent delinquency, teens) **OCEANIA** *New Zealand*: BRE Wright et al. 1999b (at age 21) | **NORTH AMERICA** *United States*: Kelly & Balch 1971; Burkett & Jensen 1975; Finnell & Jones 1975; Smith & Fogg 1978; Krohn et al. 1984; Johnston et al. 1986:29; Hawkins et al. 1988:263; McBride et al. 1991; Agnew & White 1992:486; Free 1994 |

through self-reports. As shown in Table 7.1.1a, nearly all of the available studies have concluded that such resolutions and beliefs are inversely correlated with involvement in delinquent and criminal behavior. The two exceptional studies involved self-reported illegal drug use, both of which failed to find a statistically significant relationship.

One study of children with and without conduct disorders sought to determine their commitment toward furthering their education and concluded that those with conduct disorders expressed less favorable attitudes toward becoming well educated than did children generally (Table 7.1.1b).

## 7.1.2 Occupational Aspirations

Table 7.1.2 shows that only one study was located that examined a connection between occupational aspirations and criminality. The results indicate that persons with relatively low motives regarding the kind of work they would like to do report greater criminal involvement.

## 7.1.3 Cynicism

One study was located pertaining to cynicism. This research compared delinquents and nondelinquents regarding the

**TABLE 7.1.1b Commitment to Education and Clinical or Personality Traits Associated with Criminality.**

| Nature of the relationship | Antisocial behavior |
|---|---|
| | Child & early adol. |
| Positive | |
| Not signif. | |
| Negative | **EUROPE** *Sweden*: Stattin & Magnusson 1996:621 |

**TABLE 7.1.2 Occupational Aspirations and Criminal/ Delinquent Behavior.**

| Nature of the relationship | Self-reported offenses |
|---|---|
| | Overall offenses |
| Positive | |
| Not signif. | |
| Negative | **OCEANIA** *New Zealand*: BRE Wright et al. 1999b (at age 21) |

**TABLE 7.1.3 Cynicism and Criminal/Delinquent Behavior.**

| Nature of the relationship | Self-reported offenses |
|---|---|
| | Overall offenses |
| Positive | |
| Not signif. | **NORTH AMERICA** *United States*: BRE Wright et al. 2001 (delinquency) |
| Negative | |

tendency to be cynical. As shown in Table 7.1.3, no significant difference was found regarding this trait.

## 7.1.4 Empathy/Altruism

*Empathy* refers to the capacity to vicariously experience the pain that others actually feel. To measure empathy in scientific research, subjects are typically asked to rate how easy or difficult it is to imagine the emotions that others perceive under various circumstances (Hogan 1969:308; Chlopan et al. 1985; Hanson & Mullis 1985:182).

*Altruism* can be thought of as the action component of empathy. In other words, one who experiences empathy for another is often motivated to try to help that person. To measure altruism, some studies have asked people to imagine how helpful they would be under various hypothetical conditions (Ma & Leung 1991) or how they actually reacted when confronted with situations that required self-sacrificing behavior (Benson et al. 1980; Smithson & Amato 1982; Clary & Miller 1986).

**TABLE 7.1.4b Empathy/Altruism and Clinical or Personality Traits Associated with Criminality.**

| Nature of the relationship | Antisocial behavior | Physical aggression |
|---|---|---|
| | Childhood & early adol. | |
| Positive | | |
| Not signif. | | |
| Negative | **EUROPE** *Britain*: Tranah et al. 1998:743 (empathy) **NORTH AMERICA** *United States*: Feshbach 1975; MacQuiddy et al. 1987 (empathy); Zahn-Waxler et al. 1995; D Cohen & Strayer 1996 (empathy); Krueger et al. 1996:125 | **NORTH AMERICA** *United States*: Baumrind 1991 |

Table 7.1.4a summarizes the evidence concerning the relationship between empathy and altruism and criminality. One can see that the studies are virtually unanimous in indicating that offenders are less prone toward both empathy and altruism than persons in general, regardless of whether the research is based on official crime data or self-reported offending.

A few studies have sought to determine if childhood conduct disorders and physical aggression (both well-established correlates of offending) are also related to empathy and altruism as is criminality. One can see that these are linked and that the direction (negative) is the same as in the case of criminality (Table 7.1.4b).

**TABLE 7.1.4a Empathy/Altruism and Criminal/Delinquent Behavior.**

| Nature of the relationship | Officially detected offenses | | Self-reported offenses | |
|---|---|---|---|---|
| | Delinquency | General & adult offenses | Overall offenses | Illegal drugs |
| Positive | | | | |
| Not signif. | **NORTH AMERICA** *United States*: Kendall et al. 1977 | | | |
| Negative | **EUROPE** *Britain*: Eysenck & McGurk 1980 **NORTH AMERICA** *United States*: R Hogan 1969*; Mehrabian & Epstein 1972; Rotenberg 1974; Aleksic 1976; PL Ellis 1982; Kaplan & Arbuthnot 1984; M Lee & Prentice 1988 (empathy); Chandler & Moran 1990 | **NORTH AMERICA** *United States*: Turner 1948 (altruism); Riley 1986 | **ASIA** *Hong Kong:* Ma & Leung 1991 (altruism) **EUROPE** *Spain*: Luengo et al. 1994a* **NORTH AMERICA** *United States*: R Hogan 1969*; Hogan & Jones 1983:17 | **EUROPE** *Spain*: Luengo et al. 1994a:32* |

## 7.1.5 Delayed Gratification

The inability to delay gratification corresponds to a type of "here-and-now" thinking, where future consequences are ignored in favor of short-term gains. Interesting methods have been developed for measuring delayed gratification. In one of the best known, children are asked to perform some task and when they have finished, they are given a choice of rewards: one piece of candy today or two pieces if they wait until the next day (Mischel et al. 1989:934). This and several studies (e.g., Newman et al. 1992; Krueger et al. 1996:112) have shown that some children are much more prone to take the immediate smaller reward, while others consistently opt for delayed larger rewards.

Table 7.1.5a contains a total of six studies published over a span of more than 40 years which assessed the association between delayed gratification and delinquent behavior. All of these studies reported a negative relationship, meaning that those who were least prone toward delay gratification were most delinquent.

One can see in Table 7.1.5b that a few studies also examined the link between delayed gratification and factors linked to criminality. Once again, they all reported statistically significant negative relationships.

## 7.1.6 Future Orientation

A famous fable about the ant who worked all day preparing for winter and the grasshopper who spent his time playing the fiddle dramatizes the fact that some people seem to live for today, while others carefully plan for the future. While future orientation has commonalities with the concept of delayed gratification (discussed above), this concept is broader in the sense of referring to the tendency to think generally about both the short-term and the long-term consequences of one's actions (Arbuthnot et al. 1987:146).

Several studies have been undertaken to determine if future orientation is related to delinquent behavior.

**TABLE 7.1.5a Delayed Gratification and Criminal/Delinquent Behavior.**

| Nature of the relationship | Officially detected offenses | Self-reported offenses |
|---|---|---|
| | Delinquency | Overall offenses |
| Positive | | |
| Not signif. | | |
| Negative | NORTH AMERICA<br>*Canada*: Tremblay et al. 1994; *United States*: Riddle & Roberts 1977 | NORTH AMERICA<br>*United States*: Mischel 1961; Mischel & Gilligan 1964; JL White et al. 1994:201; Wiebe 2006:525 |

**TABLE 7.1.5b Delayed Gratification and Clinical or Personality Traits Associated with Criminality.**

| Nature of the relationship | Antisocial behavior | |
|---|---|---|
| | Childhood & early adol. | Late adol. & adulthood |
| Positive | | |
| Not signif. | | |
| Negative | NORTH AMERICA<br>*United States*: Krueger et al. 1996 | NORTH AMERICA<br>*United States*: Blanchard et al. 1977; Newman et al. 1992 |

Table 7.1.6 shows that nearly all relevant studies indicate that delinquents appear to be less future oriented than are persons in general.

## 7.1.7 Feelings of External Locus of Control

Back in the 1960s, an American researcher noticed that individuals vary in the extent to which they perceive forces external to themselves controlling their lives (Rotter 1960). Since then, a multi-item questionnaire scale has been developed to measure what has come to be known as *internal/external locus of control* (Nowicki & Strickland 1973). People who believe they are very much "masters of their own fate" are said to have internal control, whereas those who think that their behavior is being manipulated by outside forces are said to have external control. The two main sources of external control are chance/fate and "powerful others" (Richter et al. 1996).

A number of studies have been conducted since the 1970s to determine if persons who are most prone toward criminality might be "internals" or "externals". As shown in Table 7.1.7, most of the research suggests that perceived external control is significantly more common among those who have engaged in delinquency and crime to the greatest extent. Studies undertaken to determine which of the two main types of external controllers seems to be perceived as most important for delinquents and criminals have concluded that "powerful others" are most often mentioned (Richter et al. 1996:340).

## 7.1.8 Liberal/Tolerant Attitudes in General

It is possible to measure the degree to which individuals hold liberal/tolerant attitudes about people in general. Liberal attitudes are thought to increase various types of antisocial behaviors. There is, however, a paucity of research investigating this link. As shown in Table 7.1.8, only one study was located that examined the relationship between liberal/tolerant attitudes and a factor often

**TABLE 7.1.6 Future Orientation and Criminal/Delinquent Behavior.**

| Nature of the relationship | Officially detected offenses | Self-reported offenses | |
|---|---|---|---|
| | Delinquency | Overall offenses | Illegal drugs |
| Positive | | | |
| Not signif. | **NORTH AMERICA** *United States*: Siegman 1961 | | |
| Negative | **NORTH AMERICA** *United States*: Quay 1965a; Siegman 1966; Stein et al. 1966; Landau 1975 | **NORTH AMERICA** *Canada*: LaGrange & Silverman 1999* (property & violent offenses, under age 18) | **NORTH AMERICA** *Canada*: LaGrange & Silverman 1999* (females, under 18) |

**TABLE 7.1.7 Feelings of External Locus of Control and Criminal/Delinquent Behavior.**

| Nature of the relationship | Officially detected offenses | | Self-reported offenses | |
|---|---|---|---|---|
| | Delinquency | Recidivism | Overall offenses | Illegal drugs |
| Positive | **NORTH AMERICA** *United States*: Conger & Miller 1966:138; Duke & Fenhagen 1975; Beck & Ollendick 1976; Kumchy & Sawyer 1980<br>**OCEANIA** *Hawaii*: EE Werner 1987:31 | **EUROPE** *Germany*: Richter et al. 1996<br>**NORTH AMERICA** *Canada*: Andrews & Friesen 1987 | **NORTH AMERICA** *United States*: Hogan & Mookherjee 1981; Parrott & Strongman 1984; Keilitz & Dunivant 1986<br>**OCEANIA** *Australia*: JM Shaw & Scott 1991 | **NORTH AMERICA** *Canada*: Currie et al. 1977; *United States*: Obitz et al. 1973; Carman 1977 |
| Not signif. | **NORTH AMERICA** *United States*: Valliant et al. 1983 | | **NORTH AMERICA** *United States*: Farley & Sewell 1976<br>**OCEANIA** *Australia*: Peiser & Heaven 1996 | |
| Negative | | | | |

**TABLE 7.1.8 Liberal/Tolerant Attitudes in General and Clinical or Personality Traits Associated with Criminality.**

| Nature of the relationship | Physical aggression |
|---|---|
| Positive | **EUROPE** *Britain*: P Smith et al. 2006 (aggressive driving) |
| Not signif. | |
| Negative | |

associated with criminality. The results of this study suggested that liberal/tolerant attitudes were positively associated with aggressive driving.

## 7.1.9 Liberal/Tolerant Attitudes toward Deviance and Nonconformity

The word *deviance* is impossible to precisely define, in part because exactly what it refers to varies from one culture or subculture to another. Nevertheless, most forms of deviance tend to be unusual and unpopular within a given society.

Table 7.1.9 summarizes the results of studies undertaken to determine if individuals who engage in delinquency and crime are more or less tolerant of deviance than those who rarely or never do. Findings suggest that liberal and tolerant attitudes toward deviance in general are positively correlated with offending.

## 7.1.10 Liberal/Tolerant Attitudes toward Drug Use

Some research has examined the potential association between liberal attitudes toward drug use and involvement in delinquency and the use of illegal drugs. Table 7.1.10 summarizes the results of these studies. As can be seen, all but one of the available studies have positively correlated offending with liberal attitudes toward illegal drug use.

**TABLE 7.1.9** Liberal/Tolerant Attitudes toward Deviance and Nonconformity and Criminal/Delinquent Behavior.

| Nature of the relationship | Officially detected offenses | | | Self-reported offenses | |
|---|---|---|---|---|---|
| | Delinquency | General & adult offenses | Recidivism | Overall offenses | Illegal drugs |
| Positive | **EUROPE** *Belgium*: Vermeiren et al. 2004:572* **NORTH AMERICA** *Canada*: Bogaert & Rushton 1989; Vermeiren et al. 2004:572* | **OCEANIA** *New Zealand*: Krueger et al. 1994 | | **EUROPE** *Belgium*: Vermeiren et al. 2004:572* (delinquency); *Britain*: Reicher & Emler 1985; *Netherlands*: Junger-Tas 1992 **NORTH AMERICA** *United States*: Hogan & Mookherjee 1981:54; Agnew 1991; Empey & Stafford 1991; Thornberry et al. 1991; Jensen & Rojek 1992; Vermeiren et al. 2004:572* (delinquency) | **NORTH AMERICA** *United States*: Suchman 1968; R Blum 1970; R Jessor & Jessor 1977; Ginsberg & Greenley 1978; CS Sellers et al. 1993 |
| Not signif. | | | **NORTH AMERICA** *Canada*: Mills & Kroner 1997 | | |
| Negative | | | | | |

**TABLE 7.1.10** Liberal/Tolerant Attitudes toward drug Use and Criminal/Delinquent Behavior.

| Nature of the relationship | Self-reported offenses | |
|---|---|---|
| | Overall offenses | Illegal drugs |
| Positive | **NORTH AMERICA** *United States*: Thornberry et al. 1994; Zhang et al. 1997 | **NORTH AMERICA** *United States*: Martino & Truss 1973; Cockerham 1977; Kohn et al. 1979; Wingard et al. 1979; Fors & Rojek 1983:214; Krohn et al. 1984; Winfree & Griffiths 1985; Burkett & Warren 1987; Blau et al. 1988; Brook et al. 1988:151; O'Donnell et al. 1995b:534; Rienzi et al. 1996:343 |
| Not signif. | **EUROPE** *Britain*: DJ West & Farrington 1973:52 | |
| Negative | | |

## 7.1.11 Liberal/Tolerant Attitudes toward Illegal Activity

The results of two studies (Table 7.1.11) indicate that liberal/tolerant attitudes toward illegal activity in general are positively associated with delinquency.

## 7.1.12 Liberal/Tolerant Attitudes toward Political Issues

According to a few studies, illegal drug use is positively correlated with having liberal (left-wing) political attitudes

**TABLE 7.1.11** Liberal/tolerant Attitudes toward Illegal Activity and Criminal/Delinquent Behavior.

| Nature of the relationship | Officially detected offenses | Self-reported offenses |
|---|---|---|
| | Delinquency | Illegal drugs |
| Positive | **NORTH AMERICA** *Canada*: SW Baron 2003 (self-control statistically controlled) | **ASIA** *Russia*: Knyazev 2004 (adol.) |
| Not signif. | | |
| Negative | | |

(Table 7.1.12). This is not entirely surprising in that liberal political views usually include permissive attitudes toward behavior that does not directly harm others.

## 7.1.13 Moral Reasoning, Levels of

Morality may seem like a topic that is too subjective to be scientifically studied. Nevertheless, morality has been of interest to criminologists due to the obvious similarity between what is generally considered immoral and what is legally defined as criminal.

Some studies dating back to the 1920s attempted to link delinquency and crime with whether individuals appeared to know right from wrong. Looking for evidence of this connection obviously required researchers to make decision as to right and wrong, and then assess how closely subjects agreed with their decisions. The results of these early studies failed to find differences between delinquents and nondelinquents in what was and was not considered wrong (Hartshorne & May 1928; Hartshorne et al. 1929, 1930).

More recent studies have generally found that those who engage in delinquency and crime consider such behavior less wrong than do those who avoid such activities (Smith & Paternoster 1987; Gertz & Gould 1995) and have generally weaker commitments to moral standards than do their nondelinquent peers (Zhang & Messner 1995:377).

In the late 1950s, psychologist Lawrence Kohlberg (1958) suggested that everyone develops a moral sense, but that they do so through identifiable stages, with some proceeding through the stages more rapidly than others. The basic idea is that what is right and wrong for a young child depends on whether it causes pain or pleasure. At intermediate levels of moral reasoning, most decisions about right and wrong depend upon the dictates of authority figures (e.g., parents, political & religious leaders, and even God). Kohlberg asserted that at the highest stages of moral reasoning, judgements depend on certain universal intuitively understood principles, the most important being respect to the life and well-being of others.

To determine where people are in terms of their levels of moral reasoning, Kohlberg and his supporters usually present subjects with a series of moral dilemmas, none of which have an obvious right or wrong solution. The subjects are then asked to explain each of their moral decisions, which gives trained researchers insight into where each subject resides along the moral reasoning continuum at a given age (Rest 1979).

Table 7.1.13a shows what research has indicated regarding an association between levels of moral reasoning and involvement in criminal/delinquent behavior. It appears that offenders generally have lower levels of moral reasoning than do their peers. In a sense, most studies indicate that delinquents and criminals are close to toddlers in their moral reasoning. The only possible exception is in the area of drug offenses, where studies have not found a significant inverse relationship (Blasi 1980:37).

It should be noted that moral reasoning is fairly strongly and positively linked to the following traits: empathy (Hogan 1973; Kuhmerker 1975; Dickstein 1979; Lee & Prentice 1988; Kozeki & Berghammer 1992:193), altruism (Hoffman 1975; Blasi 1980:30), role taking ability (Lee 1983; DeWolfe et al. 1988), and intelligence (Gregg et al. 1994). As noted elsewhere in this book, all of these traits have generally been found to be negatively associated with criminality.

A number of studies have also examined the relationship between moral reasoning and factors frequently linked to criminality. Table 7.1.13b displays the results of these studies. As can be seen, moral reasoning during childhood and early adolescence was negatively related to criminality in most of the studies. A similar pattern of findings, where moral reasoning is inversely related to criminality, has been reported by researchers samples of older adolescents and adults were analyzed.

**TABLE 7.1.12 Liberal/tolerant Attitudes toward Political Issues and Criminal/Delinquent Behavior.**

| Nature of the relationship | Self-reported offenses |
|---|---|
| | Illegal drugs |
| Positive | **NORTH AMERICA** *United States*: Gergen et al. 1972; Gordon 1972; Ritter 1972; BD Johnson 1973; Kohn et al. 1985 |
| Not signif. | |
| Negative | |

## 7.1.14 Negative Affect

It is impossible not to notice that some individuals have a much more sour attitude toward life than do others. A number of research studies have been undertaken to determine if such tendencies are correlated with involvement in criminal/delinquent behavior. As one can see from Table 7.1.14a, the evidence has rather consistently indicated that delinquents and criminals are more prone than their relatively law-abiding peers to exhibit negative attitudes toward life in general and the people around them.

As with findings surrounding criminality per se, Table 7.1.14b shows that a negative affect is positively associated with factors related to offending for children and young adolescents.

**TABLE 7.1.13a** Moral Reasoning, Levels of and Criminal/Delinquent Behavior.

| Nature of the relationship | Officially detected offenses | | | Self-reported offenses | |
|---|---|---|---|---|---|
| | Delinquency | General & adult offenses | Recidivism | Overall offenses | Illegal drugs |
| Positive | | | | | **NORTH AMERICA** *United States*: Lanza-Kaduce et al. 1983:450 |
| Not signif. | **NORTH AMERICA** *United States*: CO Weber 1926; Ruma 1967; Hudgins & Prentice 1973; Miller et al. 1974; Haviland 1977; Schmidlin 1977; Hains & Ryan 1983:1540 | | **NORTH AMERICA** *United States*: Petronio 1980 | **EUROPE** *Scotland*: Emler et al. 1978*; Renwick & Emler 1984* | **NORTH AMERICA** *United States*: Haier 1976 |
| Negative | **EUROPE** *Britain*: Eshel et al. 1968; *Scotland*: Emler et al. 1978* **MIDDLE EAST** *Israel*: Sagi & Eisikovits 1981; Addad & Leslau 1990* **NORTH AMERICA** *Canada*: Trevethan & Walker 1989; *United States*: Betke 1944; Kohlberg 1958; Rest et al. 1969; Fodor 1972; Hickey 1972; Hudgins & Prentice 1973; Hawk & Peterson 1974; McColgan 1976; McColgan 1976; Jurkovic & Prentice 1977; Hains & Miller 1980; Gavaghan et al. 1983; Hains 1984; Hanson & Mullis 1984; Basinger & Gibbs 1987; Lee & Prentice 1988; Chandler & Moran 1990 | **MIDDLE EAST** *Israel*: Addad & Leslau 1990* **NORTH AMERICA** *Canada*: Parlett et al. 1975; *United States*: Ravitch 1973; Deardorff & Finch 1975; Parlett et al. 1975; Kantner 1976; Griffore & Samuels 1978; Hartnett & Shumate 1980; Craig & Truitt 1996 | **NORTH AMERICA** *United States*: Jennings et al. 1983 | **EUROPE** *Britain*: Renwick & Emler 1984*; Palmer & Hollin 1996:180 **NORTH AMERICA** *United States*: Lanza-Kaduce et al. 1983:453 | |

**TABLE 7.1.13b** Moral reasoning, Levels of and Clinical or Personality Traits Associated with Criminality.

| Nature of the relationship | Antisocial behavior | |
|---|---|---|
| | Childhood & early adol. | Late adol. & adulthood |
| Positive | | |
| Not signif. | **NORTH AMERICA** *United States*: Richards et al. 1992 | **EUROPE** *Britain*: RJ Blair 1995:12 **NORTH AMERICA** *United States*: Chandler & Moran 1990:243 |
| Negative | **EUROPE** *Britain*: RJ Blair 1999 **NORTH AMERICA** *United States*: Campagna & Harter 1975*; Bear & Richards 1981; McColgan et al. 1983 | **NORTH AMERICA** *Canada*: Trevethan & Walker 1989; *United States*: Fodor 1973; Campagna & Harter 1975*; Kegan 1986; O'Kane et al. 1996 |

**TABLE 7.1.14a** Negative Affect and Criminal/Delinquent Behavior.

| Nature of the relationship | Officially detected offenses | | Self-reported offenses | |
|---|---|---|---|---|
| | Delinquency | General & adult offenses | Overall offenses | Illegal drugs |
| Positive | **NORTH AMERICA** *United States*: Conger & Miller 1966:144; HR White et al. 1987:729 | **OCEANIA** *New Zealand*: Krueger et al. 1994 | **NORTH AMERICA** *United States*: Stice & Gonzales 1998:21* | **NORTH AMERICA** *United States*: Lerner & Vicary 1984; Labouvie et al. 1990; Caspi et al. 1994:185; Rothbart et al. 1994 **OCEANIA** *Australia*: Heaven 1994:451* (females); Krueger et al. 1996 |
| Not signif. | | | | **NORTH AMERICA** *United States*: Stice & Gonzales 1998:21* **OCEANIA** *Australia*: Heaven 1994:451* (males) |
| Negative | | | | |

## 7.1.15 Neutralization

Engaging in acts of delinquency and crime can cause feelings of guilt, remorse, and shame. Offenders, however, are thought to use a variety of techniques to downplay or offset these feelings and delay personal culpability (Sykes & Matza 1957). Three studies were located that examined this association and, as Table 7.1.15 shows, all three found a positive relationship between neutralization and criminal and delinquent behavior.

## 7.1.16 Rebelliousness/Defiance/Negative Attitudes toward Authority

Studies have been undertaken to determine if offenders and non-offenders can be distinguished in terms of their general tendencies to be rebellious, particularly toward authority figures, which include not only government officials and police, but also teachers and even parents (Rigby et al. 1987). As seen in Table 7.1.16a, these studies have shown that when delinquents are compared with age-mates, they have more hostile attitudes toward authority (Gorsuch & Butler 1976; Kazdin 1987b:189).

Table 7.1.16b shows the studies that examined the association between hostile attitudes and factors linked to criminality. All three of the studies detected a statistically significant and positive relationship.

## 7.1.17 Role Taking/Role Playing

Some people find it easy to put themselves "in the shoes of others", while others find it difficult or impossible (Krebs & Gilmore 1982). The studies that have compared delinquents and criminals with people generally in terms of their *role taking*/role playing abilities are summarized in Table 7.1.17a. Most of the studies have indicated that people who

**TABLE 7.1.14b** Negative Affect and Clinical or Personality Traits Associated with Criminality.

| Nature of the relationship | Antisocial behavior |
|---|---|
| | Childhood & early adol. |
| Positive | **NORTH AMERICA** *United States*: Cameron 1978; Maziade et al. 1990; Carlo et al. 1998 |
| Not signif. | |
| Negative | |

**TABLE 7.1.15** Neutralization and Criminal/Delinquent Behavior.

| Nature of the relationship | Self-reported offenses |
|---|---|
| | Overall Offenses |
| Positive | **NORTH AMERICA** *United States*: Costello & Vowell 1999; Wiebe 2003; Wiebe 2006 |
| Not signif. | |
| Negative | |

**TABLE 7.1.16a Rebelliousness/Defiance/Negative Attitudes toward Authority and Criminal/Delinquent Behavior.**

| Nature of the relationship | Officially detected offenses | | Self-reported offenses | |
|---|---|---|---|---|
| | Delinquency | Recidivism | Overall offenses | Illegal drugs |
| Positive | **EUROPE** *Britain*: TC Gibbens 1962 **NORTH AMERICA** *Canada*: Le Blanc 1992:344; *United States*: J Conger & Miller 1966; K Stein et al. 1966; Hindelang 1972; S Feldman & Weinberger 1994 | **MIDDLE EAST** *Turkey*: Corapcioglu & Erdogan 2004 (in correctional centers) **NORTH AMERICA** *United States*: Tolman 1938 | **ASIA** *Russia*: Ruchkin et al. 1998b **EUROPE** *Britain*: Reicher & Emler 1985*; *Scotland*: Reicher & Emler 1985*; N Emler & Reicher 1987 **NORTH AMERICA** *United States*: GF Jensen 1969; Buffalo & Rogers 1971; Hindelang 1973; Cernkovich 1978a; Cernkovich 1978b; Ginsberg & Greenley 1978; J Brook & Newcomb 1995:406; LE Ross 1994:80; Stacy & Newcomb 1995 **OCEANIA** *Australia*: Rigby et al. 1989; Heaven 1993:71 | **EUROPE** *Finland*: Pulkkinen 1990 **NORTH AMERICA** *United States*: Blumenfield et al. 1972:607; GM Smith & Fogg 1978; R Jessor & Jessor 1977; R Jessor & Jessor 1978; DB Kandel 1978; Wingard et al. 1980; Chassin 1984; Johnston et al. 1986; Newcomb et al. 1986; Simcha-Fagan et al. 1986; J Stein et al. 1987; H White et al. 1987; Newcomb & Bentler 1988a; Cloninger et al. 1988 |
| Not signif. | | | | |
| Negative | | | | |

**TABLE 7.1.16b Rebelliousness/Defiance/Negative Attitudes toward Authority and Clinical or Personality Traits Associated with Criminality.**

| Nature of the relationship | Antisocial behavior |
|---|---|
| | Childhood & early adol. |
| Positive | **NORTH AMERICA** *United States*: de Blois & Stewart 1980; KA Dodge 1985; Maziade et al. 1985 |
| Not signif. | |
| Negative | |

can assume most readily the role of another person are less likely to become involved in crime and delinquency than those who find role taking difficult. Some studies have separated the emotional aspects of role taking from the purely cognitive or intellectual aspects, and have suggested that it is primarily the emotional aspects that are most strongly inversely correlated with involvement in delinquency (Arbuthnot et al. 1987:164).

One study examined the relationship between role taking/role playing and factors linked to criminality and, as with criminality per se, a negative association was reported (Table 7.1.17b).

**TABLE 7.1.17a Role Taking/Role Playing and Criminal/Delinquent Behavior.**

| Nature of the relationship | Officially detected offenses | | Self-reported offenses |
|---|---|---|---|
| | Delinquency | General & adult offenses | Overall offenses |
| Positive | | | |
| Not signif. | **EUROPE** *Britain*: N Emler et al. 1978 **NORTH AMERICA** *United States*: Kaplan & Arbuthnot 1984 | **NORTH AMERICA** *United States*: Griffore & Samuels 1978 | |
| Negative | **NORTH AMERICA** *United States*: Kurtines & Hogan 1972*; MJ Chandler 1973*; Rotenberg 1974; Jurkovic & Prentice 1977; V Little & Kendall 1979; Ollendick & Hensen 1979; Kaplan & Arbuthnot 1985 | **NORTH AMERICA** *United States*: Kurtines & Hogan 1972*; R Hogan 1973; Hartnett & Shumate 1980 | **NORTH AMERICA** *United States*: MJ Chandler 1973* |

**TABLE 7.1.17b Role Taking/Role Playing and Clinical or Personality Traits Associated with Criminality.**

| Nature of the relationship | Antisocial behavior |
|---|---|
| | Late adol. & adulthood |
| Positive | |
| Not signif. | |
| Negative | **NORTH AMERICA** *United States*: Jurkovic & Prentice 1977 |

## 7.1.18 Self-Esteem/Self-Concept

Self-esteem refers to whether a person largely views himself/herself favorably or unfavorably. The only way that social scientists have for measuring self-esteem is through self-reports, usually on anonymous questionnaires (Cobb et al. 1966; Bennett et al. 1971). Obviously, feelings of self-esteem tend to fluctuate as people's daily experiences vacillate from positive to negative. Nevertheless, research has shown that on average some people have much higher average feelings of self-esteem than do others (Rosenberg 1965).

Table 7.1.18a presents the results of studies undertaken to determine if delinquents and criminals have high or low self-esteem relative to persons in general of the same age. The research shows that the majority of studies indicate that the self-esteem of offenders is below that of other persons. Nonetheless, the relationship does not appear to be strong, thereby explaining why this table contains quite a few studies showing no significant relationship.

Some studies have sought to determine which appears first: low self-esteem or delinquency. To obtain an answer, researchers have interviewed large numbers of pre-adolescents. For those who eventually engaged in serious delinquency, the researchers checked to see if and when self-esteem began to drop. Generally, low self-esteem seemed to occur first (Rosenberg 1978; HB Kaplan 1975a; Bynner et al. 1981). In fact, engaging in delinquency was followed by a slight rise in self-esteem, although not quite to the level of adolescents in general (HB Kaplan 1975a; Bynner et al. 1981:429), but eventually self-esteem seems to

**TABLE 7.1.18a Self-Esteem/Self-Concept and Criminal/Delinquent Behavior.**

| Nature of the relationship | Officially detected offenses | | | Self-reported offenses | |
|---|---|---|---|---|---|
| | Drug offenses | Delinquency | Recidivism | Overall offenses | Illegal drugs |
| Positive | | | **NORTH AMERICA** *United States*: Byrd et al. 1993 | | **EUROPE** *Spain*: Luengo et al. 1994 **NORTH AMERICA** *United States*: Kinnier et al. 1994 |
| Not signif. | | **NORTH AMERICA** *United States*: Dietz 1969; Calhoun et al. 1984 | **NORTH AMERICA** *United States*: Cox 1996:21 | **EUROPE** *Spain*: Luengo et al. 1994 **NORTH AMERICA** *United States*: Atkins 1974; DW Mann 1976; M Gold 1978; McCarthy & Hoge 1984*; Jang & Thornberry 1998 (delinquency) | **NORTH AMERICA** *United States*: Bennett 1974; Galli & Stone 1975; Richek et al. 1975; R Jessor & Jessor 1977; Barrett et al. 1991; S Moore et al. 1996 |
| Negative | **NORTH AMERICA** *United States*: Pandina & Schuele 1983; Ress & Wilborn 1983 | **ASIA** *Korea*: Kim 1967 **EUROPE** *Britain*: Eyo-Isidore 1981 **MIDDLE EAST** *Saudi Arabia*: Hilmi 1988 **NORTH AMERICA** *United States*: Dorn 1968; Fitts & Hamner 1969; HB Kaplan 1975a; Martinez et al. 1979; Lund & Salary 1980; Truckenmiller 1982:84; Singh et al. 1986; Ward & Tittle 1994; Edwards 1996:980 | **NORTH AMERICA** *Canada*: Gendreau et al. 1979 | **ASIA** *China*: Leung & Lau 1989 **NORTH AMERICA** *Canada*: Annis et al. 1971; DE Riggs 1973; *United States*: Peterson et al. 1961; Matchett 1971; GF Jensen 1972a; HB Kaplan 1975a; HB Kaplan 1976; HB Kaplan 1978; HB Kaplan 1980; Bynner et al. 1981:420; Hogan & Mookherjee 1981; R Hogan & Jones 1983:17; McCarthy & Hoge 1984*; Rosenberg 1978; Schweitzer et al. 1992 **OCEANIA** *Australia*: Cole et al. 1989; Heaven 1993:73; Heaven 1996; Rigby & Cox 1996; *New Zealand*: DM Fergusson et al. 2002 **INTERNATIONAL** *Multiple Countries*: Cormier et al. 1973 | **NORTH AMERICA** *United States*: RA Ball 1977:114; Burke et al. 1978; Smith & Fogg 1978; HB Kaplan 1980; Bry et al. 1982; MG Miller et al. 1982; LS Wright & Moore 1982; Bry 1983; Chassin 1984; Dielman et al. 1984; HB Kaplan 1985; Steffenhagen & Steffenhagen 1985; Dielman et al. 1987; H White et al. 1987:729; Blau et al. 1988; Kaestner 1997:168 |

**TABLE 7.1.18b Self-Esteem/Self-Concept And Clinical or Personality Traits Associated with Criminality.**

| Nature of the relationship | Antisocial behavior | Physical aggression |
|---|---|---|
| | Childhood & early adol. | |
| Positive | **NORTH AMERICA** *United States*: Pakiz et al. 1992 | **OCEANIA** *Australia*: Rigby & Slee 1991 (school age, bullying) |
| Not signif. | | **NORTH AMERICA** *United States*: Seals & Young 2003 (adol., self-report bullying) |
| Negative | | **EUROPE** *Ireland*: O'Moore & Hillery 1989 (school age, bullying) |

continually decline among persistent delinquents as they age (McCarthy & Hoge 1984).

One can see in Table 7.1.18b that a number of studies have also examined the connection between self-esteem and factors frequently linked to criminality. One study reported a positive relationship between self-esteem and antisocial behavior for children and adolescents. For physical aggression, the results were mixed; some studies detected a positive association, others detected a negative association, and still others did not detect any association.

## 7.2 INTELLIGENCE AND LEARNING ABILITY

No matter how one defines the term, intelligence is undoubtedly one of the hallmarks of the human species. Nonetheless, there are considerable variations in intelligence from one person to another. Some aspects of intelligence pertain to academic ability, whereas other aspects are more elusive. In this section, the findings of possible relationships between criminal/delinquent behavior and intelligence (along with related concepts) are summarized.

### 7.2.1 Academic Performance (Grade Point Average, GPA)

As shown in Table 7.2.1a, over 100 studies have investigated the possible link between grades in school and involvement in crime. The vast majority of studies have found that individuals who receive high grades tend to be less criminal than those with low grades (for reviews by others see Silberberg & Silberberg 1971; Siegel & Senna 1988:302). As will be discussed more later, the academic performance of delinquents and criminals tends to be especially poor in those subject areas requiring reading and other linguistic skills, rather than in areas where the primary demands are on mathematical and scientific reasoning skills (Hogenson 1974; Sturge 1982). This basic inverse relationship between criminality and intelligence has even been found after statistically controlling for parental social status (Hawkins & Wall 1980:6).

As shown in Table 7.2.1b, several studies have documented that individuals who exhibit childhood conduct disorders and/or antisocial personality in adolescence or adulthood tend to do less well in school (according to their teachers) than do their peers. A couple of studies have also found an inverse relationship between physical aggression during childhood and poor school performance.

### 7.2.2 Intelligence

The first standardized tests of intelligence were introduced to the scientific community around the beginning of the twentieth century in France (McFarland 1981:311). The main objective of the tests' developers was to identify children who could benefit most from remedial help in achieving academic success (Stelmack et al. 1995:447; Ackerman & Heggestad 1997:219). Accordingly, scores on tests of intelligence have always correlated most strongly with academic grades, especially in core subject areas (Eysenck 1979; Scarr & Carter-Saltzman 1982:831).

While controversy still surrounds IQ tests, many studies have sought to determine if criminals and delinquents differ on average from nonoffenders in intelligence. Table 7.2.2a summarizes findings from all of the published studies based on officially detected measures of offending and clearly shows that most studies link offending with significantly lower scores on intelligence tests. This table does not provide a way of estimating the magnitude of the differences, but earlier reviews have concluded that about eight points (or half a standard deviation) separate criminals from the general population, especially for persistent serious offenders (Hirschi & Hindelang 1977; Lynam et al. 1993:187).

In Table 7.2.2b, the findings pertaining to links between intelligence and self-reported offending are summarized. As one can see, most of the evidence points toward an inverse relationship, just as does the data based on officially detected offenses. This confirmation of the official data is particularly relevant to an old argument surrounding the crime–IQ relationship that "only the dumb ones get caught" (Doleschal & Klapmuts 1973). Such a view is not supported by the evidence in that even self-reported offending tends to be negatively associated with intelligence (especially when drug offenses are excluded).

Table 7.2.2c summarizes what has been found regarding links between intelligence and antisocial behavior. Note that these studies also argue strongly against the "only dumb ones get caught" idea because it has been clearly demonstrated that children with conduct disorders have lower IQs

**TABLE 7.2.1a** Academic Performance (Grade Point Average, GPA) and Criminal/Delinquent Behavior.

| Nature of the relationship | Officially detected offenses | | | | Self-reported offenses | |
|---|---|---|---|---|---|---|
| | Violent offenses | Delinquency | General & adult offenses | Recidivism | Overall offenses | Illegal drugs |
| Positive | | | | | | |
| Not signif. | **NORTH AMERICA** *United States*: Kupersmidt & Coie 1998 | | | **NORTH AMERICA** *United States:* Myner et al. 1998:77 | **NORTH AMERICA** *United States:* Voelkl et al. 1999:82* (White students); Wright et al. 2001 (delinquency); Felson & Staff 2006 (delinquency) | **NORTH AMERICA** *United States*: Steffenhagen et al. 1969; Blumenfield et al. 1972; Simon et al. 1974; Finnell & Jones 1975; Agnew & White 1992:486 |
| Negative | **EUROPE** *Britain*: Farrington 1989 **NORTH AMERICA** *United States*: Andrew 1979 | **ASIA** *China*: Gao 1986 **EUROPE** *Britain*: Burt 1925; Burt 1931; Gibbens 1963; Offord et al. 1978; Farrington 1979*; Nagin & Land 1993:352; *Finland*: Rantakallio et al. 1995; M Cannon et al. 2002 (among schizophrenics); *Poland*: Zabczyaska 1977; *Scotland*: Ferguson 1952:29; *Sweden*: Jonsson 1975:184; Sarnecki & Sollenhag 1985 **NORTH AMERICA** *Canada*: Gomme 1982; Frechette & Le Blanc 1987; Tremblay et al. 1992; Le Blanc 1994; *United States*: Sullivan 1927; Glueck & Glueck 1934b:87; Bond & Fendrick 1936; Healy & Bronner 1936:61; Moore 1936; Moore 1937; Kvaraceus 1945:141; Glueck & Glueck 1950; | **EUROPE** *Britain*: H. Ellis 1910:132; Farrington 1993a:16; Farrington 1997b:97*; *Denmark*: Raine et al. 1994; *Sweden*: Kirkegaard-Sorensen & Mednick 1977 **NORTH AMERICA** *United States*: Polk 1975*; Robins 1979 | **EUROPE** *Germany*: Richter et al. 1996 **NORTH AMERICA** *United States*: Meade 1973:483; Niarhos & Routh 1992 | **ASIA** *China*: Ma et al. 1996 **EUROPE** *Belgium*: Born & Gavray 1994:147; *Britain*: Farrington 1973; Farrington 1979:99*; Farrington 1997b:100*; *Norway*: Cochran & Bo 1989; *Switzerland*: Killias et al. 1994:198 **NORTH AMERICA** *Canada*: WG West 1984; Le Blanc et al. 1992; *United States*: Gold 1963:44; Hirschi 1969:111; Polk 1969*; Bachman 1970; Kelly & Balch 1971*; Silberberg & Silberberg 1971; Elliott & Voss 1974; Polk et al. 1974*; Senna et al. 1974*; Polk 1975*; Jensen 1976*; Jensen & Eve 1976; Mann 1976; Bachman et al. 1978; Gold 1978:296; Offer et al. 1979; Krohn & Massey 1980; Akers et al. 1981; | **EUROPE** *Britain*: Engel et al. 1987; Miller & Plant 1996:397 **NORTH AMERICA** *Canada*: Annis et al. 1971; Moyer & Fejer 1972; Bakal et al. 1976; Killeen 1977; Hundleby 1985; *United States*: Palmore & Hammond 1964; Frumkin et al. 1969; Gossett et al. 1972; Senna et al. 1974*; Galli & Stone 1975; Brook et al. 1977; Kandel et al. 1978; Smith & Fogg 1978; Kirk 1979; Fors & Rojek 1983:213-214; Krohn et al. 1984; Mills & Noyes 1984; Friedman et al. 1985; Barnes & Welte 1986; Wolford & Swisher 1986; Newcomb et al. 1987:418; White et al. 1987:729; Marston et al. 1988; Weng et al. 1988 (including cigarettes); Elliott et al. |

(*continued*)

**TABLE 7.2.1a** Academic Performance (Grade Point Average, GPA) and Criminal/Delinquent Behavior—*cont'd*

| Nature of the relationship | Officially detected offenses | | | | Self-reported offenses | |
|---|---|---|---|---|---|---|
| | Violent offenses | Delinquency | General & adult offenses | Recidivism | Overall offenses | Illegal drugs |
| | | Reiss & Rhodes 1961:723; Slocum & Stone 1963:205; Palmore & Hammond 1964; Short & Strodtbeck 1965:238; Robins & Hill 1966:329; Polk 1969*; Rhodes & Reiss 1969; Burns 1971; Empey & Lubeck 1971; Kelly 1971; Kelly & Balch 1971*; Venezia 1971; Wolfgang et al. 1972; Feldhusen et al. 1973; Frease 1973; Kelly & Pink 1973; Swift et al. 1973; Kelly 1974; Mauser 1974; Polk et al. 1974*; Poremba 1975; GF Jensen 1976:382*; Noblit 1976; Ackerman et al. 1977; Bazemore & Noblit 1978; Jerse & Fakouri 1978; Phillips & Kelly 1979; Broder et al. 1981; Eron 1982:201; Elifson et al. 1983:521; Meltzer et al. 1984; Figueira-McDonough 1983; Plutchik 1983:70; Farnworth et al. 1985; Lawrence 1985*; Lawrence 1991; Ward & Tittle 1994; Rowe 1997:150* **OCEANIA** *Hawaii*: Werner 1987:27; Werner & Smith 1992; *New Zealand*: Williams & McGee 1994 | | | Broder et al. 1981; Hundleby 1982; Wiatrowski et al. 1982; Brook et al. 1983; Hogan & Jones 1983:17; Wells & Rankin 1983; McCarthy & Hoge 1984; Menard & Morse 1984:1371; Donovan & Jessor 1985; LaGrange & White 1985; Lawrence 1985*; Levine & Singer 1988:392; Tygart 1988; Elliott et al. 1989*; Agnew & White 1992:486; Lynam et al. 1993; Sampson & Laub 1993b; Broidy 1995:551; Joseph 1996; Rowe 1997:150*; Vazsonyi & Flannery 1997; Voelkl et al. 1999:82* (Black students); Herrenkohl et al. 2000 (violent delinquency, teens) | 1989*; Wallace & Bachman 1991:351; McGee & Newcomb 1992; Bachman & Schulenberg 1993; Shannon et al. 1993; Schulenberg et al. 1994; Brook & Newcomb 1995; Beauvais et al. 1996; Jenkins 1996; Younger et al. 1996; Dozier & Barnes 1997; DS Miller & Miller 1997; Duncan et al. 1998 |

**TABLE 7.2.1b** Academic Performance (Grade Point Average, GPA) and Clinical or Personality Traits Associated with Criminality.

| Nature of the relationship | Antisocial behavior | | Physical aggression |
|---|---|---|---|
| | Childhood & early adol. | Late adol. & adulthood | |
| Positive | | | |
| Not signif. | | | |
| Negative | **EUROPE** *Britain*: Rutter et al. 1970; Cochrane 1979:204 **NORTH AMERICA** *Canada*: Ledingham & Schwartzman 1984 *United States*: Moffitt 1990a; Dishion et al. 1991; Zoccolillo & Rogers 1991 (females, intellectual aptitude controlled); Wentzel 1993 | **EUROPE** *Britain*: Reitsma-Street et al. 1985 **NORTH AMERICA** *United States*: Pakiz et al. 1997 | **NORTH AMERICA** *United States*: Brook & Newcomb 1995 (childhood); LR Bergman & Magnusson 1997 (childhood) |

than children without conduct disorders (Rutter & Giller 1984:165).

## 7.2.3 Performance Intelligence (PIQ)

Although IQ scores are often presented as a single, unitary concept, there are actually two major distinguishable components to IQ: a verbal component and a nonverbal component. The nonverbal IQ is often referred to performance intelligence (PIQ) and captures abilities that are related to such tasks as spatial ability. Table 7.2.3 contains one study that examined the association between PIQ and criminal/delinquent behavior. This sole study, conducted on a sample of New Zealand males, revealed a negative relationship between PIQ and officially detected delinquent and adult offenders, as well as self-reported offenders.

## 7.2.4 Verbal Intelligence (VIQ)

Table 7.2.4 reveals the results of the studies that tested for a relationship between verbal intelligence (VIQ) and criminal/delinquent behavior. VIQ is typically measured by administering a standardized assessment protocol that measures vocabulary knowledge, word association ability, verbal memory, or all three. All of the studies presented in Table 7.2.4 reported a statistically significant negative effect between VIQ and criminal/delinquent behavior. Stated differently, it appears as though delinquents and criminals have lower VIQs.

## 7.2.5 Intellectual Imbalance

Intelligence (or mental ability) is not a simple or unified phenomenon (Quay 1987a:109). Over the years, researchers have repeatedly identified several different aspects of intelligence, but, as noted above, two major aspects stand out: verbal (linguistic) IQ and performance (nonlinguistic) IQ (TD Hill et al. 1985; Leckliter et al. 1986).

A number of studies have been undertaken to determine if one of these two dimensions of IQ correlates more closely with criminality than does the other. The results of these studies are reflected in Table 7.2.5a. As one can see, the vast majority of studies have indicated that criminals and delinquents score significantly lower than average only with respect to VIQ. In other words, much more of the deficits in IQ that are found among persons with criminal and antisocial tendencies have to do with language ability rather than with other aspects of intelligence. This pattern is called *intellectual imbalance* (Angenent & de Man 1996:52). Most studies that have documented this imbalance have found it to be in the range of 3–5 IQ points (Law & Faison 1996:699). Interestingly, the one study that documented the opposite pattern (i.e., a higher VIQ compared with the PIQ) compared illegal drug users with nonusers, suggesting that there is something fairly distinctive about users of illegal drugs relative to offenders.

A number of studies have also examined the association between intellectual imbalance and antisocial behavior in childhood, adolescence, and adulthood. As one can see in Table 7.2.5b most of the studies have reported that persons displaying antisocial behavior tend to have PIQ scores that are significantly higher than VIQ scores. It should be noted, however, that a number of studies have failed to detect this relationship.

## 7.2.6 Interpreting the Emotions of Others (Emotional Intelligence)

Definitions and measures of emotional intelligence vary but revolve around decoding emotional information from others (Santesso et al. 2006:312). Generally speaking, persons who have higher emotional intelligence are better able to empathize and sympathize with others. Given the amount of harm that criminals inflict on others, it seems likely that

**TABLE 7.2.2a Intelligence and Criminal/Delinquent Behavior.**

| Nature of the relationship | Officially detected offenses | | | | |
|---|---|---|---|---|---|
| | Violent offenses | Sex offenses | Delinquency | General & adult offenses | Recidivism |
| Positive | | | | | **EUROPE** *Britain*: Calhoun 1928; Hill 1936<br>**NORTH AMERICA** *United States*: Murchison 1926*; Hartman 1940* |
| Not signif. | | | **EUROPE** *Britain*: Rutter et al. 1970:227<br>**NORTH AMERICA** *Canada*: Valliant & Bergeron 1997; *United States*: Baker et al. 1929; Maller 1937a; Lichtenstein & Brown 1938<br>**OCEANIA** *New Zealand*: Black & Hornblow 1973:88 | **EUROPE** *Germany*: Richter et al. 1996*<br>**NORTH AMERICA** *United States*: Murchison 1926*; Doll 1930; Townes et al. 1981 | **EUROPE** *Britain*: Lane & Witty 1935; Marcus 1955<br>**NORTH AMERICA** *United States*: Tolman 1938; Kirkpatrick 1937; Merrill 1947; Hartman 1940*; AH Roberts et al. 1974:835<br>**OCEANIA** *New Zealand*: Black & Hornblow 1973 |
| Negative | **EUROPE** *Denmark*: Hogh & Wolf 1981*; Hodgins et al. 1996 | **NORTH AMERICA** *Canada*: Cantor 2004 (male pedophiles); Blanchard et al. 2007 (male pedophiles) | **ASIA** *India*: Shanmugam 1980<br>**EUROPE** *Britain*: Eilenberg 1961; Gibson & West 1970; Rutter et al. 1975; Moffitt et al. 1981*; Sturge 1982; Farrington 1987a:32; Nagin & Land 1993:352; Farrington 1997b:100; *Denmark*: Moffitt et al. 1981*; Kandel et al. 1988*; *Finland*: Jarvelin et al. 1995; Rantakallio et al. 1995; *Spain*: Diaz et al. 1994:313; *Sweden*: Hartelius 1965; Jonsson 1967:200; Jonsson 1975:184; Stattin et al. 1997:204*; Elmund et al. 2004 (adoptees)<br>**NORTH AMERICA** *Canada*: Rogers & Austin 1934; *United States*: Fernald 1920:527; Goddard 1921; Caldwell 1929; M Elliott 1929:574; Mendenhall 1932; Ruggles 1932; S Glueck & Glueck 1934b:292; Glueck 1935; Lane & Witty 1935; Charles 1936; Moore 1937; Owen 1937; Jameson 1938; CW Mann & Mann 1939; Lichtenstein & Brown 1938; Kvaraceus 1944c; Franklin 1945; Altus & Clark 1949; S Glueck & Glueck 1950; Shulman 1951; Diller 1952; Prentice & Kelly 1973; KM Murphy & D'Angelo 1963:345; Naar 1965; Ahmad 1966; Conger & Miller 1966:191; Robins & Hill 1966:331; Wolfgang et al. 1972:58; Miller et al. 1974; Moffitt et al. 1981*; Yeudall et al. 1982:261; Menard & Morse 1984; Lawrence 1985; Kandel et al. 1988*; Moffitt & Silva 1988a&b; Denno 1990a; Lipsitt et al. 1990; Moffitt et al. 1994; Ward & Tittle 1994; Coughlin & Vuchinich 1996:497; Rowe 1997:150; Kasen et al. 1998:58; McGloin & Pratt 2003 (blacks)<br>**OCEANIA** *Australia*: Tennison-Wood 1932; McRae 1934; *Hawaii*: Werner 1987:25; Werner & Smith 1992:104; *New Zealand*: White et al. 1989; Lynam et al. 1993* | **EUROPE** *Britain*: Goring 1913; West & Farrington 1973:123; Farrington 1993a:15; Farrington 1997b:97; *Denmark*: Hogh & Wolf 1981*; *Finland*: Tiihonen et al. 1993; *Germany*: Goppinger 1983; *Sweden*: Stattin & Klackenburg-Larsson 1993<br>**NORTH AMERICA** *United States*: Zeleny 1933; Brown & Hartman 1938; McGarvey et al. 1981; Hains & Ryan 1983:1540; Huesmann et al. 1984 (traffic violations & more serious crimes); Eisenman 1990, 1991; AD Davis et al. 1991; Schweinhart et al. 1993 | **EUROPE** *Britain*: Frank 1931; Shulman 1951; *Germany*: Schwind 1975; Richter et al. 1996:339*; *Sweden*: Stattin et al. 1997:204*<br>**NORTH AMERICA** *United States*: Tibbitts 1931; Shakow & Millard 1935 |

**TABLE 7.2.2b Intelligence and Criminal/Delinquent Behavior.**

| Nature of the relationship | Self-reported offenses | |
|---|---|---|
| | Overall offenses | Illegal drugs |
| Positive | | **NORTH AMERICA** *United States*: Kellam et al. 1980 |
| Not signif. | **NORTH AMERICA** *Canada*: Bogaert & Rushton 1989: 1075; *United States*: Broidy 1995:550; Rowe 1997:150; McGloin et al. 2004:618 | **NORTH AMERICA** *United States*: Wexler 1975; Codina et al. 1998* (males) |
| Negative | **EUROPE** *Britain*: Gibson & West 1970; West & Farrington 1973:131; Farrington 1997b:97 **NORTH AMERICA** *United States*: Hirschi 1969; Jessor 1976; Moffitt et al. 1981; Wiatrowski et al. 1981; Menard & Morse 1984; Lynam et al. 1993; Blackson & Tarter 1994:818; Ward & Tittle 1994 (IQ); Williams & McGee 1994 **OCEANIA** *New Zealand*: Moffitt & Silva 1988a; Moffitt & Silva 1988b; White et al. 1989; Moffitt et al. 1995; DM Fergusson et al. 2002 (excluding victimless offenses) | **EUROPE** *Ireland*: Timms et al. 1973 **NORTH AMERICA** *United States*: Bear & Richards 1981; Codina et al. 1998* (females) |

**TABLE 7.2.2c Intelligence and Clinical or Personality Traits Associated with Criminality.**

| Nature of the relationship | Antisocial behavior | |
|---|---|---|
| | Childhood & early adol. | Late adol. & adulthood |
| Positive | | |
| Not signif. | | |
| Negative | **EUROPE** *Britain*: Rutter et al. 1970:227; West & Farrington 1973; Rutter et al. 1975; McMichael 1979; Richman et al. 1982; Maughan et al. 1985; Farrington et al. 1990; Farrington 1993a:15 *Netherlands*: Wiegman et al. 1992; *Scotland*: May 1975 **NORTH AMERICA** *Canada*: Andre et al. 1994; *United States*: Schonfeld et al. 1988; Robins et al. 1991:278; Wentzel 1993:360; Lynam & Henry 2001 **OCEANIA** *New Zealand*: Fergusson et al. 2005 | **EUROPE** *Finland*: Virkkunen & Luukkonen 1977:222 **NORTH AMERICA** *United States*: Wiens et al. 1959; Robins 1966:156; O'Kane et al. 1996; PA Arnett et al. 1997:1424; RJ Blair et al. 2004; Epstein et al. 2006:205 |

**TABLE 7.2.3 Performance Intelligence (PIQ) and Criminal/Delinquent Behavior.**

| Nature of the relationship | Officially detected offenses | | Self-reported offenses |
|---|---|---|---|
| | Delinquency | General & adult offenses | Overall offenses |
| Positive | | | |
| Not signif. | | | |
| Negative | **OCEANIA** *New Zealand*: Moffitt et al. 1994* (males, by age 17, police contact) | **OCEANIA** *New Zealand*: Moffitt et al. 1994* (males, by age 18, visual spatial scores) | **OCEANIA** *New Zealand*: Moffitt et al. 1994* (age 18, males, visual motor scores, delinquency) |

**TABLE 7.2.4 Verbal Intelligence (VIQ) and Criminal/Delinquent Behavior.**

| Nature of the relationship | Officially detected offenses | | Self-reported offenses |
|---|---|---|---|
| | Delinquency | General & adult offenses | Overall offenses |
| Positive | | | |
| Not signif. | | | |
| Negative | **NORTH AMERICA** *United States*: CL Gibson et al. 2001:587 (blacks, early onset of delinquency) | **NORTH AMERICA** *United States*: Silverton 1988b* **OCEANIA** *New Zealand*: Moffitt et al. 1994* (verbal memory & scores) | **NORTH AMERICA** *United States*: Silverton 1988b* **OCEANIA** *New Zealand*: Moffitt et al. 1994* (verbal memory & scores, delinquency) |

antisocial persons would be less adept at decoding and interpreting the emotions of others. A number of studies have examined this possibility, the results of which are presented in Table 7.2.6a. This table suggests that emotional intelligence is inversely related to official delinquency, self-reported delinquency, and illegal drug use.

Table 7.2.6b contains the studies that tested for a connection between emotional intelligence and antisocial behavior or other factors linked to criminality. The results reported in these studies were strikingly consistent in concluding that emotional intelligence exhibits a negative relationship with antisocial behavior in adolescence and

**TABLE 7.2.5a Intellectual Imbalance and Criminal/Delinquent Behavior.**

| Nature of the relationship | Officially detected offenses | | | Self-reported offenses | |
|---|---|---|---|---|---|
| | Delinquency | General & adult offenses | Recidivism | Overall offenses | Illegal drugs |
| PIQ significantly higher than VIQ | **EUROPE** *Britain*: Payne 1960; Rutter et al. 1975; Rutter et al. 1979; Sturge 1982; *Denmark*: Buikhuisen et al. 1988 **NORTH AMERICA** *United States*: Werder et al. 1943; Wechsler 1944; Franklin 1945; Sloan & Cutts 1945:96; Altus & Clark 1949; S Glueck & Glueck 1950; Diller 1952; Doppelt & Seashore 1959; Prentice & Kelly 1973; Camp 1966; Matarazzo 1972:433; Ganzer & Sarason 1973; Andrews 1974; Ollendick 1979; Haynes & Bensch 1983; Tarter et al. 1984; Tarter et al. 1985*; Grace & Sweeney 1986; A Walsh et al. 1987; Jensen & Faulstich 1988; Culberton et al. 1989 **OCEANIA** *New Zealand*: Lynam et al. 1993:193 | **EUROPE** *Britain*: Farrington 1993:15; *Denmark*: Moffitt et al. 1981*; *Germany*: Richter et al. 1996:338; *Sweden*: Stattin & Klackenberg-Larsson 1993 | **EUROPE** *Britain*: Farrington 1995b:941; *Denmark*: Moffitt et al. 1981:155 **NORTH AMERICA** *United States*: Solway et al. 1975; Haynes & Bensch 1981; Blecker 1983 | **NORTH AMERICA** *United States*: Moffitt et al. 1981*; Maguin et al. 1993 **OCEANIA** *New Zealand*: Moffitt & Silva 1988c | |
| Not signif. | **NORTH AMERICA** *United States*: Henning & Levy 1967; Foster 1959; Davis et al. 1991; Law & Faison 1996 | **EUROPE** *Britain*: Farrington 1993a:15 **OCEANIA** *New Zealand*: Walters 1953 | | **NORTH AMERICA** *United States*: Meltzer et al. 1984; Tarter et al. 1985* | |
| VIQ significantly higher than PIQ | | | | | **NORTH AMERICA** *United States*: Fleming et al. 1982 |

**TABLE 7.2.5b Intellectual Imbalance and Clinical or Personality Traits Associated with Criminality.**

| Nature of the relationship | Antisocial behavior | |
|---|---|---|
| | Childhood & early adol. | Late adol. & adulthood |
| PIQ significantly higher than VIQ | **NORTH AMERICA** *United States*: Wechsler 1958:160; Camp 1977; Richman et al. 1982; Kender et al. 1985 **OCEANIA** *New Zealand*: McGee et al. 1986; Henry et al. 1992 | **NORTH AMERICA** *United States*: Wechsler 1944:155; Fisher 1961 |
| Not signif. | **EUROPE** *Britain*: Farrington 1993a:15 | **EUROPE** *Finland*: Virkkunen & Luukkonen 1977:222 **NORTH AMERICA** *United States*: Strother 1944:398; Naar 1965 |
| VIQ significantly higher than PIQ | | |

**TABLE 7.2.6a Interpreting the Emotions of Others (Emotional Intelligence) and Criminal/Delinquent Behavior.**

| Nature of the relationship | Officially detected offenses | Self-reported offenses | |
|---|---|---|---|
| | Sex offenses | Overall offenses | Illegal drugs |
| Positive | | | |
| Not signif. | | | |
| Negative | **NORTH AMERICA** *United States*: Moriarty et al. 2001 (adol.) | **ASIA** *China*: C Wang 2002; **OCEANIA** *Malaysia*: Liau et al. 2003 | **NORTH AMERICA** *United States*: Loeber et al. 1999; Riley & Schutte 2003 |

adulthood, physical aggression, cognitive and personality factors, drug abuse, and physiological factors. The evidence garnered from these two tables appears to indicate that antisocial persons have lower emotional intelligence.

## 7.2.7 Language Learning

The acquisition of language is one of the most fascinating, yet least understood, aspects of human development. It appears as though language may be an inborn instinct (Pinker 1994) because all healthy children who are exposed to language eventually learn it. There is, however, considerable variability in how quickly children acquire language and how well they understand it. Two studies were located that examined the association between language skills and criminal/delinquent behavior. Table 7.2.7 shows that reduced language abilities are associated with greater official and self-reported delinquency.

## 7.2.8 Learning Disabilities in General

A *learning disability* is usually defined as a significant discrepancy between an individual's IQ test score and his/her actual academic performance (Broder et al. 1981; Stelmack et al. 1995:447; Winters 1997:452). Persons who

**TABLE 7.2.6b Interpreting the Emotions of Others (Emotional Intelligence) and Clinical or Personality Traits Associated with Criminality.**

| Nature of the relationship | Antisocial behavior | Physical aggression | Cognitive & personality factors | Drug abuse | Physiological factors |
|---|---|---|---|---|---|
| | Late adol. & adult | | | | |
| Positive | | | | | |
| Not signif. | | | | | |
| Negative | **NORTH AMERICA** *United States*: D Stevens et al. 2001; Marsh et al. 2007 (fearful facial expressions, less prosocial subjects) | **NORTH AMERICA** *United States*: Dodge & Frame 1982; Denham et al. 2002 | **NORTH AMERICA** *Canada*: Santesso et al. 2006 (externalizing behavior) | **NORTH AMERICA** *United States*: Trinidad & Johnson 2002 (alcohol & tobacco use) | **NORTH AMERICA** *Canada*: Bar-On et al. 2003 (bilateral brain lesion of the ventromedial cortex and/or unilateral lesions of the amygdale) |

**TABLE 7.2.7** Language Learning and Criminal/Delinquent Behavior.

| Nature of the relationship | Officially detected offenses | | Self-reported offenses |
|---|---|---|---|
| | Delinquency | General & adult offenses | Overall offenses |
| Positive | | | |
| Not signif. | | | |
| Negative | **EUROPE** *Sweden*: Stattin & Klackenberg-Larsson 1993* | **NORTH AMERICA** *United States*: Stattin & Klackenberg-Larsson 1993* | **NORTH AMERICA** *Canada*: Brownlie et al. 2004 (delinquency) |

**TABLE 7.2.8a** Learning Disabilities in General and Criminal/Delinquent Behavior.

| Nature of the relationship | Officially detected offenses | | Self-reported offenses | |
|---|---|---|---|---|
| | Delinquency | Recidivism | Overall offenses | Illegal drugs |
| Positive | **EUROPE** *Britain*: Yule & Rutter 1968; *Sweden*: Jonsson 1967:198; Gath et al. 1970:219; Jonsson 1975:184; Virkkunen & Nuutila 1976 **NORTH AMERICA** *Canada*: Underwood 1976; *United States*: Mulligan 1972; Mauser 1974; Miller et al. 1974; Poremba 1975; Barrows et al. 1977; Bachara & Zaba 1978; Zinkus & Gottlieb 1978; Keilitz et al. 1979; Lewis et al. 1980; Broder et al. 1981; Post 1981; J Zimmerman et al. 1981; Wilgosh & Paitich 1982; Dunivant 1984; Roff & Wirt 1984:115; Epstein et al. 1985; Keilitz & Dunivant 1986; Grande 1988; Larson 1988; Leone et al. 1991 | **NORTH AMERICA** *United States*: California Youth Authority 1982 | **NORTH AMERICA** *United States*: Rubenstein 1992 | **NORTH AMERICA** *United States*: Maag et al. 1994; Katimas et al. 1996 |
| Not signif. | | | **NORTH AMERICA** *United States*: Broder et al. 1981; J Zimmerman et al. 1981 | |

perform at levels substantially below their measured ability are said to be learning disabled.

There appears to be numerous causes of learning disabilities, including brain abnormalities (John et al. 1977:1405; Kraus et al. 1996) and physical difficulties in hearing or communicating (e.g., stuttering) (Cozad & Rousey 1966). Sometimes, the causes may be due to a lack of interest in school or an inability to focus on information being communicated by teachers (Flicek 1992).

Research that has explored the possibility that persons prone toward criminal and antisocial behavior have higher rates of learning disabilities than do persons in general are summarized in Table 7.2.8a. Nearly all of the evidence supports the conclusion of a positive relationship, with two exceptions found for self-reported offending.

Studies have also been conducted to test for a connection between learning disabilities and antisocial behavior during childhood, adolescence, and adulthood. The results of these studies are presented in Table 7.2.8b and show that all of the

**TABLE 7.2.8b** Learning Disabilities and Clinical or Personality Traits Associated with Criminality.

| Nature of the relationship | Antisocial behavior | |
|---|---|---|
| | Childhood & early adol. | Late adol. & adulthood |
| Positive | **EUROPE** *Britain*: Yule & Rutter 1968; Davie et al. 1972b; Rutter et al. 1976 **NORTH AMERICA** *United States*: Harris 1961; Williams & McGee 1994 **OCEANIA** *New Zealand*: McGee et al. 1986 | **NORTH AMERICA** *United States*: FA Elliott 1978:150 |
| Not signif. | | |
| Negative | | |

located research detected a significant positive relationship between learning disabilities and antisocial behavior.

## 7.2.9 Learning from Being Disciplined

Discipline is one of the hallmarks of parenting, but not all children are equally responsive to this form of training. Some children, for example, learn to refrain from the behaviors for which they are punished, while others, no matter how much they are disciplined, will continue to engage in wayward behavior. One study was located that examined the association between learning from discipline and antisocial behavior during childhood and early adolescence (Table 7.2.9). The results of this study indicated that the learning from discipline is significantly lower among those children displaying antisocial behavior.

## 7.2.10 Passive Avoidance Learning

Passive avoidance learning refers to learning that inhibits behaviors in some contexts, but not in others. A number of studies have examined the association between passive avoidance learning and antisocial behavior in late adolescence and adulthood. Most of these studies employed the "go/no-go" task to measure passive avoidance learning. The "go/no-go" task requires subjects to respond to some signals (e.g., a green light) but to ignore other signals (e.g., a red light). The results of these studies are presented in Table 7.2.10. Most of these studies reported a negative relationship between antisocial behavior and passive avoidance learning, meaning that persons displaying antisocial behaviors were not very efficient at learning to inhibit behaviors that would be punished.

## 7.2.11 Reading Ability

Verbal ability and language development both tend to be lower in criminals and delinquents than in those who do not engage in this type of behavior. It would seem to follow then that reading ability would also be depressed in persons displaying antisocial behaviors. A few studies have examined the association between reading ability and antisocial behaviors and, for the most part, have found reading ability to be lower in antisocials. Table 7.2.11 shows, for example, four studies which detected a negative relationship between reading ability and antisocial behavior in children and young adolescents. One study failed to find a significant association between physical aggression and reading ability.

**TABLE 7.2.9** Learning from Being Disciplined and Clinical or Personality Traits Associated with Criminality.

| Nature of the relationship | Antisocial behavior |
|---|---|
| | Child & early adol. |
| Positive | |
| Not signif. | |
| Negative | **NORTH AMERICA** *United States*: Patterson 1982 |

**TABLE 7.2.10** Passive Avoidance Learning and Clinical or Personality Traits Associated with Criminality.

| Nature of the relationship | Antisocial behavior |
|---|---|
| | Late adol. & adulthood |
| Positive | |
| Not signif. | **NORTH AMERICA** *United States:* Thornquist & Zuckerman 1995 (inmates) |
| Negative | **NORTH AMERICA** *United States:* Newman & Kosson 1986 (inmates); Kosson et al. 1990 (inmates); Lynam et al. 1999; Wallace et al. 2000 (inmates); Brinkley et al. 2001 (offenders) |

## 7.2.12 Slow Reading Development

Studies undertaken to specify the type of learning disabilities most associated with criminal/delinquent behavior have often pointed specifically to reading difficulties (Jonsson 1975:184; Buikhuisen 1987:169; Williams & McGee 1994). A common form of learning difficulty linked to slow reading is known as *dyslexia*, a condition often associated with difficulty in recognizing the differences between letters with the same shapes, but only different in their positioning (e.g., *p*, *q*, *b*, *d*) (Critchley 1972). This

**TABLE 7.2.11** Reading Ability and Clinical or Personality Traits Associated with Criminality.

| Nature of the relationship | Antisocial behavior | Physical aggression |
|---|---|---|
| | Childhood & early adol. | |
| Positive | | |
| Not signif. | | |
| Negative | **EUROPE** *Britain*: Rutter & Yule 1970<br>**OCEANIA** *Australia*: D Smart et al. 1996; Prior et al. 1999; *New Zealand*: S Williams & McGee 1994 | **EUROPE** *Britain*: Maughan et al. 1996 |

condition is also sometimes called "word blindness" (Holzman 1979:78).

As one can see when examining Table 7.2.12a, the evidence is very consistent in showing that several forms of slow development in reading ability are unusually common among delinquents and criminals. These findings complement evidence that offenders are more likely to have IQ deficit of a language (VIQ) nature than of a nonlanguage nature (PIQ).

Research has also explored the potential relationship between slow reading development and antisocial behavior during childhood, adolescence, and adulthood. Table 7.2.12b summarizes the findings from this area of research. One can see that all of these studies indicated that persons displaying antisocial behaviors had slower reading development than those who did not display this type of behavior.

**TABLE 7.2.12b** Slow Reading Development and Clinical or Personality Traits Associated with Criminality.

| Nature of the relationship | Antisocial behavior | |
|---|---|---|
| | Childhood & early adol. | Late adol. & adulthood |
| Positive | **EUROPE** *Britain*: Yule & Rutter 1968 (reading retardation); Gregory 1965 (reading retardation); *Scotland*: McMichael 1979 (reading retardation); Maughan et al. 1985 (reading retardation) | **NORTH AMERICA** *United States*: Ziskind et al. 1977 (reading retardation); Rodriguez 1993 (slow language development) |
| Not signif. | | |
| Negative | | |

## 7.2.13 Spatial Span

Spatial span tests measure the ability to recall the temporal sequence of spatial events. These tests are thought to involve the right prefrontal cortex, an area of the brain that is partially responsible for behavioral regulation, the modulation of emotions, and the processing of information encountered in the social world. As a result, any impairment of this area of the brain is likely to increase the odds of careless, antisocial, and even criminal conduct. Only one study was located that examined the association between spatial span and criminal/delinquent behavior. As shown in Table 7.2.13 this study indicated an inverse relationship between spatial span and official delinquency, meaning that

**TABLE 7.2.13** Spatial Span and Criminal/Delinquent Behavior.

| Nature of the relationship | Officially detected offenses |
|---|---|
| | Delinquency |
| Positive | |
| Not signif. | |
| Negative | **NORTH AMERICA** *United States*: E Cauffman et al. 2005 |

**TABLE 7.2.12a** Slow Reading Development and Criminal/Delinquent Behavior.

| Nature of the relationship | Officially detected offenses | | | |
|---|---|---|---|---|
| | Violent offenses | Delinquency | General & adult offenses | Recidivism |
| Positive | **NORTH AMERICA** *United States*: Brearley 1932:145 (reading retardation) | **EUROPE** *Britain*: Critchley 1968 (reading retardation); Rutter et al. 1970:247 (reading retardation); *Sweden*: Jonsson 1975:184 (reading retardation) **NORTH AMERICA** *United States*: Sullivan 1927 (reading retardation); Lane & Witty 1934 (reading retardation); Hill 1935 (reading retardation); Fendrick & Bond 1936 (reading retardation); S Glueck & Glueck 1950 (illiteracy); Fabian 1955 (reading retardation); Harrower 1955 (reading retardation); Margolin et al. 1955 (reading retardation); Mulligan 1972 (dyslexia); Herjanic & Penick 1972 (reading retardation); Hogenson 1974 (reading retardation); Rizzo 1975 (dyslexia); Andrew 1978 (reading retardation); Andrew 1979 (reading retardation); Meltzer et al. 1984 (reading retardation) **OCEANIA** *New Zealand*: Moffitt et al. 1994 (reading retardation) | **EUROPE** *Sweden*: Stattin & Klackenberg-Larsson 1993 (slow language development) | **NORTH AMERICA** *United States*: Ganzer & Sarason 1973 (reading retardation) |
| Not signif. | | | | |
| Negative | | | | |

**TABLE 7.3.1a** Mental Illness in General and Officially Detected Criminal/Delinquent Behavior.

| Nature of the relationship | Officially detected offenses | | | | | |
|---|---|---|---|---|---|---|
| | Violent offenses | Property offenses | Drug offenses | Delinquency | General & adult offenses | Recidivism |
| Positive | **EUROPE** *Britain*: Wessely et al. 1994; C Wallace et al. 1998*; *Denmark*: Gottlieb et al. 1987*; Hodgins 1992*; Eronen et al. 1996* (homicides); Brennan et al. 2000; *Finland*: Tiihonen & Hakola 1994; Eronen et al. 1996*; Tiihonen et al. 1997*; *Sweden*: Lindqvist 1986; Hodgins 1992*; Adler & Lidberg 1995; Fazel & Grann 2004; Fazel & Grann 2006 **NORTH AMERICA** *Canada*: Cote & Hodgins 1992; *United States*: Giovannoni & Gurel 1967*; Sosowsky 1978*; Steadman et al. 1978*; Ribner & Steadman 1981; Gottlieb et al. 1987*; J Swanson et al. 1990; Link et al. 1992; Steadman et al. 1993; Swanson 1994:113; Steadman et al. 1998; Swartz et al. 1998 **OCEANIA** *Australia*: C Wallace et al. 1998*; Mullen et al. 2000; Wallace et al. 2004; *New Zealand*: Arseneault et al. 2000 | **EUROPE** *Sweden*: Hodgins 1992* | **EUROPE** *Netherlands*: Hendricks 1990; *Sweden*: Mueser et al. 1992; Sandell & Bertling 1996 **NORTH AMERICA** *United States*: Kosten et al. 1982; Rounsaville et al. 1982; Khantzian & Treece 1985; Woody et al. 1985; Jainchill et al. 1986; Kosten & Rounsaville 1986; Weiss et al. 1986; Christie et al. 1988; HE Ross et al. 1988; Bukstein et al. 1989; Regier et al. 1990; Rounsaville et al. 1991 **OCEANIA** *Hawaii*: Werner & Smith 1992:104 | **NORTH AMERICA** *Canada*: Andre et al. 1994; *United States*: Balla et al. 1974; Lewis et al. 1985 | **EUROPE** *Denmark*: Ortmann 1981; Hodgins 1992*; Hodgins et al. 1996; *Finland*: Joukamaa 1991; Tiihonen et al. 1993; Tiihonen et al. 1997* **NORTH AMERICA** *Canada*: Hodgins & Cote 1990; Motvik & Porporino 1991; Palermo et al. 1992; Bland et al. 1998:276; *United States*: Rappeport & Lassen 1965; Rappeport & Lassen 1966; Giovannoni & Gurel 1967*; Yarvis 1972; Sosowsky 1974; Swank & Winer 1976; Zitrin et al. 1976; Durbin et al. 1977; Sosowsky 1978*; Steadman et al. 1978*; Shore et al. 1980; Sosowsky 1980; Shanok & Lewis 1981; Lamb & Grant 1982; Schuerman & Kobrin 1984; Washington & Diamond 1985; Valdiserri et al. 1986; Hyde & Seiter 1987; Neighbors et al. 1987; Daniel et al. 1988; Harry & Steadman 1988; Holcomb & Ahr 1988; McFarland et al. 1989; Hodgins 1993; Friedman et al. 1996:399; Teplin et al. 1996 | **EUROPE** *Netherlands*: Buikhuisen & Hoekstra 1974:65 **NORTH AMERICA** *United States*: Koenigsberg et al. 1977; R Moos et al. 1994 (substance abuse, within four years) |
| Not signif. | **EUROPE** *Britain*: Modestin & Ammann 1995 | | | | **NORTH AMERICA** *United States*: Guze et al. 1969 | **NORTH AMERICA** *United States*: Lueger & Cadman 1982; Dembo et al. 1995:1444 |
| Negative | | **NORTH AMERICA** *United States*: Giovannoni & Gurel 1967* | | | | |

reduced spatial span abilities corresponded to greater delinquent involvement.

## 7.3 MENTAL ILLNESS

While difficult to define, *mental illness* is obviously an important concept in the social and behavioral sciences. The present section reviews research findings that have attempted to determine if mental illness is associated with criminality.

### 7.3.1 Mental Illness in General

The research reviewed below is controversial because few professionals in the mental health field want to see the trend toward noninstitutional treatment of the mentally ill (begun in the 1950s) reversed. However, if mentally ill people have an above average tendency to engage in criminal/delinquent behavior, the wisdom of the expanded use of community-based treatment for serious mental illness may be questioned (Abramson 1972; Solomon et al. 1994). One writer went so far as to refer to the movement toward community-based treatment of the mentally ill as the *criminalization of mental illness*, since many patients who would otherwise be receiving care and treatment in mental hospitals end up in jails or prisons instead (Teplin 1983). By examining Table 7.3.1a, one can see that the vast majority of studies have found a significant positive relationship between mental illness and officially detected involvement in criminal/delinquent behavior. This occurs despite the fact that the majority of mentally ill persons do not become involved in this type of behavior.

Table 7.3.1b shows that self-reported criminality is positively associated with mental illness in general, and that this is roughly to the same extent as seems to be true for officially detected offending.

Similar to findings about criminality per se, Table 7.3.1c indicates that antisocial behavior and possibly alcoholism are positively correlated with mental illness in general.

**TABLE 7.3.1b** Mental Illness in General and Self-Reported Criminal/Delinquent Behavior.

| Nature of the relationship | Self-reported offenses | |
|---|---|---|
| | Overall offenses | Illegal drugs |
| Positive | **NORTH AMERICA** *United States*: Steadman & Felson 1984; Swanson et al. 1990; Link et al. 1992 | **EUROPE** *Britain*: Johns 2001; *Sweden*: Andreasson et al. 1987 (among schizophrenics) **NORTH AMERICA** *United States*: Helzer 1988 **OCEANIA** *Australia*: W Hall & Solowij 1997; Degenhardt & Hall 2001; *New Zealand*: R McGee et al. 2000 |
| Not signif. | | **NORTH AMERICA** *United States*: Richek et al. 1975 |
| Negative | | |

### 7.3.2 Minor/Subclinical Depression

*Depression* refers to feelings of sadness and loneliness. Even though everyone has had these feelings over the loss of loved ones or after major setback in achieving lifetime goals, for some the feelings can be prolonged seemingly for no reason. To these cases, psychologists and psychiatrists apply the concept of depression. While there is certainly no sharp dividing line, many clinicians find it useful to distinguish between minor and major depression, with the main distinction being the depth of a depressive episode and the length of time it persists.

Table 7.3.2a provides a summary of the evidence regarding whether a relationship exists between minor depression and criminal/delinquent behavior. This table clearly shows that persons who engage in criminal/delinquent behavior are more prone to be even moderately depressed than people in general. The only possible exception is that of drug offenders.

**TABLE 7.3.1c** Mental Illness in General and Clinical or Personality Traits Associated with Criminality.

| Nature of the relationship | Antisocial behavior | | Alcoholism |
|---|---|---|---|
| | Childhood & early adol. | Late adol. & adulthood | |
| Positive | **NORTH AMERICA** *Canada*: Kutcher et al. 1989; *United States*: Biederman et al. 1997 **OCEANIA** *New Zealand*: Bardone et al. 1998 (females) | **OCEANIA** *New Zealand*: Mulder et al. 1994:283 | **NORTH AMERICA** *United States*: Regier et al. 1990 |
| Not signif. | | | |
| Negative | | | |

**TABLE 7.3.2a** Minor/Subclinical Depression and Criminal/Delinquent Behavior.

| Nature of the relationship | Officially detected offenses | | | | Self-reported offenses | |
|---|---|---|---|---|---|---|
| | Violent offenses | Delinquency | General & adult offenses | Recidivism | Overall offenses | Illegal drugs |
| Positive | **EUROPE** *France*: Benezech & Bourglois 1992 | **EUROPE** *Belgium*: Vermeiren et al. 2004:572* (delinquency) **NORTH AMERICA** *Canada:* Sas et al. 1985; Sas & Jaffe 1986; Reddon et al. 1996; M Kerr et al. 1997 (childhood depressive symptoms); *United States*: Kashani et al. 1980; Pliszka et al. 2000; Overbeek et al. 2001; *United States*: Vermeiren et al. 2004:572* (delinquency) | **EUROPE** *Switzerland*: Modestin et al. 1996b **NORTH AMERICA** *Canada*: Bland et al. 1998:276 | **NORTH AMERICA** *United States*: McManus et al. 1984 | **EUROPE** *Belgium*: Vermeiren et al. 2004:572* (delinquency); *Iceland*: Sigfusdottir et al. 2004 (delinquency preceded depression) **NORTH AMERICA** *Canada*: Hagan 1997; Hagan & Foster 2003; *United States*: De Coster & Heimer 2001; Vermeiren et al. 2004:572* (delinquency); Siennick 2007:596 (delinquency predicts depression) | **NORTH AMERICA** *United States*: Paton et al. 1977; Hogan & Jones 1983:17; Johnston & O'Malley 1986; Deykin et al. 1987; Greenbaum et al. 1991; Van Hasselt et al. 1993; Barnet et al. 1995; Aseltine et al. 1998; Krueger 1999 (negative emotions); Curran et al. 2000; Costello et al. 2003; Silberg et al. 2003; Kashdan et al. 2005; Elkins et al. 2006 **OCEANIA** *Australia*: Reynolds & Rob 1988; *New Zealand*: Fergusson & Woodward 2000 (females); Fergusson et al. 2002 (marijuana use) |
| Not signif. | | | | | | **EUROPE** *Spain*: Calafat et al. 1994 **MIDDLE EAST** *Israel*: Teichmann et al. 1989 **NORTH AMERICA** *United States*: Yamaguchi & Kandel 1984 |
| Negative | | | | | | |

**TABLE 7.3.2b** Minor/Subclinical Depression and Clinical or Personality Traits Associated with Criminality.

| Nature of the relationship | Antisocial behavior | | Physical aggression | Alcoholism | Drug abuse |
|---|---|---|---|---|---|
| | Childhood & early adol. | Late adol. & adulthood | | | |
| Positive | **NORTH AMERICA** *Canada*: Fleming et al. 1989; Hagan 1997; *United States*: Kovacs et al. 1988; Loeber et al. 1991; Patterson & Stoolmiller 1991 (males); Robins & Price 1991; Capaldi 1992 (males); Lahey et al. 1992; Hinshaw et al. 1993; Myers et al. 1993; JM Beyers & Loeber 2003 (males); Siennick 2007 **OCEANIA** *New Zealand*: Moffitt & Caspi 2001 | **EUROPE** *Britain*: Fombonne et al. 2001 **OCEANIA** *New Zealand*: Mulder et al. 1994:283* (women); Bardone et al. 1998 (women) | **NORTH AMERICA** *United States*: Seals & Young 2003* (bullies) **OCEANIA** *Australia*: Rigby & Slee 1991 (school age bullies) | **NORTH AMERICA** *United States*: KM Jackson & Sher 2003 | **NORTH AMERICA** *United States*: Patkar et al. 2003:438 (blacks, cocaine addiction) |
| Not signif. | | **OCEANIA** *New Zealand*: Mulder et al. 1994:283* (men) | **NORTH AMERICA** *United States*: Seals & Young 2003* (bullies, self-report) | | |
| Negative | | | | | |

An impressive amount of research has also examined whether minor/subclinical depression is associated with antisocial behavior and a range of factors frequently linked to criminality. As Table 7.3.2b shows, the overwhelming majority of all studies have shown that depression is positively related to antisocial behavior, physical aggression, alcoholism, and drug abuse.

## 7.3.3 Major/Clinical Depression

Table 7.3.3a displays the results of the studies that have explored the relationship between major/clinical depression and criminal and delinquent behavior. Most of the studies that examined this possible connection reported a positive relationship, with all of the failures to replicate confined to self-reported offenses.

Research has also examined the association between major/clinical depression and antisocial behavior from childhood to adulthood. One can see in Table 7.3.3b that all of the located studies revealed a positive relationship between major/clinical depression and antisocial behavior.

## 7.3.4 Bipolar Depression

One type of depression is typified by mood swings between feeling extreme sadness and lethargy to periods of exceptional exuberance. This type of depression is called *bipolar depression* or *manic depression* (MacKinnon et al. 1997:356).

**TABLE 7.3.3a** Major/Clinical Depression and Criminal/Delinquent Behavior.

| Nature of the relationship | Officially Detected Offenses | | | Self-reported offenses | |
|---|---|---|---|---|---|
| | Violent offenses | Drug offenses | Delinquency | Overall offenses | Illegal drugs |
| Positive | **EUROPE** *Finland*: Eronen et al. 1996 (homicide) | **NORTH AMERICA** *United States*: Kleinman et al. 1990 | **NORTH AMERICA** *United States*: Chiles et al. 1980; McManus et al. 1984 | **EUROPE** *Switzerland*: Modestin et al. 1996b | **NORTH AMERICA** *United States*: Kandel & Davies 1986; Regier et al. 1990; Swanson et al. 1992; Lin et al. 1996 |
| Not signif. | | | | **OCEANIA** *New Zealand*: Bardone et al. 1996:820 | **NORTH AMERICA** *United States*: Garber et al. 1988; Harrington et al. 1990 |
| Negative | | | | | |

**TABLE 7.3.3b** Major/Clinical Depression and Clinical or Personality Traits Associated with Criminality.

| Nature of the relationship | Antisocial behavior | |
|---|---|---|
| | Childhood & early adol. | Late adol. & adulthood |
| Positive | **NORTH AMERICA** *United States*: Puig-Antich 1982; Herkov & Myers 1996; Clark et al. 1997; Whitmore et al. 1997:93 | **OCEANIA** *New Zealand*: Bardone et al. 1996:820; Kasen et al. 2001 (childhood depression); Loeber et al. 2002 (childhood depression) |
| Not signif. | | |
| Negative | | |

While not nearly as many studies have involved manic depression as have considered unipolar depression, the number of studies is sufficient to consider manic depression as a separate correlate of crime. Table 7.3.4a shows that studies have either found sufferers from manic depression to be at increased risk of engaging in crime or that they and individuals without the disorder do not differ significantly in offending risks. Whatever increased risk may exist seems to be confined to the manic phase to the illness rather than to the depressed phase.

Some studies were located that tested for an association between bipolar depression and antisocial behavior. As Table 7.3.4b shows, all of the studies reported a positive relationship between bipolar depression and antisocial behavior in childhood, adolescence, and adulthood.

**TABLE 7.3.4a** Bipolar Depression and Criminal/Delinquent Behavior.

| Nature of the relationship | Officially detected offenses | | |
|---|---|---|---|
| | Drug offenses | Delinquency | General & Adult offenses |
| Positive | **NORTH AMERICA** *United States*: Estroff et al. 1985 | **EUROPE** *Switzerland*: Modestin et al. 1996b **NORTH AMERICA** Canada: Bland et al. 1998:276 | |
| Not signif. | | **NORTH AMERICA** *United States*: Guze et al. 1969 | **EUROPE** *Sweden*: Petterson 1977 |
| Negative | | | |

**TABLE 7.3.4b** Bipolar Depression and Clinical or Personality Traits Associated with Criminality.

| Nature of the relationship | Antisocial behavior | |
|---|---|---|
| | Childhood & early adol. | Late adol. & adulthood |
| Positive | **NORTH AMERICA** *Canada*: Kutcher et al. 1989; *United States*: Biederman et al. 1996a; Wozniak et al. 1995; Biederman et al. 1997 | **NORTH AMERICA** *United States*: Thorneloe & Crews 1981; Robins et al. 1991:288; McElroy et al. 1992 |
| Not signif. | | |
| Negative | | |

## 7.3.5 Posttraumatic Stress Disorder

Post-traumatic stress disorder (PTSD) is a psychological disorder that typically occurs in response to an unusually traumatic event. Soldiers engaged in combat, for example, are at risk for developing PTSD as are seriously abused children. Whether PTSD is related to crime and antisocial behaviors is an under-researched line of inquiry. Table 7.3.5 shows that the pertinent studies all concluded that there was a positive relationship between PTSD and antisocial behavior assessed during late adolescence and adulthood.

## 7.3.6 Schizophrenia

*Schizophrenia* refers to mental disorders that are most often associated with auditory hallucinations, delusions, and paranoia. Determination of who is and is not afflicted with schizophrenia is nearly always based on clinical interviews with patients and/or their relatives. The evidence for a link between schizophrenia and criminal/delinquent behavior is summarized in Table 7.3.6a, which predominantly supports the view that a positive relationship exists.

A handful of studies were also located that had examined the association between schizophrenia and antisocial

**TABLE 7.3.5** Posttraumatic Stress Disorder and Clinical or Personality Traits Associated with Criminality.

| Nature of the relationship | Antisocial behavior |
|---|---|
| | Late adol. & adulthood |
| Positive | **NORTH AMERICA** *United States*: Mueser et al. 2002; Schnurr et al. 2002; Sareen et al. 2004 |
| Not signif. | |
| Negative | |

**TABLE 7.3.6a** Schizophrenia and Criminal/Delinquent Behavior.

| Nature of the relationship | Officially detected offenses | | | | | Self-reported offenses |
|---|---|---|---|---|---|---|
| | Violent offenses | Drug offenses | Delinquency | General & adult offenses | Recidivism | Illegal drugs |
| Positive | **EUROPE** *Austria*: Schanda et al. 2004 (homicide); *Britain:* PJ Taylor 1985; Wallace et al. 1998 (males, homicide); Mullen et al. 2000 (homicide, males); EA Walsh et al. 2001 (males, homicide); Cannon et al. 2002; *Denmark*: Eronen et al. 1996* (homicide); Brennen et al. 2000; Gosden et al. 2005 (among male juvenile offenders); *Finland*: Eronen et al. 1996* (males); Tiihonen et al. 1997*; Rasanen et al. 1998; *Germany*: Boeker & Haefner 1973; *Iceland*: Petursson & Gudjonsson 1981 (homicide); *Sweden*: Lindqvist 1989 (males); Lindqvist & Allebeck 1990; Fazel & Grann 2006 **MIDDLE EAST** *Isreal*: Stueve & Link 1997 **NORTH AMERICA** *United States*: J Swanson et al. 1990*; Cirincione et al. 1992; Monahan 1992; Eronen 1995; Erb et al. 2001 (males, homicide) **OCEANIA** *Australia*: Mullen et al. 2000; *New Zealand*: Arseneault et al. 2000 | **EUROPE** *Sweden*: Lindqvist & Alleback 1989 **NORTH AMERICA** *United States*: Panton 1958; Mueser et al. 1990*; Regier et al. 1990; Mueser et al. 1992 | **EUROPE** *Germany*: H Gross & Kaltenback 1975; DO Lewis & Shanok 1978 | **EUROPE** *Britain*: Coid et al. 1993; *Denmark:* Silverton 1985; *Finland*: Tiihonen et al. 1997*; *Sweden*: Lindqvist & Allebeck 1990:346* **NORTH AMERICA** *Canada*: Bland et al. 1998:276; *United States*: Dunham et al. 1939; Roth & Erwin 1971; Link et al. 1992: Wessely et al. 1994 | | **NORTH AMERICA** *United States*: Breakey et al. 1974; Richard et al. 1985; Barbee et al. 1989; Drake et al. 1989; Test et al. 1989; Mueser et al. 1990*; Swanson et al. 1990*; Dixon et al. 1990 |
| Not signif. | | | | **NORTH AMERICA** *United States*: Kloek 1968; Guze et al. 1969; Teplin et al. 1996 (females) | | |
| Negative | | | | | | **NORTH AMERICA** *Canada*: Rice & Harris 1995:339; *United States*: Lidz et al. 1993 |

**TABLE 7.3.6b** Schizophrenia and Clinical or Personality Traits Associated with Criminality.

| Nature of the relationship | Antisocial behavior | | Physical aggression |
|---|---|---|---|
| | Childhood & early adol. | Late adol. & adulthood | |
| Positive | **NORTH AMERICA** *United States*: Morriss et al. 1956; O'Neil & Robins 1958; Robins & Price 1991 | **EUROPE** *Sweden*: Bland et al. 1987; Jackson et al. 1991 **NORTH AMERICA** *United States*: Robins et al. 1991:288 | **EUROPE** *Britain*: Done et al. 1994 (childhood); M Cannon et al. 2001 (childhood); PM Miller et al. 2002 (childhood) **NORTH AMERICA** *United States*: Swanson et al. 1990; Monahan 1992; Link et al. 1994 (delusional schizophrenia) |
| Not signif. | | | **EUROPE** *Britain*: P Jones et al. 1994 (childhood) |
| Negative | | | |

behavior and physical aggression, the results of which are presented in Table 7.3.6b. As can be seen, all of the studies reported that schizophrenics were more likely than nonschizophrenics to display antisocial behaviors during childhood, adolescence, and adulthood. Similarly, most of the studies of physical aggression and schizophrenia reported a positive relationship.

### 7.3.7 Suicide

It is not entirely appropriate to think of suicide as a form of mental illness. However, for lack of a better place within which to categorize it, and because suicide is often linked to depression (Apter et al. 1988; Hoberman & Garfinkel 1988), it is being considered here. Suicidal behavior is measured in three main ways: the most obvious is the actual completion of suicide; the second is an attempt to do so, often based on self-reports. The third way is called suicide ideation and refers to self-reports of giving serious thought to committing suicide.

Table 7.3.7a shows that quite a number of studies have investigated possible links between suicidal behavior and criminal tendencies. As one can see, all of these studies found a significant positive relationship. The link between suicidal behavior and criminality appears to be especially strong in the case of persons with lengthy histories of alcohol and drug abuse (Woodruff et al. 1972).

In addition to looking for links between suicide and crime at an individual level, some studies have also explored links at the ecological level. Time series studies have shown that suicide rates and delinquency/crime rates within countries tend to fluctuate together, both in the United States (Loeber 1990:2) and in Ireland (McKenna et al. 1997). Similarly, within the United States, one study found that states with the highest crime rates also had higher average suicide rates (Boor 1981). Similarly, across countries, two studies found murder rates and suicide rates to be positively correlated (Palmer 1968; Holinger 1979), although one earlier study found the opposite to be true (Henry & Short 1954).

Several studies were located that had examined the relationship between suicide and antisocial behavior. As shown in Table 7.3.7b, all of these studies reported a positive relationship between suicide and antisocial behaviors. One study found a positive link between physical aggression and the commission of suicide using violent means.

## 7.4 MENTAL DISORDER

*Mental disorders* refer to a general state of cognitive difficulties often resulting in inappropriate social behavior. A "fuzzy" distinction can be made between mental disorder and mental illness. Basically, persons are less likely to voluntarily seek help for mental disorders than for mental illnesses, and are less likely to be treated in an institutional setting.

The mental disorders that have been frequently examined with respect to criminal/delinquent behavior are attention deficit hyperactivity disorder (ADHD), oppositional defiant disorder (ODD), alcoholism, and drug dependence. Two other widely recognized mental disorders – conduct disorder and antisocial personality disorder – will be considered only indirectly since these two conditions are considered clinical manifestations of what is legally defined as criminal and delinquent behavior.

### 7.4.1 Attention Deficit Hyperactivity Disorder

While every child at least occasionally fails to pay attention to parents and teachers, those with the greatest difficulties are given the diagnosis of *attention deficit disorder* (*ADD*). This disorder is often accompanied by high degrees of unruly and disruptive behavior, in which case it is known as *attention deficit hyperactivity disorder* (*ADHD*). Until the 1980s, the name most commonly given to ADHD was *hyperactivity* or *hyperkinesis*. Even though the restless motor movements that constitute a key feature of ADHD usually diminish as affected children become adolescent,

**TABLE 7.3.7a** Suicide and Criminal/Delinquent Behavior.

| Nature of the relationship | Officially detected offenses | | | | Self-reported offenses |
|---|---|---|---|---|---|
| | Drug offenses | Delinquency | General & adult offenses | Overall offenses | Illegal drugs |
| Positive | **EUROPE** *Sweden*: Allebeck & Allgulander 1990 (completed)<br>**NORTH AMERICA** *United States*: McKenry et al. 1983 (attempted); RC Fowler et al. 1986 (completed); Rich et al. 1988 (completed); Rich et al. 1989 (completed); Deykin et al. 1994 (ideation) | **NORTH AMERICA** United States: Alessi et al. 1984 (attempted) | **EUROPE** *Sweden*: Belfrage 1991 (completed); Lidberg 1993 (completed); Belfrage 1994 (completed)<br>**NORTH AMERICA** *Canada*: Deptepartment of the Solicitor General 1976 (completed); Bland et al. 1998:276 (attempted); Placido et al. 2001 (completed)<br>**OCEANIA** *Australia*: O'Toole & Stankov 1992:713 (attempted) | **NORTH AMERICA** *United States*: Frances et al. 1987 (ideation); Juon & Ensminger 1997 (ideation and attempted) | **EUROPE** *Britain*: Morgan et al. 1976; *Sweden*: Casey 1989 (attempted); Bukstein et al. 1993 (attempted)<br>**NORTH AMERICA** *Canada*: R Simon 1991 (ideation); De Man et al. 1993 (ideation); *United States*: Chabrol & Moron 1988 (ideation); Dukes & Lorch 1989 (ideation); Levy & Deykin 1989 (ideation); Berman & Schwartz 1990 (attempted); Ravinus 1990 (attempted); Anonymous 1991 (attempted); Kandel et al. 1991 (ideation); Kirkpatrick-Smith et al. 1991 (ideation); Felts et al. 1992 (ideation); DM Adams & Overholser 1992 (ideation); Kaminer 1992 (attempted and completed); AR Rich et al. 1992 (ideation); JW Swanson et al. 1992 (attempted); Garrison et al. 1993 (ideation and attempted); CA King et al. 1993 (attempted); DM Adams et al. 1994 (attempted); Kinnier et al. 1994 (attempted); Young et al. 1994 (attempted); V Burge et al. 1995; Juon & Ensminger 1997 (ideation and attempted); Mezzich et al. 1997 (ideation and attempted); Windle & Windle 1997:925 (attempted); Trammel et al. 1998 (attempted); R Garofalo et al. 1999 (high school students, attempted); Prinstein et al. 2000 (ideation); Rowan 2001 |
| Not signif. | | | | | |
| Negative | | | | | |

TABLE 7.3.7b Suicide and Clinical or Personality Traits Associated with Criminality.

| Nature of the relationship | Antisocial behavior | | Physical aggression |
|---|---|---|---|
| | Childhood & early adol. | Late adol. & adulthood | |
| Positive | **EUROPE** *Britain*: Shaffer 1974 (attempted)<br>**NORTH AMERICA** *United States*: Shafii et al. 1985 (completed); Apter et al. 1988 (attempted) | **EUROPE** *Iceland*: Helgason 1964 (completed)<br>**NORTH AMERICA** *United States*: Dorpat & Ripley 1960 (completed); Rich et al. 1986 (completed); SA Hill et al. 2005 (attempted)<br>**OCEANIA** *New Zealand*: Mulder et al. 1994:283 (attempted) | **EUROPE** *Finland*: Linnoila and Virkkunen 1992 (violent suicide) |
| Not signif. | | | |
| Negative | | | |

their abilities to maintain a focus on long term tasks assigned by others continue to be abnormally low throughout life (Gittelman et al. 1985, Klein & Mannuzza 1991; Mannuzza et al. 1991; Faigel et al. 1995).

In the United States, ADHD is estimated to affect about 2–9% of the childhood population (JC Anderson et al. 1987; Safer & Krager 1988), with estimates in a similar range for other countries as well (HR Bird et al. 1988; Bauermeister et al. 1994). A major reason the estimates will vary from one study to the next is that ADHD reveals itself in a substantial range of severities, and not all clinicians will use the same degree of severity in making a diagnosis.

Many studies have examined the possible connection between ADHD and criminal and antisocial behavior, and as shown in Table 7.4.1a, the link is well established. ADHD is especially predictive of persistent criminality (Farrington et al. 1990:73). The only possible exception involves self-reported drug offenses.

Very similar results were observed for the studies that had examined the relationship between ADHD and other factors linked to criminality. All of the studies reported in Table 7.4.1b reported a statistically significant and positive relationship between ADHD and antisocial behavior, alcoholism, and drug abuse. Taken together, the studies contained in Tables 7.4.1a and 7.4.1b provide strong and compelling evidence linking ADHD to criminal and antisocial behaviors. It is important to note that these findings were garnered from studies using different methodological techniques and which analyzed heterogeneous samples collected on different continents during different time periods. ADHD, in short, is one of the most robust correlates to criminal conduct and related behavior yet identified.

## 7.4.2 Compulsive Gambling

Most people who gamble do so occasionally as a form of recreation. However, some people seem to become addicted to the activity, and since the odds are always in favor of the gambling establishments, individuals who gamble have the greatest chances of losing substantial amounts of money. According to surveys conducted in the United States (Volberg 1994) and Great Britain (Blumel 1995), about 2% of adult gamblers are considered to be compulsive (or pathological).

A number of studies have been undertaken to determine if compulsive gambling is associated with involvement in criminal/delinquent behavior. The results of these studies, summarized in Table 7.4.2a, have been consistent in indicating that there is a significant positive correlation, both in terms of gambling addiction and even in terms of the frequency and addition of gambling.

Research has also explored the link between antisocial behavior and compulsive gambling. As Table 7.4.2b shows, four studies conducted in Canada, the United States, and Australia reported a positive and statistically significant association between compulsive gambling and antisocial behavior during late adolescence and adulthood.

## 7.4.3 Enuresis

*Enuresis*, more commonly known as *bed wetting*, refers to tendencies beyond early childhood to involuntarily urinate while sleeping. Studies conducted in the United States have indicated that most children stop wetting their beds by around age 4, with only about a third persisting through age 5, and 20% continuing to at least occasionally wet their beds beyond the age of 7 (Byrd et al. 1996). Children who are among the last to stop nighttime urination are diagnosed as having enuresis.

Over the years, researchers have sought to determine if enuretics have an elevated probability of exhibiting criminal and antisocial tendencies. The results are shown in Table 7.4.3a. As one can see, the majority of studies support the view that enuresis is significantly more common among offenders.

Research has also found some evidence linking enuresis to antisocial behavior. Table 7.4.3b shows, for example, that studies conducted in Britain, the United States, and New

**TABLE 7.4.1a** Attention deficit Hyperactivity Disorder (ADHD) and Criminal/Delinquent Behavior.

| Nature of the relationship | Officially detected offenses | | | | | Self-reported offenses | |
|---|---|---|---|---|---|---|---|
| | Violent offenses | Drug offenses | Delinquency | General & adult offenses | Recidivism | Overall offenses | Illegal drugs |
| Positive | **EUROPE** *Sweden*: B Klinteberg et al. 1993* | **EUROPE** *Sweden*: B Klinteberg et al. 1993* **NORTH AMERICA** *United States*: Blouin et al. 1978; Barkley et al. 1990; Crowley & Riggs 1995; Wilens et al. 1998 | **EUROPE** *Norway*: Troland 1988 **NORTH AMERICA** *Canada*: Offord et al. 1989; Tremblay et al. 2003; *United States*: Mendelson et al. 1971; Weiss et al. 1971; Huessy et al. 1974; Borland & Heckman 1976; Ackerman et al. 1977; Milman 1979; Weiss et al. 1979*; Loney et al. 1981; Mattes et al. 1982:115; Satterfield et al. 1982*; Loney et al. 1983; Roff & Wirt 1984:115; Gittelman et al. 1985; Mannuzza et al. 1989*; B Shaywitz & Shaywitz 1989; Zagar et al. 1989; Barkley et al. 1990; Barkley et al. 1991; Loeber 1990; Armistead et al. 1992; Biederman et al. 1996a; J Taylor et al. 2000 **OCEANIA** *New Zealand*: Moffitt 1990a | **EUROPE** *Britain*: Farrington 1990; Farrington 1993a; *Sweden*: Nylander 1979 **NORTH AMERICA** *United States*: Satterfield et al. 1982*; Weiss et al. 1985; Satterfield 1987; Mannuzza et al. 1989*; Lilienfeld & Waldman 1990; Mannuzza et al. 1991; Satterfield & Schell 1997 | **EUROPE** *Britain*: Knight & West 1975; Farrington et al. 1990:73 **NORTH AMERICA** *United States*: Satterfield et al. 1982*; Wierson & Forehand 1995:64 | **NORTH AMERICA** *United States*: Stewart et al. 1973; Peeples & Loeber 1994; Herrenkohl et al. 2000 (violent delinquency, teens, teacher & parent rated) **OCEANIA** *New Zealand*: Fergusson & Horwood 1995:482*; BR Wright et al. 1999b (parent–teacher rated, delinquency at age 15 & crime at age 21) | **MIDDLE EAST** *Israel*: Teichmann et al. 1989 **NORTH AMERICA** *United States*: Gittelman et al. 1985; Kellam et al. 1989; Friedman et al. 1991; Biederman et al. 1996a*; Wilens et al. 1997; HR White et al. 2001 **OCEANIA** *New Zealand*: Fergusson & Horwood 1995:482* |
| Not signif. | | | | | | | **NORTH AMERICA** *United States*: Weiss et al. 1979*; Halikas et al. 1990 (among delinquents) |
| Negative | | | | | | | |

**TABLE 7.4.1b Attention Deficit/Hyperactivity Disorder (ADHD) and Clinical or Personality Traits Associated with Criminality.**

| Nature of the relationship | Antisocial behavior | | Alcoholism | Drug abuse |
|---|---|---|---|---|
| | Childhood & early adol. | Late adol. & adulthood | | |
| Positive | **EUROPE** *Britain*: Sandberg et al. 1978, Sandberg et al. 1980; Schachar et al. 1981; August et al. 1983; Schachar 1991; Taylor et al. 1996; *Norway*: Backe-Hansen & Ogden 1996 **NORTH AMERICA** *Canada*: Offord & Bennett 1994; *United States*: Prinz et al. 1981; Stewart et al. 1981; McGee et al. 1985; Johnston et al. 1985; Munir et al. 1987; Walker et al. 1987; Wallander 1988; Mannuzza et al. 1989; Barkley et al. 1990; Biederman et al. 1991; Faraone et al. 1991b; Abikoff & Klein 1992; Mannuzza et al. 1993; McDermott 1993:422; Crowley & Riggs 1995; Biederman et al. 1996a; MacDonald & Achenbach 1996; Greene et al. 1997:763; Jensen et al. 1997; Satterfield & Schell 1997; Whitmore et al. 1997:93; Wilens et al. 1997; Disney et al. 1999*; Lahey et al. 1999; Sanford et al. 1999; Lahey et al. 2000; HR White et al. 2001; McCabe et al. 2004 | **NORTH AMERICA** *Canada*: Hare 1970:67; *United States*: Porges 1977; Ziskind et al. 1977:256; Satterfield 1978; Loney et al. 1981; Hechtman et al. 1984; Weiss et al. 1985; Loeber 1990; Mannuzza et al. 1993; Biederman et al. 2006 | **EUROPE** *Germany*: Johann et al. 2003 | **NORTH AMERICA** *United States*: Disney et al. 1999* (clinical diagnosis) |
| Not signif. | | | | |
| Negative | | | | |

**TABLE 7.4.2a Compulsive Gambling and Criminal/Delinquent Behavior.**

| Nature of the relationship | Officially detected offenses | | Self-reported offenses |
|---|---|---|---|
| | Drug offenses | Delinquency | Illegal drugs |
| Positive | **NORTH AMERICA** *United States*: Ramirez et al. 1983 (diagnosed gambling addiction); McCormick 1993 (diagnosed gambling addiction) | **EUROPE** *Britain*: Farrington 1988:72 (diagnosed gambling addiction) **NORTH AMERICA** *United States*: Nagin & Land 1993:353 (diagnosed gambling addiction) | **NORTH AMERICA** *United States*: Lesieur et al. 1986 (frequent gambling); Proimos et al. 1998 (frequent gambling) |
| Not signif. | | | |
| Negative | | | |

**TABLE 7.4.2b Compulsive Gambling and Clinical or Personality Traits Associated with Criminality.**

| Nature of the relationship | Antisocial behavior |
|---|---|
| | Late adol. & adulthood |
| Positive | **NORTH AMERICA** *Canada*: Bland et al. 1993 (diagnosed gambling addiction); *United States*: McCormick et al. 1987 (diagnosed gambling addiction) **OCEANIA** *Australia*: Blaszczynski et al. 1989 (diagnosed gambling addiction); Blaszczynski & McConaghy 1994 (diagnosed gambling addiction) |
| Not signif. | |
| Negative | |

Zealand have found a positive association between enuresis and antisocial behavior in childhood, adolescence and adulthood. However, two studies, one in the Netherlands and one in the United States, failed to detect a statistically significant relationship between enuresis and childhood antisocial behavior.

## 7.4.4 Externalizing Behavior

Externalizing behaviors is a term often used to describe children who display visible signs of misconduct. Only one study was located pertaining to a possible link between externalizing behavior problems (assessed at the age of 3) and officially detected offenses during adulthood. As Table 7.4.4 shows, this single study reported the relationship to be positive.

**TABLE 7.4.3a Enuresis and Criminal/Delinquent Behavior.**

| Nature of the relationship | Officially detected offenses | | | | Self-reported offenses |
|---|---|---|---|---|---|
| | Property offenses | Delinquency | General & adult offenses | Recidivism | Illegal drugs |
| Positive | **EUROPE** *France*: Bachet 1948 | **EUROPE** *Britain*: Argyle 1964:63; Rutter et al. 1970; *Sweden*: Hartelius 1965:113; Jonsson 1967:197; Jonsson 1975:184 **NORTH AMERICA** *United States*: Michaels 1938; Michaels 1934; S Glueck & Glueck 1950; Michaels 1955; Hader 1965 | **EUROPE** *Britain*: Stevenson & Goodman 2001 (at age 3) | **EUROPE** *Finland*: Repo et al. 1997 | **EUROPE** *Spain*: Calafat et al. 1997:17 |
| Not signif. | | | **NORTH AMERICA** *United States*: Rosenow 1920 | | |
| Negative | | | | | |

**TABLE 7.4.3b Enuresis and Clinical or Personality Traits Associated with Criminality.**

| Nature of the relationship | Antisocial behavior | |
|---|---|---|
| | Childhood & early adol. | Late adol. & adulthood |
| Positive | **EUROPE** *Britain*: Rutter et al. 1973; *Sweden*: Hallgren 1957; Jarvelin et al. 1990 **NORTH AMERICA** *United States*: Pillay et al. 1989; Freehan et al. 1990; Byrd et al. 1996 **OCEANIA** *New Zealand*: Fergusson & Horwood 1994 | **NORTH AMERICA** *United States*: Ziskind et al. 1977:256 |
| Not signif. | **EUROPE** Netherlands: Hirasing et al. 1997 **NORTH AMERICA** *United States*: Warzak 1993 | |
| Negative | | |

## 7.4.5 Oppositional Defiant Disorder

Persons who are extremely defiant and hostile toward those in authority (such as parents and teachers) are said to have a condition known as *oppositional defiant disorder* (ODD). Diagnosis of ODD is nearly always based on clinical interviews (Lahey et al. 1994). Obviously, not everyone will draw the line between ODD and simply being stubborn and rude, but clinicians agree that some children and adolescents are so extreme in their tendencies to defy authority and thereby bring despair to themselves and others that a clinical diagnosis is warranted (Angold & Costello 1996).

In recent years, a number of researchers have sought to determine if ODD is more prevalent among persons who engage in criminal/delinquent behavior. The findings summarized in Table 7.4.5a, are quite consistent with the conclusion that ODD symptoms are positively associated with offending behavior.

Table 7.4.5b summarizes the findings of studies that examined the association between ODD and antisocial behavior. As one can see, all of the studies reported a positive relationship between ODD and both antisocial behavior and physical aggression.

**TABLE 7.4.4 Externalizing Behavior and Criminal/Delinquent Behavior.**

| Nature of the relationship | Officially detected offenses |
|---|---|
| | General & adult offenses |
| Positive | **EUROPE** *Britain*: Stevenson & Goodman 2001 (at age 3) |
| Not signif. | |
| Negative | |

## 7.4.6 Phobias

A phobia is an irrational fear that produces intense anxiety and panic. Some phobias, such as the fear of snakes

**TABLE 7.4.5a** Oppositional Defiant Disorder and Criminal/Delinquent Behavior.

| Nature of the relationship | Officially detected offenses | | Self-reported offenses | |
|---|---|---|---|---|
| | Delinquency | General & adult offenses | Overall offenses | Illegal drugs |
| Positive | **NORTH AMERICA** *United States*: Russo et al. 1994; Simons et al. 1994a; Biederman et al. 1996a | **NORTH AMERICA** *United States*: Hirschfield et al. 2006 (males) | **NORTH AMERICA** *United States*: Simons et al. 1998 | **NORTH AMERICA** *Canada*: Dobkin et al. 1995:1210 |
| Not signif. | | | | |
| Negative | | | | |

**TABLE 7.4.5b** Oppositional Defiant Disorder and Clinical or Personality Traits Associated with Criminality.

| Nature of the relationship | Antisocial behavior | Physical aggression |
|---|---|---|
| | Childhood & early adol. | Late Adol. & adulthood |
| Positive | **NORTH AMERICA** *Canada*: Tremblay et al. 1994; *United States*: Reich et al. 1979; JC Anderson et al. 1987; Hinshaw et al. 1993; McDermott 1993:422; Lahey et al. 1995; MacDonald & Achenbach 1996; Christian et al. 1997; Faraone et al. 1997; Hewitt et al. 1997:960 **LATIN AMERICA** *Puerto Rico*: Bird et al. 1988 | **NORTH AMERICA** *United States*: Langbehn et al. 1998 **NORTH AMERICA** *Canada*: Tremblay et al. 2003 (males) |
| Not signif. | | |
| Negative | | |

(ophidophobia) or the fear of spiders (arachnophobia), are quite common, while others, like the fear of vegetables (lachanophobia) or the fear of sitting (cathisophobia), are not nearly as pervasive. Whether phobias, in general, are associated with crime and delinquency is relatively unknown; no studies were located that addressed this issue. One study was identified that had investigated the association between phobias and antisocial behavior during late adolescence/adulthood. As shown in Table 7.4.6, this lone study reported a positive relationship between phobias and antisocial behavior, meaning that antisocial behavior was

**TABLE 7.4.6** Phobias and Clinical or Personality Traits Associated with Criminality.

| Nature of the relationship | Antisocial behavior |
|---|---|
| | Late adol. & adult |
| Positive | **NORTH AMERICA** *United States*: Sareen et al. 2004 |
| Not signif. | |
| Negative | |

**TABLE 7.4.7a** Somatization Disorders and Criminal/Delinquent Behavior.

| Nature of the relationship | Officially detected offenses | Self-reported offenses |
|---|---|---|
| | Delinquency | Overall offenses |
| Positive | | **EUROPE** *Belgium*: Vermeiren et al. 2004:572* **NORTH AMERICA** *United States*: Vermeiren et al. 2004:572* |
| Not signif. | **EUROPE** *Belgium*: Vermeiren et al. 2004:572* **NORTH AMERICA** *United States*: Vermeiren et al. 2004:572* | |
| Negative | | |

**TABLE 7.4.7b Somatization Disorders and Clinical or Personality Traits Associated with Criminality.**

| Nature of the relationship | Antisocial behavior |
|---|---|
| | Late adol. & adult |
| Positive | **NORTH AMERICA** *United States*: Cloninger & Guze 1970a; Swartz et al. 1991a |
| Not signif. | |
| Negative | |

more common among people with, as opposed to without, phobias.

### 7.4.7 Somatization Disorders

Somatization disorder is a psychiatric disorder where people persistently complain of having physical problems without any identifiable cause. The basis of somatization disorder is unknown and, perhaps as a result, treatment for this disorder is not very effective. The research examining the association between somatization disorders and criminal/delinquent behaviors is decidedly mixed; two studies reported a significant positive relationship, while two studies failed to detect any association (Table 7.4.7a).

The studies that were located regarding the possible association between somatization disorders and clinical factors linked to criminality are summarized in Table 7.4.7b. These studies revealed a statistically significant positive relationship.

## 7.5 DRUG ADDICTION/DEPENDENCE

While people will never agree on exactly where minor alcohol and drug use gives way to alcoholism and drug dependency, no one doubts that a legitimate distinction can be made. Basically, individuals who feel compelled to consume several drinks every day are considered alcoholic, especially if their drinking adversely affects family and social relationships (Helzer et al. 1991:81; American Psychiatric Association 1994:195). Drug dependence is similarly defined.

### 7.5.1 Drug Dependence/Substance Abuse in General

Without claiming that there are sharp dividing lines, nearly all scientists agree that a distinction between drug use and drug dependency (or drug addiction) is warranted (Jurich & Polson 1984). The latter terms mean that drug use must have become fairly habitual and accompanied by feelings of discomfort whenever use is stopped even for

**TABLE 7.5.1a Drug Dependence/Substance Abuse in General and Criminal/Delinquent Behavior.**

| Nature of the relationship | Officially detected offenses | | | | | Self-reported offenses |
|---|---|---|---|---|---|---|
| | Violent offenses | Property offenses | Delinquency | General & adult offenses | Recidivism | Overall offenses |
| Positive | **EUROPE** *Britain*: H Scott et al. 1998; Soyka 2000; *Denmark*: Brennan et al. 2000; *Finland*: Tiihonen et al. 1997; *Sweden*: Grann & Fazel 2004 **NORTH AMERICA** *United States*: Felthous & Kellert 1986; Steadman et al. 1998 | **OCEANIA** *Australia*: Dobinson & Ward 1986 | **EUROPE** *Britain*: Dimond 1964; Backhouse & Pierce James 1969; *Sweden*: Stattin et al. 1997:204 **NORTH AMERICA** *United States*: A Gordon 1973 | **EUROPE** *Britain*: IP James 1969; *Sweden*: Hodgins 1992:480 **NORTH AMERICA** *Canada*: Bland et al. 1998:276; *United States*: Rappeport & Lassen 1966; Giovannoni & Gurel 1967; Guze et al. 1969; Plair & Jackson 1970; Roth & Ervin 1971; McGlothlin 1979; Inciardi 1980; Ball et al. 1981; Ball 1982; Leukfield 1985; Speckart & Anglin 1985 | **EUROPE** *Sweden*: DeJong et al. 1992; Stattin et al. 1997:204 **NORTH AMERICA** *United States*: Vold 1931; Cloninger & Guze 1970a; Babst et al. 1971; Cloninger & Guze 1973; Palmer & Carlson 1976; DM Gottfredson et al. 1978; Brown 1978; SD Gottfredson & Gottfredson 1979; Eisenberg 1985; Wish & Johnson 1986:80; Wierson & Forehand 1995:64 | **EUROPE** *Britain*: Hammersley & Morrison 1987; Otero-Lopez et al. 1994; *Germany*: Stadtland and Nedopil 2003 (recidivism) **NORTH AMERICA** *United States*: Hundleby 1982; Elliott et al. 1985; Watters et al. 1985; Swanson et al. 1990; Dembo et al. 1991; Horney et al. 1995; Uggen & Thompson 2003 (property offending) |
| Not signif. | | | | | | |
| Negative | | | | | | |

**TABLE 7.5.1b Drug Dependence/Substance Abuse in General and Clinical or Personality Traits Associated with Criminality.**

| Nature of the relationship | Antisocial behavior | | Mental disorders |
|---|---|---|---|
| | Childhood & early adol. | Late adol. & adulthood | |
| Positive | **EUROPE** *Britain*: Farrington et al. 1989; *Sweden*: Storm-Mathisen & Vaglum 1994*; Spak et al. 1997 **NORTH AMERICA** *Canada*: Boyle et al. 1993; Reebye et al. 1995; *United States*: Loney et al. 1981; Cadoret et al. 1986 (clinical diagnosis); Kandel et al. 1986; Dimileo 1989; Robins & McEvoy 1990; Friedman et al. 1991; Greenbaum et al. 1991; Keller et al. 1992; Stowell & Estroff 1992; Cohen et al. 1993a; Mannuzza et al. 1993; Martin et al. 1993; Crowley & Riggs 1995; Lynskey & Fergusson 1995; Steele et al. 1995; SE Young et al. 1995; Greenbaum et al. 1996; JB Rowe et al. 1996; Milberger et al. 1997:325; Whitmore et al. 1997 **OCEANIA** *New Zealand*: Henry et al. 1993b; Bardone et al. 1996 | **EUROPE** *Norway*: Storm-Mathisen & Vaglum 1994* **NORTH AMERICA** *United States*: Kosten et al. 1982; Rounsaville et al. 1982 (psychiatric diagnosis); Boyd et al. 1984; Stabenau 1984 (clinical diagnosis); Hesselbrock et al. 1985; Cadoret et al. 1986; JJ Collins et al. 1988 (substance abuse disorder); Jaffe et al. 1988; HE Ross et al. 1988; Grove et al. 1990; Kleinman et al. 1990; Regier et al. 1990; LN Robins et al. 1991:288; Brooner et al. 1992; Luthar et al. 1992 (relatives of opiate addicts); Mueser et al. 1997; Myers et al. 1998 **OCEANIA** *New Zealand*: Mulder et al. 1994:283 | **NORTH AMERICA** *Canada*: Hechtman & Weiss 1986 (ADHD); *United States*: Mendelson et al. 1971 (ADHD); Goodwin et al. 1975 (ADHD); Tarter et al. 1977(ADHD); Loney et al. 1981 (ADHD); Loney et al. 1983 (ADHD, males); Gittelman et al. 1985 (ADHD); Cloninger et al. 1988 (ADHD); Comings 1989 (Tourette syndrome); DE Comings & Comings 1990 (Tourette syndrome); Mannuzza et al. 1991 (ADHD, males); Molina & Pelham 2003 (ADHD) |
| Not signif. | | | |
| Negative | | | |

a few days. Social scientists usually assess drug dependency though clinical interviews or via self-reports on anonymous questionnaires (Stacy et al. 1985; Midanik 1988).

Many studies have been undertaken to determine if, apart from casual drug use, drug dependency is a correlate of crime. As one can clearly see by viewing Table 7.5.1a, the answer is definitely yes.

As revealed in Table 7.5.1b, there is also a strikingly consistent positive relationship between drug dependence/ substance abuse and antisocial behavior and mental disorders linked to criminality. All of the studies in this table reported a statistically significant positive relationship, indicating that persons with drug/substance abuse problems displayed more antisocial behavior and were more likely to have a mental disorder compared with persons without these problems.

**TABLE 7.5.2 Alcohol Abuse and Criminal/Delinquent Behavior.**

| Nature of the relationship | Officially detected offenses | | Self-reported offenses |
|---|---|---|---|
| | Violent offenses | General & adult offenses | Overall offenses |
| Positive | **EUROPE** *Austria*: Schanda et al. 2004; *Britain*: Mullen et al. 2000; *Denmark*: Brennan et al. 2000; *Finland*: Eronen et al. 1996 (schizophrenics); Rasanen et al. 1998; *Germany*: Erb et al. 2001; *Sweden*: Gottlieb et al. 1987 **NORTH AMERICA** *Canada*: Cote & Hodgins 1992 (males, prisoners/murders); *United States*: Kantor & Strauss 1987 (domestic violence); Gelles & Cornell 1990 (domestic violence); Swartz et al. 1998; DR White & Chen 2002 (domestic violence) | **EUROPE** *Sweden*: Bohman 1996 | **EUROPE** *Britain*: G Robertson 1990 (female prisoners) |
| Not signif. | | | |
| Negative | | | |

**TABLE 7.5.3a** Alcoholism and Criminal/Delinquent Behavior.

| Nature of the relationship | Officially detected offenses | | | | | Self-reported offenses | |
|---|---|---|---|---|---|---|---|
| | Violent offenses | Property offenses | Delinquency | General & adult offenses | Recidivism | Overall offenses | Illegal drugs |
| Positive | **EUROPE** *Finland*: Eronen et al. 1996 (homicide); *Switzerland*: Modestin et al. 1996* **NORTH AMERICA** *United States*: Eronen 1995 | **EUROPE** *Switzerland*: Modestin et al. 1996* **NORTH AMERICA** *United States*: Cordilia 1985 | **EUROPE** *Britain*: Backhouse & Pierce James 1969; *Sweden*: Andreasson et al. 1993 | **EUROPE** *Britain*: Glatt 1967; *Czech Republic*: Kubicka et al. 1992; *Denmark*: Baker 1986; *Sweden*: Amark 1951; Lindelius & Salum 1973 **NORTH AMERICA** *Canada*: Elliott-Harper & Harper 1981; Bland et al. 1998:276; *United States*: Banay 1942; W McCord & McCord 1962; Guze et al. 1968; Guze et al. 1969; Roth & Ervin 1971; Mayfield 1976; Frances et al. 1980; McCord 1981a; Martin et al. 1982a; Martin et al. 1982b; Swanson et al. 1990*; Greenfield & Weisner 1995* | **EUROPE** *Britain*: Mannheim & Wilkins 1955; Farrington & Hawkins 1991; *Denmark*: Schroder 1917; *Finland*: Repo et al. 1997 **NORTH AMERICA** *Canada*: Rice & Harris 1995; *United States*: Vold 1931; Hakeem 1948; Glaser 1954; Babst et al. 1972; Palmer & Carlson 1976; Brown 1978; SD Gottfredson & Gottfredson 1979; Schmidt & White 1979 | **EUROPE** *Britain*: Cookson 1992 **NORTH AMERICA** *United States*: BA Miller et al. 1989; Swanson et al. 1990*; Windle 1990; Greenfield & Weisner 1995:99* | **NORTH AMERICA** *United States*: Helzer et al. 1991; S Wilsnack & Wilsnack 1991; Rhee et al. 2006 |
| Not signif. | | | | | | | |
| Negative | | | | | | | |

TABLE 7.5.3b Alcoholism and Clinical or Personality Traits Associated with Criminality.

| Nature of the relationship | Antisocial behavior | | Physical aggression | Drug abuse | Mental disorder |
|---|---|---|---|---|---|
| | Childhood & early adol. | Late adol. & adulthood | | | |
| Positive | **EUROPE** *Czech Republic*: Kubicka et al. 1992; *Sweden*: Spak et al. 1997 **NORTH AMERICA** *United States*: Bukstein et al. 1989; Buydens-Branchey et al. 1989; Glenn & Parsons 1989; Stowell & Estroff 1992; Fergusson et al. 1994a; Myers et al. 1995; Nixon et al. 1995 | **EUROPE** *Britain*: Vaillant 1983b; *Sweden*: Schulsinger et al. 1986 **NORTH AMERICA** *United States*: Schuckit 1973; Gorenstein 1979; Lewis et al. 1982; Rounsaville et al. 1982; Lewis et al. 1983; Lewis et al. 1985; Schuckit et al. 1986; Cadoret et al. 1987; Helzer et al. 1991; Hesselbrock 1991; Robins et al. 1991:288; Sher & Trull 1974 **OCEANIA** *New Zealand*: Mulder et al. 1994:283 | **NORTH AMERICA** *United States*: McCord 1988 | **EUROPE** *Sweden*: von Knorring et al. 1985:51 **NORTH AMERICA** *United States*: Morrison 1979; Morrison 1980 | **EUROPE** *Germany*: Johann et al. 2003 (ADHD) |
| Not signif. | | | | | |
| Negative | | | | | |

## 7.5.2 Alcohol Abuse

Alcohol abuse refers to the frequent consumption of alcohol in sufficient amounts to become intoxicated. A common example would be binge drinking as well as drinking repeatedly to the point of drunkenness. Alcohol abuse can lead to alcoholism (discussed below).

Given that a large proportion of crimes are committed when people are under the influence of alcohol, it seems likely that alcohol abuse would be positively associated with criminal and delinquent behaviors. This is exactly what the research in Table 7.5.2 indicates, all of the studies located reported a statistically significant positive association between alcohol abuse and involvement in official crime as well as self-reported offenses.

## 7.5.3 Alcoholism

In recent decades, two types of alcoholics have been identified, called Type I and Type II (von Knorring et al. 1987:307; Sigvardsson et al. 1996). *Type I alcoholics* rarely begin drinking excessively until their mid 20s or 30s, and they do so in response to devastating social or family circumstances. In contrast, *Type II alcoholics* have nearly always established a pattern of heavy drinking by their teens or early 20s, and this pattern is not related to an obvious personal tragedy (Anthenelli & Tabakoff 1995:178). Type II alcoholism has been found to run in families much more than Type I alcoholism, especially among the males (Hallman et al. 1990; Mutzell 1993). This strong family transmission patterns for Type II alcoholism has implicated genetic factors as making a substantial contribution to this form of the disease (Cloninger et al. 1981).

As shown in Table 7.5.3a, many studies have found higher rates of alcoholism among persons who are criminal as well as delinquent. Only a few of these studies distinguished between Type I and Type II alcoholics, but those that did all concluded that offending is more closely associated with Type II than Type I alcoholism (von Knorring et al. 1987:307; Sigvardsson et al. 1996).

There is also strong evidence linking alcoholism with antisocial behavior, physical aggression, and mental disorders. In fact, all of the studies that were located revealed a positive statistically significant relationship between alcoholism and these additional clinical and personality traits (Table 7.5.3b).

## 7.5.4 Age of Onset of Alcoholism (Early)

A few studies sought to determine if early age of onset of alcoholism (a symptom of Type II alcoholism as discussed above) is associated with antisocial personality. As shown in Table 7.5.4, the evidence suggests a clear positive association.

TABLE 7.5.4 Age of Onset of Alcoholism (Early) and Clinical or Personality Traits Associated with Criminality.

| Nature of the relationship | Antisocial behavior | |
|---|---|---|
| | Child & early adol. | Late adol. & adult |
| Positive | **NORTH AMERICA** *Canada*: Murdoch et al. 1990 (alcoholism); *United States*: MP Dawkins 1997 (alcoholism) | **NORTH AMERICA** *United States*: Rimmer et al. 1972; Schuckit & Morrissey 1979; CE Lewis et al. 1983 (convicts) |
| Not signif. | | |
| Negative | | |

Chapter 8

# Biological Factors

Contents

*Biology* is the study of life. Because behavior is essentially unique to just one form of life – animals – it is reasonable to argue that behavior, even social behavior, is a biological phenomenon. In this sense, criminologists are de facto biologists. Nevertheless, many exclude behavior, especially human social behavior, from the realm of "mere" biology. With this narrowed definition in mind, the present chapter reviews evidence connecting biological variables with criminal and delinquent behavior.

## 8.1 GENETIC FACTORS

The first factors to be considered are those of a strictly genetic nature. Some of the evidence relevant to the influence of genetics on criminality was reviewed in Chapter 4, with reference to comparing identical and fraternal twins and comparing parents to their adopted and nonadopted offspring. Below are tables containing citations to the studies relating to (a) percentage estimates of the extent of genetic influence on a particular aspect of behavioral correlates of criminality and (b) specific genes that have been implicated in causing criminality or closely related behavioral traits.

### 8.1.1 Estimated Genetic Contribution

A meta-analysis of twin and adoption studies concluded that genes definitely have an influence on criminal and delinquent behavior (Rhee & Waldman 2002). With the mounting evidence of genetic influences have come a few researchers who have attempted to provide percentage estimates of genetic influences on antisocial behavior and other frequent behavioral correlates of criminality. Table 8.1.1 shows that the estimates of genetic influences on traits frequently associated with offending vary roughly from 35 to 75%.

### 8.1.2 Androgen Receptor Gene

The androgen receptor gene plays an important role in the transcription and regulation of androgen receptors. These receptors are needed to ensure that testosterone and other androgens are able to promote the expression of male sex traits throughout the body, including the brain. The short allele version of the androgen receptor gene has been associated with increased androgen activity (Comings et al. 2002).

No evidence was found directly linking the androgen receptor gene to criminality. However, as shown in Table 8.1.2, the gene has been found to be positively related to antisocial behavior in childhood and early adolescence. In the same study, the androgen receptor gene was also linked with ADHD.

**TABLE 8.1.1** Estimated Genetic Contribution and Clinical or Personality Traits Associated with Criminality.

| Extent of contribution | Antisocial behavior | Aggression | Cognitive and personality factors associated with criminality |
|---|---|---|---|
| | Childhood or early adol. | | |
| 0–9% | | | |
| 10–19% | | | |
| 20–29% | | | |
| 30–39% | **INTERNATIONAL** *Multiple Countries*: van der Valk et al. 1998* (35%, adoption study, clinical assessment) | **INTERNATIONAL** *Multiple Countries*: van der Valk et al. 1998* (40%, adoption study) | **INTERNATIONAL** *Multiple Countries*: Van den Oord et al. 1994 (adoption study, externalizing behavior); van der Valk et al. 1998* (40%, adoption study, externalizing behavior) |
| 40–49% | | **NORTH AMERICA** *United States*: DR Miles & Carey 1997 (40%) | |
| 50–59% | | | |
| 60–69% | | | |
| 70–79% | **NORTH AMERICA** *United States*: Schmitz et al. 1995 (75%, clinical assessment) | | |
| 80–89% | | **NORTH AMERICA** *Canada*: Dionne et al. 2003 (80%, at 17 months, infants, twins) | |
| 90–100% | | | |

**TABLE 8.1.2 Androgen Receptor Gene and Clinical or Personality Traits Associated with Criminality.**

| Nature of the relationship | Antisocial behavior | Mental disorder |
|---|---|---|
| | Childhood & early adol. | |
| Positive | **NORTH AMERICA** *United States*: Comings et al. 2002* (short allele version) | **NORTH AMERICA** *United States*: Comings et al. 2002* (ADHD, short allele version) |
| Not signif. | | |
| Negative | | |

## 8.1.3 Catechol-O-Methyltransferase (COMT) Gene

Catechol-O-methyltransferase (COMT) plays an important role in executive functioning by the prefrontal lobes. It does so by helping to degrade dopamine, epinephrine, and norepinephrine (Winterer & Goldman 2003). The available evidence indicates that the presence of the homozygous low COMT producing gene (called the *val/val COMT allele*) is positively associated with a history of violent criminality, at least among schizophrenics, as shown in Table 8.1.3a.

According to one study, the val/val COMT allele version of the COMT gene was positively associated with antisocial behavior among children (Table 8.1.3b).

## 8.1.4 A1 Allele of the DRD2 Gene

Persons with the A1 allele of the DRD2 gene appear to have fewer D2 dopamine receptors, reduced dopamine activity, and lower glucose metabolism in the brain. The DRD2 gene is located on chromosome 11 (K Blum et al. 1995) and has been implicated in the rewards and satisfaction people feel in their daily lives. Individuals with the A1 allele do not appear to respond to drugs and alcohol in the same way as those without the A1 allele.

**TABLE 8.1.3a Catechol-O-Methyltransferase (COMT) Gene and Criminal/Delinquent Behavior.**

| Nature of the relationship | Officially detected offenses |
|---|---|
| | Violent offenses |
| Positive | **MIDDLE EAST** *Israel*: Kotler et al. 1999 (among schizophrenics) **NORTH AMERICA** *United States*: Strous et al. 1997 (low activity allele, among schizophrenics); Lachman et al. 1998 (among schizophrenics) |
| Not signif. | |
| Negative | |

**TABLE 8.1.3b Catechol-O-Methyltransferase (COMT) Related Genes and Clinical or Personality Traits Associated with Criminality.**

| Nature of the relationship | Antisocial behavior |
|---|---|
| | Child & early adol. |
| Positive | **EUROPE** *Wales*: Thapar et al. 2005:1277 (val/val genotype, as opposed to val/met & met/met genotypes) |
| Not signif. | |
| Negative | |

No studies have examined possible links between the A1 allele of the DRD2 gene and criminal offending, but it is mentioned here because several factors associated with elevated rates of crime have been associated with this allele. These studies are documented in Table 8.1.4 along with a nearly equal number of studies that have failed to find a significant relationship.

## 8.1.5 DRD4 Gene

The DRD4 gene has been linked to motivation and attention via the dopamine network in the brain (Asghari et al. 1995). As shown in Table 8.1.5a, one study of schizophrenics who had committed murders failed to find any significant difference in DRD4 gene configurations than was true for schizophrenics in general.

A personality trait that has been frequently associated with involvement in crime is novelty seeking. Table 8.1.5b indicates that DRD4 configurations were more common among persons who scored high in novelty seeking as opposed to those who scored low.

## 8.1.6 Serotonin-Linked Genes (Except the 5-HTTLPR Polymorphism)

Serotonin is an important inhibitory neurotransmitter that is expressed in the brain and central nervous system. The serotonergic system is highly complex and appears to require a "balance" to achieve optimal human behavioral performance. Too much or too little serotonin has been found to be associated with a range of problem behaviors. As shown in Table 8.1.6a, with one exception, a short allele for serotonin production has been associated with offending in studies conducted to date.

**TABLE 8.1.4 A1 Allele of the DRD2 Gene and Clinical or Personality Traits Associated with Criminality.**

| Nature of the relationship | Antisocial behavior | Alcoholism | Drug abuse | Mental disorder |
|---|---|---|---|---|
| | Childhood & early adol. | | | |
| Positive | **NORTH AMERICA** *United States*: Comings et al. 1991a* | **ASIA** *Japan*: Arinami et al. 1993; Ishiguro et al. 1998; *Russia*: Ovchinnikov et al. 1999* **EUROPE** *Britain*: CC Cook et al. 1992; *Finland*: Hietala et al. 1997; *France*: Amadeo et al. 1993; *Slovakia*: Ovchimikov et al. 1999*; *Sweden*: Berggren et al. 2006 **NORTH AMERICA** *United States*: Blum et al. 1990; Blum et al. 1991; Comings et al. 1991b; Parsian et al. 1991; Noble et al. 1994; Neiswanger et al. 1995; Lawford et al. 1997*; Ritchie & Noble 2003 **SOUTH AMERICA** *Brazil*: Freire et al. 2006 | **NORTH AMERICA** *United States*: Comings et al. 1994* | **NORTH AMERICA** *United States*: Comings et al. 1991 (ADHD & Tourette's syndrome); Blum et al. 1995 (pathological gambling); Ozkaragoz & Noble 2000 (externalizing behavior) |
| Not signif. | | **ASIA** *Japan*: MS Lee et al. 1997; Kono et al. 1997; Anghelescu et al. 2001; *Taiwan*: Chen et al. 1996; Lu et al. 1996; Chen et al. 1997 **EUROPE** *Germany*: Heintz et al. 1996; Sander et al. 1999; Samochowiec et al. 2000; *Sweden*: Geijer et al. 1994 **MIDDLE EAST** *Turkey*: Karaoguz et al. 2004 **NORTH AMERICA** *United States*: Bolos et al. 1990; Gelernter et al. 1991; Schwab et al. 1991; BL Cook et al. 1992; Goldman et al. 1992; Turner et al. 1992; Comings et al. 1994*; Suarez et al. 1994; Lawford et al. 1997*; Gelernter & Kranzler 1999; Limosin et al. 2002; Foley et al. 2004; Konishi et al. 2004 (Mexican Americans) **SOUTH AMERICA** *Brazil*: Bau et al. 2000 | | |
| Negative | | | | |

**TABLE 8.1.5a DRD4 Gene and Criminal/Delinquent Behavior.**

| Nature of the relationship | Officially detected offenses |
|---|---|
| | Violent offenses |
| Positive | |
| Not signif. | **MIDDLE EAST** *Israel*: Kotler et al. 1999 (among schizophrenics, homicide convicts) |
| Negative | |

**TABLE 8.1.5b DRD4 Gene and Clinical or Personality Traits Associated with Criminality.**

| Nature of the relationship | Cognitive & personality factors |
|---|---|
| Positive | **NORTH AMERICA** *United States*: Fassino et al. 2002 (novelty seeking) |
| Not signif. | |
| Negative | |

**TABLE 8.1.6a** Serotonin-Linked Genes (Except the 5-HTTLPR Polymorphism) and Criminal/Delinquent Behavior.

| Nature of the relationship | Officially detected offenses | | |
|---|---|---|---|
| | Violent offenses | Drug offenses | Delinquency |
| Long allele | | | **ASIA** *Korea*: JH Lee et al. 2003 (males) |
| Not signif. | | | |
| Short allele | **ASIA** *Taiwan*: Liao et al. 2004 (short allele, 5-HTT) **EUROPE** *Finland*: Hallikainen et al. 1999 | **OCEANIA** *Australia*: Gerra et al. 2005 (teenagers) | |

Table 8.1.6b indicates that the short allele of the 5-HTT gene has also been linked to antisocial behavior and alcoholism.

## 8.1.7 5-HTTLPR Polymorphism

The serotonin transporter gene (5-HTT) is responsible for carrying serotonin from the synaptic cleft to the presynaptic neuron during reuptake. The 5-HTT gene that makes this possible has a 44-base pair insertion/deletion polymorphism in the promoter region of the gene. The 5-HTTLPR polymorphism has two allele types: a long type and a short type. The short allele has been linked to lower transcriptional efficiency of the promoter region, desensitized 5-HT receptors, and consequently lower concentrations of serotonin in the brain. It is believed that individuals who carry the short allele will be less inhibited in their actions than individuals who possess the long allele. As shown in Table 8.1.7a, one study did not find a relationship between the 5-HTTLPR polymorphism and violent crime among schizophrenics.

**TABLE 8.1.7a** 5-HTTLPR Polymorphism Allele and Criminal/Delinquent Behavior.

| Nature of the relationship | Officially detected offenses |
|---|---|
| | Violent offenses |
| Positive | **ASIA** *China*: Liao et al. 2004 (short allele) |
| Not signif. | **MIDDLE EAST** *Israel*: Kotler et al. 1999 (homicide, among schizophrenics) |
| Negative | |

As indicated in Table 8.1.7b, the short allele 5-HTTLPR genotype is associated with physical aggression and violent suicidal behavior, while it was not significantly associated with antisocial behavior or alcoholism. Oddly, the long allele version of 5-HTTLPR was found linked to ADHD.

## 8.1.8 Tryptophan Hydroxylase-1 Gene

The tryptophan hydroxylase-1 (TPH-1) gene is located on the short arm of chromosome 11 (Nielsen et al. 1992) and appears to regulate an enzyme that aids in the regulation of serotonin levels in the body, including the brain. Researchers speculate that TPH-1 may be related to aggressive and criminal behavior through its effects on the serotonergic system.

Table 8.1.8 reveals that different variants on the TPH-1 gene has been statistically linked to impulsive aggression or to impulsiveness in general. Whether criminality itself is linked to any variants of this gene remains to be determined.

**TABLE 8.1.6b** Serotonin-Linked Genes (Except 5-HTTLPR polymorphism) and Clinical or Personality Traits Associated with Criminality.

| Nature of the relationship | Antisocial behavior | | Cognitive & personality factors | Alcoholism |
|---|---|---|---|---|
| | Child & early adol. | Late adol. & adulthood | | |
| Long allele | | | | |
| Not signif. | | | | |
| Short allele | **NORTH AMERICA** *United States*: Cadoret et al. 2003 (males, adoptees) | **EUROPE** *Finland*: Hallikainen et al. 1999* | | **EUROPE** *Finland*: Hallikainen et al. 1999*; *Germany*; Sander et al. 1998 |

**TABLE 8.1.7b** 5-HTTLPR Polymorphism and Clinical or Personality Traits Associated with Criminality.

| Nature of the relationship | Antisocial behavior<br>Late adol. & adulthood | Physical aggression | Alcoholism | Mental illness | Mental disorder |
|---|---|---|---|---|---|
| Positive | | **EUROPE** *Finland*: Hallikainen et al. 1999 (short allele, impulsive violence); *Germany*: Retz et al. 2004 (short allele, impulsive violence) | | **EUROPE** *France*: Bayle et al. 2003 (violent suicide); *Germany*: Preuss et al. 2001 (violent suicide) | **EUROPE** *Germany*: Seeger et al. 2001 (ADHD, long allele); Retz et al. 2002 (ADHD, long allele)<br>**NORTH AMERICA** *United States*: Manor et al. 2001 (ADHD, long allele) |
| Not signif. | **NORTH AMERICA** *United States*: EM Hill et al. 2002* (5-HTTLPR, males) | | **NORTH AMERICA** *United States*: EM Hill et al. 2002* (5-HTTLPR, males) | | |
| Negative | | | | | |

**TABLE 8.1.8** Tryptophan Hydroxylase-1 Gene and Clinical or Personality Traits Associated with Criminality.

| Nature of the relationship | Physical aggression | Cognitive & personality factors |
|---|---|---|
| Positive | **NORTH AMERICA** *United States*: New et al. 1998 (LL allele, A779A/C TPH-1 polymorphism; impulsive aggression); Manuck et al. 1999 (U allele) | **NORTH AMERICA** *United States*: J Evans et al. 2000 (L allele, impulsiveness) |
| Not signif. | | |
| Negative | | |

## 8.2 BIRTH AND DEVELOPMENT FACTORS

Among the most basic of all biological variables are those associated with development. Below, these types of variables are considered with respect as to how they may be related to criminality.

### 8.2.1 Birth Weight

Studies have found that birth weight is statistically associated with a variety of traits that manifest themselves later in life. For instance, people who weigh less at birth tend to be less healthy as adults (McCormick 1989; Hadders-Algra & Touwen 1990; Hack et al. 1993), to get lower grades in school (Lagerstrom et al. 1989; McCormick et al. 1990), and to score lower on IQ tests (Saigal et al. 1991; Marlow et al. 1993; Roussounis et al. 1993; Pharoah et al. 1994a). Since health, grades, and IQ scores all appear to be correlates of crime (as discussed elsewhere in this book), one would not be surprised to find that low birth weight would also be associated with offending.

Several studies have investigated the possible link between criminal/delinquent behavior and birth weight. As shown in Table 8.2.1a, evidence concerning the relationship is mixed. One study found a positive relationship between birth weight and criminal behavior, while four studies found no relationship. Most studies, however, have indicated that persons who weigh the least at birth have a higher probability of offending and/or exhibiting conduct disorders during childhood than do those who weigh the most.

Table 8.2.1b summarizes the research on birth weight and various antisocial factors. Studies show that birth weight is negatively associated with attention deficit disorder (ADD), motor skills, intelligence, and learning disabilities. In addition, the cognitive and behavioral deficits of low birth weight extend from childhood into adolescence.

### 8.2.2 Fetal Alcohol Exposure

Exposure to alcohol during pregnancy may interfere with development of the central nervous system. Studies have revealed that prenatal alcohol use inhibits growth of the corpus callosum, cerebellum, hippocampus, and basal ganglia (Mattson et al. 2001). These regions are thought to be related to motor skills, memory, and integration of sensory information. *In utero* exposure to alcohol may thereby cause various cognitive and behavioral problems including poor problem-solving skills, verbal and spatial memory deficits, impulsivity, and aggression (Cone-Wesson 2005).

**TABLE 8.2.1a Birth Weight and Criminal/Delinquent Behavior.**

| Nature of the relationship | Officially detected offenses | | Self-reported offenses |
|---|---|---|---|
| | Delinquency | General & adult offenses | Overall offenses |
| Positive | **EUROPE** *Finland*: M Cannon et al. 2002 (among schizophrenics) | | |
| Not signif. | **EUROPE** *Finland*: Rantakallio et al. 1992 (males); Rantakallio et al. 1995:117 **NORTH AMERICA** *United States*: Pasamanick & Knoblock 1966 | **NORTH AMERICA** *United States*: McGloin et al. 2006 | |
| Negative | **EUROPE** *Denmark*: Mednick et al. 1988; *Britain*: JWB Douglas 1960; JWB Douglas & Ross 1968; Wadsworth 1979:42; *Sweden*: Jonsson 1967:191; *Wales*: Thapar et al. 2005 **NORTH AMERICA** *Canada*: Offord et al. 1979 **OCEANIA** *Hawaii*: Werner 1987 | | **NORTH AMERICA** *United States*: Tibbetts & Piquero 1999 (early onset of offending) |

**TABLE 8.2.1b Birth Weight and Clinical or Personality Traits Associated with Criminality.**

| Nature of the relationship | Antisocial behavior | Cognitive & personality factors | Mental disorder |
|---|---|---|---|
| | Childhood & early adol. | | |
| Positive | | | |
| Not signif. | | | |
| Negative | **EUROPE** *Britain*: Drillien & Wilkinson 1964; Thapar et al. 2005:1277; *Denmark*: Rogers et al. 1955 **NORTH AMERICA** *Canada*: Breslau et al. 1988; Szatmari et al. 1990; Andre et al. 1994; *United States*: Breslau 1995; Pharoah et al. 1994b **OCEANIA** *New Zealand*: McGee et al. 1984 | **NORTH AMERICA** *United States*: Julkowski-Cherkes 1998* (learning disabilities, children) | **NORTH AMERICA** *United States*: Julkowski-Cherkes 1998* (ADHD, children) |

As shown in Table 8.2.2, four studies found a positive relationship between fetal alcohol exposure and criminal behavior. For instance, Mattson and Riley's (2000) analysis of fetal alcohol exposed youths and matched controls found that even after controlling for several personal and environmental factors the prevalence of delinquency was significantly higher among those who had been exposed.

**TABLE 8.2.2 Fetal Alcohol Exposure and Criminal/Delinquent Behavior.**

| Nature of the relationship | Officially detected offenses | Self-reported offenses |
|---|---|---|
| | Delinquency | Overall offenses |
| Positive | **NORTH AMERICA** *United States*: Fast et al. 1999; Mattson & Riley 2000 (IQ controlled); Schonfeld et al. 2005 (except those with full-FAS) | **NORTH AMERICA** *United States*: Roebuck et al. 1999 (rated by parents) |
| Not signif. | | |
| Negative | | |

## 8.2.3 Perinatal Trauma/Birth Complications

Perinatal trauma (including birth complications or birth stress) refers to any injuries or other difficulties encountered at or around the time of birth. Among the two most common

**TABLE 8.2.3a Perinatal Trauma/Birth Complications and Criminal/Delinquent Behavior.**

| Nature of the relationship | Officially detected offenses | | | | Self-reported offenses |
|---|---|---|---|---|---|
| | Violent offenses | Property offenses | Delinquency | General & adult offenses | Overall offenses |
| Positive | **EUROPE** *Denmark*: Kandel & Mednick 1991* (with rejection of parents); Raine et al. 1994*; *Sweden*: Hodgins et al. 2001* (when combined with poor parenting) **NORTH AMERICA** *Canada*: Arsenlault et al. 2002* (juveniles); *United States*: Lewis et al. 1979; Mungas 1983; Kandel & Mednick 1991*; Piquero & Tibbetts 1999* (with weak family environment) | | **EUROPE** *Denmark*: Raine et al. 1997 (with rejection of parents); *Britain*: Stott & Latchford 1976; *Finland*: Rantakallio et al. 1992 **NORTH AMERICA** *Canada*: Offord et al. 1979; Pagani et el. 1998b; *United States*: Healy & Bronner 1936; Piquero & Tibbetts 1999*(with rejection of parents) **OCEANIA** *New Zealand*: Moffitt 1990 | **EUROPE** *Denmark*: Litt 1971; Brennan et al. 1999:218; *Sweden*: S Hodgins et al. 2001 | **NORTH AMERICA** *Canada*: Arseneault et al. 2002* |
| Not signif. | **EUROPE** *Denmark*: Raine et al. 1994*; *Sweden*: Hodgins et al. 2001* (when parenting was good or adequate) **NORTH AMERICA** *United States*: Raine et al. 1994* | **EUROPE** *Denmark*: Kandel & Mednick 1991* (with rejection of parents); Raine et al. 1994* | **EUROPE** *Britain*: Wadsworth 1979; *Sweden*: Jonsson 1967:190 **NORTH AMERICA** *United States*: Pasamanick & Knobloch 1966; Lewis & Shanok 1977:1021; Shanok & Lewis 1981 | | |
| Negative | | | | | |

types of such trauma are caused by physical blows to the mother's abdomen during pregnancy (such as in falls, motor vehicle accidents, or spousal assaults) and oxygen deprivation during the birth process (called *hypoxia*) (Bakan 1990:60). Researchers most often measure perinatal trauma and birth complications using reports by mothers or an attending physician.

Table 8.2.3a summarizes the findings from studies undertaken to assess the links between birth traumas and/or complications, and offspring involvement in criminal/delinquent behavior. As one can see, while several studies have detected no significant links, most of the evidence indicates that these perinatal conditions are more prevalent in samples of criminals than in the population at large. Furthermore, studies have found that the negative effects of perinatal conditions may be exacerbated when paired with harsh or rejecting parent–child relationships following birth (Raine et al. 1997; Hodgins et al. 2001).

Table 8.2.3b shows that the effects of birth complications are presumably not limited to criminality. The table shows that most studies have found perinatal trauma to be associated with higher levels of antisocial behavior during childhood and early adolescence.

**TABLE 8.2.3b Perinatal Trauma/Birth Complications and Clinical or Personality Traits Associated with Criminality.**

| Nature of the relationship | Antisocial behavior | Cognitive & personality factors |
|---|---|---|
| | Childhood & early adol. | |
| Positive | **EUROPE** *Britain*: Drillien 1964; *Denmark*: Rogers et al. 1955; RL Baker & Mednick 1984 **NORTH AMERICA** *United States*: Pasamanick et al. 1956; McNeil et al. 1970 | **EUROPE** *Denmark*: Raine et al. 1997 (externalizing behavior); *Germany*: Barnow et al. 2005 (novelty seeking) **NORTH AMERICA** *United States*: Allen et al. 1998 (externalizing behavior) |
| Not signif. | **NORTH AMERICA** *Canada*: Szatmari et al. 1986 | |
| Negative | | |

**TABLE 8.2.4a** Minor Physical Anomalies and Criminal/Delinquent Behavior.

| Nature of the relationship | Officially detected offenses | | | | |
|---|---|---|---|---|---|
| | Violent offenses | Property offenses | Drug offenses | Delinquency | Recidivism |
| Positive | **NORTH AMERICA** *Canada*: Arseneault et al. 2000*; *United States*: Mednick & Kandel 1988; Kandel et al. 1990 | | **NORTH AMERICA** *United States*: Durfee 1974 | **NORTH AMERICA** *Canada*: Arseneault et al. 2000*; *United States*: Wallace 1940 **OCEANIA** *Hawaii*: EE Werner & Smith 1992:108 | **NORTH AMERICA** *United States*: Kandel et al. 1989 |
| Not signif. | | **NORTH AMERICA** *Canada*: Arseneault et al. 2000* | | | |
| Negative | | | | | |

## 8.2.4 Minor Physical Anomalies

Minor physical anomalies (MPAs) refer to a number of unusual physical traits, none of which are life threatening. These include asymmetrical or malformed ears, multiple hair whorls, widely spaced eyes, high-arched palate, and webbed or widely spaced toes (Eysenck & Gudjonsson 1989:20; Pine et al. 1997:395). The causes of MPAs are largely unknown, but are likely to include genetic factors as well as maternal consumption of various drugs and exposure to environmental pollutants during pregnancy.

Research pertaining to MPAs and criminal/delinquent behavior is indicated in Table 8.2.4a. As one can see, several studies have found a significant positive relationship. MPAs appear to be strongly connected to criminal aggression among individuals reared in unstable home environments (Mednick & Kandel 1988). These links also seem to be more pronounced in the case of males than for females (Eysenck & Gudjonsson 1989:20).

Two studies suggested that MPAs are linked to conduct disorders among offspring from homes steeped in dissension and turmoil (Sandberg et al. 1980; Pine et al. 1997).

**TABLE 8.2.4b** Minor Physical Anomalies and Clinical or Personality Traits Associated with Criminality.

| Nature of the relationship | Antisocial behavior | Physical aggression | Cognitive & personality factors | Mental illness | Mental disorder |
|---|---|---|---|---|---|
| | Childhood & early adol. | | | | |
| Positive | **EUROPE** *Britain*: Sandberg et al. 1980 **NORTH AMERICA** *United States*: Halverson & Victor 1976; O'Donnell & Van Tuinan 1979; Pine et al. 1997 | **NORTH AMERICA** *Canada*: Arseneault et al. 2002 (adol.); *United States*: Waldrop et al. 1978 (childhood) | **NORTH AMERICA** *United States*: Rosenberg & Weller 1973 (poor school performance); Steg & Rapaport 1975 (learning disabilities); Halverson & Victor 1976 (low IQ); Firestone & Prabhu 1983 (low IQ); Schonfeld et al. 1988 (low VIQ); Pine et al. 1997:398 (low VIQ) **OCEANIA** *New Zealand*: Moffitt 1993 (low VIQ) | **NORTH AMERICA** *United States*: Campbell et al. 1978 (schizophrenia); Guy et al. 1983 (schizophrenia); Green et al. 1994 (schizophrenia) | **EUROPE** *Denmark*: Fogel et al. 1985 (ADHD); Mednick & Kandel 1988 **NORTH AMERICA** *United States*: Waldrop & Halverson 1971 (ADHD); Waldrop et al. 1978 (ADHD); O'Donnell et al. 1979a (ADHD); Firestone & Prabhu 1983 (ADHD); Gillberg et al. 1983 (ADHD); Fogel et al. 1985 (ADHD); Satterfield 1987 (ADHD) |
| Not signif. | | | | | |
| Negative | | | | | |

**TABLE 8.2.5a Prenatal Stress and Perinatal Depression by the Mother and Criminal/Delinquent Behavior.**

| Nature of the relationship | Officially detected offenses |
|---|---|
| | General & adult offenses |
| Positive | **EUROPE** *Finland*: Huttunen & Niskanen 1978 (prenatal stress); Maki et al. 2003 (postpartum depression) |
| Not signif. | |
| Negative | |

This finding reinforces the idea that many biological correlates of crime probably have stronger associations with criminality when interacting with social variables than when present in isolation.

According to most studies, MPAs besides being linked to criminality, have been found to be associated with several behavioral correlates of crime (Table 8.2.4b). In particular, studies have found MPAs correlated with poor school performance, schizophrenia, ADHD, and low intelligence, especially that of the verbal type.

### 8.2.5 Prenatal Stress and Perinatal Depression by the Mother

Prenatal and perinatal environments may shape an offspring's behavior and/or cognitive performance across the life course. Animal studies have found that prenatal stress is associated with anxiety, greater sensitivity to negative stimuli, memory impairments, and aggressive behavior among offspring (Fride et al. 1986; Clarke et al. 1994; Lemaire et al. 2001). In addition, maternal depression early in the life of a child may inhibit the child's cognitive and behavioral development. Table 8.2.5a suggests that prenatal stress and perinatal depression by mothers are more common for adult offenders than for persons in general.

As shown in Table 8.2.5b, limited research has linked prenatal stress and perinatal depression with cognitive and behavioral problems during childhood, adolescence, and adulthood.

### 8.2.6 Maternal Smoking during Pregnancy

Since the 1990s, several studies have found a statistical link between smoking by an expectant mother during her pregnancy and criminality among her offspring (Table 8.2.6a).

Besides being frequently associated with criminality and delinquency, many studies have found maternal smoking to be statistically associated with several established correlates of crime, including childhood conduct disorders, low IQ, and ADHD symptoms (Table 8.2.6b).

**TABLE 8.2.5b Prenatal Stress and Perinatal Depression by the Mother and Clinical or Personality Traits Associated with Criminality.**

| Nature of the relationship | Antisocial behavior |
|---|---|
| | Child & early adol. |
| Positive | **EUROPE** *Finland*: Luoma et al. 2001 (8–9 year olds, prenatal depression)<br>**OCEANIA** *New Zealand*: Kim-Cohen et al. 2005 |
| Not signif. | |
| Negative | |

## 8.3 HEALTH FACTORS

Links between overall health or between specific diseases and criminal/delinquent behavior have captured the attention of not only criminologists but also of public health officials. The studies to be reviewed in the following section pertain to overall health, life expectancy, accidental injuries, and three specifically recognized disorders: hypoglycemia, the perimenstrual syndrome (PMS), and epilepsy.

### 8.3.1 Morbidity

Over the years, numerous studies have compared the health of criminals with that of the general population. Various methods have been used to objectively assess health including asking people to rate their health from excellent to poor. Other measures have entailed determining how many times in the past year visits were made to physicians or time spent in the hospital for specific ailments.

Are persons who engage in crime and delinquency more or less healthy than persons in general? Table 8.3.1a shows that the research results are fairly consistent in suggesting that the physical health of offenders is poorer than that of the general population.

The studies that have sought to assess the health of persons who demonstrate antisocial behavior and those who do not have all concluded that the former have poorer overall health and exhibit higher rates of morbidity than do persons not displaying such behavior (Table 8.3.1b).

### 8.3.2 Mortality (Life Expectancy)

It is not unreasonable to think that just because crime-prone individuals become ill more often than people in general, their life expectancy might still be longer. When men and women are compared, most studies have found that males feel healthier, have fewer annual physician visits, and fewer disability days per year than do women, even when all

TABLE 8.2.6a Maternal Smoking during Pregnancy and Criminal/Delinquent Behavior.

| Nature of the relationship | Officially detected offenses | | | |
|---|---|---|---|---|
| | Violent offenses | Drug offenses | Delinquency | General & adult offenses |
| Positive | **EUROPE** *Denmark*: Brennan et al. 1999*; *Finland*: Rasanen et al. 1999* | **EUROPE** *Denmark*: Brennan et al. 2002* | **EUROPE** *Britain*: Bagley 1992; *Finland*: Rantakallio et al. 1992b* (several social & demographic variables controlled); *Sweden*: Rantakallio et al. 1992b* | **EUROPE** *Denmark*: Brennan et al. 1999*; Brennan et al. 2002*; *Finland*: Rasanen et al. 1999* **NORTH AMERICA** *United States*: Brennan et al. 1999*; Gibson et al. 2000; Piquero et al. 2002:244 (blacks); McGloin et al. 2006 |
| Not signif. | | | **EUROPE** *Denmark*: Brennan et al. 1999* **NORTH AMERICA** *United States*: Gibson & Tibbetts 1998 (Apgar scores controlled) | |
| Negative | | | | |

pregnancy-related factors are excluded from consideration. Yet, nearly all research has shown that men have shorter lives by several years, especially in modern industrial countries (reviewed by Ellis et al. 2008:131–142).

What about criminal/delinquent behavior and mortality? Is it consistent with the research on morbidity or does it go in the opposite direction, as is the case of gender? Table 8.3.2a provides the answer: persons with criminal tendencies have greater morbidity than those with minimal criminal tendencies. Thus, offenders are not only less healthy but also die at earlier ages than do people in general.

The link between criminality and poor health has even been found to run in families. Specifically, studies have reported that parents of criminals die at earlier average ages than do parents of persons with no serious criminal record (Slawson 1926; F Brown & Epps 1966).

As with its link to offending per se, mortality tends to be higher (life expectancy tends to be shorter) among persons

TABLE 8.2.6b Maternal Smoking during Pregnancy and Clinical or Personality Traits Associated with Criminality.

| Nature of the relationship | Antisocial behavior | Cognitive & personality factors | Drug abuse | Mental disorder |
|---|---|---|---|---|
| | Childhood & early adol. | | | |
| Positive | **EUROPE** *Netherlands*: Orlebeke et al. 1997* (child behavior checklist) **NORTH AMERICA** *Canada*: Makin et al. 1991; Fried et al. 1992; Weitzman et al. 1992; *United States*: Fergusson et al. 1993; Orlebeke et al. 1997*; Wakschlag et al. 1997 (maternal social status controlled) **OCEANIA** *New Zealand*: D Fergusson et al. 1998 (mostly males) | **NORTH AMERICA** *Canada*: Fried et al. 1988* (low IQ); Fried & Watkinson 1990 (low IQ); *United States*: Olds et al. 1994 (low IQ) | | **NORTH AMERICA** *United States*: Naeye & Peters 1984 (ADHD); Milberger et al. 1996a (ADHD); Mick et al. 2002 |
| Not signif. | **OCEANIA** *New Zealand*: Maughan et al. 2004 | | **NORTH AMERICA** *Canada*: Fried et al. 1988* (marijuana smoking) | |
| Negative | | | | |

**TABLE 8.3.1a Morbidity and Criminal/Delinquent Behavior.**

| Nature of the relationship | Officially detected offenses | | | Self-reported offenses |
|---|---|---|---|---|
| | Violent offenses | Delinquency | General & adult offenses | Overall offenses |
| Positive (more ill health) | **NORTH AMERICA** *United States*: Palmer 1962:71 | **EUROPE** *Britain*: Burt 1925; Eilenberg 1961; Gibbens 1963; Stott 1966; Sweden: E Johanson 1968:78 **NORTH AMERICA** *Canada*: Andre et al. 1994; *United States*: Christie 1934; Chaiklin et al. 1977; DO Lewis & Shanok 1977; Shanok & Lewis 1981:226; DO Lewis et al. 1985:164 | **EUROPE** *Britain*: Farrington 1993a:16 **NORTH AMERICA** *United States*: Christie 1934 | **EUROPE** *Britain*: Farrington 1995a |
| Not signif. | | **EUROPE** *Sweden*: G Jonsson 1967:194; G Jonsson 1975:184; Stattin et al. 1997:204 **NORTH AMERICA** *United States*: Glueck & Glueck 1950:81 | **NORTH AMERICA** *United States*: McCord et al. 1959 | |
| Negative | | | | |

diagnosed with antisocial personality disorders (Table 8.3.2b).

## 8.3.3 Accidental Injuries

Accidental injuries refer to significant bodily harm (trauma) resulting from unintended natural or man-made events. A large number of studies have been conducted to determine if persons exhibiting serious criminal or delinquent behavior sustain accidental injuries at rates that are higher or lower than for people in general. Table 8.3.3a clearly shows that offending and accidental injuries are positively correlated.

Research pertaining to accidental injuries and antisocial behavior is quite consistent with that on criminality per se in showing that these behavioral conditions are associated with higher rates of injury (Table 8.3.3b).

## 8.3.4 Diabetes

No research linking criminality with diabetes was located. However, as shown in Table 8.3.4, two studies have indicated that this disorder is more common among adults diagnosed with antisocial personality disorder than with persons not so diagnosed.

**TABLE 8.3.1b Morbidity and Clinical or Personality Traits Associated with Criminality.**

| Nature of the relationship | Antisocial behavior | |
|---|---|---|
| | Childhood & early adol. | Late adol. & adulthood |
| Positive (more ill health) | **NORTH AMERICA** *United States*: Zoccolillo et al. 1992 **OCEANIA** *New Zealand*: Bardone et al. 1998 (females) | **EUROPE** *Britain*: J Shepherd & Farrington 2003 **NORTH AMERICA** *United States*: Robins 1966:92; PS Frick et al. 1995; DW Black et al. 1996 |
| Not signif. | | |
| Negative | | |

**TABLE 8.3.2a Mortality (Life Expectancy) and Criminal/ Delinquent Behavior.**

| Nature of the relationship | Officially detected offenses | |
|---|---|---|
| | Delinquency | General & adult offenses |
| Longer lives | | |
| Not signif. | | |
| Shorter lives | **NORTH AMERICA** *United States*: Douglas et al. 1968; FJ Miller et al. 1985; Yeager & Lewis 1990; Laub & Vaillant 2000 (males) | **EUROPE** *Finland*: Joukamaa 1995; Rasanen et al. 1998 **OCEANIA** *Australia*: NS Thomson & McDonald 1993 |

**TABLE 8.3.2b** Mortality (Life Expectancy) and Clinical or Personality Traits Associated with Criminality.

| Nature of the relationship | Antisocial behavior | |
|---|---|---|
| | Childhood & early adol. | Late adol. & adulthood |
| Longer lives | | |
| Not signif. | | |
| Shorter lives | **NORTH AMERICA** *United States*: Pajer 1998 | **NORTH AMERICA** *United States*: LN Robins 1966:92; Martin et al. 1985; DW Black et al. 1985; DW Black et al. 1996 |

**TABLE 8.3.3b** Accidental Injuries and Clinical or Personality Traits Associated with Criminality.

| Nature of the relationship | Antisocial behavior | |
|---|---|---|
| | Childhood & early adol. | Late adol. & adulthood |
| Positive | **EUROPE** *Sweden*: Rydelius 1988 **NORTH AMERICA** *United States*: LN Robins 1966:295; Suchman 1970; Langley et al. 1983 | **NORTH AMERICA** *United States*: Nordstrom et al. 2001 |
| Not signif. | | |
| Negative | | |

## 8.3.5 Epilepsy

Epilepsy is a neurological disorder typified by *seizures*, which can be thought of as "electrical storms" in the brain. While people vary in genetic susceptibility, seizures occur as a result of various environmental factors, including physical injuries to the brain, viral infections, low birth weight, and birth trauma (Cummings 1985:99). Seizures can also be induced by hypoglycemia (Laron 1998:117).

The main behavioral symptoms of epilepsy are convulsions (or *fits*), although not all epileptics have full-blown convulsive episodes (Previc 1996:484). Mild epileptic episodes may manifest themselves as little more than momentary pauses in on-going activities accompanied by a glazed stare. Seizures that do not have noticeable debilitating effects on coordination are called *subconvulsive* (or *subclinical*) *seizures*.

About one person in every 150–200 will be diagnosed with epilepsy in their lifetime (Kurland 1959; Hauser & Kurland 1975; Merritt 1973:740; Kolb & Whishaw 1980:78; Rwiza et al. 1992; Sander & Shorvon 1996:435). In prisons, however, the rates of epilepsy are closer to 1/50 (Roth & Erwin 1971; L Ellis 1987:504). The evidence of higher

**TABLE 8.3.3a** Accidental Injuries and Criminal/Delinquent Behavior.

| Nature of the relationship | Officially detected offenses | | | Self-reported offenses | |
|---|---|---|---|---|---|
| | Delinquency | General & adult offenses | Recidivism | Overall offenses | Illegal drugs |
| Positive | **EUROPE** *Britain*: SW Douglas et al. 1968; FS Miller et al. 1985; Meadows et al. 1998 **NORTH AMERICA** *United States*: Healy & Bronner 1936:57; Fuller 1948; DO Glueck & Glueck 1950; Kraus et al. 1970; Lewis & Shanok 1977:1021; Shanok & Lewis 1981:226; Langley et al. 1987 **OCEANIA** *Hawaii*: EE Werner & Smith 1992:106 | **NORTH AMERICA** *United States*: Tillman & Hobbs 1949; CP Hansen 1988; Mawson et al. 1988 **OCEANIA** *Australia*: O'Toole & Stankov 1992:713 | **EUROPE** *Britain*: DS West & Farrington 1977:72 | **EUROPE** *Britain*: DS West & Farrington 1973:72; Farrington 1995b; Lawton et al. 1997; *Netherlands*: Junger & Wiegersma 1995:165* | **EUROPE** *Netherlands*: Junger & Wiegersma 1995:165* |
| Not signif. | | | | | |
| Negative | | | | | |

**TABLE 8.3.4 Diabetes and Clinical or Personality Traits Associated with Criminality.**

| Nature of the relationship | Antisocial behavior |
|---|---|
| | Late adol. & adulthood |
| Positive | **NORTH AMERICA** *United States*: Popkin et al. 1988; DW Black et al. 1996 |
| Not signif. | |
| Negative | |

**TABLE 8.3.5a Epilepsy and Criminal/Delinquent Behavior.**

| Nature of the relationship | Officially detected offenses | | |
|---|---|---|---|
| | Violent offenses | Delinquency | General & adult offenses |
| Positive | **EUROPE** *Britain*: D Hill & Pond 1952 **NORTH AMERICA** *United States*: S Palmer 1962:71; Okasha et al. 1975:39; Mungus 1983; Mendez et al. 1993 | **ASIA** *Ceylon*: Fernando 1965 | **EUROPE** *Britain*: Gunn & Fenton 1971; Gunn 1977 **NORTH AMERICA** *United States*: Healy 1915:147; Roth & Ervin 1971; Derro 1978; LN King & Young 1978; DO Lewis et al. 1982; Whitman et al. 1984 |
| Not signif. | | **EUROPE** *Finland*: Rantakallio et al. 1992; Rantakallio et al. 1995:117; *Germany*: H Gross & Kaltenback 1975 **NORTH AMERICA** *United States*: Osgood & Trapp 1936 | |
| Negative | | | |

epilepsy rates among offenders is summarized in Table 8.3.5a. As one can see, with exception of delinquency, there can be little doubt that epilepsy and offending are positively correlated.

Table 8.3.5b shows that epilepsy appears to be associated with other correlates of crime in ways that make any simple deductions about causation difficult to identify.

## 8.3.6 Hypoglycemia

The main fuel used by the brain to perform its various functions is a sugar known as *glucose*. Brain glucose levels are regulated by the blood system, which in turn responds to chemical messages from a small region of the brain's hypothalamus (Bonnet & Pfeiffer 1978:196). When the hypothalamus detects glucose levels getting either too high or too low, it sends chemical signals to the pancreas to either curtail or increase the release of insulin into the blood. This regulatory process helps to maintain brain glucose levels at fairly stable levels for most people.

For a variety of reasons, some people have difficulty maintaining glucose levels within a narrow range. These people are said to suffer from *hypoglycemia*. Although the

**TABLE 8.3.5b Epilepsy and Clinical or Personality Traits Associated with Criminality.**

| Nature of the relationship | Antisocial behavior | | Cognitive factors | Mental disorders |
|---|---|---|---|---|
| | Childhood & early adol. | Late adol. & adulthood | | |
| Positive | **EUROPE** *Britain*: Holdsworth & Whitmore 1974 | **EUROPE** *Britain*: Herzberg & Fenwick 1988 | **NORTH AMERICA** *United States*: Piness et al. 1937:170 (low IQ); Green & Hartlage 1971 (poor school performance); Holdsworth & Whitmore 1974 (poor school performance); Pazzaglia & Frank-Pazzaglia 1976 (poor school performance) | **NORTH AMERICA** *United States*: Mendez et al. 1993 (schizophrenia) |
| Not signif. | | | | |
| Negative | | | | |

prefix *hypo* means low, hypoglycemia can be best thought of as referring to unusually unstable glucose levels.

When most people consume sweets, the concentrations of sugar in their blood rise temporarily but in most individuals, it is quickly normalized. For hypoglycemics, consumption of sugar can have roller-coaster effects on brain glucose levels, i.e., a dramatic rise followed by a deep plunge (Chollar 1988:33). Dramatic fluctuations in brain glucose can cause temporary disturbances in people's thoughts and moods, with the most common symptoms being confusion, difficulty concentrating, and irritability (Adlersberg & Dolger 1939:1805; Virkkunen 1988:153).

Since the 1970s, a number of studies have been conducted to determine if there is any connection between hypoglycemia and the probability of criminal/delinquent behavior. Table 8.3.6a indicates that hypoglycemia is significantly more common among those with serious criminal histories than for persons in general, particularly in the case of those crimes of a violent nature.

In addition, a series of population-wide studies of a Native American tribe in Peru where the homicide rate is extraordinarily high found that nearly 50% of the adults in that tribal group suffer from mild forms of hypoglycemia (Bolton 1973, 1974; Bolton & Bolton 1975). Also, two studies in which adolescents were injected with high "challenge" dosages of sugar, found that delinquents responded with a higher insulin release than was true for their nondelinquent peers (Gans et al. 1990; Matykiewicz et al. 1997).

According to studies cited in Table 8.3.6b, hypoglycemia has also been found to be associated with antisocial and aggressive behaviors. Overall, the current evidence largely supports the view that hypoglycemia plays a role in causing criminality and violence. Nevertheless, because it is a rare disease, especially in its severe forms, it can be considered only a contributor to a small proportion of violent offenses (Tardiff 1985:636).

**TABLE 8.3.6a** Hypoglycemia and Criminal/Delinquent Behavior.

| Nature of the relationship | Officially detected offenses | |
|---|---|---|
| | Violent offenses | General & adult offenses |
| Positive | **EUROPE** *Finland*: Virkkunen & Huttunen 1982; Virkkunen 1986 **NORTH AMERICA** *United States*: Yaruara-Tobias & Neziroglu 1975 | **NORTH AMERICA** *United States*: Groesbeck et al. 1975 |
| Not signif. | | |
| Negative | | |

## 8.3.7 Perimenstrual Syndrome

During the reproductive years, sex hormone levels in females tend to fluctuate on a roughly 28–30 day cycle. Coinciding with these hormonal vacillations, many women report changes in mood associated with their menstrual cycle. The most common pattern reported by women is greater depression, irritability, and anxiety in the period shortly before and during menstruation (i.e., perimenstrum) (Horney 1978:26). For approximately one-third of women, the negative moods associated with perimenstrum are sufficiently severe as to constitute a condition known as the *perimentrual* (or *premenstrual*) *syndrome* (PMS) (Dougherty et al. 1997:381). As shown in Table 8.3.7, several studies have found that female crime is most probable during the perimenstrum period.

## 8.3.8 Sexually Transmitted Diseases

No research pertaining specifically to criminal behavior and sexually transmitted diseases was found. However, as shown in Table 8.3.8, some evidence linking antisocial behavior to a relatively high prevalence of such diseases has been published.

# 8.4 PHYSIOLOGY AND MORPHOLOGY

Physiology primarily has to do with the body's functioning, while morphology refers to the body's external appearance. This section reviews evidence of relationships between physiological and morphological factors being related to criminal and delinquent behavior.

## 8.4.1 Blood Pressure

One study was located pertaining to blood pressure and self-reported delinquency. As shown in Table 8.4.1, this study suggested that delinquency was associated with relatively high blood pressure.

**TABLE 8.3.6b** Hypoglycemia and Clinical or Personality Traits Associated with Criminality.

| Nature of the relationship | Antisocial behavior | Aggressive behavior |
|---|---|---|
| | Late adol. & adulthood | |
| Positive | **EUROPE** *Finland*: Virkkunen 1982; Virkkunen 1983a | **NORTH AMERICA** *United States*: Benton et al. 1982 |
| Not signif. | | |
| Negative | | |

**TABLE 8.3.7 Perimenstrual Syndrome and Criminal/Delinquent Behavior.**

| Nature of the relationship | Officially detected offenses | | | |
|---|---|---|---|---|
| | Violent offenses | Property offenses | Delinquency | General & adult offenses |
| Higher during perimenstrum | **EUROPE** *France*: Cooke 1945; *Britain*: d'Orban & Dalton 1980 **NORTH AMERICA** *United States*: Morton et al. 1953 | **EUROPE** *France*: Pollack 1950:128 | **EUROPE** *Britain*: Dalton 1960 | **EUROPE** *Britain*: Dalton 1961 |
| Not signif. | | **EUROPE** *Britain*: Epps & Parnell 1952 | | |
| Lower during perimenstrum | | | | |

## 8.4.2 Height

A few studies have sought to determine if height is associated with involvement in criminal behavior. From Table 8.4.2a, one can see that there tends to be more criminality among individuals who are taller.

According to the one relevant study located, males who were taller tended to be more physically aggressive than those who were shorter (Table 8.4.2b).

## 8.4.3 Body Type

Research on the possible association between basic body types and criminality first began to appear in the early decades of the twentieth century. Three extreme body types are recognized: *Endomorphy* refers to persons who are extremely rotund (fat) and non-muscular. *Mesomorphy* refers to individuals who are unusually muscular in their body build. *Ectomorphy* denotes the tendency to be thin and nonmuscular. Finally, in the middle of these three extremes are persons who have a *balanced body type*, which includes the majority of people. Since the earliest work regarding body types, researchers have used a "bulging triangular" diagram to represent the range of possibilities, with the three extremes at each point of the triangle and the balanced type in the center.

As indicated in Table 8.4.3a, all available studies have reported significant tendencies for criminals and delinquents to be more mesomorphic than their nonoffending peers. In one recent study, comparisons were simply made among prisoners. This study found that those who were convicted of violent offenses were more mesomorphic than those convicted of nonviolent offenses.

As shown in Table 8.4.3b, one study of antisocial personality disorder concluded that the body type profile for those affected with this condition exhibited more mesomorphic features than did persons in general.

## 8.4.4 Physical Attractiveness

Physical attractiveness refers to the fact that human beings have preferences about the physical appearances of other people, particularly with reference to facial features and body proportions. Some aspects of these preferences appear to be arbitrarily derived from ever-changing cultural standards, while other aspects seem to be unlearned (Buss 1994:52). Evidence of unlearned preferences is a result of studies of neonates (new born infants who have obviously not had time to learn their cultural standards of beauty).

**TABLE 8.3.8 Sexually Transmitted Diseases and Clinical or Personality Traits Associated with Criminality.**

| Nature of the relationship | Antisocial behavior |
|---|---|
| | Late adol. & adulthood |
| Positive | **NORTH AMERICA** *United States*: D Ellis et al. 1995; Woody et al. 1997 (HIV/AIDS); WM Compton et al. 1998 (HIV/AIDS); Erbelding et al. 2004; Tubman et al. 2003 |
| Not signif. | |
| Negative | |

**TABLE 8.4.1 Blood Pressure and Criminal/Delinquent Behavior.**

| Nature of the relationship | Self-reported offenses |
|---|---|
| | Overall offenses |
| Positive | **NORTH AMERICA** *United States*: Pine et al. 1996 (parental rated, at-risk males, adol.) |
| Not signif. | |
| Negative | |

**TABLE 8.4.2a Height and Criminal/Delinquent Behavior.**

| Nature of the relationship | Officially detected offenses |
|---|---|
| | Delinquency |
| Positive | **NORTH AMERICA** *Canada*: Tremblay et al. 1998 (males); *United States*: RB Felson 1996 (violent delinquency) |
| Not signif. | |
| Negative | |

**TABLE 8.4.2b Height and Clinical or Personality Traits Associated with Criminality.**

| Nature of the relationship | Physical aggression |
|---|---|
| Positive | **ASIA** *India*: J Archer & Thanzami 2007 (males) |
| Not signif. | |
| Negative | |

These studies have shown that infants stare longer and smile more at what adults generally consider "pretty" faces than they do at "average" or "unattractive" faces (Langlois et al. 1987, 1990).

Regarding the relationship between physical attractiveness and criminality, Table 8.4.4 shows that several studies have found the link to be negative, meaning that those considered most attractive are less involved in criminal and delinquent behavior than persons who are considered least attractive.

## 8.4.5 Reaction Response Speed

Reaction response speed refers to the speed at which one responds to the introduction of environmental stimuli, and can reflect one's level of cognitive and emotional processing. For instance, individuals go through a series of mental steps (i.e., recognize, analyze, and create a response) when a stimulus is introduced into their environment. People who complete these steps efficiently and accurately show signs of higher cognitive functioning than individuals who are inefficient and/or inaccurate. Reaction speed can also reflect an individual's level of emotional processing. Those who have difficulty correctly identifying the emotions of others will take longer to understand them. Thus, the reaction response speed captures dimensions of both cognitive and emotional processing. No research directly linking reaction speed to criminality was located, but, among criminals, one study was found indicating that those who were diagnosed as psychopaths were slower to exhibit a neurological response to most stimuli presented than were non-psychopathic offenders (Table 8.4.5).

## 8.4.6 Skin Conductivity

When humans sweat, they excrete what is tantamount to diluted urine, containing substantial levels of salt water, a good electrical conductor. A device, called a *Galvanic Skin Response* (GSR) meter, has been developed to monitor moment-to-moment changes in the amount of sweat on the skin's surface. While temperature obviously affects how

**TABLE 8.4.3a Body Type and Criminal/Delinquent Behavior.**

| Nature of the relationship | Officially detected offenses | | | Self-reported offenses |
|---|---|---|---|---|
| | Violent offenses | Delinquency | General & adult offenses | Overall offenses |
| Highest among mesomorphs | **NORTH AMERICA** *United States*: Maddan et al. 2008 (versus nonviolent offenders) | **EUROPE** *Britain*: Epps & Parnell 1952; Gibbens 1963 **NORTH AMERICA** *United States*: Seltzer 1950; Glueck & Glueck 1956; Cortes & Gatti 1972; McCandless et al. 1972 | **NORTH AMERICA** *United States*: WH Sheldon 1949; Hartl et al. 1982:499 | **NORTH AMERICA** *United States*: Blackson & Tarter 1994:818; Ellis et al. 2007 (degree of muscularity) |
| Highest among endomorphs | | | | |
| Highest among ectomorphs | | | | |
| Highest among balanced types | | | | |
| No signif. diff. | | | | |

**TABLE 8.4.3b Body Type and Clinical or Personality Traits Associated with Criminality.**

| Nature of the relationship | Antisocial behavior |
|---|---|
| | Late adol. & adulthood |
| Highest among mesomorphs | **NORTH AMERICA** *United States*: Hartl et al. 1982:494 |
| Highest among endomorphs | |
| Highest among ectomorphs | |
| Highest among balanced types | |
| No signif. diff. | |

much we sweat, so too do emotions. The more emotionally aroused an individual becomes (especially in terms of strong "negative" emotions such as stress and fear), the more he or she sweats. The GSR meter detects these changes usually on the tips of the fingers.

As shown in Table 8.4.6a, several studies suggest that offenders sweat less under stressful conditions than do persons in general. This has been interpreted as indicating that they experience less feeling of stress than do most people.

The evidence of a possible association between skin conductivity and antisocial behavior is much less clear-cut than in the case of criminality and delinquency per se (Table 8.4.6b).

**TABLE 8.4.4 Physical Attractiveness and Criminal /Delinquent Behavior.**

| Nature of the relationship | Officially detected offenses | | Self-reported offenses |
|---|---|---|---|
| | Delinquency | General & adult offenses | Overall offenses |
| Positive | | | |
| Not signif. | | | |
| Negative | **NORTH AMERICA** *United States*: Cavior & Howard 1973 | **EUROPE** *Britain*: Masters &Greaves 1967 **NORTH AMERICA** *United States*: Kurtzberg et al. 1969; JE Stewart 1985 | **NORTH AMERICA** *United States*: Agnew 1984 |

**TABLE 8.4.5 Reaction Response Speed and Clinical or Personality Traits Associated with Criminality.**

| Nature of the relationship | Antisocial behavior |
|---|---|
| | Late adol. & adult |
| Positive | |
| Not signif. | |
| Negative | **NORTH AMERICA** *United States*: Loney et al. 2003 (to negative words, among prisoners) |

**TABLE 8.4.6a Skin Conductivity and Criminal/Delinquent Behavior.**

| Nature of the relationship | Officially detected offenses | | Self-reported offenses |
|---|---|---|---|
| | Delinquency | General & adult offenses | Overall offenses |
| Positive | | | |
| Not signif. | | | |
| Negative | **EUROPE** *Britain*: Siddle et al. 1971 (resting conditions); *Denmark*: Siddle et al. 1976 (resting conditions) **NORTH AMERICA** *United States*: RS Fox & Lippert 1963; Lippert & Senter 1966; Borkovec 1970; Kruesi et al. 1992 | **EUROPE** *Britain*: Raine et al. 1990a (males); Raine et al. 1996 (startling/ threatening conditions); *Netherlands*: Buikhuisen et al. 1985 (startling/ threatening conditions); Buikhuisen et al. 1989 (startling/ threatening conditions) **NORTH AMERICA** *United States*: Hemming 1981 (startling/ threatening conditions); Delameter & Lahey 1983 (resting conditions) | **EUROPE** *Britain*: Raine et al. 1995 (resting and startling/ threatening conditions) |

TABLE 8.4.6b Skin Conductivity and Clinical or Personality Traits Associated with Criminality.

| Nature of the relationship | Antisocial behavior | |
|---|---|---|
| | Childhood & early adol. | Late adol. & adulthood |
| Positive | | |
| Not signif. | **EUROPE** *Britain*: Raine & Venables 1984a (startling/threatening conditions) **NORTH AMERICA** *United States*: Schmidt et al. 1985 (startling/threatening conditions) | **NORTH AMERICA** *Canada*: RD Hare 1978 (resting conditions); *United States*: Sutker 1970 (startling/threatening conditions); Damasio et al. 1990 (startling/threatening conditions) |
| Negative | **EUROPE** *Britain*: Raine & Venables 1981 (startling/threatening conditions); Raine & Venables 1988 (startling/threatening conditions) **NORTH AMERICA** *United States*: Delamater & Lahey 1983 | **NORTH AMERICA** *United States*: Fung 2005 (psychopaths, adol.) |

## 8.4.7 Slow Resting Heart (or Pulse) Rate

Fear and other intense emotions can initiate a rapid heart rate. By monitoring changes in the heart rate of individuals who are not physically active, researchers are able to measure emotional responses to various stimuli (Raine 1996:157). Research findings suggest that under most conditions, offenders have lower heart rates than do persons in general (Table 8.4.7a). A couple of studies have even been prospective in their design, meaning that the heart and pulse rates were assessed several years prior to the assessment of any criminal/delinquent behavior, and the same tendency to exhibit less intense emotionality to environmental stimuli was found (Raine 1988; Raine et al. 1990b).

As shown in Table 8.4.7b, studies have also consistently found traits associated with offending to be linked to relatively slow heart rates.

## 8.4.8 Strength

Are the physically strong more criminal than the weak? The evidence already reviewed earlier on muscularity (mesomorphy) being related to criminality implies that there would be a positive correlation between physical strength and offending. As shown in Table 8.4.8a, the one available study supports this line of reasoning.

TABLE 8.4.7a Slow Resting Heart (or Pulse) Rate and Criminal/Antisocial Behavior.

| Nature of the relationship | Officially detected offenses | | | Self-reported offenses |
|---|---|---|---|---|
| | Violent offenses | Delinquency | General & adult offenses | Overall offenses |
| Positive | **EUROPE** *Britain*: Farrington 1997a:94 (heart rate) **NORTH AMERICA** *United States*: Raine 1996:49 (heart rate) | **EUROPE** *Britain*: Wadsworth 1976* (heart rate, boys from intact homes); Farrington 1987 (heart rate); Maliphant et al. 1990 (heart rate, middle class girls); Cauffman et al. 2005 **NORTH AMERICA** *United States*: Raine & Venables 1984b* (heart rate, upper status boys) | **EUROPE** *Britain*: Wadsworth 1976:249* (heart rate); Farrington 1987:55* (pulse rate); Raine et al. 1990a (males, heart rate); Raine et al. 1995 (heart rate); Brennan et al. 1997* (males, heart rate); Raine et al. 1997a* (males, heart rate) **NORTH AMERICA** *United States*: Raine et al. 1990a (heart rate); Raine et al. 1990b (heart rate) | **EUROPE** *Britain*: West & Farrington 1973:71 (pulse rate); Raine et al. 1995* (heart rate); Farrington 1997a:100* (heart rate) **NORTH AMERICA** *Canada*: Mezzacappa et al. 1997:463 (heart rate) |
| Not signif. | | **EUROPE** *Britain*: Wadsworth 1976* (heart rate, boys from broken homes) **NORTH AMERICA** *United States*: Raine & Venables 1984b* (heart rate, low status boys) | | |
| Negative | | | | |

**TABLE 8.4.7b** Slow Resting Heart (or Pulse) Rate and Clinical or Personality Traits Associated with Criminality.

| Nature of the relationship | Antisocial behavior | | Physical aggression | Personality traits | Family factors |
|---|---|---|---|---|---|
| | Childhood & early adol. | Late adol. & adulthood | | | |
| Positive | **EUROPE** *Britain*: Raine & Venables 1984b (heart rate); Farrington 1997a:100 (heart rate) **NORTH AMERICA** *Canada*: Kindlon et al. 1995 (heart rate); *United States*: Davies & Maliphant 1971 (pulse rate); Raine & Jones 1987 (heart rate); Rogeness et al. 1990b (heart rate); Maliphant et al. 1990 (heart rate) | **NORTH AMERICA** *Canada*: Hare 1982 (heart rate); *United States*: Raine 1988 (heart rate) | **NORTH AMERICA** *Canada*: Kindlon et al. 1995 (adol. fighting); *United States*: Gottman et al. 1995 (wife battering by males); Kindlon et al. 1995 (bullying) | **NORTH AMERICA** *United States*: Resznick et al. 1986 (impulsiveness); Kagan et al. 1988 (impulsiveness) | **EUROPE** *Britain*: Wadsworth 1976 (coming from a broken home) |
| Not signif. | | | | | |
| Negative | | | | | |

As with delinquency, one study suggests that physical aggression is positively correlated with physical strength (Table 8.4.8b).

## 8.5 CELLULAR RECEPTORS, TRANSPORTERS, AND BINDING SITES

The biological factors to be considered in this section explore the body's subcellular level. Cellular receptors are biochemicals configured in certain ways as to bond to other biochemicals. Cellular transporters are biochemicals that aid in delivering hormones and other biochemicals throughout the body. Binding sites in the cells are locations that combine with specific biochemicals to perform some bodily function.

Most cellular binding sites for hormones and other biochemicals are largely controlled by genes, some of which have now been identified. Earlier in this chapter, research findings pertaining to some of these genes were discussed. In this section, the actual binding sites are explored.

**TABLE 8.4.8a** Strength and Criminal/Delinquent Behavior.

| Nature of the relationship | Self-reported offenses |
|---|---|
| | Overall offenses |
| Positive | **NORTH AMERICA** *Canada*: Tremblay et al. 1998 (males, delinquency) |
| Not signif. | |
| Negative | |

### 8.5.1 Dopamine Receptors

D2 dopamine receptors are a key substrate for alcohol and other drug-related reward behaviors (Koob & LeMoal 1997; Tanda et al. 1997). Individuals with a variant of this receptor known as DRD2 do not appear to be affected by rewards like people with other variants of the receptor. DRD2 individuals tend to seek out environments or substances that strongly stimulate the brain's reward circuitry. While no research directly linking the DRD2 variant to criminality was found, several studies have linked this receptor to factors frequently associated with criminality (Table 8.5.1).

### 8.5.2 Paroxetine Binding Sites

Paroxetine is a serotonin reuptake inhibitor that can be used to label serotonin uptake sites on blood platelets (Laruelle

**TABLE 8.4.8b** Strength and Clinical or Personality Traits Associated with Criminality.

| Nature of the relationship | Physical aggression |
|---|---|
| Positive | **ASIA** *India*: J Archer & Thanzami 2007 (males) |
| Not signif. | |
| Negative | |

**TABLE 8.5.1 Dopamine Receptors and Clinical or Personality Traits Associated with Criminality.**

| Nature of the relationship | Antisocial behavior | Cognitive & personality factors | Alcoholism |
|---|---|---|---|
| | Late adol. & adult | | |
| Positive | **EUROPE** *Italy*: Ponce et al. 2003 (DRD2, alcoholics) | **NORTH AMERICA** *United States*: EP Noble et al. 1998 (DRD2, novelty seeking); Comings et al. 2001 (pathological gambling) | **EUROPE** *Britain*: Connor et al. 2002 (DRD2)<br>**LATIN AMERICA** *Brazil*: Bau et al. 2000 (DRD2) |
| Not signif. | | | **EUROPE** *Finland*: Adamson et al. 1995 (DRD4) |
| Negative | | | |

et al. 1988). Studies have revealed that the number of paroxetine binding sites is positively associated with the uptake of 5-HT in blood platelets (Maguire et al. 1993). Similarly, researchers have hypothesized that fewer paroxetine binding sites are associated with the decreased density of 5-HT transporter sites, the reduced sensitivity of 5-HT postsynaptic receptors, and lower serotonergic neurotransmission within the body (Patkar et al. 2003). As discussed in a later section of this chapter, serotonin is an inhibitory neurotransmitter that helps regulate and control behavior. When there is not enough serotonin in the body, individuals may be more likely to engage in irrational, impulsive, or criminal behaviors. Therefore, given the relationship between paroxetine and serotonin neurotransmission, it may be expected that the density of paroxetine binding sites may be negatively correlated with antisocial and criminal behaviors. Table 8.5.2 shows that three studies have found a negative relationship between paroxetine binding and behavior that is frequently associated with criminality.

## 8.5.3 Serotonin Platelet-Binding Sites

Due to the high cost of neuroimaging studies and the invasiveness of cerebrospinal fluid tapping methods, researchers during the 1960s began measuring serotonin reuptake via blood-platelet methods. Blood-platelet specimens can be easily collected, and platelets can give researchers the same type of information that typically comes from examining neurons directly. For instance, researchers may gather information on serotonin uptake, serotonin binding, 5-HT receptors, and the metabolism of serotonin from both blood platelets and neurons (Hrdina, 1994). The benefits of blood-platelet analysis make this an attractive option for researchers.

Similar to the hypotheses concerning the reuptake of serotonergic neurons (discussed above), it is reasonable to believe that blood-platelet serotonin reuptake has a negative relationship with antisocial and criminal behaviors. Table 8.5.3 shows that there is some evidence to support this hypothesis although no study yet has directly linked

**TABLE 8.5.2 Paroxetine Binding Sites and Antisocial Behavior or Factors Frequently Linked to Criminality.**

| Nature of the relationship | Physical aggression | Cognitive & personality factors |
|---|---|---|
| Positive | | |
| Not signif. | | |
| Negative | **NORTH AMERICA** *United States*: Coccaro et al. 1996 (tritiated platelet binding, impulsive aggression); H Steiger et al. 2000 (tritiated platelet binding, impulsive aggression); Patkar et al. 2003:438* (blacks) | **NORTH AMERICA** *United States*: Patkar et al. 2003:438* (sensation seeking, blacks) |

**TABLE 8.5.3 Serotonin Platelet-Binding Sites and Antisocial Behavior or Factors Frequently Linked to Criminality.**

| Nature of the relationship | Antisocial behavior | Physical aggression |
|---|---|---|
| | Child & early adol. | |
| Positive | | |
| Not signif. | | |
| Negative | **NORTH AMERICA** *United States*: Stoff et al. 1987 | **NORTH AMERICA** *United States*: CS Brown et al. 1989 (episodic aggression); Birmaher et al. 1990 (impulsive aggression); Coccaro et al. 1996 (impulsive violence) |

the number of serotonin platelet-binding sites to criminality per se.

### 8.5.4 Serotonin Transporters (5-HTT)

Serotonin transporters (5-HTT) are responsible for transporting excess serotonin back to the axon during the reuptake process. Dysfunction in serotonin transporter synthesis or binding may cause disruptions in serotonergic neurotransmission. That is, the reuptake of serotonin relies upon an adequate amount of serotonin transporters synthesized by the body along with an adequate amount of transporter binding sites to capture the serotonin neurotransmitters. Disruptions in either of these components may prevent the reuptake of serotonin, desensitize postsynaptic receptors, and reduce serotonergic neurotransmission within the body. Reduced serotonergic neurotransmission has been linked to increases in impulsive, violent, and criminal behavior. This line of reasoning is supported by the study cited in Table 8.5.4, indicating a negative correlation between physical aggression and serotonin neurotransmission.

## 8.6 BIOCHEMICAL FACTORS (EXCEPT HORMONES)

A *biochemical* is any substance naturally produced by living organisms. Even though there are literally thousands of distinguishable biochemicals in nearly all forms of life, thus far only a handful have been implicated as possible correlates of crime. This section deals primarily with nonhormonal biochemicals.

### 8.6.1 Catechol-O-Methyl Transferase (COMT)

Catechol-O-methyl transferase (COMT) is an enzyme that functions within the synaptic gap (between neurons) to deactivate neurotransmitters collectively known as catecholamines. One study suggested that the COMT activity levels among schizophrenics who had committed homicide were usually low when compared with schizophrenics in general (Table 8.6.1a). A specific low-activity COMT genetic allele appears to control COMT activity in the brain.

With one failure to replicate, some research suggests that physical violence among schizophrenics is linked to low COMT activity in the brain (Table 8.6.1b).

**TABLE 8.5.4 Serotonin Transporters (5-HTT) and Antisocial Behavior or Factors Frequently Linked to Criminality.**

| Nature of the relationship | Physical aggression |
|---|---|
| Positive | |
| Not signif. | |
| Negative | **EUROPE** *Finland*: Tiihonen et al. 1997 (males, impulsive violence) |

**TABLE 8.6.1a Catechol-O-Methyl Transferase (COMT) and Criminal/Delinquent Behavior.**

| Nature of the relationship | Officially detected offenses |
|---|---|
| | Violent offenses |
| Positive | |
| Not signif. | |
| Negative | **NORTH AMERICA** *United States*: Kotler et al. 1999 (homicide, among schizophrenics) |

### 8.6.2 Cholesterol

Cholesterol is a fat-like substance found in all animal tissue. Studies have revealed that from one human to another, there is a fourfold variation in blood cholesterol levels (Fox 1961:84). While many people simply think of cholesterol in connection with heart disease, there are in fact different types of cholesterol, not all of which cause fatty deposits to accumulate in the arteries, eventually leading to strokes or other cardiovascular problems (Tierney 1987:83).

Interestingly, several studies have investigated the possibility of cholesterol being associated with criminality. Table 8.6.2a summarizes the evidence which shows that offenders have lower cholesterol levels in the blood than do nonoffenders.

As shown in Table 8.6.2b, low cholesterol levels are also associated with various behavioral and mental conditions associated with criminality.

**TABLE 8.6.1b Catechol-O-Methyl Transferase (COMT) and Clinical or Personality Traits Associated with Criminality.**

| Nature of the relationship | Physical aggression |
|---|---|
| Positive | |
| Not signif. | **EUROPE** *Britain*: Zammit et al. 2004 (among schizophrenics) |
| Negative | **NORTH AMERICA** *United States*: Strous et al. 1997 (among schizophrenics); Lachman et al. 1998 (among schizophrenics) |

**TABLE 8.6.2a** Cholesterol and Criminal/Delinquent Behavior.

| Nature of the relationship | Officially detected offenses | |
|---|---|---|
| | Violent offenses | General & adult offenses |
| Positive | | |
| Not signif. | | |
| Negative | **EUROPE** *Finland*: Virkkunen 1979; Virkkunen 1983c; Virkkunen 1987; *Sweden*: Golomb et al. 2000 | **NORTH AMERICA** *United States*: Hatch et al. 1966; Hillbrand et al. 1995 |

**TABLE 8.6.3** DHEA Sulfate Levels and Clinical or Personality Traits Associated with Criminality.

| Nature of the relationship | Antisocial behavior |
|---|---|
| | Childhood & early adol. |
| Positive | **EUROPE** *Netherlands*: Van Goozen et al. 1998 (boys) |
| Not signif. | |
| Negative | |

## 8.6.3 Dehydroepiandrosterone (DHEA) Sulfate Levels

Dehydroepiandrosterone (DHEA) sulfate is a neurosteroid that peaks in production during adolescence and decreases in density with age. As shown in Table 8.6.3, one study reported that DHEA sulfate levels for conduct-disordered boys were higher than for boys generally.

## 8.6.4 5-HIAA Levels in Cerebrospinal Fluid

Serotonin (also called *5-hydroxytryptamine* or *5-HT* for short) is an important neurotransmitter. When 5-HT is active in the brain, people usually report feeling calm and contented; and when inactive, they feel anxious and depressed (Kalus et al. 1989; Plaznik et al. 1989). Unfortunately, it is very difficult to measure serotonergic functioning directly without seriously damaging the brain in the process. However, animal studies have revealed that one can fairly accurately infer serotonergic functioning by measuring a chemical by-product in the urine, a metabolite known as *5-HIAA* (*5-hydroxy indoleacetic acid*).

Several studies have investigated the possibility that serotonergic brain functioning might be related to criminal/delinquent behavior. As shown in Table 8.6.4a, all of these studies have found 5-HIAA levels to be lower in criminal populations than in the general public. This is especially true for individuals whose offenses are impulsive in nature as opposed to crimes that are carefully planned (Linnoila et al. 1983; Bloch & Thompson 1993:53).

Table 8.6.4b indicates that, with only a few exceptions, a very large number of studies have documented the inverse relationship between 5-HIAA and traits frequently associated with criminality. Physical aggression, in particular, has been statistically linked to low 5-HIAA levels in nearly all studies in both humans and other animals.

## 8.6.5 Glucose Nadir

Glucose nadir refers to the lowest level to which blood glucose levels decline. Persons who have unusually low glucose after receiving glucose infusions are diagnosed as hypoglycemic. As shown in Table 8.6.5a, persons who exhibit a drop in blood glucose after receiving a glucose infusion appear to have a high probability of criminal behavior.

**TABLE 8.6.2b** Cholesterol and Clinical or Personality Traits Associated with Criminality.

| Nature of the relationship | Antisocial behavior | | Physical aggression | Mental illness |
|---|---|---|---|---|
| | Childhood & early adol. | Late adol. & adulthood | | |
| Positive | | | | |
| Not signif. | | | | |
| Negative | **EUROPE** *Sweden*: Virkkunen & Penttinen 1984 | **EUROPE** *Finland*: Virkkunen 1987 (among personality disordered persons) | **NORTH AMERICA** *United States*: Mufti et al. 1998 (psychiatric patients) **PRIMATES** *Monkey*: Kaplan et al. 1991; Muldoon et al. 1992 | **EUROPE** *France*: Zureik et al. 1996; *Sweden*: Horsten et al. 1997 (with suicide) |

**TABLE 8.6.4a** 5-HIAA Levels in the Cerebral Spinal Fluid and Criminal/Delinquent Behavior.

| Nature of the relationship | Officially detected offenses | | | | |
|---|---|---|---|---|---|
| | Violent offenses | Property offenses | Delinquency | General & adult offenses | Recidivism |
| Positive | | | | | |
| Not signif. | | | | | |
| Negative | **EUROPE** *Finland*: Linnoila et al. 1983; Virkkunen et al. 1987; Virkkunen et al. 1989; Virkkunen et al. 1995; *Sweden*: Lidberg et al. 1985 (spousal homicide) **MIDDLE EAST** *Israel*: Blumensohn et al. 1995 **NORTH AMERICA** *United States*: DT George et al. 2001 (CSF levels, domestic violence offenders) | **EUROPE** *Finland*: Virkkunen et al. 1987 (arson) | **NORTH AMERICA** *United States*: Pliszka et al. 1988; Matykiewicz et al. 1997 | **EUROPE** *Finland*: Virkkunen et al. 1994a; Virkkunen et al. 1994b; *Sweden*: Cloninger et al. 1982a | **EUROPE** *Finland*: Virkkunen et al. 1989; Linnoila & Virkkunen 1992; Virkkunen et al. 1996 |

Table 8.6.5b suggests that in addition to being linked to criminality, low glucose after glucose challenges is more common in children with conduct disorders than in children in general.

## 8.6.6 Homovanillic Acid (HVA)

Neurotransmitters degraded by enzymes, such as MAO-A or COMT, are converted into by-products called metabolites. The metabolite for dopamine is homovanillic acid (HVA). As shown in Table 8.6.6a, two studies have found a negative relationship between HVA and recidivism, while one study of arsonists failed to identify a significant difference between them and offenders generally in HVA levels. Lower levels of HVA may reflect dopamine deficiencies in the brain (Gabel et al. 1993) which could in turn lead to antisocial conduct (Moffitt et al. 1996).

Research pertaining to frequent correlates of criminality has also found that low levels of HVA are linked to antisocial behavior and frequent physical aggression (Table 8.6.6b).

## 8.6.7 HVA:5-HIAA Ratio

The ratio of HVA to 5-HIAA is thought to reflect a disruption of serotonin's regulation of dopamine activity in the brain. This disruption may create behavioral problems due to the imbalance between the inhibitory capabilities of serotonin and/or the excitory properties of dopamine. One study, reported in Table 8.6.7 found an association between the HVA:5-HIAA ratio and antisocial behavior in late adolescence/adulthood among male offenders.

## 8.6.8 L-Tryptophan/Competing Amino Acid Plasma

Tryptophan is an essential amino acid for producing serotonin. The ratio of tryptophan relative to competing amino acids in the blood was assessed in one study. It revealed that the ratio was higher in offenders than in nonoffenders (Table 8.6.8).

## 8.6.9 3-Methoxy 4-Hydroxyphenylglycol (MHPG)

3-Methoxy 4-hydroxyphenylglycol (MHPG) is a metabolite of norepinephrine, a neurotransmitter that is released into the brain (especially in the prefrontal cortex) when an individual is confronted with a stressful or negative situation. The most common assaying source for MHPG is the cerebrospinal fluid (CSF). Elevating brain levels of norepinephrine increases one's heart rate and primes the body for a fight-or-flight response. Overactivity of this neurotransmitter can interfere with cognitive functioning within the prefrontal cortex and lead to impulsive and aggressive behavior (Birnbaum et al. 1999; Haden & Scarpa 2007).

It is reasonable to suspect them that elevated MHPG would be associated with impulsivity and aggression, thereby increasing the chances of violent forms of criminality. Only a few studies are available thus far, none of which pertain to criminality per se. Nevertheless, the evidence is supportive. As shown in Table 8.6.9, studies have found higher MHPG levels associated with aggressive behavior, especially that of an impulsive nature.

**TABLE 8.6.4b** 5-HIAA Levels in the Cerebral Spinal Fluid and Clinical or Personality Traits Associated with Criminality.

| Nature of the relationship | Antisocial behavior | | Physical aggression | Cognitive & personality factors | Alcoholism | Mental illness | Mental Disorder |
|---|---|---|---|---|---|---|---|
| | Childhood & early adol. | Late adol. & adulthood | | | | | |
| Positive | | | | | | | |
| Not signif. | | | **NORTH AMERICA** *United States*: DL Gardner et al. 1990 (among borderline personality disorder patients); Castellanos et al. 1994 (among ADHD males); Moller et al. 1996; Coccaro et al. 1997 (among mental patients) | | | | **NORTH AMERICA** *United States*: Shetty & Chase 1976 (ADHD); DJ Cohen et al. 1977b (ADHD); Shaywitz et al. 1977 (ADHD) |
| Negative | **NORTH AMERICA** *United States*: GL Brown et al. 1986; Kruesi et al. 1990; Kruesi et al. 1992 | **EUROPE** *Finland*: Virkkunen & Linnoila 1993* **NORTH AMERICA** *United States*: G Brown et al. 1979; G Brown et al. 1982* | **EUROPE** *Britain*: Coccaro 1989*; Coccaro & Kavoussi 1996; *Finland*: Linnoila et al. 1983 (impulsive violent offenders); Roy et al. 1988*; Virkkunen et al. 1989; Virkkunen & Linnoila 1990; Virkunnen et al. 1994b **NORTH AMERICA** *United States*: G Brown et al. 1979a; G Brown 1979b; GL Brown et al. 1982; Brown & Goodwin 1984; Stanley et al. 1985; Roy et al. 1988; CS Brown et al. 1989; Kruesi et al. 1989; Linnoila et al. 1989; G Brown et al. 1990; G Brown & Linnoila 1990; Limson et al. 1991; Kruesi et al. 1992 (two year olds); Halperin et al. 1997 (among ADHD boys); Stanley et al. 2000 (psychiatric patients); AJ Bond et al. 2001 (women, inferred from low typtophan); Placido et al. 2001 **PRIMATES** *Monkeys*: McGuire et al. 1983b; Raleigh et al. 1984; Higley et al. 1990; Higley et al. 1992; Higley et al. 1994; Mehlman et al. 1994; Raleigh & McGuire 1994; Mehlman et al. 1995; Higley et al. 1996c | **EUROPE** *Britain*: Coccaro et al. 1989 (impulsivity); Coccaro et al. 1991 (impulsivity); *Finland*: Linnoila et al. 1983 (among violent offenders); Virkkunen et al. 1994b (impulsivity) **NORTH AMERICA** *United States*: Asberg et al. 1987* (impulsivity); Kent et al. 1988 (impulsivity); Apter et al. 1990 (impulsivity); Coccaro & Kavoussi 1996 | **EUROPE** *Finland*: Virkkunen & Linnoila 1993 **NORTH AMERICA** *United States*: Moss et al. 1990; Limson 1991 | **NORTH AMERICA** *United States*: Asberg et al. 1976 (suicide); Traskman et al. 1981 (suicide); Brown et al. 1982 (suicide); Goodwin & Post 1983 (depression); Asberg et al. 1986 (suicide); Asberg et al. 1987* (suicide); Roy et al. 1991 (suicide) | **NORTH AMERICA** *United States*: Winston 1973 (PMS); Rausch & Janowsky 1982 (PMS); Moreno et al. 1991(pathological gambling) |

**TABLE 8.6.5a** Glucose Nadir and Criminal/Delinquent Behavior.

| Nature of the relationship | Officially detected offenses | |
|---|---|---|
| | Violent offenses | Property offenses |
| Higher after glucose challenge | | |
| Not signif. | | |
| Lower after glucose challenge | **EUROPE** *Finland*: Virkkunen 1982; Virkkunen & Huttunen 1982; Virkkunen et al. 1994b* | **EUROPE** *Finland*: Virkkunen et al. 1994b* (arsonists) |

**TABLE 8.6.5b** Glucose Nadir and Clinical or Personality Traits Associated with Criminality.

| Nature of the relationship | Antisocial behavior |
|---|---|
| | Child & early adol. |
| Higher after glucose challenge | |
| Not signif. | |
| Lower after glucose challenge | **EUROPE** *Finland*: Virkkunen & Penttinen 1984 |

## 8.6.10 Monoamine Oxidase (MAO) Activity in General

Monoamine oxidase (MAO) is a type of enzyme found throughout the body, including the brain. The role of MAO in the brain is not fully understood, but it appears to help breakdown and disperse neurotransmitters from the synaptic regions between neurons to avoid accumulation of excessive amounts of these neurotransmitters in the synaptic cleft. MAO comes in two slightly different forms, termed *MAO-A* and *MAO-B*. Both forms are discussed separately below.

Unfortunately, it is impossible to measure brain levels of MAO activity directly without damaging the brain in the process (Redmond et al. 1976:316). Therefore, most studies of MAO derive their samples from the blood, known as *platelet MAO*. Studies have revealed that people exhibit up to a sixfold variation in the amount of platelet MAO they possess (Robinson et al. 1971; Murphy et al. 1976), which appears to be almost entirely due to genetic factors (Fowler et al. 1982; Alexopoulos et al. 1983:1501; Revely et al. 1983; Oxenstierna et al. 1986).

**TABLE 8.6.6a** Homovanillic Acid (HVA) and Criminal/Delinquent Behavior.

| Nature of the relationship | Officially detected offenses | |
|---|---|---|
| | General & adult offenses | Recidivism |
| Positive | | |
| Not signif. | **EUROPE** *Finland*: Virkkunen et al. 1987 (among male arsonists) | |
| Negative | | **EUROPE** *Finland*: Virkkunen et al. 1989; Virkkunen et al. 1994a |

**TABLE 8.6.6b** Homovanillic Acid (HVA) and Clinical or Personality Traits Associated with Criminality.

| Nature of the relationship | Antisocial behavior | Physical aggression |
|---|---|---|
| | Late adol. & adulthood | |
| Positive | | |
| Not signif. | | |
| Negative | **EUROPE** *Finland*: Linnoila et al. 1983 | **NORTH AMERICA** *United States*: Limson et al. 1991 |

**TABLE 8.6.7** HVA:5-HIAA Ratio and Clinical or Personality Traits Associated with Criminality.

| Nature of the Relationship | Antisocial behavior |
|---|---|
| | Late adol. & adulthood |
| Positive | **NORTH AMERICA** *United States*: Soderstrom et al. 2003 (male offenders) |
| Not signif. | |
| Negative | |

**TABLE 8.6.8** L-Tryptophan/Competing Amino Acid Plasma and Criminal/Delinquent Behavior.

| Nature of the relationship | Officially detected offenses |
|---|---|
| | General & adult offenses |
| Positive | **EUROPE** *Finland*: Tiihonen et al. 2001 |
| Not signif. | |
| Negative | |

**TABLE 8.6.9** MHPG (3-Methoxy 4-Hydroxyphenylglycol) and Clinical or Personality Traits Associated with Criminality.

| Nature of the relationship | Physical aggression |
|---|---|
| Positive | **NORTH AMERICA** *United States*: GL Brown et al. 1979 (impulsive aggression in personality disordered males); Castellanos et al. 1994 (impulsive aggression in ADHD adol. males) **PRIMATE** *Rhesus Macaque*: Higley et al. 1992 |
| Not signif. | |
| Negative | |

The research linking platelet MAO in general to criminality is shown in Table 8.6.10a. As one can see, all but one study concluded that unusually low levels of MAO activity are found in the blood of criminals.

Complementing the research findings linking low MAO activity with criminality are findings of various studies of traits closely associated with offending. Table 8.6.10b shows that antisocial behavior, physical aggression, impulsiveness, and sensation seeking appear to be inversely associated with MAO.

## 8.6.11 Monoamine Oxidase A (MAO-A) Activity

Monoamine oxidase A (MAO-A) is an enzyme that is responsible for removing or degrading excess neurotransmitters (specifically serotonin, dopamine, and

**TABLE 8.6.10a** Monoamine Oxidase (MAO) Activity in General and Criminal/Antisocial Behavior.

| Nature of the relationship | Officially detected offenses | | | | Self-reported offenses |
|---|---|---|---|---|---|
| | Violent offenses | Drug offenses | General & adult offenses | Recidivism | Illegal drugs |
| Positive | | | | | **NORTH AMERICA** *United States*: Gabel et al. 1994 |
| Not signif. | | | | | |
| Negative | **EUROPE** *Greece*: Skondras et al. 2004; *Sweden*: Linnoila et al. 1983; Belfrage et al. 1992; Garpenstrand et al. 2002 **NORTH AMERICA** *United States*: Yu et al. 1984 | **NORTH AMERICA** *United States*: Stillman et al. 1978 | **EUROPE** *Sweden*: Alm et al. 1996a; Alm et al. 1996b; af Klinteberg 1996 **NORTH AMERICA** *United States*: Buchsbaum et al. 1976 | **EUROPE** *Sweden*: Alm et al. 1994 | **EUROPE** *Sweden*: von Knorring et al. 1987 **NORTH AMERICA** *United States*: Stillman et al. 1978 |

**TABLE 8.6.10b** Monoamine Oxidase (MAO) Activity in General and Clinical or Personality Traits Associated with Criminality.

| Nature of the relationship | Antisocial behavior | | Physical aggression | Cognitive & personality factors |
|---|---|---|---|---|
| | Childhood & early adol. | Late adol. & adulthood | | |
| Positive | | | | |
| Not signif. | | | | |
| Negative | **NORTH AMERICA** *Canada:* Bowden et al. 1988 | **EUROPE** *Sweden*: von Knorring et al. 1984*; Lidberg et al. 1985; von Knorring et al. 1987 **NORTH AMERICA** *United States*: Haier et al. 1980:341; BA Davis et al. 1983 | **EUROPE** *Denmark*: Schalling et al. 1987 (criminals); Belfroge et al. 1991 (among the mentally ill) | **EUROPE** *Sweden*: von Knorring et al. 1984* (impulsivity & sensation seeking); Stallenheim et al. 1997 (impulsivity & sensation seeking) |

norepinephrine) from the synaptic cleft after the electrochemical message has been passed onto the next brain cell. Dysfunction in MAO-A can be caused by its presence in the synaptic cleft being too prevalent or too insufficient. For instance, overactivity in MAO-A leads to abnormally low levels of neurotransmitter activity, while underactivity of MAO-A leads to unusually high concentrations of neurotransmitters in the brain. Both situations can lead to disruptions in communication between brain cells. Therefore, MAO-A levels must stay within the 'normal' range for optimal cognitive functioning.

MAO-A activity is regulated by a gene located on the X chromosome. The MAO-A gene is a polymorphic gene, meaning that at least two allelic variants of the gene are involved. The low activity allele is the one that has been most often associated with antisocial behavior.

Three studies were found that attempted to associate MAO-A activity and antisocial behavior. Table 8.6.11a shows that two of these studies reported a negative relationship while one reported no significant relationship.

With several exceptions, some studies point toward an inverse association between MAO-A activity and antisocial behavior and physical aggression (Table 8.1.11b).

**TABLE 8.6.11a Monoamine Oxidase A (MAO-A) Activity and Criminal/Delinquent Behavior.**

| Nature of the relationship | Officially detected offenses | |
|---|---|---|
| | Violent offenses | General & adult offenses |
| Positive | | |
| Not signif. | | **EUROPE** *Finland*: Sjoberg et al. 2006 (females) |
| Negative | **EUROPE** *Netherlands*: Brunner et al. 1993<br>**OCEANIA** *New Zealand*: Caspi et al. 2002* (combined with maltreatment by parents) | **EUROPE** *Finland*: Nilsson et al. 2006 (males) |

As shown in Table 8.6.12, while quite a few studies have found no significant MAO-B activity relationships with physical aggression or alcoholism, most studies have found significant inverse relationships.

## 8.6.12 Monoamine Oxidase B (MAO-B) Activity

Monoamine Oxidase B (MAO-B) seems only to degrade dopamine and is therefore a more specialized enzyme than MAO-A. Researchers have hypothesized that MAO-B levels may be associated with a range of problem behaviors and traits linked to dopamine. The evidence is limited to behavior associated with criminality, not criminality itself.

## 8.7 HORMONES OR NEAR-HORMONES

Hormones are biochemicals produced in one part of the body which travel via the blood system to other parts of the body where their primary effects occur. The two main hormones thus far investigated in criminological research are testosterone and cortisol, but, as this section documents, several other hormones have also been explored.

**TABLE 8.1.11b MAO-A Activity and Antisocial Factors or Factors Frequently Linked to Criminality.**

| Nature of the relationship | Antisocial behavior | | Physical aggression |
|---|---|---|---|
| High activity | Child & early adol. | Late adol. & adulthood | |
| Not signif. | **NORTH AMERICA** *United States*: Haberstick et al. 2005 (males, in combination with child abuse); SE Young et al. 2005 (males, in conjunction with child maltreatment) | **EUROPE** *Finland*: Ducci et al. 2006 (males)<br>**OCEANIA** *New Zealand*: Caspi et al. 2002* (MAO-A) | **EUROPE** *Britain*: Zammit et al. 2004 (among schizophrenics)<br>**PRIMATE** *Rhesus Macaque*: T Newman et al. 2005* (females, codes for low MAO activity) |
| Low activity | **NORTH AMERICA** *United States*: Foley et al. 2004 (males, when combined with adversity in childhood); Kim-Cohen et al. 2006 (males, when combined with adversity in childhood); Nilsson et al. 2006 (males, in combination with childhood adversity); Widom & Brzustowicz 2006 (in combination with child abuse)<br>**OCEANIA** *New Zealand*: Caspi et al. 2002 | **EUROPE** *Finland*: Sjoberg et al. 2007* (males, CSF levels, when combined with high testosterone) | **EUROPE** *Finland*: Sjoberg et al. 2007* (males, CSF levels, when combined with high testosterone)<br>**PRIMATE** *Rhesus Macaque*: T Newman et al. 2005* (males, codes for low MAO activity) |

**TABLE 8.6.12** Monoamine Oxidase B (MAO-B) Activity and Clinical or Personality Traits Associated with Criminality.

| Nature of the relationship | Physical aggression | Cognitive & personality factors | Alcoholism | Drug abuse | Mental illness | Mental disorder |
|---|---|---|---|---|---|---|
| Positive | | | | | | |
| Not signif. | **EUROPE** *Britain*: Zammit et al. 2004 (among schizophrenics) | **EUROPE** *Sweden*: Propping et al. 1981 (extroversion); Berggren et al. 2002 (males, Type I) **NORTH AMERICA** *United States*: Coursey et al. 1980 (sensation seeking); Zeller & Davis 1980 (learning disability); Ballenger et al. 1983 (sensation seeking) | **EUROPE** *Sweden*: Soyka et al. 2000 **NORTH AMERICA** *United States*: Tabakoff et al. 1988; Mezzich et al. 1994 (females); Parsian et al. 1995 (Type II); Anthenelli et al. 1998 (Type II); Farren et al. 1998 (Type II); Whitfield et al. 2000 | | | |
| Negative | | **EUROPE** *Germany*: Demisch et al. 1982 (males, extroversion); *Sweden*: Fowler et al. 1980 (sensation seeking); Gattaz & Beckman 1981; Oreland et al. 1984 (impulsivity & academic performance); AF Klinteberg et al. 1987a (impulsivity) **NORTH AMERICA** *United States*: Murphy et al. 1977 (sensation seeking); Buchsbaum et al. 1978:216; Schooler et al. 1978 (sensation seeking); Coursey et al. 1982 (academic performance); von Knorring et al. 1984 (sensation seeking); Ward et al. 1987 (sensation seeking) | **ASIA** *Japan*: Takahashi et al. 1976 **EUROPE** *Sweden*: Gottfries et al. 1975; von Knorring et al. 1985; von Knorring & Oreland 1978; Hallman et al. 1990; Hallman et al. 1996 (Type II) **NORTH AMERICA** *United States*: JB Brown 1977; Major & Murphy 1978; Shaskan 1983; Dolinski et al. 1985; Paney et al. 1988; Sullivan et al. 1978; Yates et al. 1990; Calhoon-Grange et al. 1993; Devor et al. 1993 (Type II); Rommelspacher et al. 1994 (Type II); von Knorring & Oreland 1996 (Type II) | **EUROPE** *Sweden*: Oreland et al. 1981a; von Knorring et al. 1987 **NORTH AMERICA** *United States*: Stillman et al. 1978; Norman et al. 1982; Yong & Perry 1986 | **EUROPE** *Sweden*: Oreland et al. 1981b (depression) **NORTH AMERICA** *United States*: BA Davis et al. 1983 (among schizophrenics) | **EUROPE** *Sweden*: Hallman et al. 1987 (PMS) **NORTH AMERICA** *United States*: Shekim et al. 1982 (ADHD) |

**TABLE 8.7.1 Estrogen Levels and Clinical or Personality Traits Associated with Criminality.**

| Nature of the relationship | Physical aggression |
|---|---|
| Positive | **RODENT** *Mouse*: Hilakivi-Clarke et al. 1997 (adult); *Rat*: NG Simon & Whalen 1986 (adult) |
| Not signif. | |
| Negative | |

## 8.7.1 Estrogen Levels

Although estrogen is often referred to as a female sex hormone, males also have measurable levels of estrogen. In females, estrogen is essential to the development of secondary sexual characteristics such as breast development, and also plays an important role during a woman's menstrual cycle. While many criminological studies have examined the relationship between the main "male" sex hormone, testosterone, and/or criminal behavior (see below), no study directly linking estrogen and antisocial and criminal behavior was located. Using rodents, however, researchers have found estrogen levels to be positively correlated with aggression (Table 8.7.1).

## 8.7.2 Testosterone Levels

Testosterone is a sex hormone that helps to differentiate the sexes. While both males and females produce measurable quantities of testosterone throughout most of their lives, as noted in more detail below, males produce much higher levels both perinatally and following the onset of puberty.

Male levels of testosterone are also much higher than that of females throughout most of the gestation period. During childhood, testosterone production in both sexes subsides to nearly undetectable levels. Then, following the onset of puberty, male testosterone production skyrockets some 10–15 times higher than what it was for both sexes during childhood (Khan & Cataio 1984:10; Malasanos et al. 1986:702).

Scientists have been interested in testosterone as a possible correlate of crime over the years for various interrelated reasons, with the following being most notable:

**(1)** In most species, males are more overtly aggressive than females (L Ellis et al. 2008:707–708), a difference that is difficult to attribute to social training.

**(2)** Castration (removal of the testes, the main organ producing testosterone) usually has "pacifying effects" on aggressive behavior in males (Potegal et al. 1980; Bernstein et al. 1983).

**(3)** Among humans, males engage in crime, especially that of the violent type, more than do females, and this involvement in crime usually rises in the early to mid teens (documented in Chapter 2). This rise in male crime rates coincides with the distinct rise in male testosterone levels.

To measure testosterone levels in most studies, the two main assaying sources are blood and saliva. Neither of these methods are ideal from the standpoint of determining what effect testosterone might have on criminality because behavior is controlled not by the blood or saliva, but by the brain. About the only way to determine how much testosterone is in the brain itself is through a spinal tap, a painful invasion of the body not undertaken simply for research purposes.

Another difficulty concerning the use of blood and saliva samples to measure testosterone levels involves the distinction between what is known as bound and unbound testosterone. *Bound testosterone* refers to testosterone molecules that are chemically bonded to other biochemical molecules. In the blood, these bound molecules are too large to cross the blood–brain barrier (O'Dea et al. 1979; Franks et al. 1991). Only unbound testosterone enters the brain and thereby potentially affects behavior.

Also worth mentioning is that outside the brain, testosterone levels fluctuate a great deal throughout the day, usually being highest soon after waking from a night of sleep (Foreman & Goodyear 1988; Butler et al. 1989; Dabbs 1990). For this reason, subjects in most studies are tested at usually the same time of day, usually early morning. Despite the instability and difficulties in measuring testosterone outside the brain in order to make inferences about how this hormone might be affecting the brain itself, quite a number of studies have investigated the possibility that testosterone and involvement in criminal/delinquent behavior are related.

Despite the above-noted evidence that testosterone is related to aggression and peaks in males around the same time as their peak probabilities of offending, the only theory which puts the effects of testosterone on the brain as a centerpiece in its explanation of criminality is the *evolutionary neuroandrogenic (ENA) theory* (L Ellis 2003a, 2003b, 2005, 2007, 2008). According to ENA theory, evolutionary forces have favored males who are more aggressive and competitive relative to females, especially when males are beginning to accumulate resources with which to attract mates. This theory asserts that the testes have evolved the capability to produce high levels of testosterone, a hormone that alters brain functioning in ways that cause males to be more capable of long-term competition for mates and resources. Criminality is hypothesized to be one of the main early manifestations of this competitiveness. Males who learn most efficiently, according to ENA theory, shift rather quickly to relatively subtle methods of competition, while slow learners often persist at criminal forms of competition well into full adulthood.

TABLE 8.7.2a Testosterone Levels and Criminal/Delinquent Behavior.

| Nature of the relationship | Officially detected offenses | | | | | | Self-reported offenses |
|---|---|---|---|---|---|---|---|
| | Violent offenses | Sex offenses | Drug offenses | Delinquency | General & adult offenses | Recidivism | Illegal drugs |
| Positive | **EUROPE** *Finland*: Virkkunen et al. 1994 (males); *Greece*: Giotakos et al. 2004 (male rapists); *Italy*: D'Alessandro et al. 1972 (females) **NORTH AMERICA** *Canada*: Brooks & Reddon 1996; *United States*: Kreuz & Rose 1972 (males); Dabbs et al. 1987 (males); Dabbs et al. 1988 (female prisoners than other offenders); Dabbs et al. 1991 (males); Bergman & Brismar 1994 (male alcoholics, domestic violence); Dabbs et al. 1995 (males); Dabbs & Hargrov 1997 (female prisoners); George et al. 2001 (males, spousal abuse); Dabbs et al. 2001 (male prisoners) | **NORTH AMERICA** *Canada*: Studer et al. 2005; *United States*: K Christiansen & Knussmann 1987 (males, sexual aggression) | **NORTH AMERICA** *United States*: Dabbs et al. 1990 (males) | **EUROPE** *Sweden*: Mattsson et al. 1980 (males) **NORTH AMERICA** *United States*: Banks & Dabbs 1996 (males & females) | **EUROPE** *Denmark*: Schiavi et al. 1988; *Sweden*: Stalenheim et al. 1998 (males) **NORTH AMERICA** *Canada*: van Bokhoven et al. 2006 (saliva sample); *United States*: Dabbs et al. 1987 (females); Dabbs et al. 1988* (males); Dabbs & Morris 1990 (males); Dabbs et al. 1990 (males); Booth & Osgood 1993; Mazur 1995:289 (males) | **EUROPE** *Finland*: Rasanen et al. 1999 (prisoners with personality disorders); *Sweden*: Mattsson et al. 1980 (males) **NORTH AMERICA** *Canada*: Studer et al. 2005 (male sex offenders); *United States*: Dabbs et al. 1987 (prison violations, males); Dabbs et al. 1995 (prison violations, males); Dabbs & Hargrove 1997 (prison violations, females) | **NORTH AMERICA** *United States*: Udry 1989 (Males); Dabbs & Morris 1990 (males, military personal) |
| Not signif. | | **EUROPE** *Finland*: Aromaki et al. 2002 (saliva levels); *Sweden*: Rada et al. 1983 (rapists versus other sex offenders) **NORTH AMERICA** *United States*: Rada et al. 1976 | | **NORTH AMERICA** *United States*: Susman et al. 1987 (males); Inoff-Germain et al. 1988 (males) | **NORTH AMERICA** *United States*: Dabbs et al. 1988* (females) | | |
| Negative | | | | **NORTH AMERICA** *Canada*: Schaal et al. 1996 (males) | | | |

As shown in Table 8.7.2a, most studies support the idea of a link between testosterone and adult criminality, although when analyses are performed separately by sex, the relationships are of only modest strength (Book et al. 2001). Nearly all of the studies of juvenile delinquency, however, are not statistically significant.

Turning to traits associated with high probabilities of criminal behavior, Table 8.7.2b reveals that most studies have concluded that these traits are positively correlated with testosterone levels. It is worth adding that the blood levels of testosterone have been found to be more similar for identical twins than for fraternal twins, at least among males (JA Harris et al. 1998; Sluyter et al. 2000), suggesting that genetic factors contribute to human variations in testosterone levels. If so, this could at least partly explain how genes appear to be linked to variations in criminality (discussed earlier in Chapter 4).

Because of the tremendous amount of both human and animal research on the relationship between testosterone and various forms of aggression, the relevant findings are presented in a separate table. As one can see by examining Table 8.7.2c, results have been mixed regarding any links between these two variables, with roughly half of the studies documenting a positive relationship and the remaining ones failing to find any significant relationship. Interestingly, the proportions of positive versus nonsignificant relationships are roughly equal for human and nonhuman samples.

## 8.7.3 Androgens other than Testosterone

Testosterone is not the only hormone to be produced in larger quantities in males than in females. Other so-called male hormones include dihydrotestosterone and androstenedione. No research was found which attempted to determine if either of these hormones is associated with criminality, but some studies have investigated these hormones in connection with behavioral factors frequently associated with criminality. As shown in Table 8.7.3, some of the findings indicate that these two male hormones are, like testosterone, somehow associated with antisocial behavior and physical aggression.

## 8.7.4 Cortisol

Cortisol is generally considered a stress hormone, with its most active release taking place during times of physical or emotional stress (Stanton et al. 1987:141; Wittling & Pfluger 1990:244). For instance, two- to threefold increases in cortisol levels have been found for persons anticipating serious forms of surgery (Shannon et al. 1961; Czeisler et al. 1976), while speaking in public (Kirschbaum et al. 1992), and when asked to solve challenging arithmetic problems while classmates watch (Bossert et al. 1988; Brantley et al. 1988).

To measure cortisol levels, most researchers use blood or saliva samples (King et al. 1990; Kirschbaum & Hellhammer 1994; Ockenfels et al. 1995). However, a few investigators have used urine and cerebral spinal fluid levels (Mason et al. 1986).

In addition to emotional stress triggered by challenging social circumstances, physical pain often causes a rise in the release of cortisol. For example, cortisol in the blood has been shown to rise more than five times the normal levels for male newborns who have just experienced circumcision (Gunnar et al. 1981, 1985; Stang et al. 1988). Nonetheless, if stress persists for prolonged periods of time (several days or weeks), eventually the release of cortisol subsides to below-normal levels (Bourne et al. 1968; Bauer et al. 1994). As revealed in Table 8.7.4a, most research suggests that offenders tend to have levels of cortisol that are lower than for persons in general.

Regarding factors frequently linked to criminality, low cortisol levels appear to be more common among persons who are antisocial as well as unusually aggressive and impulsive, but there may be an exception relative to alcoholism (Table 8.7.4b).

## 8.7.5 Prolactin

Prolactin is a hormone that plays a major role in prompinglactation in female mammals. Nevertheless, both sexes produce prolactin and it appears to affect many other aspects of mammalian bodily functioning, including that of the brain. By altering the brain, prolactin also impacts emotions and behavior. As shown in Table 8.7.5a, one study reported that male sex offenders appeared to have above normal levels of prolactin.

Minimal and somewhat inconsistent findings have been reported concerning any relationship between physical aggression and prolactin levels (Table 8.7.5b).

## 8.7.6 Prolactin Response to Buspirone

Buspirone is an anti-anxiety drug which affects the functioning of neurotransmitters such as serotonin and dopamine. Once ingested, buspirone activity can be measured through prolactin release into the blood stream (Lane & Cherek 2000). Table 8.7.6 reveals that, according to one study, individuals with aggressive personality disorder tend to have significantly lower than normal levels of prolactin released following the administration of buspirone. This finding may indicate that individuals characterized as aggressive have diminished serotonin activity even when given anti-anxiety medication.

## 8.7.7 Prolactin Response to Fenfluramine

Fenfluramine is a drug that affects the production of the hormone prolactin. Researchers have administered fenfluramine to various subjects and noted whether the production

**TABLE 8.7.2b** Testosterone Levels and Clinical or Personality Traits Associated with Criminality.

| Nature of the relationship | Antisocial behavior | | Cognitive & personality factors | Alcoholism | Mental disorder |
|---|---|---|---|---|---|
| | Childhood & early adol. | Late adol. & adulthood | | | |
| Positive | **EUROPE** *Germany*: Maras et al. 2003* (males, DHT also higher); *Netherlands*: Van Goozen et al. 1998 (males, saliva sample) **NORTH AMERICA** *United States*: Scerbo & Kolko 1994 (males) | **EUROPE** *Britain*: Dolan et al. 2001 (adult males); *Finland*: Virkkunen et al. 1994 (males, CSF levels); Aromaki et al. 1999; Aromaki et al. 2002; Sjoberg et al. 2007* (males, CSF levels, when combined with low MAO-A activity); *Sweden*: Stalenheim et al. 1998 (males, SHBG also higher) **NORTH AMERICA** *United States*: Dabbs & Morris 1990 (males); Dabbs et al. 1990 (male) | **EUROPE** *Germany*: Maras et al. 2003*(adol. boys, externalizing behavior) **NORTH AMERICA** *United States*: La Grange et al. 1995 (college students, sensation seeking); Bjork et al. 2001 (impulsivity, women); Maras et al. 2003 (externalizing behavior, adol.); Loney et al. 2006 (adol. callous-unemotionality) Coccaro et al. 2007* (venturesomeness) | **EUROPE** *Sweden*: Stalenheim et al. 1998 (males, Type II, total T & SHBG but not unbound levels in the blood) | **EUROPE** *Britain*: Dolan et al. 2001 (male prisoners); *Sweden*: Stalenheim et al. 1998 (males) **NORTH AMERICA** *United States*: SE Chance et al. 2000 (5–11 year olds, saliva sample) |
| Not signif. | **EUROPE** *Germany*: Maras et al. 2003* (females); *Netherlands*: van Goozen et al. 1998 (males, 8–12 years old) **NORTH AMERICA** *United States*: Susman et al. 1987 (males); Constantino et al. 1993 (males) | | **EUROPE** *Germany*: Maras et al. 2003*(adol. girls, externalizing behavior) **NORTH AMERICA** *United States*: Coccaro et al. 2007* (impulsivity, males with personality disorders) | | |
| Negative | | | | | |

**TABLE 8.7.2c** Testosterone Levels and Aggressive/Combative Tendencies in Humans and Other Animals.

| Nature of the relationship | Direct observation of aggression and violence | Self-reported offenses | | |
|---|---|---|---|---|
| | | Physical aggression | Verbal aggression | Feelings of hostility and anger |
| Positive | **EUROPE** *Finland*: Sjoberg et al. 2007* (males, CSF levels, when combined with low MAO-A activity); *Italy*: Gerra et al. 1996; *Sweden*: Bergman & Brismar 1994 **NORTH AMERICA** *United States*: Dabbs et al. 1987 (male prisoners, peer rated toughness); Dabbs et al. 1988; Dabbs et al. 1995; Scerbo & Kolko 1994 (male children, staff-rated); Dabbs & Hargrove 1997* (males) **FOWL** *Chicken*: Watson & Moss 1971 **PRIMATE** *Chimpanzee*: Clark & Birch 1946; *Cynomolgus Monkey*: Rejeski et al. 1988 (males, blood); *Rhesus Monkey*: Rose et al. 1971, 1972; Eaton & Resko 1974; Higley et al. 1996a; Mehlman et al. 1997; *Talipoin Monkey*: Dixson & Herbert 1977; Eberhart et al. 1980 (males); *Vervet Monkey*: Steklis et al. 1985 **RODENT** *Hamster*: Payne & Swanton 1973; Jasnow et al. 2000 (male); *Mouse*: Erpino & Chappelle 1971; *Rat*: Beeman 1947; Barfield et al. 1972; Albert et al. 1986 **REPTILE** *Lizard*: Woodley & Moore 1999 (female) **MAMMALS OTHER THAN PRIMATES & RODENTS** *Deer*: Lincoln et al. 1972; *Dog*: Le Boeuf 1970 | **AFRICA** *Namibia*: Christiansen & Winkler 1992 (among San males) **EUROPE** *Britain*: Dolan et al. 2001 (males); *Finland*: von der Pahlen et al. 2002 (free testosterone among women, blood sample); *Germany*: Christiansen & Knussmann 1987; Maras et al. 2003*(adol. boys); *Italy*: Cotrufo et al. 2000 (female, bulimics); *Netherlands*: von der Pahlen et al. 2002 (adult females); *Spain*: Salvador et al. 1999 (male, judo participants); Sanchez-Martin et al. 2000* (preschool boys); *Sweden*: Olweus et al. 1980; Olweus et al. 1986; Lindman et al. 1987 (males); Olweus 1987 (males); Schalling 1987 (male delinquents, self-rated); Susman et al. 1987* (males rated by mothers); Olweus et al. 1988 **NORTH AMERICA** *Canada*: JA Harris et al. 1996 (both sexes, salivary levels); *United States*: Persky et al. 1971 (males); Kreuz & Rose 1972 (male criminal offenders); Ehrenkranz et al. 1974; Kedenberg 1977 (males, destructiveness); Monti et al. 1977 (males); Scaramella & Brown 1978; Ehlers et al. 1990 (female mental patients); A Gray et al. 1991; Constantino et al. 1993 (male children); Scerbo & Kolko 1994 (children); Kouri et al. 1995; Higley et al. 1996 (males); Dougherty et al. 1997 (women); Orengo et al. 1997 (elderly males); SE Chance et al. 2000 (male children, especially among low IQ); Pope et al. 2000 (males, computer game aggression); RK Strong & Dabbs 2000 (saliva sample, childhood) | **EUROPE** *Sweden*: Lindman et al. 1997 | **EUROPE** *Britain*: O'Connor et al. 2004* (males, experimental); *Italy*: Gerra et al. 1997:39 **NORTH AMERICA** *United States*: Persky et al. 1971; A Gray et al. 1991 |
| Not signif. | **NORTH AMERICA** *United States*: Persky et al. 1982 (females); Wu et al. 1982 (Kleinfelter's syndrome, adult males, clinical treatment); O'Carroll et al. 1985 (hypogonadal males, clinical treatment); Susman et al. 1987 (males only); Inoff-Germain et al. 1988 (males only); RA Anderson et al. 1992 (normal adult males); Dabbs & Hargrove 1997 (males) **PRIMATE** *Bonobo*: Sannen et al. 2004; *Rhesus Monkey*: Mirsky 1955; Eaton & Resko 1974 (males); Gordon et al. 1976; *Japanese Monkeys*: Rostal et al. 1986; *Squirrel Monkey*: Green et al. 1972; Coe et al. 1985 (males); *Stumptail Monkey*: Nievwenhuijsen et al. 1987; *Talipoin Monkey*: Epple 1978; Eberhart et al. 1980 **RODENT** *Hamster*: Payne & Swanson 1972 (female) | **EUROPE** *Britain*: Campbell et al. 1997; *Germany*: Maras et al. 2003* (adol. girls); *Spain*: Sanchez-Martin et al. 2000* (preschool girls); *Sweden*: Susman et al. 1987* (objectively assessed); Inoff-Germain et al. 1988 (saliva sample, childhood); Aromaki et al. 1999 (young adult males) **NORTH AMERICA** *United States*: Monti et al. 1977; Brain et al. 1987 (males); Dougherty et al. 1997b (females); Coccaro et al. 2007 (males with personality disorders) | **EUROPE** *Britain*: Campbell et al. 1997; O'Connor et al. 2004* (males, experimental) | **EUROPE** *Britain*: Campbell et al. 1997; *Italy*: Gerra et al. 1996; *Spain*: Aluja & Torrubia 2004 (males) **NORTH AMERICA** *United States*: Doering et al. 1974; Albert et al. 1993; Banks & Dabbs 1996:54 |
| Negative | | **NORTH AMERICA** *Canada*: Schaal et al. 1996 (males, 6–13 years old) | **NORTH AMERICA** *United States*: Gladue 1991a | |

**TABLE 8.7.3 Androgens Other than Testosterone and Clinical or Personality Traits Associated with Criminality.**

| Nature of the relationship | Antisocial behavior | Physical aggression | Cognitive & personality factors |
|---|---|---|---|
| | Childhood & early adol. | | |
| Positive | **EUROPE** *Netherlands*: van Goozen et al. 1998 (androstenedione, boys) | **AFRICA** *Namibia*: Christiansen & Winkler 1992 (dihydrotestosterone, San males) **EUROPE** *Finland*: von der Pahlen et al. 2002 (dihydrotestosterone & androstenedione, among women, blood sample); *Germany*: Maras et al. 2003* (dihydrotestosterone, boys); *Spain*: Azurmendi et al. 2006* (male children, androstenedione); *Sweden*: Christiansen & Knussmann 1987 (dihydrotestosterone, blood levels) | **NORTH AMERICA** *United States*: Nottelmann et al. 1987 (androstenedione, 9–14 year olds, psychosocial adjustment problems) |
| Not Signif. | | **EUROPE** *Germany*: Maras et al. 2003* (dihydrotestosterone, girls, 8–14 years old); *Spain*: Azurmendi et al. 2006* (female children, androstenedione) | |
| Negative | | | |

**TABLE 8.7.4a Cortisol and Criminal/Delinquent Behavior.**

| Nature of the relationship | Officially detected offenses | | | Self-reported offenses |
|---|---|---|---|---|
| | Violent offenses | Drug offenses | Delinquency | Overall offenses |
| Positive | | | | |
| Not signif. | | **NORTH AMERICA** *United States*: Banks & Dabbs 1996 | | |
| Negative | **EUROPE** *Finland*: Virkkunen 1985; Lindman et al. 1997; *Sweden*: Bergman & Brismar 1994 | **NORTH AMERICA** *United States*: King et al. 1990 | **NORTH AMERICA** *United States*: Moss et al. 1995 (males only, drug use) | **NORTH AMERICA** *United States*: Pajer et al. 2001 (adol.) |

**TABLE 8.7.4b Cortisol and Clinical or Personality Traits Associated with Criminality.**

| Nature of the relationship | Antisocial behavior | | Physical aggression | Cognitive & personality factors | Alcoholism | Drug abuse | Mental disorder |
|---|---|---|---|---|---|---|---|
| | Childhood & early adol. | Late adol. & adulthood | | | | | |
| Positive | | | | | **NORTH AMERICA** *United States*: Buydens-Branchey & Branchey 1992 | | |
| Not signif. | **NORTH AMERICA** *United States*: Kruesi et al. 1989; McBurnett et al. 1991 | **NORTH AMERICA** *United States*: Moss et al. 1990 | **NORTH AMERICA** *United States*: KP Schulz et al. 1997 (among boys with ADHD) | **NORTH AMERICA** *United States*: Loney et al. 2006* (females) | | | |
| Negative | **NORTH AMERICA** *United States*: Tennes & Kreye 1985*; Tennes et al. 1986; McBurnett et al. 1991; Susman et al. 1991; Vanyukov et al. 1993; Moss et al. 1995; McBurnett et al. 2000* (saliva levels); Pajer et al. 2001 (females only); Pajer et al. 2002 (females) | **EUROPE** *Britain*: Dolan et al. 2001 (male prisoners); *Finland*: Virkkunen 1985* **NORTH AMERICA** *United States*: Fishbein et al. 1992; Vanyokov et al. 1993 | **EUROPE** *Finland*: Virkkunen 1985* (males); *Netherlands*: Van Goozen et al. 1998* (male children) **NORTH AMERICA** *United States*: Ballenger et al. 1983 (sexual promiscuity); Tennes & Kreye 1985 (children); Tennes et al. 1986 (children); McBurnett et al. 2000* (males, saliva levels) | **NORTH AMERICA** *United States*: Ballenger et al. 1983* (impulsivity); RJ King et al. 1990* (impulsivity); Rosenblitt et al. 2001 (sensation seeking); Loney et al. 2006* (males) | **NORTH AMERICA** *United States*: RJ King et al. 1990* | **EUROPE** *Netherlands*: Van Goozen et al. 1998* (oppositional defiant disorder, boys, when frustrated) | |

**TABLE 8.7.5a Prolactin and Criminal/Delinquent Behavior.**

| Nature of the relationship | Officially detected offenses |
|---|---|
| | Sex offenses |
| Positive | **NORTH AMERICA** *Canada*: Studer & Aylwin 2006 |
| Not signif. | |
| Negative | |

**TABLE 8.7.5b Prolactin and Clinical or Personality Traits Associated with Criminality.**

| Nature of the relationship | Physical aggression |
|---|---|
| Positive | **NORTH AMERICA** *United States*: Halperin et al. 1997 (prepubertal males with ADHD) |
| Not signif. | **NORTH AMERICA** *United States*: Stoff et al. 1992 (in pre- and postpubertal children) |
| Negative | |

**TABLE 8.7.6 Prolactin Response to Buspirone and Clinical or Personality Traits Associated with Criminality.**

| Nature of the relationship | Antisocial behavior |
|---|---|
| | Late adol. & adult |
| Positive | |
| Not signif. | |
| Negative | **NORTH AMERICA** *United States*: Kavoussi et al. 1997 (aggressive personality disordered patients, blunted prolactin response) |

**TABLE 8.7.7 Prolactin Response to Fenfluramine and Clinical or Personality Traits Associated with Criminality.**

| Nature of the relationship | Physical aggression |
|---|---|
| Positive (increased response) | **NORTH AMERICA** *United States*: Fishbein et al. 1989 (among adult substance abusers); Bernstein & Handelsman 1995 (among substance abusers, response to fenfluramine); DS Pine et al. 1997 (prepubertal males) |
| Not signif. | **NORTH AMERICA** *United States*: Stoff et al. 1992 (in pre- and postpubertal children) |
| Negative (decreased response) | **EUROPE** *Britain*: O'Keane et al. 1992 **NORTH AMERICA** *United States*: Coccaro et al. 1989 (among persons with personality disorders); Coccaro et al. 1995 (males with personality disorders); Coccaro et al. 1997 |

**TABLE 8.7.8 Sex Hormone-Binding Globulin and Clinical or Personality Traits Associated with Criminality.**

| Nature of the relationship | Antisocial behavior | Alcoholism |
|---|---|---|
| | Late adol. & adulthood | |
| Positive | **EUROPE** *Sweden*: Stalenheim et al. 1998a* (males) | **EUROPE** *Sweden*: Stalenheim et al. 1998a* (males) |
| Not signif. | | |
| Negative | | |

of prolactin increases or decreases as a result. No research has directly linked this response to criminality per se, but, as shown in Table 8.7.7. Some studies have found an increased prolactin response to fenfluramine associated with physical aggression, while other studies have reported the exact opposite.

## 8.7.8 Sex Hormone-Binding Globulin

Sex hormone-binding globulin (SHBG) plays an important biochemical role in producing and maintaining the production of testosterone. As shown in Table 8.7.8, one study found that relatively high levels of SHBG were positively associated with adult antisocial personality and alcoholism.

## 8.7.9 Triiodothyronine Levels

Triiodothyronine is a thyroid hormone that circulates in the blood and interacts with testosterone and MAO-A in ways that are currently not understood. Table 8.7.9a shows that one study found triiodothyronine levels to be higher in adult offenders than in adults in general.

One study reported higher triiodothyronine levels among alcoholics when compared with nonalcoholics (Table 8.7.9b).

TABLE 8.7.9a Triiodothyronine Levels and Criminal/ Delinquent Behavior.

| Nature of the relationship | Officially detected offenses |
|---|---|
| | General & adult offenses |
| Positive | **EUROPE** *Sweden*: Alm et al. 1996 |
| Not signif. | |
| Negative | |

TABLE 8.7.9b Triiodothyronine Levels and Clinical or Personality Traits Associated with Criminality.

| Nature of the relationship | Alcoholism |
|---|---|
| Positive | **EUROPE** *Sweden*: Stalenheim et al. 1998b (Type II) |
| Not signif. | |
| Negative | |

## 8.8 OTHER CHEMICALS

Research findings on the relationship between one non-biochemical chemical and criminal behavior are reported below.

### 8.8.1 Lead

Lead is a neurotoxin, meaning that it causes the brain to function in very inappropriate ways. Among the consequences of exposing the body to abnormally high levels of lead is a lowering of intelligence scores, at least among young children (J Schwartz 1994, meta-analysis). The more general effects of lead exposure are the diminishing of the brain's ability to make well-planned judgments. As shown in Table 8.8.1a, quite a number of studies have found a positive correlation between levels of lead in the body and involvement in crime.

As shown in Table 8.8.1b, at least two studies have reinforced the connection between high lead levels in the blood and criminality by suggesting that physical aggression and hyperactivity are also positively correlated with lead.

TABLE 8.8.1a Lead and Criminal/Delinquent Behavior.

| Nature of the relationship | Officially detected offenses | | Self-reported offenses |
|---|---|---|---|
| | Violent offenses | Delinquency | Overall offenses |
| Positive | **NORTH AMERICA** *United States*: RD Masters et al. 1998 (in blood); Nevin 2000* (time series on gasoline lead sales & violent crime, unemployment and age of population controlled); Stretesky & Lynch 2001 (ecological study of county homicide rates) | **NORTH AMERICA** *United States*: Denno 1990 (black males); Dietrich et al. 2001 (in blood); Needleman et al. 2002 (levels in bones) | **NORTH AMERICA** *United States*: Needleman et al. 1996 (bone-levels); Dietrich et al. 2001 (parental reported delinquency, prenatal exposure) |
| Not signif. | | | |
| Negative | | | |

TABLE 8.8.1b Lead and Clinical or Personality Traits Associated with Criminality.

| Nature of the relationship | Physical aggression | Mental disorder |
|---|---|---|
| Positive | **EUROPE** *Scotland*: GO Thompson et al. 1989 (in blood, children, teacher parent ratings) | **NORTH AMERCIA** *United States*: David et al. 1972 (hyperactivity) |
| Not signif. | | |
| Negative | | |

## 8.9 NEUROLOGICAL FACTORS

Neurological factors pertain to the brain and its functioning. As one might suspect, several neurological factors have been investigated with reference to criminality and related phenomena as this section will show.

### 8.9.1 Abnormal Brain Wave Patterns

Not long after the development of a method for measuring brain waves by attaching electrodes to the scalp, called *electroencephalograph* (EEG), researchers in the 1940s began testing samples of criminals and psychopaths to determine if any unusual patterns might be found.

**TABLE 8.9.1a Abnormal Brain Wave Patterns and Criminal/Delinquent Behavior.**

| Nature of the relationship | Officially detected offenses | |
|---|---|---|
| | Violent offenses | Delinquency |
| Positive | **EUROPE** *Britain*: Hill & Pond 1952; Sayer et al. 1969 **NORTH AMERICA** *United States*: Stafford-Clark & Taylor 1949 | **NORTH AMERICA** *Canada*: Yeudall et al. 1982; *United States*: Lewis et al. 1987:749 |
| Not signif. | **EUROPE** *Britain*: Driver et al. 1974 | **NORTH AMERICA** *United States*: Hsu et al. 1985 |
| Negative | | |

**TABLE 8.9.1b Abnormal Brain Wave Patterns and Clinical or Personality Traits Associated with Criminality.**

| Nature of the relationship | Antisocial behavior | |
|---|---|---|
| | Childhood & early adol. | Late adol. & adulthood |
| Positive | **EUROPE** *Sweden*: Forssman & Frey 1953:68 | **EUROPE** *Britain*: Stafford-Clark et al. 1951 **NORTH AMERICA** *United States*: Silverman 1943; Diethelm & Simons 1945; Kennard 1953; Knott et al. 1953; Arthurs & Cahoon 1964; Monroe & Mickle 1967; Ohlesen et al. 1970 |
| Not signif. | | **EUROPE** *Britain*: Hill & Watterson 1942 **NORTH AMERICA** *United States*: FA Gibbs et al. 1945 |
| Negative | | |

Unfortunately for research purposes, brain wave patterns are exceedingly complex, making it very difficult for even trained observers of EEG read-outs to recognize anything but the most "abnormal" patterns (Mednick & Volavka 1980:125).

In addition to the complexity of brain waves themselves, affixing electrodes to the skull only allows researchers to detect what is happening near the surface of the brain (Kligman & Goldberg 1980:336). As one writer put it, "There are over 10 billion separate nerve cells in the brain, woven in a tight latticework of reciprocal interconnections. Even the most precise EEG recordings inevitably detect the chatter of hundreds of thousands of the cells, muted and distorted by the skull" (Hassett 1978:102). Other writers described the use of EEG recordings for studying the workings of the brain as being "like blind men trying to understand the workings of a factory by listening outside its walls" (Margerison et al. 1967). To reduce the risk of bias, most of the studies that compared EEG patterns required clinicians to make the ratings of abnormality "blind" as to whether their ratings were of offenders or nonoffenders.

Table 8.9.1a summarizes evidence concerning abnormal brain wave patterns. One can see that most studies revealed that higher proportions of criminals exhibited abnormal brain waves than did their relatively law-abiding peers. The studies that simply compared different types of offenders with one another are not presented.

As with research on criminality itself, most of the studies of the links between abnormal brain wave patterns and antisocial behavior have concluded that higher proportions of abnormal patterns were present among those exhibiting antisocial behavior (Table 8.9.1b). Despite evidence that criminals and psychopaths have a higher incidence of "abnormal" EEG patterns compared with persons in general, it is worth mentioning that no significant differences have been documented when comparing psychopathic criminals with criminals not so diagnosed (Small 1966; Murdoch 1972).

## 8.9.2 Brain Wave Speed

Clinicians who interpret EEG readings generally recognize four basic bands within which to classify most EEG brain waves. These bands are called alpha, beta, theta, and delta (Kooi et al. 1978; John et al. 1980:1255). Alpha brain waves are the most rapid and tend to be unusually rhythmical and consistent in amplitude. When alpha brain waves are emitted (especially in the most rapid range), individuals are usually alert and focused on some intellectual or manual task.

With respect to beta waves, which are somewhat slower than alpha waves, the attention of the individual is usually sustained on some train of thought, but to a lesser degree than for alpha waves. Brain waves in the theta range are slower than for alpha or beta, and are commonly emitted when a subject is dozing or falling asleep or allowing his mind to wonder as a result of boredom. Finally, delta brain waves are the slowest and are usually associated with deep sleep. Most EEG read-outs contain combinations of all four wave patterns, varying over time and according to what specific area of the brain is being monitored. With these qualifications in mind, Table 8.9.2a suggests that criminals exhibit slower brain wave patterns under most testing conditions than is true for generally law-abiding persons.

In the case of antisocial behavior, most research is consistent with the conclusion derived from the study of criminality itself. Both the childhood and adult forms of this disorder appear to be associated with relatively slow brain wave patterns (Table 8.9.2b).

TABLE 8.9.2a Brain Wave Speed and Criminal/Delinquent Behavior.

| Nature of the relationship | Officially detected offenses | | | | Self-reported offenses |
|---|---|---|---|---|---|
| | Violent offenses | Delinquency in general | General & adult offenses | Recidivism | Overall offending |
| Positive | | | | | |
| Not signif. | | | | | **EUROPE** *England*: Raine et al. 1995 |
| Negative | **AFRICA** *Egypt*: Okasha et al. 1975:39 | **EUROPE** *Denmark*: Mednick et al. 1981; *France*: Verdeaux & Verdeaux 1955 **NORTH AMERICA** *United States*: Low & Dawson 1961 | **NORTH AMERICA** *United States*: Raine et al. 1990b | **EUROPE** *Denmark*: Petersen et al. 1982 | |

TABLE 8.9.2b Brain Wave Speed and Clinical or Personality Traits Associated with Criminality.

| Nature of the relationship | Antisocial behavior | | Alcoholism |
|---|---|---|---|
| | Childhood & early adol. | Late adol. & adult | |
| Positive | | **NORTH AMERICA** *United States*: Bauer & Hesselbrock 1993 | |
| Not signif. | **NORTH AMERICA** *United States*: Lucas et al. 1965 | | |
| Negative | **EUROPE** *Sweden*: Foreman & Frey 1981:68 **NORTH AMERICA** *Canada*: Bay-Rakal 1965 | **EUROPE** *Britain*: Hill & Watterson 1942; Hill 1952 **NORTH AMERICA** *Canada*: Hare 1970b (psychopathy); *United States*: Knott et al. 1953; Ellington 1954; Syndulko et al. 1975 | **NORTH AMERICA** *United States*: Deckel et al. 1995 |

## 8.9.3 Behavioral Activating/Inhibiting System Factor

The reward dominance theory states that behavior is regulated by two neurological systems: the behavioral activating system (BAS) and the behavioral inhibition system (BIS). BAS is the motivating system that seeks pleasure and reward, while BIS is the inhibiting system that determines the appropriate time at which to refrain from these stimuli. Some have described the BAS as behavior's equivalent to an accelerator and the BIS as its break. It is argued that a defective BIS or an overactive BAS could lead to antisocial behavior, especially that of an impulsive nature. Abnormalities in the dopaminergic reward pathway are thought to be the key to the BAS neurological substrate (Pickering et al. 1997).

TABLE 8.9.3 Behavioral Activating/Inhibiting System Factor and Clinical or Personality Traits Associated with Criminality.

| Nature of the relationship | Antisocial behavior | Drug abuse |
|---|---|---|
| | Child & early adol. | |
| Stronger BAS than BIS | **NORTH AMERICA** *United States*: JL Walker et al. 1991 | **ASIA** *Russia*: Knyazev 2004 (adol.) |
| Not signif. | | |
| Stronger BIS than BAS | | |

Measuring these theoretical concepts has been difficult, but to the degree measurement has been done, Table 8.9.3 suggests that conduct-disordered children and drug abusers may have a more powerful BAS than BIS relative to persons generally. Comparable research pertaining to criminality per se was not located.

## 8.9.4 Blood Flow to the Brain

The two neuroimaging techniques often used to assess the functional properties of the brain are the positron emission tomography (PET) and the single photon emission computed tomography (SPECT). Both instruments are capable of measuring cerebral blood flow to the brain to

**TABLE 8.9.4 Blood Flow to the Brain and Antisocial Behavior or Other Factors Frequently Linked to Criminality.**

| Nature of the relationship | Antisocial behavior | Physical aggression |
|---|---|---|
| | Late adol. & adult | |
| Positive | | |
| Not Signif. | | |
| Negative | **ASIA** *Japan*: Nakano et al. 2006 (to orbitofrontal cortex) | **NORTH AMERICA** *United States*: Amen & Carmichael 1996 (to frontal lobe, ADHD patients) |

assess brain functioning. No research was found directly linking blood flow to the brain with criminality per se, but two studies have indicated that persons with antisocial and aggressive behaviors have diminished blood flow to the frontal region of the brain (Table 8.9.4) where executive functioning primarily resides.

## 8.9.5 Brain Damage (Head Injury)

The relationship between head injury and antisocial behavior was first illustrated in the case study of Phineas Gage (Harlow, 1848). Phineas, a railroad worker, experienced an iron rod blown through his lower cheek and upper forehead. After the accident, his personality and behavior reportedly changed from being sociable and responsible to extremely impulsive and antisocial. In addition to accidents,

**TABLE 8.9.5a Brain Damage (Head Injury) and Criminal/Delinquent Behavior.**

| Nature of the relationship | Officially detected offenses | | | |
|---|---|---|---|---|
| | Violent offenses | Drug offenses | Sex offenses | General & adult offenses |
| Positive | **EUROPE** *Spain*: Leon-Carrion & Ramos 2003 (offenders in general)<br>**NORTH AMERICA** *United States*: Rosenbaum et al. 1994 (later spouse abuse) | **NORTH AMERICA** *United States*: Ommaya et al. 1996* (military personnel) | **NORTH AMERICA** *Canada*: Blanchard et al. 2002 (childhood injury) | **NORTH AMERICA** *United States*: Ommaya et al. 1996* (military personnel) |
| Not signif. | | | | |
| Negative | | | | |

**TABLE 8.9.5b Brain Damage (Head Injury) and Antisocial Behavior or Other Factors Frequently Linked to Criminality.**

| Nature of the relationship | Antisocial behavior | Physical aggression | Mental illness |
|---|---|---|---|
| | Late adol. & adulthood | | |
| Positive | **NORTH AMERICA** *United States*: Damasio et al. 1994 (prefrontal lobe) | **NORTH AMERICA** *United States*: Levin et al. 1991 (brain injury patients, prefrontal lobe); Grafman et al. 1996 (war injury patients, males, prefrontal lobe)<br>**FELINE** *Domestic Cat*: Egger & Flynn 1967 (prefrontal lobe, experimental)<br>**RODENT** *Rat*: de Bruin et al. 1993 (male, prefrontal lobe, experimental) | **NORTH AMERICA** *United States*: Abdel Malik et al. 2003 (schizophrenia) |
| Not signif. | | | |
| Negative | | | |

**TABLE 8.9.6a Brain Glucose Metabolism and Criminal/Delinquent Behavior.**

| Nature of the relationship | Officially detected offenses |
|---|---|
| | Violent offenses |
| Positive | |
| Not signif. | |
| Negative | **NORTH AMERICA** *United States*: Raine et al. 1997b (homicide, adult males, PET scan, in corpus callosum & prefrontal cortex); George et al. 2004 (domestic violent offenders, right hypothalamus) |

**TABLE 8.9.6b Brain Glucose Metabolism and Clinical or Personality Traits Associated with Criminality.**

| Nature of the relationship | Physical aggression |
|---|---|
| Positive | |
| Not signif. | |
| Negative | **NORTH AMERICA** *United States*: Seidenwurm et al. 1997 (in temporal lobe) |

head injuries can also result from a variety of experiences including child abuse. The studies presented in Table 8.9.5a suggest that there is a positive relationship between brain damage and criminal behavior.

As with criminality per se, several studies have also linked brain damage with antisocial behavior and physical aggression (Table 8.9.5b). Damage to the prefrontal area of the brain seems to be especially prominent regarding such behavior.

## 8.9.6 Brain Glucose Metabolism

Two of the most widely used neuroimaging techniques for assessing brain functioning are the positron emission tomography (PET) and single photon emission computed tomography (SPECT). Both methods are able to determine which areas of the brain are most active according to the amount of glucose flowing to these brain regions. Two studies were located which used these techniques to compare violent offenders to persons in general. According to both studies, the offenders were utilizing unusually low amounts of glucose in one or more brain regions when compared with control subjects (Table 8.9.6a).

According to one study, unusually aggressive individuals exhibited significantly lower glucose metabolism in at least one portion of the brain (Table 8.9.6b).

## 8.9.7 Corpus Callosum Connectivity

The corpus callosum is a bundle of nerve fibers connecting the two hemispheres of the brain, allowing them to communicate with one another. As shown in Table 8.9.7, males characterized as antisocial were more likely to have reduced collasal thickness relative to males in general.

## 8.9.8 P300 Decrements in Evoked Potentials

Evoked potentials (or average event-related potentials) refer to changes in electrical brain activity in response to external stimuli. To assess these potentials, electrodes are attached to a subject's scalp, then he/she is presented with a series of clicks or beeps whereupon the subject must make some sort of response, such as pressing a button (Roschke & Fell 1997:108). After averaging several dozen EEG responses to a specific type of stimulus, subjects exhibit a distinct "dip" in their brain response after 300 milliseconds (i.e., 1/3 of a second) have lapsed. In some people however the overall brain response is less pronounced (Kalat 1992:91). Most but not all of the studies that have compared the evoked potentials with offending and nonoffending subjects have

**TABLE 8.9.7 Corpus Callosum Connectivity and Clinical or Personality Traits Associated with Criminality.**

| Nature of the relationship | Antisocial behavior |
|---|---|
| | Late adol. & adult |
| Positive | **NORTH AMERICA**: *United States*: Raine et al. 2003 (psychopaths, males) |
| Not signif. | |
| Negative | |

**TABLE 8.9.8a P300 Decrements in Evoked Potentials and Criminal/Delinquent Behavior.**

| Nature of the relationship | Officially detected offenses | Self-reported offenses |
|---|---|---|
| | Violent offenses | Drug offenses |
| Positive | | **NORTH AMERICA** *United States*: Biggins et al. 1997 (cocaine); Iacono 1998; J Taylor et al. 1999 |
| Not signif. | **NORTH AMERICA** *United States*: Branchey et al. 1988 | |
| Negative | | |

**TABLE 8.9.8b** P300 Decrements in Evoked Potentials and Clinical or Personality Traits Associated with Criminality.

| Nature of the relationship | Antisocial behavior: Childhood & early adol. | Antisocial behavior: Late adol. & adulthood | Physical aggression | Cognitive & personality factors | Alcoholism |
|---|---|---|---|---|---|
| Positive | **NORTH AMERICA** *United States*: Bauer 1997 | **NORTH AMERICA** *Canada*: Jutai et al. 1987; Forth & Hare 1989; *United States*: Raine & Venables 1987; Raine & Venables 1988; Raine et al. 1990; Bauer et al. 1994; Bauer 1997 | **NORTH AMERICA** *United States*: Barratt et al. 1997 (impulsive aggression) | **NORTH AMERICA** *United States*: SR Carlson et al. 1999 (impulsiveness) | **NORTH AMERICA** *United States*: Begleiter et al. 1984 (family history of); Branchey et al. 1988 |
| Not signif. | | | | | |
| Negative | | | | | |

**TABLE 8.9.9** Right (versus Left) Brain Activity and Clinical or Personality Traits Associated with Criminality.

| Nature of the relationship | Mental illness or disability |
|---|---|
| Right more | **NORTH AMERICA** *Canada*: Santesso et al. 2006 (externalizing behavior, frontal EEG activity); *United States*: Baving et al. 2003* (externalizing behavior, frontal EEG activity, females) |
| Not signif. | **NORTH AMERICA** *United States*: Baving et al. 2003* (externalizing behavior, frontal EEG activity, males) |
| Left more | |

found greater P300 decrements in the offending subjects (Table 8.9.8a).

In addition to the research on criminal and antisocial behavior, Table 8.9.8b shows that numerous studies have linked P300 decrements in evoked potential with antisocial behavior and other traits frequently associated with criminality.

## 8.9.9 Right (versus Left) Brain Activity

No research was found directly linking functional brain laterality to criminality. However, as shown in Table 8.9.9, a couple of studies have found externalizing behavior to be associated with a greater activation of the right hemisphere than the left hemisphere (Table 8.9.9).

**TABLE 8.10.1a** Handedness and Criminal/Delinquent Behavior.

| Nature of the relationship | Officially detected offenses: Violent offenses | Officially detected offenses: Delinquency | Officially detected offenses: General & adult offenses | Officially detected offenses: Recidivism | Self-reported offenses: overall offenses |
|---|---|---|---|---|---|
| Left/mixed handers more | **NORTH AMERICA** *United States*: Krynicki 1978 | **EUROPE** *Sweden*: Elmund et al. 2004 (adoptees) **NORTH AMERICA** *Canada*: Yeudall et al. 1982; *United States*: Fitzhugh 1973 | **EUROPE** *Britain*: H Ellis 1910:118; *Italy*: Lombroso 1903 **NORTH AMERICA** *Canada*: Bogaert 2001; *United States*: Virkkunen et al. 1976; Gabrielli & Mednick 1980 | **EUROPE** *Britain*: West cited in Ellis 1990a:486 | **NORTH AMERICA** *Canada*: Coren 1998; *United States*: Ellis & Ames 1989 **OCEANIA** *New Zealand*: Feehan et al. 1990 |
| Not signif. | | **EUROPE** *Britain*: West & Farrington 1977 **NORTH AMERICA** *Canada*: Yeudall et al. 1982 | **EUROPE** *Britain*: Goring 1913:214 **NORTH AMERICA** *Canada*: Hare & Forth 1985; Hare & Connolly 1987:225; *United States*: Denno 1985:773 | | |
| Right handers more | | | **NORTH AMERICA** *United States*: Nachshon & Denno 1987 | | |

## 8.10 OTHER BIOLOGICAL OR BEHAVIORAL FACTORS

Two difficult-to-classify variables have been investigated with reference to criminality: handedness and pain tolerance.

### 8.10.1 Handedness

In all known human societies, the vast majority of people rely predominantly on the right hand to perform most tasks requiring precise coordination, such as writing, drawing, or throwing objects (Hollis 1875; Coren & Porac 1977a; Spennemann 1984). Depending on exactly how handedness is defined, the proportions of left or mixed-handed people are between 5 and 15% (LJ Harris 1990:217). The reasons for variations in handedness remain controversial, but at least part of the answer may reside in the fact that the left hemisphere of the brain controls the right side of the body and most aspects of our language abilities.

As shown in Table 8.10.1a, several studies have investigated the possibility that handedness is a correlate of crime. The findings have been mixed, but have predominantly suggested that left or mixed-handed people are more likely than right handers to have had a criminal history.

Table 8.10.1b shows that all the studies of antisocial behavior have concluded that left or mixed handedness is more prevalent in these individuals than in right handers.

### 8.10.2 Pain Tolerance

Pain tolerance (the opposite of *pain sensitivity*) refers to the ability to withstand painful stimuli at relatively strong intensities. Scientists assess pain tolerance in a number of ways, among them being a *cold water emersion test*. With this test, subjects have their arm strapped to a lever that they can lower into a container of circulating ice cold water. The subjects are instructed to hold down the level until the pain is too much to tolerate. Other devices for measuring pain tolerance involve asking subjects to press their bare foot as hard as they can for as long as they can against a fairly sharp object (but not sharp enough to break the skin) (Fowler-Kerry & Lander 1991). The one study of pain tolerance and criminality indicates that offenders have a higher degree of tolerance than do persons in general (Table 8.10.2a).

Several studies of antisocial behavior and one of physical aggression indicate that these traits are positively associated with pain tolerance, although one exception was found (Table 8.10.2b).

**TABLE 8.10.1b Handedness and Clinical or Personality Traits Associated with Criminality.**

| Nature of the relationship | Antisocial behavior | |
|---|---|---|
| | Childhood & early adol. | Late adol. & adulthood |
| Left/mixed handers more | **NORTH AMERICA** *United States*: Grace 1987<br>**OCEANIA** *New Zealand*: Feehan et al. 1990 | **EUROPE** *Britain*: Standage 1983<br>**NORTH AMERICA** *United States*: Mayer & Kosson 2000 (psychopaths) |
| Not signif. | | |
| Right handers more | | |

**TABLE 8.10.2a Pain tolerance and Criminal/Delinquent Behavior.**

| Nature of the relationship | Officially detected offenses |
|---|---|
| | General & adult offenses |
| Positive | **NORTH AMERICA** *Canada*: Fedora & Reddor 1993 |
| Not signif. | |
| Negative | |

**TABLE 8.10.2b Pain tolerance and Clinical or Personality Traits Associated with Criminality.**

| Nature of the relationship | Antisocial behavior | | Physical aggression |
|---|---|---|---|
| | Childhood & early adol. | Late adol. & adulthood | |
| Positive | **NORTH AMERICA** *Canada*: Seguin et al. 1996 (boys) | **EUROPE** *Sweden*: Schalling 1971 **NORTH AMERICA** *Canada*: Hare 1968; Hare & Thorvaldson 1970; *United States*: Lykken 1957; Fowles 1993 | **NORTH AMERICA** *Canada*: Seguin et al. 1995 (boys) |
| Not signif. | | **NORTH AMERICA** *United States*: Schachter & Latane 1964 | |
| Negative | | | |

Chapter 9

# Crime Victimization and Fear of Crime

**Contents**



As a general rule, the crimes that people fear the most are those for which there are clearly identifiable victims – so-called *victimful offenses*. This chapter explores findings pertaining to traits of victims that have been found to be associated with crimes.

## 9.1 CRIME VICTIMIZATION

Victimology is a relatively new branch of criminology, with its formal origins arising during the 1960s. A main goal of victimology is to understand why some people are more likely to be victimized by crime than are other people. The following section summarizes findings pertaining to traits that have been found to be associated with crime victimization.

### 9.1.1 Gender and Crime Victimization

Which sex is more likely to be a crime victim? Numerous studies have investigated this question, and except for sex offenses, nearly all studies agree that males are more often the victims of crime than females. The findings for offenses other than those of a sexual nature are shown in Table 9.1.1a. One can see that regarding murder, all but one study have reported that males are victimized more than females. The lone exception reported that a greater number of females than males were homicide victims in Italy during the 1800s, a finding that may be questioned in light of so many more recent studies to the contrary. Regarding property offenses, the available research also indicates that males have a higher victimization rate, although not to the extent that is typical of violent offenses.

Offenses of a sexual (or sex-related) nature are summarized in Table 9.1.1b. In this table, one can see that sexual assault victimization, whether reported to police or simply reported in surveys, is more common among females than among males. Nonetheless, there appears to be some relatively minor forms of violence such as self-reported assault victimization among both domestic and dating partners where most research suggests that there are either no sex differences in victimization or that males may be victimized more than females.

Besides strict criminal victimization, several studies have been conducted to determine if a sex difference exists in being the victim of aggression or violence, even

**TABLE 9.1.1a Gender and Crime Victimization in General.**

| Nature of any difference | Officially detected offenses | | | |
|---|---|---|---|---|
| | Homicide | Violent crimes other than homicide | Property offenses | Offenses in general |
| Higher male victimization | **AFRICA** *South Africa*: Butchart & Brown 1991; Meel 2003; *Uganda*: Mushanga 1970; *Various Tribal Societies*: Bohannan 1967:219; Hewlett 1991:20 **ASIA** *Ceylon*: Jayewardene & Ranasinghe 1963; *India*: Elwin 1943; Driver 1961; Rao 1968; *Russia*: Shkolinikov & Mesle 1996 **EUROPE** *Britain*: McClintock 1963:42; Hair 1971 (sixteenth century); Givern 1977 (thirteenth-century); Hanawalt 1979:153 (fourteenth century); *Denmark*: Svalastoga 1956; *France*: Peyeferitte 1976; *Germany*: Sessar 1973; Stephan 1976; Johnson 1985; *Netherlands*: van Dijk &Vianen 1978:17; *Sweden*: von Hofer 1990:31 (nineteenth century) **NORTH AMERICA** *Canada*: RE Mann et al. 2006:1745; *United States*: Brearley 1932:79; Langberg 1967:2; Voss & Hepburn 1968:501; Shin et al. 1977:400; Tardiff 1985:632; U.S. Department of Justice 1988:28; CR Block 1993:284; National Center for Health Statistics 1993; Smith & Kuchta 1995:669; Spergel 1995:108 (gang-related homicide); Geronimus et al. 1996; Andon 1997:25; Powell 1997 **OCEANIA** *Australia*: Wallace 1986; Day & Sherrand 1996:286 **INTERNATIONAL** *Multiple Countries*: Verkko 1967:38 | **EUROPE** *Britain*: Hough & Mayhew 1983; Gottfredson 1984; Hough & Mayhew 1985; Shepherd 1990; *Netherlands*: Wiegman et al. 1983:208 **NORTH AMERICA** *Canada*: Moyer 1992:398; *United States*: U.S. Department of Justice 1976:7; U.S. Department of Justice 1977:5; Curtis 1977:165; Hindelang et al. 1978:188; Balkan & Berger 1979; Gordon et al. 1980:S145; Bowker 1981:161; R Simon 1981:35; Empey 1982:136; U.S. Department of Justice 1988:27; U.S. Bureau of Justice Statistics 1993:18; Reiss & Roth 1993:69; Kruttschnitt 1994 (violent offense); Kingery et al. 1995:341; Kachur et al. 1996; Farrell & Bruce 1997 (adolescents); Mustaine & Tewkasbury 2000 (violent crimes); Lauritsen & Heimer 2008 **INTERNATIONAL** *Multiple Countries*: van Dijk et al. 1991:49 | **NORTH AMERICA** *Canada*: Keane & Arnold 1996:466; *United States*: Empey 1982:138 | **EUROPE** *Scotland*: Monaghan 1997:22 **NORTH AMERICA** *United States*: Lebowitz 1975; Warr 1984; Jensen & Brownfield 1986; Akers et al. 1987; Harlow 1991; Karmen 1991; Mayhew et al. 1993; Sacco et al. 1993; EJ Christiansen & Evans 2005 |
| No signif. diff. | **EUROPE** *Sweden*: Ekman et al. 2007 (age 1–20, "fatal violence") | | | |
| Higher female victimization | **EUROPE** *Italy*: Pollack 1950:81 (nineteenth century) | | | |

if non-criminal. As shown in Table 9.1.1c, most of the evidence suggests that males are more often victimized by bullying as well as other forms of aggression.

## 9.1.2 Age and Crime Victimization

Results of studies regarding how age correlates with crime victimization are shown in Table 9.1.2. Contrary to popular beliefs, criminals do not prey primarily on the elderly (Evans & Himelfarb 1987:67). Instead, research has consistently shown that individuals in the teens through the early 30s are most likely to be victimized. This holds true for murder, assaults, robberies, and, to a lesser degree, all property crimes. In the case of murder, for example, the predominant age of victims ranges is the 15 year period of 25 and 40 (Wolfgang 1967:19; Farley 1980:181). Also, based on surveys in numerous countries, researchers have found violent crime victimization rates for 16–24 year olds to be approximately three times higher than for persons 65 or older (van Dijk et al. 1991:64).

## 9.1.3 Black–White Differences in Crime Victimization

As shown in Table 9.1.3, the majority of these studies have indicated that blacks are more likely than whites to be the

**TABLE 9.1.1b Gender and Sex/Dating/Domestic Crime Victimization.**

| Nature of any difference | Officially detected offenses | | Self-reported offenses | | | |
|---|---|---|---|---|---|---|
| | Forcible rapes | Domestic/ spousal attacks | Sexual assaults | Domestic/spousal attacks | Dating violence | Stalking |
| Higher male victimization | | | | **NORTH AMERICA** *United States*: Vivian & Langhinrichsen-Rohling 1994 | **NORTH AMERICA** *United States*: Merrill & Hervig 1997 | |
| No signif. diff. | | | | **NORTH AMERICA** *United States*: Pan et al. 1994 | **NORTH AMERICA** *United States*: Makepeace 1983; Riggs 1993 | |
| Higher female victimization | **NORTH AMERICA** *United States*: Hall & Flannery 1984; Sigelman et al. 1984:538; Calderwood 1987:53; Sorenson & Siegel 1992:96; Frazier 1993 | **EUROPE** *Britain*: Mirrlees-Black et al. 1988 (repeated serious attacks by domestic partners) | **EUROPE** *Britain*: Hartless et al. 1995:119 (adol.) **NORTH AMERICA** *United States*: Groth & Burgess 1980:806 (calls to rape crisis center); Kaufman et al. 1980 (calls to rape crisis center); Lott et al. 1982:312; Sigelman et al. 1984:538; Calderwood 1987:53; Struckman-Johnson 1988:297; Anonymous 1989; L Ellis et al. 1990:1210; Laumann et al. 1994:335 | | | **NORTH AMERICA** *United States*: Tjaden & Thoennes 2000 (stalking) |

**TABLE 9.1.1c Gender and Crime Victimization of General Aggression.**

| Nature of any difference | Aggression |
|---|---|
| Higher male victimization | **EUROPE** *Estonia*: Peets & Kikas 2006 (young adol., direct & indirect aggression); *Germany*: Scheithauer et al. 2006 (physical bullying*, 5–10th graders, self-report) **NORTH AMERICA** *United States*: Whitney & Smith 1993 (adol., self-report, physical bullying); Russell & Owens 1999 (childhood, direct & indirect aggression); Khoury-Kassabri et al. 2004 (physical bullying); Van Dorn 2004 (physical bullying) **OCEANIA** *Australia*: Owens et al. 2005 (physical bullying) |
| No signif. diff. | **EUROPE** *Germany*: Scheithauer et al. 2006* (all types of bullying, 5–10th graders, self-report) |
| Higher female victimization | **EUROPE** *Finland*: Olafsen & Viemero 2000 (indirect/relational bullying, teens, self-report) |

victims of crime. This is especially true of violent offenses, where blacks have a probability of being murdered that has been found to be close to six times greater than that for whites (Farley 1980:186; Kachur et al. 1996). In the case of most property crimes, blacks are about one and a half times more likely to be victimized.

### 9.1.4 Hispanic–Anglo Differences in Crime Victimization

The only studies that were located pertaining to differences between Hispanics and non-Hispanics (Anglos or Whites) in crime victimization involved homicides. As shown in Table 9.1.4, one of these studies concluded that Hispanics were more often the victims of murder than was true for non-Hispanics. The remaining studies concluded that homicide victimization was higher among Anglos. To account for this inconsistency, it is worth noting that the majority of Hispanics in the United States are of Mexican ancestry. All of the studies that reported higher victimization for Anglos were conducted in Florida where the majority of Hispanics are of Cuban descent.

**TABLE 9.1.2** Age and Crime Victimization.

| Nature of the relationship | Officially detected offenses | | | | Self-reported |
|---|---|---|---|---|---|
| | Homicide | Violent crimes other than homicide | Property crimes | General & adult offenses | Offenses in general |
| Highest in the mid teens to the mid 30s; Lowest among the elderly | **AFRICA** *South Africa*: Butchart & Brown 1991 **NORTH AMERICA** *United States*: Brearley 1932:79; Langberg 1967:4; Wolfgang 1967:19; Voss & Hepburn 1968:502; Shin 1977:402; Farley 1980:181; Rachuba et al. 1995 | **NORTH AMERICA** *Canada:* Evans & Himelfarb 1987:68; *United States*: Jaycox 1978; Empey 1982:136; Lee 1982; Reiss & Roth 1993:69 **INTERNATIONAL** *Multiple Countries*: van Dijk et al. 1991 | **NORTH AMERICA** *Canada:* Evans & Himelfarb 1987:69; Keane & Arnold 1996:466; *United States*: Empey 1982:138 | **EUROPE** *Britain*: Hough & Mayhew 1983; *Germany*: Stephan 1976; *Netherlands*: van Dijk & Vianen 1978:16; *Scotland*: Monaghan 1997:22 **NORTH AMERICA** *Canada*: Gartner 1995:207; *United States*: Hindelang et al. 1978; Liang & Sengstock 1981; Bachman 1992; HN Snyder & Sickmund 1999 | **NORTH AMERICA** *United States*: Warshaw 1988 (rape, women 16–24) |
| Not signif. | | | | | |
| Lowest in the mid teens to the mid 30s; Highest among the elderly | | | | | |

**TABLE 9.1.3** Black–White Differences in Crime Victimization.

| Nature of the relationship | Officially detected offenses | | | |
|---|---|---|---|---|
| | Homicide | Violent crimes other than homicide | Property offenses | General & adult offenses |
| Higher among blacks | **NORTH AMERICA** *United States*: Brearley 1932:97; B. Garfinkel 1967:46; Langberg 1967:3; Lalli & Turner 1968:192; Voss & Hepburn 1968:501; Shin et al. 1977:400; Farley 1980:186; Centerwall 1984; O'Carroll & Mercy 1986; Lowry et al. 1988; Muscat 1988; CR Block 1993:294; National Center for Health Statistics 1993; Reiss & Roth 1993:70; Segall & Wilson 1993:347; Kachur et al. 1996:1731; Lattimore et al. 1997:202; R Martinez 1997 (homicide, Miami FL) | **AFRICA** *South Africa*: Butchart & Brown 1991 **EUROPE** *Britain*: Smith 1997:116 **NORTH AMERICA** *United States*: Henry & Short 1967:258; Curtis 1975:21; Hindelang et al. 1978; Hindelang 1981; Empey 1982:139; Wilbanks 1985; Rao & Rao 1988; Christoffe 1990; Rose & McClain 1990; Potter 1991; Rachuba et al. 1995 | **NORTH AMERICA** *United States*: Conklin 1986:125 | **NORTH AMERICA** *United States*: Conklin 1986:125; Blue & Griffith 1995:574 |
| Not signif. | | | | |
| Higher among whites | | **NORTH AMERICA** *United States*: Norris 1992 | **NORTH AMERICA** *United States*: Empey 1982:139 | |

TABLE 9.1.4 Hispanic–Anglo Differences in Crime Victimization.

| Nature of the relationship | Officially detected offenses |
|---|---|
| | Homicide |
| Higher among Hispanics | **NORTH AMERICA** *United States*: Texas Dept. of Health 1990 (males) |
| Not signif. | |
| Higher among Anglos | **NORTH AMERICA** *United States*: Martinez 1997a (Cuban Hispanics); Martinez 1997b (Cuban Hispanics); Martinez & Lee 1998:297 (mainly Cuban–Hispanics, Miami FL) |

## 9.1.5 Native American–White Differences in Crime Victimization

A number of studies conducted in Canada and the United States have contrasted crime victimization rates of Native (aboriginal) Americans with the remainder of the population. Table 9.1.5 shows that findings have revealed consistent overall ethnic differences. The Canadian studies have all concluded that aboriginals have homicide victimization rates that are more than five times higher than rates for Canadians in general (Millan et al. 1996). U.S. studies have put the homicide victimization rate of Native Americans at about twice the average for the country as a whole (Reiss & Roth 1993:70).

## 9.1.6 Immigrant–Nonimmigrant Status and Crime Victimization

Only one study was found which compared victimization rates according to immigrant status. Table 9.1.6 shows that non-immigrants suffered higher rates of victimization than did immigrants. However, after controlling for variations in age, gender, and race, the same study concluded that insignificant differences existed between immigrants and non-immigrants.

TABLE 9.1.5 Native American–White Differences in Crime Victimization.

| Nature of the relationship | Homicide |
|---|---|
| Higher among native Americans | **NORTH AMERICA** *Canada*: Statistics Canada 1987; Kennedy et al. 1989; Moyer 1992:389; Doob et al. 1994; Gartner 1995:205; *United States*: Reiss & Roth 1993:70 |
| Not signif. | |
| Higher among whites | |

TABLE 9.1.6 Immigrant–Nonimmigrant Status and Crime Victimization.

| Nature of the relationship | Officially detected offenses |
|---|---|
| | Violent offenses |
| Higher among immigrants | |
| Not signif. | **NORTH AMERICA** *United States*: Toussaint & Hummer 1999* (homicide, controlled for age, gender & race) |
| Higher among nonimmigrants | **NORTH AMERICA** *United States*: Toussaint & Hummer 1999* (homicide, without statistical controls) |

## 9.1.7 Associating with Delinquent Peers

As shown in Table 9.1.7, all of the available studies indicate that persons who report having one or more delinquent friends are more likely than those with nondelinquent friends to be the victim of a criminal act.

## 9.1.8 Being an Offender and Crime Victimization

Numerous studies have inquired about a possible link between an offender and a crime victim. The evidence, summarized in Table 9.1.8, unequivocally supports the conclusion that criminal offenders are more likely to be crime victims than are persons in general (Singer 1981; Sampson & Lauritsen 1994).

TABLE 9.1.7 Associating with Delinquent Peers and Crime Victimization.

| Nature of the relationship | Offenses not officially detected |
|---|---|
| | Offenses in general |
| Higher for those who have delinquent friends | **NORTH AMERICA** *United States*: Lauritsen et al. 1992; Schreck et al. 2002; Schreck & Fisher 2004; Schreck et al. 2004 |
| Not signif. | |
| Higher for those who have no delinquent friends | |

TABLE 9.1.8 Being an Offender and Crime Victimization.

| Nature of the relationship | Officially detected offenses | | | Offenses not officially detected |
|---|---|---|---|---|
| | Violent offenses | Drug offenses | General & adult offenses | Offenses in general |
| Offenders have higher rates of victimization | **NORTH AMERICA** *United States*: Goldstein 1985 (homicide victim); Wolfgang et al. 1987; Lauritsen et al. 1992; RT Wright & Decker 1994 (homicide victim); Lattimore et al. 1997; DA Hines & Saudino 2004 (intimate partner violence) **OCEANIA** *New Zealand*: Woodward & Fergusson 2000 (assault) | **NORTH AMERICA** *United States*: Cottler et al. 1992; S Menard 2002 (drug abusers) | **EUROPE** *Britain*: Rivara et al. 1995 **NORTH AMERICA** *United States*: Wolfgang et al. 1987:169; Budd 1989; Esbensen & Huizinga 1991; Lauritsen et al. 1991:286; Lauritsen et al. 1992; RT Wright & Decker 1997; S Baron & Hartnagel 1998; Mustaine & Tewksbury 1998 | **EUROPE** *Britain*: MR Gottfredson 1984 **NORTH AMERICA** *United States*: Singer 1979:10; Jensen & Brownfield 1986:97; Miethe & Meier 1990; Sampson & Lauritsen 1990; Esbensen & Huizinga 1991; Widom 1994; DS Miller & Miller 1997; Smith 1997:117; BS Fisher et al. 1998 (delinquency); Mustaine & Tewksbury 1998 (delinquency) |
| Not signif. | | | | |
| Offenders have lower rates of victimization | | | | |

## 9.1.9 Drug or Alcohol Use and Crime Victimization

The few studies of how the use of recreational drugs and alcohol is related to crime victimization have all pertained to violent offenses. As shown in Table 9.1.9, these studies have all concluded that drug use is more common among victims of violence than among persons in general.

## 9.1.10 Marital Status and Crime Victimization

A limited amount of research has sought to determine if marital status and crime victimization are related. As shown in Table 9.1.10, the two relevant studies both concluded that unmarried persons are more often victimized than are married persons.

TABLE 9.1.9 Drug or Alcohol Use and Crime Victimization.

| Nature of the relationship | Officially detected offenses |
|---|---|
| | Violent crimes |
| Higher for drug and/or alcohol users | **EUROPE** *Britain*: J Shepherd 1998 (emergency room drug-overdose patients) **NORTH AMERICA** *United States*: RE Mann et al. 1993 (alcohol use, homicide); Zanarini et al. 1999 (drug users); DR White & Chen 2002 (domestic violence) |
| Not signif. | |
| Lower for drug and/or alcohol users | |

## 9.1.11 Mental Illness

Table 9.1.11 suggests that the mentally ill are more often victims of crime than is true for persons in general.

## 9.1.12 Self-Control and Crime Victimization

Self-control refers to the ability to maintain one's behavior within the limits prescribed by one's social environment. As shown in Table 9.1.12, all of the pertinent research suggests that persons with low levels of self-control are more likely to be crime victims than individuals with high levels of self-control.

TABLE 9.1.10 Marital Status and Crime Victimization.

| Nature of the relationship | Officially detected offenses |
|---|---|
| | General & adult offenses |
| Higher among married individuals | |
| Not signif. | |
| Lower among married individuals | **NORTH AMERICA** *United States*: Weis & Hennly 1980; Gottfredson & Hindelang 1981; Klaus et al. 1983 |

**TABLE 9.1.11 Mental Illness and Crime Victimization.**

| Nature of the relationship | Officially detected offenses |
|---|---|
| | General & adult offenses |
| Higher | **NORTH AMERICA** *United States*: New & Berliner 2000; F Robinson & Keithley 2000 |
| Not signif. | |
| Lower | |

## 9.1.13 Social Status and Crime Victimization

Studies of how social status relates to the likelihood of being victimized by crime are summarized in Table 9.1.13. The studies do not provide a consistent picture except in the case of homicide where the available evidence suggests that lower status persons are more often victimized than those in the middle and upper strata. For non-homicidal violent offenses, however, the evidence has been mixed.

In the case of property crime victimization, two studies found middle and upper status persons to be more frequently victimized while a third study found no significant link between status and victimization. For offenses in general, findings have been divided between those reporting no significant differences and one suggesting that lower status persons are most often victimized.

## 9.1.14 Sex Differences in Status as It Relates to Rape Victimization

Several ecological studies have sought to determine if rape rates are higher or lower in geographic regions where males and females are relatively equal in social status (usually measured in terms of average earnings). These studies have not reached consistent conclusions (Table 9.1.14).

**TABLE 9.1.12 Self-Control and Crime Victimization.**

| Nature of the relationship | Officially detected offenses | |
|---|---|---|
| | Violent offenses | General & adult offenses |
| Positive | | |
| Not signif. | | |
| Negative | **NORTH AMERICA** *United States*: Piquero et al. 2005 | **NORTH AMERICA** *United States*: Forde & Kennedy 1997; Schreck 1999; Schreck et al. 2002; EA Stewart et al. 2004 (black females); Schreck et al. 2006 |

**TABLE 9.1.13 Social Status and Crime Victimization.**

| Nature of the relationship | Officially detected offenses | | |
|---|---|---|---|
| | Violent offenses other than homicide | Property offenses | Offenses in general |
| Higher in middle & upper strata than in the lower strata | **EUROPE** *Sweden*: Aromaa 1974 **NORTH AMERICA** *United States*: Skogan 1981 | **EUROPE** *Netherlands*: van Dijk & Vianen 1978:17 **NORTH AMERICA** *United States*: Empey 1982:143 | |
| Not signif. | | **NORTH AMERICA** *United States*: Cohen et al. 1981:522 | **EUROPE** *Netherlands*: Fiselier 1978; van Dijk & Vianen 1978:18 |
| Higher in lower strata than in middle & upper strata | **NORTH AMERICA** *United States*: Lalli & Turner 1968:192 (homicides); McDermott & Hindelang 1981; Empey 1982:143; Reiss & Roth 1993:70 (homicides); US Bureau of Justice Statistics 1991 | | **EUROPE** *Multiple European Countries*: van Dijk et al. 1991:51 |

**TABLE 9.1.14 Sex Differences in Status Inequality (Related to Rape Victimization).**

| Nature of the relationship | Officially detected offenses |
|---|---|
| | Sex offenses |
| Greater equality associated with higher rates | **NORTH AMERICA** *United States*: Ellis & Beattie 1983 (in 26 large cities); Baron & Straus 1984 (states); Baron & Straus 1989 (states); Whiley 2001* (short-term, states) |
| Not signif. | |
| Greater equality associated with lower rates | **NORTH AMERICA** *United States*: Whiley 2001* (long-term, states) **INTERNATIONAL** *Multiple Countries*: Sanday 1981 (preliterate societies); Yodanis 2004 (female victims only, 27/27 countries) |

**TABLE 9.1.15** Taking Crime Victimization Avoidance Measures.

| Nature of the relationship | Officially detected offenses |
|---|---|
| | General & adult offenses |
| Higher with taking measures | **NORTH AMERICA** *United States*: Skogan & Maxfield 1981; Rountree & Land 1996; Keane 1998; Dugan 1999 |
| Not signif. | |
| Higher without taking measures | |

## 9.1.15 Taking Crime Victimization Avoidance Measures

A few studies have sought to determine if persons who report taking specific measures to avoid being the victims of crime have lower or higher rates of victimization than those who take few if any such precautions. Somewhat surprisingly, the studies all indicate that those who take active avoidance measures actually report higher rates of victimization than those who do not (Table 9.1.15).

# 9.2 FEAR OF CRIME

Quite a number of studies have been devoted to identifying traits associated with people's varying degrees of fear of becoming a crime victim. Nearly all of these studies have been related to fear for one's self (as opposed to fear for others – so-called *altruistic fear*). Findings pertaining to traits associated with the fear of crime are summarized below.

## 9.2.1 Gender and Fear of Crime

As noted earlier in this chapter, the overwhelming evidence indicates that males are more likely than females to be victimized by crime. Even so, Table 9.2.1 shows that males report a fear of being victimized by crime less than do females. Studies have generally found women to be at least twice as likely as men to be afraid of crime. In fact, gender has been repeatedly shown to be the strongest demographic predictor of fear of crime *yet* identified (Lira & Andrade-Palos 1993:47; Snedker 2006:164).

As to why women would fear crime more than men, women's greater concern with being sexually assaulted appears to be part of the reason. Nevertheless, even when asked to exclude sex offenses from consideration, two studies still found women expressing greater fear of crime than was true for men (Karmen 1991; Ferraro 1995:89).

**TABLE 9.2.1** Gender and Fear of Crime.

| Nature of Any difference | Fear of crime in general |
|---|---|
| Higher for males | |
| Not signif. | |
| Higher for females | **EUROPE** *Britain*: Hough & Mayhew 1983; Box et al. 1988; Mayhew 1989; Crawford et al. 1990; Stanko 1990:122; N Bennett 1996; *Scotland*: Monaghan 1997:22<br>**LATIN AMERICA** *Mexico*: Ramos & Andrade 1990; Lira & Andrade-Palos 1993<br>**NORTH AMERICA** *United States*: Erskine 1974; Lebowitz 1975; Clemente & Kleiman 1977:527; Baumer 1978; Hindelang et al. 1978; Riger et al. 1978; Smith 1988; Balkan 1979; Baumer 1979; DuBow et al. 1979; Garofalo 1979; Braungart et al. 1980:56; Garofalo 1981; Riger & Gordon 1981:78; Skogan & Maxfield 1981:14; Lee 1982; Stafford & Galle 1984; Warr 1984; Akers et al. 1987:499; Ortega & Myles 1987; Liska et al. 1988; Moore & Trojanowitz 1988; Parker 1988; Bankston & Thompson 1989; LaGrange & Ferraro 1989:713; Parker & Ray 1990; Ferraro & LaGrange 1992; VD Young 1992; Maguire & Pastore 1996:188; Parker et al. 1993; Taylor & Covington 1993:390; Ferraro 1996; Chiricos et al. 1997:122; DC May & Dunaway 2000 (adol.) Culbertson et al. 2001; BS Fisher & Sloan 2003; Reid & Konrad 2004; Wesely & Gaarder 2004<br>**OCEANIA** *Australia*: Mugford 1984; Rossini 1988; *Japan*: Ito 1993:387<br>**INTERNATIONAL** *Multiple Countries*: van Dijk et al. 1991:78; Yodanis 2004:664 (27/27 countries) |

## 9.2.2 Age and Fear of Crime

Studies of how age relates to fear of crime are summarized in Table 9.2.2. The results show that most research has found the elderly expressing significantly greater fear than is true for persons in other age ranges, and that the lowest amount of fear usually comes from persons in their teens and 20s. Ironically, as noted earlier in this chapter, persons in their teens and 20s have the highest rates of victimization and the elderly have the lowest, according to most studies.

## 9.2.3 Black–White Differences in Fear of Crime

Regarding black–white differences in the fear of crime, studies have largely concluded that blacks fear crime more than do whites (Table 9.2.3). The one study conducted in England, however, found the opposite pattern.

**TABLE 9.2.2** Age and Fear of Crime.

| Nature of the Relationship | Fear of crime in general |
|---|---|
| Highest in the mid teens to the mid 30s; lowest among the elderly | |
| Not significant or a complex pattern | **NORTH AMERICA** *United States*: LaGrange & Ferraro 1987, 1989:713; Taylor & Covington 1993:390 |
| Lowest in the mid teens to the mid 30s; Highest among the elderly | **EUROPE** *Britain*: Clarke & Lewis 1982; Hough & Mayhew 1983 **NORTH AMERICA** *United States*: Clemente & Kleiman 1976, 1977:527; Cook & Cook 1976; Antunes et al. 1977; Hindelang et al. 1978; Jaycox 1978; Braungart et al. 1979, 1980; Cutler 1980; Yin 1980; Ollenburger 1981:101; Lee 1982; Lindquist & Duke 1982; Warr 1984; Mullen & Donnermeyer 1985; Lewis & Salem 1986; Ortega & Myles 1987:144; Moeller 1989 **INTERNATIONAL** *Multiple Countries*: van Dijk et al. 1991:78 |

**TABLE 9.2.3** Black–White Differences in Fear of Crime.

| Nature of the relationship | Fear of crime in general |
|---|---|
| Higher among blacks | **NORTH AMERICA** *United States*: Erskine 1974; Akers et al. 1987:499; Clemente & Kleiman 1977:527; Garofalo 1977; Hindelang et al. 1978; Braungart et al. 1980:61; Skogan & Marfield 1981:74; Ortega & Myles 1987; Liska et al. 1988; Parker 1988; Rao & Rao 1988; Parker & Ray 1990; Thompson et al. 1992; Anonymous 1994; Chiricos et al. 1997:123; May & Dunaway 2000 (males only) |
| Not signif. | **NORTH AMERICA** *United States*: May & Dunaway 2000 (females only) |
| Lower among blacks | **EUROPE** *Britain*: Walker 1994:377 |

One study considered gender, age, and race at the same time. It found that the least fearful of all groups were young black males (even though they have been shown to have the highest crime victimization rates) (Ortega & Myles 1987:144).

## 9.2.4 South Asian–White Differences in Fear of Crime

Only one study was located that compared South Asians (mainly from the former British colonies now encompassing India and Pakistan) and whites regarding fear of crime. Table 9.2.4 shows South Asians to be more fearful than whites.

## 9.2.5 Social Status and Fear of Crime

Studies of the fear of crime as it relates to social status are shown in Table 9.2.5. This research indicates that persons of

**TABLE 9.2.4** South Asian–White Differences in Fear of Crime.

| Nature of the relationship | Fear of crime in general |
|---|---|
| Higher among South Asians | **EUROPE** *Britain*: Walker 1994:377 |
| Not signif. | |
| Lower among South Asians | |

**TABLE 9.2.5** Social Status and Fear of Crime.

| Nature of the relationship | Fear of crime in general |
|---|---|
| Higher in the middle & upper strata than in the lower strata | |
| No signif. diff. | |
| Higher in the lower strata than in the middle and upper strata | **EUROPE** *Britain*: Pantazis 2000 (years of education) **NORTH AMERICA** *United States*: Clemente & Kleinman 1977:527; Kennedy & Silverman 1985 (less education); Akers et al. 1987:499; Kanan & Pruitt 2002 (years of education) |

**TABLE 9.2.6** Urban–Rural Residency and Fear of Crime.

| Nature of the relationship | Fear of crime in general |
|---|---|
| Higher in urban areas | **EUROPE** *Italy*: Mela 2003; Miceli et al. 2004 **NORTH AMERICA** *United States*: Ennis 1967; Clemente & Kleiman 1977:527; Braungart et al. 1980:60; Skogan & Maxfield 1981:75; Perkins et al. 1993; Kuo et al. 1998 |
| Not signif. | |
| Higher in rural areas | |

**TABLE 9.2.7 Having Been a Recent Victim of Crime and One's Fear of Crime.**

| Nature of the relationship | Of violent crime | Of property crime | Of crime in general |
|---|---|---|---|
| Greater fear among victims | | **NORTH AMERICA** *United States*: Dull & Wint 1997* | **EUROPE** *Britain*: Maguire & Corbett 1987; *Germany*: Stephan 1976; *Netherlands*: Cozijn & van Dijk 1976 **NORTH AMERICA** *United States*: McIntyre 1967; MK Block & Long 1973; Balkin 1979; Friedman et al. 1982; Liska et al. 1988 **OCEANIA** *Australia*: Mawby & Gill 1987 |
| Not signif. | **NORTH AMERICA** *United States*: Dull & Wint 1997* | | **EUROPE** *Netherlands*: Fiselier 1978 **NORTH AMERICA** *United States*: DuBow et al. 1979; Skogan & Maxfield 1981 **OCEANIA** *Australia*: Carcach et al. 1995 |
| Greater fear among nonvictims | | | |

lower social status have more fear of crime than do persons of middle and upper status.

## 9.2.6 Urban–Rural Residency and Fear of Crime

Several studies have investigated urban–rural variations in people's fear of crime. All have found that persons living in large urban areas express more fear than do those living in rural areas (Table 9.2.6).

## 9.2.7 Having Been a Recent Crime Victim and Fear of Crime

Over the years, quite a number of studies have been conducted to determine if persons who have been recent victims of crime express greater fear of crime revictimization than do those who have not been victims. (Recency is usually defined as victimization within the past 12 months.) As shown in Table 9.2.7, studies have indicated a greater fear of crime reported by crime victims or that there is no significant difference in fear of crime associated with recent victimization experiences.

Chapter 10

# Grand Summary

**Contents**



The overarching goal of this book is to identify variables that are most certainly associated with criminality. Toward that end, findings from over 5200 scientific studies were organized into tables to allow readers to readily determine whether the correlations with offending were positive, negative, or not significant. In this final chapter, a grand summary of the preceding chapters is presented to further distill the currently available scientific evidence.

Why identify well-established crime correlates? Criminologists and other scientists who are serious about understanding criminal behavior are wise to begin with "known facts" and then proceed to explore relationships that are less well established. Ultimately, the objective is to develop and refine theories of criminality that accurately predict as many currently "known facts," as well as "facts" yet to be established, as possible. This book is intended to assist in improving criminological theorizing by identifying the "known facts" currently are based on available evidence.

Most theories of criminal behavior that are still driving research today were proposed in or before the mid-twentieth century and they have limited predictive power, generating less than half a dozen obvious hypotheses for testing. Theories that can generate dozens of testable hypotheses are sorely needed. By pointing toward the types of relationships that are now well established, this book should guide criminologists toward formulating more powerful theories. For example, as will be noted below, the evidence is now overwhelming that throughout the world, males are more involved in crime than females and offending is highly concentrated in the second and third decades of life. Theories that do not explicitly predict such sex and age patterns in offending must be considered deficient. Similarly, theories that fail to explain most of the other facts identified in this summary chapter would be best laid to rest except as historic relics of a still emerging science.

## 10.1 GRAND TABLES

The scientific method is not perfect for uncovering truth, but it is probably as close as humans will ever get. To identify the variables that research suggests are irrefutably associated with crime, this closing chapter presents a series of *grand tables*. These tables are based on the individual tables appearing in Chapters 2 through 9 which contain 10 or more citations.

Within each grand table are five main columns, the headers for which are as follows:

- Variable name
- Table number
- Number of citations in each table separately (for official data and self-reported data)
- Consistency scores (defined below)
- Generalization derived from the current evidence

Consistency scores reflect the extent to which 10 or more studies support a specific conclusion regarding how criminality is related to another variable. These scores can range from 0.000 to 1.000, with the latter meaning that every study listed leads to the same conclusion. Throughout the grand tables, consistency scores that exceed 0.9000 are bolded, since these must be considered highly suggestive of a well-established relationship.

The following procedures were used to calculate the consistency scores: The total number of citations in every table dealing with crime was determined and the direction (either positive or negative) of the majority of the citations was noted. Then the number of citations in the majority direction was divided by the total plus a doubling of any citations that were in the opposite direction. For example, if there were a total of 12 studies concerning a particular relationship and nine of the studies suggested that the relationship was positive, one suggested it was negative, and two found no significant relationship, the following calculation was made to derive the consistency score: 9/13 = 0.692.

The main focus of this chapter will be on consistency scores between 0.9000 and 1.000. Scores in this range are highly consistent with the conclusion that a substantial relationship exists between whatever variables were being correlated.

### 10.1.1 Frequently Researched Intra-Offending and Clinical Correlates of Crime

Chapter 1 differs from the remaining Chapter in this book by focusing mainly on how different measures of criminality (and closely related phenomena) interrelate with one another. Some well-established generalizations that are revealed in Chapter 1 can be summarized as follows.

Officially detected offending is positively correlated with clinical disorders linked to antisocial behavior, most notably childhood conduct disorder and adult antisocial personality disorder. Offending during adolescence (delinquency) is positively associated with offending in adulthood (criminality), although most adolescent offenders desist by the time they have attained adulthood. Self-reported offending is positively correlated with officially detected offending, although the latter tends to focus much more than the former on the most serious types of crimes.

Overall, research has established that criminality, delinquency, childhood conduct disorder, and adult antisocial behavior are all positively correlated with one another. These studies do not suggest that such are interchangeable concepts, but that the relationships are sufficiently strong so that any variable found related to one will almost certainly be related to the others.

### 10.1.2 Frequently Researched Crime Correlates Concerning Demographic Variables

Chapter 2 pertained to the basic demographic characteristics of human beings. As one can see by viewing Grand

**GRAND Subtable 10.1.2a Generalizations from Tables in Chapter 2 with 10 or More Studies Pertaining to Gender and Age.**

| Variable name | Chapter section number | Number of studies | | Consistency score | | | Generalization |
|---|---|---|---|---|---|---|---|
| | | Official | Self | Official | Self | Total | |
| Gender and homicide | 2.1.1 | 55 | – | 1.000 | – | – | Compared to females, males commit more homicides |
| Gender and violent offenses generally | 2.1.2 | 48 | – | **1.000** | – | – | Males commit more violent crimes overall than females |
| Gender and property offenses | 2.1.3 | 25 | – | 0.724 | – | – | Males commit more property offenses except shoplifting |
| Gender and delinquency | 2.1.6 | 67 | – | **1.000** | – | – | Males engage in more overall delinquency |
| Gender and overall or adult crime | 2.1.7 | 85 | – | **1.000** | – | – | Males are more involved in overall and adult crime |
| Gender and recidivism | 2.1.8 | 18 | – | 0.722 | – | – | Males appear to be more likely to recidivate |
| Gender and self-reported offending | 2.1.9 | – | 87 | – | 0.866 | – | Males appear to be more involved in self-reported offending |
| Gender and intimate violence | 2.1.10 | – | 32 | – | 0.262 | – | Uncertain sex differences in courtship and domestic violence |
| Gender and Self-reported drug offending | 2.1.11 | – | 77 | – | 0.605 | – | Males appear to be more involved with illegal drugs (except mere use) |
| Age | 2.2.1 | 136 | 16 | **1.000** | **1.000** | **1.000** | Crime is most likely in the second and third decades of life |

Table 10.1.2 (divided into three subtables), several of these characteristics have been examined by more than 10 studies and found to be well-established crime correlates.

Regarding sex (gender), one can see in Grand Subtable 10.1.2a that there is no doubt as far as official data are concerned that males engage in criminal activities more than females, especially regarding violent offenses. In the case of property crimes, males also dominate in offending with the exception of shoplifting, where the difference between the sexes is insignificant.

The research pertaining to self-reported offenses is less clear regarding any consistent sex difference. However, in the specific table in Chapter 2, one can see that nearly all of the pertinent studies casting doubt on male dominance in self-reported drug offenses.

Findings surrounding the relationship between age and criminality are extremely consistent with the conclusion that throughout the world, criminality (including delinquency) is heavily concentrated in the teens and 20s. By approximately age 30, the probability of offending is nearly the same as it was around age 12.

A large number of studies have been published comparing the crime rates of blacks and whites, allowing separate calculations to be made for (a) officially detected violent crime, (b) officially detected crimes as a whole, and (c) self-reported offenses (Grand Subtable 10.1.2b). One can see that the official data are very consistent in suggesting that crime is more common among blacks than among whites, especially regarding violent offenses. However, in the case of self-reported offending, the evidence of any significant black–white difference is highly tenuous, particularly in the case of drug offenses.

Official data regarding differences in offending between Hispanics and non-Hispanic whites (Anglos) clearly indicates that the offending rate of Hispanics is higher. However, differences surrounding self-reported offending are not statistically detectable. With regard to Native Americans, both official and self-reported data are nearly unanimous in indicating higher offending rates than for whites.

Grand Subtable 10.1.2b compares people of Asian and South Pacific descent with whites living in the same

**GRAND Subtable 10.1.2b Generalizations from Tables in Chapter 2 with 10 or More Studies Pertaining to Race, Ethnicity, and Immigrant Status.**

| Variable name | Chapter section number | Number of studies | | Consistency score | | | Generalization |
|---|---|---|---|---|---|---|---|
| | | | | Official | Self | Total | |
| Black–white comparisons regarding violent crimes | 2.3.2a | 96 | 0 | **1.000** | – | – | Blacks exhibit higher rates of violent criminality |
| Black–white comparisons for crimes in general | 2.3.2b | 115 | 0 | **0.948** | – | – | Blacks are more involved in crime (with the possible exception of criminal recidivism) |
| Black–white comparisons, self-reports | 2.3.2c | – | 78 | – | 0.383 | – | Uncertain black–white differences, especially regarding drug offenses |
| Hispanic–Anglo comparisons, official data | 2.3.3a | 33 | 0 | **1.000** | – | – | Hispanics are more involved in all types of officially recorded crime than Anglos (non-Hispanic whites) |
| Hispanic–Anglo comparisons, self-reports | 2.3.3b | – | 32 | – | 0.342 | – | Uncertain Hispanic–Anglo differences |
| Native American–white comparisons, official data | 2.3.4a | 48 | 0 | **0.980** | – | – | Native Americans almost certainly have higher rates of official crime than do whites |
| Native American–white comparisons, self-reports | 2.3.4b | – | 30 | – | **0.935** | – | Self-reported offending is almost certainly higher for Native Americans than for whites |
| East Asian–white comparisons | 2.3.5 | 37 | 0 | **1.000** | 0.769 | – | Whites exhibit higher rates of crime than do East Asians except possibly with regard to self-reported offenses |
| South Asian–white comparisons | 2.3.6 | 12 | 4 | 0.267 | – | 0.421 | Uncertain South Asian–white (European) differences |
| Oceanic Islander–white comparisons | 2.3.7 | 20 | 5 | **1.000** | – | **1.000** | Oceanic Islanders are more involved in crime than are whites |
| Immigrant versus nonimmigrant comparisons | 2.3.8 | 68 | 3 | 0.568 | – | 0.560 | Uncertain differences between immigrants and nonimmigrants |

**GRAND Subtable 10.1.2c Generalizations from Tables in Chapter 2 with 10 or More Studies Pertaining to Social Status.**

| Variable name | Chapter section number | Number of studies | | Consistency score | | | Generalization |
|---|---|---|---|---|---|---|---|
| | | | | Official | Self | Total | |
| Individual social status (composite or unspecified) | 2.4.1 | 27 | 1 | **1.000** | – | **0.929** | Individuals of low social status are more involved in official crime than those of high status |
| Individual social status (years of education) | 2.4.2 | 22 | 14 | **0.955** | 0.800 | 0.892 | Low status persons appear to be more involved in official crime and may be more involved in self-reported crime |
| Individual social status (income/wealth) | 2.4.3 | 8 | 4 | – | – | 0.667 | An inverse correlation appears to exist except for drug offenses |
| Parental social status (composite or unspecified) | 2.5.1 | 2 | 10 | – | – | 0.700 | Probably an inverse relationship between parental social status and self-reported offending |

countries. These comparisons allow the following generalizations to be made: First, East Asians (Orientals) exhibit lower official crime rates than whites according to all official data and most self-reported data. Second, the official offending rates for south Asian populations appear to be statistically indistinguishable from those of whites, although the inhabitants of these countries self-reported offending rates which are higher. Third, all of the studies of people from various Pacific and Indian Islands have concluded that they exhibit higher rates of crime than do whites.

For immigrants, the evidence is mixed with regard to any differences in offending probabilities relative to those who are indigenous to the country in question.

Grand Subtable 10.1.2c pertains to the four social status variables with 10 or more relevant studies. This research shows that all three of the individual status measures suggest that there is an inverse correlation between social status and

**GRAND Subtable 10.1.3a Generalizations from Tables in Chapter 3 with 10 or More Studies Pertaining to Basic Ecological Factors.**

| Variable name | Chapter section number | Number of studies | | Consistency score | | | Generalization |
|---|---|---|---|---|---|---|---|
| | | | | Official | Self | Total | |
| Ethnic/racial heterogeneity/diversity | 3.1.1 | 33 | 1 | 0.794 | – | 0.824 | Regions that are ethnically/racially diverse probably have higher crime rates |
| Black percentage | 3.1.3 | 72 | 1 | 0.875 | – | 0.851 | Areas with high percentages of blacks appear to exhibit higher crime rates, especially for violent offenses |
| Foreign born/immigrant percentage | 3.1.4 | 10 | 0 | 0.600 | – | – | Inconsistent evidence with a trend toward a positive relationship |
| Teenagers & young adults percentage | 3.1.9 | 28 | 0 | 0.433 | – | – | Inconsistent evidence |
| Alcohol consumption per capita | 3.2.1 | 14 | 0 | 0.687 | – | – | Violent crime rates appear to increase in high alcohol-consuming areas |
| Taverns and liquor stores per capita | 3.2.2 | 12 | 0 | 0.917 | – | – | Crime rates are higher in areas where taverns & liquor stores are most prevalent |
| Gun ownership/firearm availability per capita | 3.2.6 | 11 | 0 | 0.818 | – | – | There is either an inverse or no relationship between the availability of firearms in a area |
| Single-parent households per capita | 3.3.1 | 44 | 0 | 0.867 | – | – | Areas with the highest percentages of single-parent households probably have higher crime rates, especially for violence |

criminality, especially regarding official data. For the one measure of parental social status containing 10 or more studies, the evidence provides somewhat weaker support for the same conclusion.

## 10.1.3 Frequently Researched Crime Correlates Concerning Ecological and Macro-Economic Variables

Grand Table 10.1.3 (in three parts) identifies the ecological and macro-economic variables that have received attention from at least 10 studies. As one might expect, very few of these studies were based on self-reported offenses.

None of these variables attained a consistency score of 1.000, but four attained a score of 0.900 or higher. The first of these strong scores suggests that as a city's (or county's) population size increases, so too does its official crime rate. Second, deteriorated neighborhood conditions in an urban area were almost always associated with higher rates of official crime. Third, nearly all of the relevant studies have concluded that residential instability is positively associated with officially detected criminality. Fourth, geographic regions with the greatest religious memberships have nearly always been found to have lower crime rates than regions with low religious affiliation (Grand Subtable 10.1.3a).

According to Grand Subtable 10.1.3b, city (or county) population size was positively correlated with crime rates, achieving a consistency score of 0.900. Even high scores were attained by the neighborhood condition and residential instability, with the direction being inverse for the first and positive for the second. The last variable to reach a 0.900 consistency score was religious membership, with most studies indicating that where it was highest, crime rates tended to be relatively low.

**GRAND Subtable 10.1.3b** Generalizations from Tables in Chapter 3 with 10 or more Studies Pertaining to Additional Ecological Factors.

| Variable name | Chapter section number | Number of studies | | Consistency score | | | Generalization |
|---|---|---|---|---|---|---|---|
| | | | | Official | Self | Total | |
| City (or county) population size | 3.4.1 | 30 | 0 | **0.900** | – | – | Cities or counties with large populations have higher crime rates |
| Neighborhood conditions | 3.4.4 | 79 | 19 | **0.975** | 0.750 | **0.921** | As neighborhood conditions worsen, so too do crime rates |
| Owner occupied housing per capita | 3.4.5 | 14 | 0 | 0.867 | – | – | The per capita ownership of houses is associated with less crime |
| Geographic population density | 3.4.6 | 52 | 1 | 0.510 | – | 0.518 | There is either a positive association between geographic population density and crime or no significant association |
| Residential instability/ mobility | 3.4.11 | 24 | 0 | **0.958** | – | – | Crime is higher in areas with the greatest residential mobility |
| Technological development/ modernization/ industrialization | 3.4.14 | 20 | 0 | 0.400 | – | – | Inconsistent evidence concerning any link between technological development, modernization, etc. on crime rates |
| Tourism and Gambling Regions | 3.4.15 | 11 | 0 | 0.818 | – | – | Crime rates appear to be higher in areas with high tourist or gambling establishments |
| Urban/rural residency (percent urban) | 3.4.16 | 87 | 30 | 0.800 | 0.813 | – | Highly urbanized communities appear to have more crime than rural areas; suburban areas are intermediate (except for self-reported crime) |
| Religious membership per capita | 3.5.1 | 12 | 0 | **0.917** | – | – | Crime rates are higher in areas where religious membership is low |
| Education of residents, average level | 3.6.1 | 12 | 1 | 0.667 | – | 0.692 | Crime appears to be higher where years of education are lowest |

**GRAND Subtable 10.1.3c Generalizations from Tables in Chapter 3 with 10 or More Studies Pertaining to Macro-Economic and Nonsocial Ecological Factors.**

| Variable name | Chapter section number | Number of studies | | Consistency score | | | Generalization |
|---|---|---|---|---|---|---|---|
| | | | | Official | Self | Total | |
| Income of residents, median level | 3.6.2 | 39 | 3 | 0.651 | – | 0.636 | Violent crimes and crimes overall may decrease as the average income of residents increases; inconsistent evidence for property crimes |
| Income/economic inequality | 3.6.3 | 23 | 1 | 0.682 | – | 0.667 | In areas where economic inequality is high, crime rates are either high or there is no significant link between these factors |
| Poverty among residents, percent below poverty line | 3.6.4 | 75 | 1 | 0.688 | – | 0.691 | Most studies indicate that residential poverty rates are positively associated with crime rates |
| Unemployment rate between regions | 3.6.6 | 80 | 0 | 0.482 | – | – | Inconsistent findings |
| Unemployment rate over time | 3.6.7 | 82 | 0 | 0.539 | – | – | A slight tendency for unemployment to be positively associated with crime rates in the majority of studies |
| State of the economy over time | 3.6.8 | 35 | 0 | 0.378 | – | – | Inconsistent findings |
| Distance from the equator (southernness) | 3.7.3 | 35 | 0 | 0.761 | – | – | There appears to be higher crime rates in geographic regions that are closest to the equator |
| Seasonality | 3.7.7 | 21 | 0 | 0.636 | – | – | Crime rates appear to be highest in spring and summer |

Grand Subtable 10.1.3c primarily pertains to macroeconomic factors such as average incomes, degrees of income inequality, poverty rates, and unemployment rates. One can see that the consistency scores for these variables are all well below 0.9000, rather surprising given the emphasis that many criminologists have put on macroeconomic factors as a cause of criminal behavior. The highest macroeconomic consistency score is for poverty rates with the lowest scores for the two unemployment rates (one by region, the other over time).

Regarding the two nonsocial ecological variables, neither distance from the equator nor seasonality achieved notably high consistency scores.

## 10.1.4 Frequently Researched Crime Correlates Concerning Family and Peer Variables

Grand Table 10.1.4 (in two parts) identifies the crime correlates in connection with family and peer relationships for which 10 or more official data or self-report studies were located. The first part of this table pertains to the family while the other involves peer relationships.

The associations identified in Grand Subtable 10.1.4a with a consistency score of 0.9000 or higher suggest that crime is more prevalent as family size and births increase and further indicated that parents and offspring tend to resemble one another in criminality. This resemblance (or concordance) is also true when the criminality of siblings is compared. Alcoholism, drug abuse, depression, and family discord are all more common in families where criminality is found in at least one member. Parent–child attachment and the careful monitoring of children by parents tends to be low while child maltreatment by parents is usually high in families with criminality.

Grand Subtable 10.1.4b shows that offenders have relatively few friends. The friends that offenders do have also exhibit high rates of delinquency and are more likely than the friends of persons in general to be gang members.

## 10.1.5. Frequently Researched Crime Correlates Concerned with Institutional Factors

Institutional factors such as those involving school, work, and religion have received considerable research attention by criminologists. Grand Table 10.1.5 summarizes what these studies have found.

**GRAND Subtable 10.1.4a Generalizations from Tables in Chapter 4 with 10 or More Studies Pertaining to Family Variables.**

| Variable name | Chapter section number | Number of studies | | Consistency Score | | | Generalization |
|---|---|---|---|---|---|---|---|
| | | | | Official | Self | Total | |
| Married versus unmarried | 4.1.1 | 24 | 5 | 0.720 | – | | Unmarried persons appear to be more involved in crime |
| Family size | 4.2.4 | 51 | 13 | **0.904** | 0.500 | | Persons from large families appear to be more involved in crime |
| Birth order | 4.2.5 | 10 | 2 | **1.000** | – | | Later born are more criminal than first born |
| Concordance between parent and offspring (excluding adoptees) | 4.3.1 | 55 | 14 | **0.982** | 0.857 | | Criminality in one or both parents tends to be positively correlated with criminality in offspring |
| Concordance between siblings (excluding twins) | 4.3.3 | 11 | 15 | **1.000** | **0.933** | | Siblings are concordant for criminality |
| Concordance among twins | 4.3.4 | 17 | 2 | 0.882 | – | | Monozygotic twins tend to be more concordant in criminality than dizygotic twins |
| Alcoholism within the family | 4.3.5 | 15 | 7 | **1.000** | – | | Criminality is positively correlated with alcoholism in the family |
| Drug use within the family | 4.3.6 | 6 | 42 | – | **0.905** | | Criminality appears positively correlated with drug use in the family |
| Depression within the family | 4.4.1 | 161 | 84 | **0.901** | 0.581 | | Depression within the family appears to be associated with official criminality, and possibly with self-reported offending |
| Marital/family discord | 4.4.3 | 27 | 28 | **1.000** | **1.000** | | Criminality is more common in dysfunctional families |
| Parent–child attachment | 4.4.6 | 20 | 52 | **0.950** | 0.885 | | Criminality is inversely correlated with parent–child attachment |
| Child maltreatment by parents | 4.5.1 | 45 | 9 | **0.978** | – | | Maltreated children tend to be more involved in crime |
| Parental supervision/monitoring | 4.5.2 | 22 | 48 | 0.833 | **0.979** | | Close parental supervision is inversely associated with offspring offending |

The generalizations one can make with the greatest confidence regarding institutional factors and crime concern education. Studies have repeatedly shown that individuals who attend school regularly, are not disruptive in class, and remain through high school graduation are less criminal and delinquent than truants, children with discipline problems, and high school dropouts. No religious institutional variables attained a consistency score of 0.900, but two job-related variables did: Being unemployed or changing jobs frequently are both positively correlated with involvement in crime.

## 10.1.6 Frequently Researched Crime Correlates Concerned with Personality and Behavior

Many studies have investigated the possible connection between criminality and personality and behavioral traits. Those traits that have received the attention of at least 10 studies are summarized in Grand Table 10.1.6.

Both aggression and bullying during childhood were linked to criminality in nearly all relevant studies. Surprisingly, however, aggression in general was not connected, mainly because it was not found to be significantly correlated with self-reported drug use.

Research has consistently linked criminality with four personality traits, which are impulsiveness, psychoticism, lack of self-control, and sensation seeking. Regarding drug use, the use of alcohol is a correlate of criminal behavior, and the use of illegal drugs of all types is positively associated with other forms of criminality.

Three aspects of sexuality have been linked to involvement in crime. One is premarital sex, another is the number of different sex partners, and the third is the age of the first experience of sexual intercourse. Individuals who have

**GRAND Subtable 10.1.4b Generalizations from Tables in Chapter 4 with 10 or More Studies Pertaining to Peer Factors.**

| Variable name | Chapter section number | Number of studies | | Consistency score | | | Generalization |
|---|---|---|---|---|---|---|---|
| | | | | Official | Self | Total | |
| Involvement in extracurricular activities | 4.6.1 | 1 | 15 | – | 0.471 | | Inconsistent findings |
| Number of friends | 4.6.2 | 10 | 15 | **1.000** | **0.933** | | Having more friends is inversely associated with criminal involvement |
| Associating with delinquent peers | 4.6.3 | 8 | 145 | – | **1.000** | | Offending is more common among those who associate with other offenders |
| Gang membership | 4.6.4 | 10 | 23 | **1.000** | 0.826 | | Members of gangs offend more |

**GRAND Table 10.1.5 Generalizations from Tables in Chapter 5 with 10 or More Studies Pertaining to Institutional Factors.**

| Variable name | Chapter section number | Number of studies | | Consistency score | | | Generalization |
|---|---|---|---|---|---|---|---|
| | | | | Official | Self | Total | |
| Dropping out of high school (versus graduating from high school) | 5.1.1 | 14 | 22 | **1.000** | **0.955** | | High school dropouts engage in more crime than do persons who graduate |
| Truancy | 5.1.4 | 19 | 11 | **1.000** | **1.000** | | Truants are more likely to commit crimes than are persons who attend school regularly |
| School discipline problems | 5.1.5 | 10 | 8 | **1.000** | – | | Persons who exhibit discipline problems in school engage in more crime and delinquency |
| Employment during adolescence | 5.2.1 | 1 | 18 | – | 0.889 | | Persons who have paying jobs during adolescence appear to engage in more delinquency than those who do not |
| Employment by the mother outside the home | 5.2.3 | 14 | 9 | 0.429 | – | | There may be a very slight tendency for working mothers to have children who are more delinquent |
| Frequently changing jobs | 5.2.4 | 17 | 3 | **0.941** | – | | Those who change jobs most appear to be more criminal |
| Frequently being unemployed | 5.2.5 | 23 | 1 | **0.913** | – | | Persons who are often unemployed appear to be more criminal |
| Religious involvement | 5.3.1 | 17 | 95 | 0.824 | 0.874 | | Persons who are most involved in religion appear to be less criminal |
| Religious saliency (importance of religion to ones life) | 5.3.2 | 2 | 29 | – | 0.892 | | Persons for who religion is most central to their lives appear to be less involved in crime |
| Religious membership | 5.3.3 | 9 | 14 | – | 0.857 | | Members of an organized religion appear to be less criminal than nonmembers |
| Orthodox religious beliefs | 5.3.4 | 1 | 17 | – | 0.882 | | Persons with orthodox religious beliefs may be less criminal |
| Jews compared to non-Jews | 5.3.11 | 24 | 4 | 0.846 | – | | Jews appear to engage in less crime overall than non-Jews |

**GRAND Table 10.1.6 Generalizations from Tables in Chapter 6 with 10 or More Studies Pertaining to Personality and Behavior.**

| Variable name | Chapter section number | Number of studies | | Consistency score | | | Generalization |
|---|---|---|---|---|---|---|---|
| | | | | Official | Self | Total | |
| Aggression in general, except childhood aggression | 6.1.1 | 4 | 7 | – | – | 0.692 | Overall aggressive behavior is positively correlated with crime with the possible exception of drug offenses |
| Aggression in childhood | 6.1.2 | 40 | 19 | **0.950** | **.900** | **.933** | Childhood aggression is positively correlated with criminality |
| Bullying | 6.1.5 | 8 | 2 | – | – | **1.000** | Bullying behavior is positively associated with offending |
| Extroversion | 6.1.7 | 29 | 25 | 0.516 | .880 | 0.678 | Offenders (especially self-reported) may be more extroverted |
| Impulsivity | 6.1.10 | 53 | 33 | **0.981** | **.970** | **0.977** | Criminals are unusually impulsive |
| Psychoticism | 6.1.14 | 11 | 9 | **0.910** | – | **0.950** | Psychoticism is positively correlated with criminal behavior |
| Self-control | 6.1.16 | 5 | 40 | – | **0.975** | **0.978** | Self-control is inversely associated with involvement in crime |
| Sensation seeking | 6.1.17 | 19 | 41 | **1.000** | **0.905** | **0.919** | Offending is positively correlated with sensation seeking |
| Alcohol use | 6.2.1 | 39 | 16 | **0.974** | **1.000** | **0.982** | Alcohol consumption is positively associated with criminality |
| Illegal drug use in general | 6.2.2 | 39 | 38 | **0.974** | **0.974** | **0.974** | Use of illegal drugs is positively related to criminality in general |
| Premarital sexual intercourse | 6.3.2 | – | 17 | – | **1.000** | – | Having premarital sex is positively correlated with criminality |
| Number of sex partners | 6.3.3 | 19 | 20 | **1.000** | **1.000** | **1.000** | As the number of sex partners one has increases, so too does involvement in criminal activities |
| Age of onset of sexual intercourse (early) | 6.3.4 | 3 | 20 | – | **1.000** | **1.000** | Those who experience sexual intercourse at the youngest ages are most involved in criminal behavior |

premarital sex, especially with many partners, and begin doing so at an early age, are more involved in crime on average than their less sexually active counterparts.

## 10.1.7 Frequently Researched Crime Correlates Concerned with Cognition

Are cognitive factors associated with criminal and delinquent behavior? Grand Table 10.1.7 (presented in three parts) indicates the answer to be "yes". Three categories of cognitive variables attitudes, intellectual traits, and mental health/illness traits will be reviewed, each in a different subtable.

Beginning with attitudes, Grand Subtable 10.1.7a suggests that criminals have a low commitment to education, are below average in empathy and altruism, and are more likely than most people to hold liberal or tolerant attitudes toward nonconformity in general and toward drug use in particular. Research has also unanimously shown that offenders tend to be unusually rebellious and prone to defy authority.

In Grand Subtable 10.1.7b, one can see that five variables were found with respect to intelligence and academic ability for which 10 or more studies were located. This research provides strong evidence that academic performance as measured by grade point average was inversely associated with both official and

**GRAND Subtable 10.1.7a Generalizations from Tables in Chapter 7 with 10 or More Studies Pertaining to Attitudes.**

| Variable name | Chapter section number | Number of studies | | Consistency score | | | Generalization |
|---|---|---|---|---|---|---|---|
| | | | | Official | Self | Total | |
| Commitment to education | 7.1.1 | 12 | 36 | **1.000** | **0.944** | **0.958** | Offenders are less committed to education as an appealing activity |
| Empathy/altruism | 7.1.3 | 10 | 5 | **0.900** | **1.000** | **0.933** | Criminals are less empathetic and altruistic |
| Feelings of external locus of control | 7.1.6 | 8 | 9 | – | – | 0.824 | Among those who offend most often, feelings of external locus (rather than internal locus) of control tends to be greater |
| Liberal/tolerant attitudes toward deviance and nonconformity | 7.1.8 | 5 | 14 | 0.800 | **1.00** | **0.947** | Individuals who are more liberal or tolerant of deviance and nonconformity tend to be more involved in offending |
| Liberal/tolerant attitudes toward drug use | 7.1.9 | 0 | 15 | – | **0.933** | – | Persons with liberal/tolerant attitudes toward drug use appear to be more involved in crime |
| Levels of moral reasoning | 7.1.12 | 42 | 7 | 0.762 | – | 0.700 | Those who think at low levels of moral reasoning seem to be involved in more crime |
| Negative affect | 7.1.13 | 3 | 8 | – | – | 0.818 | Offenders appear to be less friendly and sour toward live |
| Rebelliousness/defiance of authority | 7.1.17 | 8 | 38 | – | **1.000** | **1.000** | Rebellious and defiant attitudes toward authority are positively correlated with criminality |
| Role Taking/role playing | 7.1.18 | 13 | 1 | 0.769 | – | 0.786 | Difficulty in taking the role of others seems to increase offending |
| Self-esteem/self-concept | 7.1.19 | 19 | 52 | 0.750 | 0.704 | 0.726 | Low self-esteem tends to be associated with high involvement in crime |

**GRAND Subtable 10.1.7b Generalizations from Tables in Chapter 7 with 10 or More Studies Pertaining to Intellectual Ability and Academic Performance.**

| Variable name | Chapter section number | Number of studies | | Consistency score | | | Generalization |
|---|---|---|---|---|---|---|---|
| | | | | Official | Self | Total | |
| Academic performance/ GPA | 7.2.1 | 80 | 97 | **0.975** | **0.918** | **0.944** | Those who do poorly in school engage in more crime |
| Intelligence | 7.2.2 | 118 | 26 | 0.800 | 0.704 | 0.793 | Low intelligence tends to be associated with increased offending |
| Intellectual imbalance | 7.2.5 | 40 | 6 | 0.846 | – | 0.783 | Those whose PIQ exceeds their VIQ appears to be more involved in crime |
| Learning disabilities | 7.2.8 | 27 | 5 | **1.000** | – | **0.938** | Learning disabilities are positively correlated with offending |
| Slow reading development | 7.2.12 | 21 | 0 | **1.000** | – | – | Persons whose reading ability develops slowly offend more |

self-reported criminality in nearly all investigations. Learning disabilities and slow reading development were both positively correlated with involvement in crime and delinquency.

Regarding intelligence, most studies found an inverse correlation with criminality. However, many studies failed to document a significant correlation so that the consistency score was below 0.900 for both official and self-report studies. Intellectual imbalance likewise failed to reach a 0.900 consistency score, and therefore cannot qualify as a virtually certain correlate of crime.

Grand Subtable 10.1.7c shows that several psychological/psychiatric conditions, not including antisocial disorders themselves, are all associated with criminality. These conditions include mental illness in general along with other minor forms of mental discrders. All research pertaining to suicide, attempted suicide, and frequent thoughts of suicide indicate that offenders are more suicide-prone than nonoffenders.

Regarding mental disorders, two appear to be positively linked beyond doubt to criminality. These are attention deficit hyperactivity disorder (ADHD) and enuresis. Drug abuse, general drug dependency, alcohol abuse, and alcoholism are also unquestionably associated with increased criminal behavior.

### 10.1.8 Frequently Researched Crime Correlates Concerned with Biology

The crime correlates of a biological nature are highlighted in Grand Table 10.1.8. As before, tables in Chapter 8 containing fewer than 10 citations are excluded from this grand table.

One can see that six variables have a consistency score of at least 0.900. The first such variable is accidental injury, which all studies have shown to be more common among offenders of than of persons in general. Body type is another well-established crime correlate, with all pertinent studies concluding that offenders are unusually mesomorphic (muscular).

With respect to "internal" biological correlates, four have been studied: skin conductivity, heart rate, 5-HIAA levels, and monoamine oxidase activity. All of these correlates tend to be unusually low in offenders relative to the general human population.

**GRAND Subtable 10.1.7c Generalizations from Tables in Chapter 7 with 10 or More Studies Pertaining to Mental Illness, Mental Disorders, and Drug Dependency.**

| Variable name | Chapter section number | Number of studies | | Consistency score | | | Generalization |
|---|---|---|---|---|---|---|---|
| | | | | Official | Self | Total | |
| Mental illness in general | 7.3.1 | 95 | 10 | **0.938** | **0.900** | **0.934** | Offending is more common among the mentally ill |
| Minor/subclinical depression | 7.3.2 | 13 | 27 | **1.000** | **0.889** | **0.925** | Minor depression is more likely among offenders |
| Major/clinical depression | 7.3.3 | 4 | 8 | – | – | 0.750 | Criminality is probably positively correlated with clinical depression |
| Schizophrenia | 7.3.6 | 45 | 8 | 0.851 | – | 0.873 | Schizophrenia and criminality appear to be positively correlated |
| Suicide (actual/attempted/ ideation) | 7.3.7 | 14 | 33 | **1.000** | **1.000** | **1.000** | Criminals are more likely to be suicidal |
| Attention deficit hyperactivity disorder | 7.4.1 | 47 | 15 | **1.000** | 0.867 | **0.968** | ADHD is a positive correlate of criminality |
| Enuresis | 7.4.3 | 13 | 1 | **1.000** | 0.000 | **0.929** | Offenders are more likely to be enuretic, with the possible exception of self-reported drug offenders |
| Drug dependence/substance abuse | 7.5.1 | 39 | 10 | **1.000** | **1.000** | **1.000** | Drug dependency is more common among offenders |
| Alcohol abuse | 7.5.2 | 13 | 1 | **1.000** | – | **1.000** | Offenders are more likely to abuse alcohol |
| Alcoholism | 7.5.3 | 39 | 8 | **1.000** | – | **1.000** | Alcoholism is positively correlated with involvement in crime |

**GRAND Table 10.1.8** Generalizations from Tables in Chapter 8 with 10 or More Studies Pertaining to Biology.

| Variable name | Chapter section number | Number of studies | | Consistency score | | | Generalization |
|---|---|---|---|---|---|---|---|
| | | | | Official | Self | Total | |
| Birth weight | 8.2.1 | 12 | 1 | 0.538 | – | 0.571 | Low birth weight may be associated with high criminality |
| Perinatal Trauma/birth complications | 8.2.4 | 29 | 1 | 0.655 | – | 0.667 | Prenatal trauma is probably more prevalent among offenders |
| Maternal smoking during pregnancy | 8.2.7 | 15 | 0 | 0.867 | – | 0.867 | Maternal smoking is more common among offenders |
| Morbidity | 8.3.1 | 18 | 1 | 0.722 | – | 0.737 | Offenders probably suffer from more illnesses |
| Accidental injuries | 8.3.4 | 16 | 5 | **1.000** | – | **1.000** | Criminals are more often accidentally injured |
| Epilepsy | 8.3.6 | 18 | – | 0.778 | – | 0.778 | Epilepsy appears to be positively correlated with offending |
| Body type | 8.4.3 | 9 | 2 | – | – | **1.000** | Mesomorphs are more involved in crime |
| Skin conductivity | 8.4.6 | 12 | 1 | **1.000** | – | **1.000** | Low skin conductivity is typical of offenders |
| Heart rate | 8.4.7 | 17 | 4 | 0.880 | – | **0.905** | Heart rates appear to be below normal among criminals |
| 5-HIAA levels in cerebral spinal fluid | 8.6.6 | 16 | 0 | **1.000** | – | **1.000** | Low 5-HIAA levels are found among offenders |
| Monamine oxidase activity in general | 8.6.12 | 12 | 3 | **1.000** | – | 0.875 | Monoamine oxidase activity in low among offenders |
| Testosterone | 8.7.2 | 41 | 2 | 0.810 | – | 0.818 | Testosterone appears to be positively correlated with criminality |
| Handedness | 8.10.1 | 18 | 3 | 0.500 | – | 0.565 | Left-handers (or mixed-handers) may be more criminal |

## 10.1.9 Frequently Researched Correlates of Crime Victimization

Grand Table 10.1.9 shows that several variables are well-established correlates of crime victimization. For example, there can be virtually no doubt that males are more likely to be the victims of homicide than females, but that females are more likely to be the victims of sex crimes as well as dating or domestic offenses, as the official statistics indicate. Also, the age of greatest crime victimization has been repeatedly shown to be between the teens and mid 30s, and blacks are more often the victims of crime than whites.

Regarding fear of crime, gender and age have been shown to be almost certainly linked. Females fear crime more than males do, and this fear is greatest among the elderly and lowest among individuals in their teens, 20s, and early 30s.

# 10.2 CLOSING COMMENTS

This book summarizes most of what is currently known about variables that are (and are not) associated with criminality. Such information should be of value to professionals and graduate students in criminology, criminal justice, and allied fields of study who seek a nonselective and impartial overview of research findings.

Because the subject areas of criminology are vast and research is continually growing, no claim can be made that this book such as this is comprehensive. However, it is a serious start, and assurance can be given that the studies cited throughout were not "cherry picked" to support a particular perspective. We welcome other scholars to consider joining us in updating and expanding this book for future editions. Also, if any errors need to be corrected or additions made, readers are invited to provide specifics to the authors or the publisher.

**GRAND Table 10.1.9 Generalizations from Tables in Chapter 9 with 10 or More Studies Pertaining to Crime Victimization.**

| Variable name | Chapter section number | Number of studies | | Consistency score | | | Generalization |
|---|---|---|---|---|---|---|---|
| | | | | Official | Unofficial | Total | |
| Gender and homicide victimization | 9.1.1a | 76 | – | **0.980** | – | – | Males are murder victims more than females |
| Gender and sex/dating/ domestic crime victimization | 9.1.1b | 6 | 16 | **1.000** | 0.611 | 0.708 | Females are victimized more according to official data, but the evidence is mixed for self-reported victimization |
| Age and crime victimization | 9.1.2 | 27 | 0 | **1.000** | – | – | Victimization is highest for teens through mid 30s and lowest for the elderly |
| Black–white differences in victimization | 9.1.3 | 36 | 0 | **0.900** | – | – | Blacks have higher rates of victimization especially for murder |
| Being an offender and victimization | 9.1.8 | 18 | 11 | **1.000** | **1.000** | **1.000** | Offenders are more often crime victims |
| Social status and victimization | 9.1.15 | 13 | – | 0.353 | – | – | No consistent relationship |
| Gender and fear of crime | 9.2.1 | – | 51 | – | **1.000** | – | Females fear crime more |
| Age and fear of crime | 9.2.2 | – | 22 | | **0.909** | – | Fear is lowest in the mid teens through the mid 30s and highest among the elderly |
| Black–white differences in fear of crime | 9.2.3 | – | 18 | – | 0.842 | – | Blacks appear to fear crime more |
| Having been a recent crime victim and fear of crime | 9.2.7 | – | 15 | – | 0.667 | – | There may be a slight tendency for recent crime victims to fear crime more than nonvictims |

# Index